Men Against McCarthy

Contemporary American History Series
William E. Leuchtenburg, *General Editor*

MEN AGAINST
McCARTHY

RICHARD M. FRIED

Columbia University Press   *New York*

Library of Congress Cataloging in Publication Data

Fried, Richard M   1941–
  Men Against McCarthy.

  Bibliography: p.
  Includes index.
  1. McCarthy, Joseph Raymond, 1908–1957.
2. United States—Politics and government—1945–
1953.   3. United States—Politics and government
—1953–1961.   I. Title.
E748.M143F74   320.9′73′0918   75-40447
ISBN 0-231-03872-0

ISBN 0-231-08360-2 (paperback)

Columbia University Press
New York   Guildford, Surrey

For My Mother and Father
and
for Barbara

CONTENTS

PREFACE

THE STORMY ERA of Joseph R. McCarthy has generated a freshet of works dealing with his career and the "ism" to which he gave his name. This essay focuses upon the McCarthy problem as his political foes perceived it and examines their strategy and tactics. I hope that my endeavor will shed some light on the limitations under which McCarthy's opponents functioned, the parameters within which McCarthy himself operated, and the boundaries of national politics during the heyday of the cold war.

In recent years, historians who can be loosely categorized as "revisionists" have striven to shift emphasis from the study of McCarthy's own activities to the cold-war foreign and domestic policies which facilitated his rise. In so doing, these scholars have ascribed responsibility for the onset of McCarthyism less to the Wisconsinite's particular demagogic talents than to the Truman administration and its liberal supporters who, promoting the cold-war consensus, laid themselves open to the repressive political atmosphere which unavoidably accompanied it.

There is much truth to this cluster of contentions; however, other forces conducive to a politics of anticommunism sometimes preceded and often transcended tendencies in that direction on the part of the Truman administration. Even before the cold war jelled or Harry Truman took office, the germs of anticommunist politics were visible: the "red" issue enjoyed an independent growth pattern of its own. While the Truman administration, through its foreign policies, the loyalty program, and the attending strident rhetoric, bears some blame for the rise of McCarthyism, the exigencies and rhythms of partisan politics of the New Deal/Fair Deal era had greater effect. The cues, if he took any, and the necessary legitimization for McCarthy's anticommunist politics came not from Democrats who may have attacked Henry A. Wallace's associations in 1948 but from the more seasoned redbaiters in his own party.

Because McCarthyism was preeminently a partisan weapon deployed by Republicans to end the Democratic hegemony, the bulk of the coverage of McCarthy's opposition is devoted to the Democrats. Not always wisely, perhaps, Democrats perceived McCarthy to lie at the intersection of a number of impinging political problems, including the decline of foreign-policy bipartisanship, impatience with "containment," and the vexing internal security issue. As a consequence, they expended vast energies in devising and executing strategies in regard to the Wisconsin Senator; in many cases, equal energies went into the construction of positions permitting the avoidance of confrontations with McCarthy.

During the Truman administration, there were several phases of the Democratic response to McCarthy: the reaction to his initial charges and the resulting Tydings Committee investigation; the 1950 elections; subsequent White House efforts to recapture the initiative from McCarthy and the Republican right in the area of internal security; scattered senatorial opposition (chiefly from Senator William Benton) in 1951–1952; and the 1952 campaign. After that, most Democrats abided by the strategic formulation that McCarthy had become a "Republican problem." The initiative now lay squarely with the GOP; only when his own party was ready, would McCarthy's sway be ended. Indeed, the political tides coursing between and within the parties had generally made for such a circumstance during the McCarthy era. Throughout their five-year running fight with McCarthy, the Democrats had made many errors, but at most stages their prospects for success had been sharply limited by the fact that McCarthy's power arose from long-term political trends over which they had only slight control.

I would like to declare my gratitude to the many individuals without whose aid this book would not have been possible. Librarians and archivists far beyond numbering provided assistance, hospitality, and, in one case, even a ride to the airport. I am especially indebted to the staffs of the Library of Congress, the Illinois State Historical Library, the Minnesota Historical Society, and the Eisenhower Library; to Philip Lagerquist and others at the Harry S. Truman Library; to Josephine Harper at the State Historical Society of Wisconsin. I would also like to acknowledge gratefully the Harry S. Truman Library Institute and the Graduate College of the University of Illinois at Chicago Circle, whose grants-in-aid expedited my research. Franklin Watts, Inc., kindly granted permission to use in this book portions of an essay which appeared in *The Specter,* edited by Robert Griffith and Athan Theoharis, copyright 1974.

I owe a debt to many fellow-historians, particularly among my colleagues at the University of Illinois at Chicago Circle, whose suggestions were of great value. Lon Hamby of Ohio University provided a critique of an early version of this work and shared the fruits of his own research with me. Charles C. Colley at Arizona State University and Richard Chenoweth at Dakota Wesleyan University led me through the intricacies of manuscript collections under their care. Among those who provided valuable information about manuscript sources were James T. Patterson of Brown University, Thomas G. Paterson of the University of Connecticut, and Richard Jensen of Chicago Circle.

I wish also to thank those who squeezed time for interviews into their busy schedules and those who granted me permission to examine their personal papers, including the late Senators Bourke Hickenlooper and Frank P. Graham, former Senators J. William Fulbright and Paul Douglas, Congressman Claude D. Pepper, former Congressman Walter Judd, the Honorable Jonathan Daniels, and Senator Hubert H. Humphrey. Mr. Maurice Rosenblatt was hospitable beyond the call of duty in allowing me to forage through the files of the National Committee for an Effective Congress.

Professor William E. Leuchtenburg directed the dissertation which preceded this book and provided valuable advice at every stage. To him goes my deep gratitude for his patience, care, and kind assistance in helping shape an investigation at times as rambling as any undertaken by the central figure in this book. I wish also to thank Bernard Gronert and Joan McQuary, two knowledgeable, long-suffering, and extremely able editors. My thanks also to Mrs. Barbara Rutherford for exemplary typing, and to the extremely helpful staff of the UICC Interlibrary Loan Office.

Lastly, I would like to express my appreciation to my wife Barbara, who shared a den, a dinner table, and much of the past decade with the documentary and anecdotal remains of the Senator from Wisconsin. She helped with research, typing, and conceptualization; with two delightful children, Rocky and Gail, who for years assumed that all daddies left home each day to "work on footnotes"; and in other ways which words cannot express. McCarthy himself may have provided a label: "the most unheard-of thing I ever heard of."

R.M.F.

Glendale Heights, Illinois

Men Against McCarthy

CHAPTER 1

The Red Perennial

MAY DAY, 1950: at dawn, Communist cadres infiltrated the sleeping hamlet of Mosinee, Wisconsin, to carry out their coup. With dispatch they captured the mayor, "shot" the chief of police and incarcerated his men, seized the power plant, rounded up clergymen, and began the task of pulling "objectionable" books from the shelves of the public library. Mosinee's burghers awakened to find three roadblocks interdicting access to their town and to learn that they had fallen under Communist rule. The newly installed commissars halted trains and harassed the passengers. The stores were nationalized. Parading children brandished signs bearing such inscriptions as "Religion is the opium of the people," and raised their arms in the clenched-fist salute. Rushed off the presses, the first issue of *The Red Star* heralded the new communist labor code. All citizens shared a uniform socialist diet of potato soup, dark bread, and coffee.

Actually, it was members of the American Legion, assisted by two former Communist Party leaders, who plotted Mosinee's putsch, hoping thus to dramatize the horrors of life under Soviet rule. By distributing leaflets which debunked the picture of communism presented by Legion "big shots" and profiteering "money-men," a handful of authentic Communists added some disruptive and dismaying spontaneity the day before, but they failed to dispel the booster spirit attending the pageant. On the big day, the authorities, having secured the town against real Reds, anticipated little trouble—except perhaps from "some of the boys" in the taverns. Those who could not stomach the spartan communist diet could sneak away to nearby Wausau, still in capitalist hands, for a square meal.[1]

For the theme of its political passion play, Mosinee had isolated an anxiety that was disturbing countless Americans: the communist menace. Less than three months earlier, on the strength of this concern, Senator Joseph R. McCarthy had launched a career and the era which would bear his name. The pressures of the cold war had converted "communism" into a catch-all charge encompassing anything that was suspect or deviant. Even oleomargarine, according to author Louis Bromfield, constituted an oily adjunct to the Soviet conspiracy (since it was the product of monopoly, "the best friend of communism"). Conversely, "McCarthyism," which within a few short years would enter the dictionaries, received the blame for numerous shortcomings and extravagances in American life. Brooks Atkinson attributed a poor Broadway season to its influence. By 1952 it had reached a point where a Milwaukee tippler, confronted in court by his wife's charges of drunkenness, dismissed them as "a lot of McCarthyism." [2]

During the years after World War II, events in a dislocated world intruded upon the nation's consciousness with unwonted persistence. In 1945, the euphoria of victory had been fleeting. The Grand Alliance which was to serve as the foundation for postwar peace had developed rifts before the fighting ended. The hope of postwar collaboration between the United States and the Soviet Union soon proved illusory. While President Harry S. Truman, other leaders, and broad sectors of the public continued to entertain thoughts about the possibility of settling differences with Stalin through diplomacy, the Truman administration moved—however fitfully—toward a "get-tough" policy vis-á-vis Russia. Soon the citizenry were required to live with a new and pessimistic-sounding language which included terms such as "cold war," "Iron Curtain," and "containment." They watched with mounting apprehension the solidification of Soviet control over the nations of Eastern Europe, culminating in the Czech coup of 1948 and the blockade of Berlin. With some exceptions, Henry Wallace for one, Americans generally approved the first halting signs of a stiffening response to events in Eastern Europe, and they consented to such unprecedented interventionist policies as aid to Greece and Turkey, the Marshall Plan, and NATO.

Many people, however, harbored doubts about the Truman administration's foreign policy despite its growing firmness. For them the taste of victory lacked sweetness—victory was too remote in Greece and Turkey, too partial in beleaguered Berlin, still too prospective in the case of the Marshall Plan. Americans had taxed themselves to supply foreign aid, sent their sons into the military under peacetime conscription, entered an alliance which entangled them in the fortunes of Europe, played host to the United Nations Organization. While they would listen to sermons about the "responsibilities" they now bore, they awaited clear-cut results from these new foreign involvements; if the outcome proved uncertain, many might succumb to the temptation to seek villains and scapegoats.

The drift of the postwar world bred measurable unease. In March 1945, 38 percent of the respondents to a Gallup poll foresaw their country's embroilment in a war within the next twenty-five years; three years later the proportion who feared such a likelihood had doubled. The source of trouble was readily identified. In September 1945, 39 percent described the Soviet Union as a "peaceloving" country; two years later, only 12 percent concurred in that appraisal. During the same period, the proportion who considered the Soviets "aggressive" rose from 38 to 66 percent. Increasing numbers viewed the confrontation with pessimism. While 17 percent believed America was winning the cold war as of December 1948, by March 1950, 16 percent held such a conviction; early in 1951, only 9 percent thought so. Meanwhile, the percentage who felt the Russians were winning the struggle increased from 15 to 23 and eventually to 30 percent during the same period.* [3]

In 1949 transpired a series of events which exacerbated these gen-

---

* It should be noted that public opinion initially was somewhat fluid. Thus the number of respondents to a Gallup poll who believed the Soviets would cooperate with the United States ranged from a wartime high of 55 percent to lows of 35 and 32 percent (March and October 1946) back to intermediate readings of 45 and 43 percent (May 1946, and January 1947). *Public Opinion Quarterly,* 10 (Spring 1946): 115, and 11 (Spring 1947): 151. For a finding that public opinion was relatively tolerant of Russia, see Athan Theoharis, "The Rhetoric of Politics: Foreign Policy, Internal Security, and Domestic Politics in the Truman Era, 1945–1950," in Barton J. Bernstein, ed., *Politics and Policies of the Truman Administration* (Chicago, 1970), pp. 199–200, 207n, and passim. Also see Theoharis, *Seeds of Repression: Harry S. Truman and the Origins of McCarthyism* (Chicago, 1971), ch. 1. In my view, the consensus regarding communism and the Soviet Union was less permissive.

eral suspicions regarding the nation's security and prompted the historian Eric F. Goldman to label it the "Year of Shocks." In August, the State Department issued its White Paper on China, heralding the impending collapse of the regime of Chiang Kai-shek. In his letter of transmittal, Secretary of State Dean Acheson cautioned that "the material aid, the military and technical assistance, and the good will of the United States, however abundant, could not of themselves put China on her feet." China's salvation lay in her own hands, but her grip was palsying rapidly: the "crusading spirit" of the now corrupt Kuomintang had withered, while Chiang set his face against all suggestions of reform. Upholding the policy of disengagement initiated after the failure of General George C. Marshall's peace mission in 1947, the White Paper opposed further aid to the Nationalists.[4]

Although the Republicans, like the Democrats, had generally treated the China question in a gingerly fashion, some of them protested the "contradictions" between the administration's interventionist policies in Europe and its standoffishness in Asia. "They can't urge that we kiss the Communists in China and kick them in Greece," Senator Owen Brewster expostulated. As part of their price for support of the Marshall Plan, Republicans had insisted that China, too, be given aid. Now, as the administration endeavored to write off the Nationalists, a number of Republicans gave vent to cries of "betrayal" and "sellout." Starting from the assumption that China was America's to "lose" in the first place, they reasoned that the Nationalists had been traduced by wrongheaded, if not disloyal, diplomats who had undercut Chiang while praising Mao Tse-tung and his Communist followers as innocent "agrarian reformers." "If ever a nation—half decimated by twenty years of struggle against organized Communist and Japanese aggression—was laid low by assassination and innuendo, by charges and lies and half truths, by a campaign of clever defamation," it was China, exclaimed Senator Styles Bridges. "China asked for a sword, and we gave her a dull paring knife." Senator Robert A. Taft entertained "not the slightest doubt . . . that the proper kind of sincere aid to the Nationalist Government a few years ago could have stopped communism in China." From 1949 on, Republicans castigated all the China observers and policy-makers associated with the White Paper as dupes or traitors.[5]

In the China crisis, the Republicans found an attractive political issue which dovetailed with certain party attitudes. During the late 1930s some Republicans such as Henry L. Stimson and Wendell Willkie had joined the Democrats in fixing their attention upon the fascist menace in Europe, but the isolationists, who exerted great leverage upon the party, resisted intervention in Europe. However, from the halcyon days of William McKinley and Manila Bay, the GOP had held to a more Pacific- and China-oriented set of priorities in foreign policy. While grudgingly giving up their classical isolationist position during World War II, many Republicans, retaining this Asian predilection, had urged that more resources be poured into the theater of war commanded by General Douglas MacArthur and made the latter a peculiarly Republican hero. They shook their heads knowingly at the charges leveled by General Patrick J. Hurley, who, upon resigning as envoy to China in 1945, claimed that officials of the Foreign Service had sabotaged his mission and favored the Chinese Communists. This Asia-first attitude constituted one aspect of what Norman Graebner has labeled the "new isolationism." [6]

Republicans could both exploit and deny responsibility for the China debacle: the umbrella of bipartisanship which protected the postwar program in Europe had never covered Asia. "We Republicans," Congressman Walter Judd noted, "have had no part either in formulating or carrying out" the administration's China policy. Lacking any feasible alternative, however, Republicans generally muffled their opposition until the White Paper was published. Senator Arthur H. Vandenberg, for instance, advocated strong "moral support" for the Nationalists and an end to any notions of coalition with the Communists, but he had "no illusions about China's future under any prospectus." He resisted the cutting off of aid—not out of hope that the Nationalists could be rescued, but for fear that its cessation would ratify the charge "that *we* are the ones who gave poor China the final push into disaster." [7]

As the Nationalists were surrendering their U.S.-made arms to the forces of Mao, Communists elsewhere had acquired, it seemed, a more awesome American weapon: on September 23, 1949, President Truman announced that the Soviet Union had detonated an atomic bomb. The nation's nuclear monopoly had ended; security had vanished in the familiar mushroom cloud. How, the question occurred to many, had the Soviet Union, presumably so far behind in technology, managed to accomplish this feat a scant four years after America had? Had espionage played a part? In 1946 a Canadian Royal Commission had uncovered evidence that men engaged in the joint Anglo-American projects of World War II had passed secrets to the Russians. Further revelations of nuclear spying did not emerge until 1950, but anxiety lest Russia acquire the bomb was endemic. The House Committee on Un-American Activities, for instance, expressed concern over those "trying to dissipate" what it called "our atomic bomb know-how." [8]

As early as 1945, the celebrated *Amerasia* incident had given the nation a premonitory hint of the coming concern with Soviet spying. *Amerasia* was a journal dealing with Far Eastern affairs which had a readership numbering less than two thousand. In March 1945, operatives of the Office of Strategic Services discovered hundreds of classified government documents in its offices. Although most of the stolen documents were routine, one dealt with American plans for bombing Japan; another detailed the "intimate relations" between Chiang Kai-shek and his wife. The FBI entered the case, and shortly Philip Jaffe and Kate Mitchell, the editors of *Amerasia,* were arrested along with Emmanuel S. Larsen, a minor State Department employee, John Stewart Service, a State Department China expert, and two other suspects. A grand jury declined, however, to indict three of the six, and the Justice Department allowed the remaining charges to shrink from espionage to unlawful possession of government documents. The two defendants who went before a judge—Jaffe and Larsen—pled guilty and *nolo* respectively and got off with fines.

Tongues clucked at this outcome, but the government's case, clumsily handled, had unraveled—chiefly because the Justice Department had relied upon evidence obtained through illegal entry. When one of the defendants learned of this circumstance, the government had to scramble even to get Jaffe and Larsen to plead to minor charges before the entire case evaporated. As for Service, in passing documents to Jaffe he had apparently exercised not evil intent, but indiscretion in cultivating a man he thought to be a legitimate journalist. [9] Nobilled by the grand jury, Service was reinstated in his job, but the *Amerasia* case, plus his connection with China policy, would subject him to recurrent attacks by Republicans including, latterly, Senator Joseph R. McCarthy. Periodically after 1945, for want of live prey, conservatives would flush the *Amerasia* case and take a few potshots before it once again fell soddenly to earth. By 1950, "Amerasia" had entered the litany of the Right.[10]

Well before *Amerasia,* enemies of the New Deal had aired warnings of Communist infiltration and subversive activity within the administration. The American Liberty League and those of similar persuasion had characterized the New Deal as communistic—and sometimes socialistic and fascist as well. Congressman Clare Finerty charged that Roosevelt presided over "the only willfully subversive Government in our history." Al Smith, climaxing his break with FDR, sounded the alarm in 1936. There could be but "one capital, Washington or Moscow. There can be only the clear, pure, fresh air of free America, or the foul breath of communistic Russia." [11] Most conservatives condemned New Deal "communism" in rather vague terms, but some critics had been more explicit. Dr. William A. Wirt, a Hoosier school superintendent, briefly captured headlines in 1934 with charges that Roosevelt's radical advisors were busily sovietizing the country; for the brain-trusters, according to Wirt, Roosevelt served merely as "the Kerensky of this revolution," which awaited its Stalin. Wirt's charges fizzled under congressional scrutiny, but the genre survived, and Wirt remained a hero to those who eventually buttressed the McCarthyite right wing.[12]

In the 1936 campaign, some GOP spokesmen followed Liberty League prescriptions and labeled the New Deal as socialist and/or communist. Vice-Presidential nominee Frank Knox charged that FDR "has been leading us toward Moscow," while Republican National Chairman John D. M. Hamilton taxed the President for letting David Dubinsky, "a man who has rendered financial aid to the Communists in Spain," serve as a Roosevelt elector. William Randolph Hearst inveighed against the "imported autocratic Asiatic Socialist party of Karl Marx and Franklin Delano Roosevelt." Such salvos failed to hit their target. Lacking as yet any concrete evidence of the presence of Communists in government, Republicans who attacked subversion were firing blank ammunition. Other allegations, relying either upon hyperbole (H. L. Mencken asserted that FDR's advisors made Stalin look like a Liberty Leaguer) or upon broad warnings like those of Alf Landon against "dictatorship," "class feeling," or "regimentation," exploded as airbursts; they served to silhouette the GOP's opposition to all the social gains achieved under the New Deal and to allow Roosevelt to seize the political center for liberalism while offering the conservative advice to "reform if you would preserve." [13] In subsequent elections Republicans faced a recurrent dilemma: whether to follow "moderate" leadership and accept sizable portions of Democratic programs or to heed more conservative counsel and oppose the New Deal and all its works. Implicitly, the first of these approaches made it more difficult to employ "communist" charges in a campaign.

Wendell Willkie in 1940 and Thomas E. Dewey in 1948 indulged in little red-baiting, but the heated anticommunist rhetoric of the 1944 contest bore a similarity to that of the McCarthy era. Republicans attacked the newly-formed CIO Political Action Committee (PAC), spotlighting the links between its chairman Sidney Hillman (in that year of "Clear it with Sidney") and the Democratic Party. To the New Deal bandwagon they also yoked Earl Browder, the Communist leader whom FDR had recently pardoned from his prison term for perjury. Governor John Bricker, the GOP vice-presidential nominee, alleged that Browder had been released from jail to line up Communist support for the Democratic Party, which had become "the Hillman-Browder communistic party with Franklin Roosevelt as the front"; he named seven federal employees who belonged to "subversive organizations" to prove that FDR and the New Deal were "in the hands of the radicals and the Communists." [14]

More cautiously, Governor Dewey too warmed to the issue of communism in 1944. He claimed that Roosevelt was "indispensable" to both Browder and Hillman; he pledged that his administration would promptly oust all Communists from federal jobs. In response, Roosevelt angrily denied ever seeking Communist support and charged that purveyors of this "fear propaganda" were "dragging red herrings across the trail of the national election." Dewey rejoined that this "soft disclaimer" could not conceal the fact that Roosevelt's election was, according to Browder himself, "essential" to the Communist cause. "In Russia," Dewey explained, "a communist is a man who supports his Government. In America a Communist is a man who supports the fourth term so our form of government may more easily be changed." Roosevelt retorted that anyone who insinuated "a danger that the Government . . . could be sold out to Communists" revealed "a shocking lack of trust in America." [15]

In the 1946 campaign, too, Republicans busily decried the presence of Communists or near-Communists in high places. B. Carroll Reece, Chairman of the Republican National Committee, charged that sympathizers of Henry A. Wallace who accepted "every tune wafted from Moscow by way of the CIO/PAC" infested the opposition party. He asserted that "red-Fascists" who were "beholden to the political ideology of Moscow" had seized control of the Democratic Party. Congressmen Joe Martin warned of a trend "toward communism on the one hand and fascism on the other" and promised that a Republican Congress would put a high priority on ending "boring from within by subversionists high up in government." Although Senate Majority Leader Alben Barkley derided charges of communism as a "political scarecrow," a number of observers believed the issue carried considerable weight in the GOP victory.[16]

The Republicans who triumphed in that off-year election had campaigned at the height of the nation's ill humor over the problems of the immediate postwar era. They had run while vexation at Russia was growing and—more importantly—when public discontent with the administration's wildly yawing policies of price control and reconversion was most outspoken. Several members of the "Class of 1946" would subsequently distinguish themselves for arch-conservatism on domestic issues, displeasure with bipartisanship in foreign policy, and support for the activities of Senator McCarthy. While in some cases these attributes were prefigured in 1946, other candidacies in that year were noteworthy for little beyond an emphasis upon engaging, youthful vigor and attractive war records. Joseph R. McCarthy, for instance, while occasionally dabbling in red-baiting in his Wisconsin Senate race, seemed more often to personify these virtues and to stand behind the moderate Republicanism of Harold L. Stassen and a bipartisan, internationalist foreign policy. Nonetheless, the 1946 elections had made a number of Republicans literate in the issue of communism.[17]

Anticommunism had usually flourished more luxuriantly on Capitol Hill than in the blast of electoral activities. The conservative coalition which emerged during Roosevelt's second term found in anticommunism a handy weapon against the New Deal. In particular, the House of Representatives Special Committee to Investigate Un-American Activities, under the leadership of Congressman Martin Dies, spearheaded attacks against the Roosevelt administration. From its founding in 1938, the House Un-American Activities Committee wore but the thinnest of veils over its hostility to the New Deal's liberalism and to the new militancy of the CIO. With colleagues and retainers on the committee, Dies frequently charged that the federal government swarmed with Communists and radicals. "Stalin baited his hook with a 'progressive' worm, and the New Deal suckers swallowed bait, hook, line, and sinker," the Congressman exclaimed. He warned that the "plan" under the New Deal was "to sabotage the capitalistic system by placing upon that system burdens of restrictive legislation and staggering taxation." Republican J. Parnell Thomas, later chairman of HUAC, accused the Federal Theatre Project under Hallie Flanagan of putting on "only the productions containing Communistic or New Deal theories." [18]

The Dies group struck a responsive chord in the electorate. Dies's individual road-show investigation during the 1938 congressional campaign reputedly affected elections in several states. In Michigan, Governor Frank Murphy, under attack by witnesses before the committee, went down to defeat. (Other issues, however, had greater effect upon the outcome.) Soon after the elections, 74 percent of those who hazarded an opinion felt that Dies's investigations should go on. A year later, despite world events, about the same percentage believed that HUAC should focus on Communist activities rather than those of the Nazis.

So mandated, the committee managed to obtain appropriations to continue its pursuit of Communist, Communist-front, leftist, and liberal organizations, seldom bothering to distinguish among them. Giving a pinch of attention to Nazi and fascist activities and to the Japanese internment program, the Dies panel carried on its search for Communists during World War II. Although Dies, facing a difficult campaign, chose to retire from Congress in 1944, others conversant in the politics of anticommunism did not intend to let the committee die. In 1945, John Rankin, race-baiter and anti-Semite extraordinary from Mississippi, managed by astute parliamentary maneuvering to make HUAC a permanent committee. Thus reborn, the group cast its net widely and randomly—for Reds in Hollywood, in the schools, in the unions, in the nation's atomic energy program and among scientists generally. Aware that allegations of espionage were political trump cards, HUAC searched sporadically for spies. In 1948, they achieved apparent success.[19]

Whittaker Chambers, a Communist agent until he broke with the party in 1938, appeared before the committee in August and named one Alger Hiss as a former close friend and fellow Communist. Hiss had served in the upper-middle echelons of the State Department until 1946. He denied ever having been a Communist or even having known Chambers. The man confronting him, Hiss eventually conceded, did resemble a shabby character he had once known under the name of George Crosley. When Chambers repeated his charges without the immunity which shielded his congressional testimony, Hiss, after some delay, sued for libel, to all appearances an innocent man wronged.

Gradually, however, as Chambers recalled details of his association with Hiss and added the new charge that Hiss had given him secret State Department documents for transmission to the Russians, the web of suspicion tightened. What had begun as an accusation of Communist Party membership became a charge of treachery. From an abandoned dumbwaiter in a Brooklyn apartment Chambers retrieved papers purporting to be copies of the purloined documents typed on the Hiss family typewriter. Out of the same cache came several microfilms; these Chambers first hid in a hollowed-out pumpkin on his Maryland farm, then surrendered to HUAC in December 1948. With this evidence, a federal grand jury indicted Hiss on two counts of perjury for having falsely stated that he had not seen Chambers after January 1, 1937, nor passed secret papers to him. (The statute of limitations for the crime of espionage had lapsed.) The first trial produced a hung jury; at the end of the second, on January 21, 1950, Hiss was found guilty; four days later he received a five-year prison sentence.[20]

Not just a man, but a symbol was convicted. The verdict thrust at the twenty-year Democratic ascendancy, the New Deal, and the Roosevelt-Truman foreign policies. Hiss personified everything that opponents of the New and Fair Deals had loathed.[21] Having served in the Agricultural Adjustment Administration and in the Office of the Solicitor General during the 1930s, he possessed ample New Deal credentials. He had moved on to the State Department, which became the continuing repository for much of the unpopularity of the New Deal after Roosevelt's domestic experiments ended. Hiss had gone to Yalta and there had stood, the Republicans claimed, at FDR's right hand while freedom-loving inhabitants of Eastern Europe and China were "sold down the river." Hiss and Roosevelt alone, Senator Homer Capehart cried, had given the Soviets three votes in the UN General Assembly. "What a triumvirate," Senator Karl Mundt exclaimed sarcastically. "Poor Gladwin Jebb, with Gromyko and Alger Hiss" at Yalta, "trying to figure out what to do to help free men." Impeached with Hiss were his charm, intellect and wit, his handsome features and trim tailoring, his Ivy League background and sophistication. Congressmen who had bridled at the jaunty, patronizing glibness of bureaucrats testifying before them over the past decade and a half now relished this comeuppance. Senator Mundt mused incredulously that some people still thought it "inconceivable that a man who looks so smooth and intelligent and speaks such an effective Harvard accent, could be considered guilty." To them Hiss was "just a nice young man with a neat crease in the front of his trousers." Harry Truman added to his party's woes with his early dismissal of the affair as a "red herring" dragged across the trail of the Republican Eightieth Congress. "This cooks President Truman's 'red herring,'" quipped Harold Velde, a Republican member of HUAC, after the second trial. "I hope he enjoys eating it." [22]

Attacks on the New Deal past did not end with Hiss.* After the 1948 testimony of Chambers and another ex-Communist, Elizabeth Bentley, there were more names to bandy about. Harry Dexter White, a high-ranking official of the Treasury Department and the International Monetary Fund, received the attentions of HUAC. Three days after testifying in August 1948, he died of a heart ailment; while his defenders agreed with Henry A. Wallace that White had perished a martyr, conservative opponents of the administration considered his death just one more frustration in the search for subversion. A grislier episode unfolded in the case of Lawrence Duggan, a former State Department functionary mentioned peripherally in HUAC testimony

* By wrapping themselves in the banners of New Deal liberalism, several of the accused managed to make this symbolism more explicit. See Goodman, *The Committee,* pp. 250–51, 260–61.

and then questioned by the FBI. On December 20, 1948, ten days after his interrogation, Duggan's body was found beneath his sixteenth-floor office window. Karl Mundt said that HUAC would release names of other suspects "as they jump out of windows." [23]

On the strength of its activities in 1948, HUAC soared to a new pinnacle of prestige. While the committee had enjoyed its more responsible moments, in times of less restraint it had provided models for unscrupulous, ambitious politicians. By the time Joe McCarthy reached national prominence, most of the paraphernalia of witchhunting—the lists, the letterheads, even the vocabulary—had been in use for years. Moreover, HUAC had shown that in the buried drifts and fissures of the "red decade" of the New Deal lay political nuggets of pure gold.

If 1949 had been a year of shocks,* 1950 brought more tremors. On January 12, 1950, Secretary Acheson gave a major address before the National Press Club for which Republicans would berate him over the next three years. In defining America's defense perimeter in the Far East, Acheson excluded the Republic of Korea and Taiwan from among those nations to whose protection the United States would unilaterally commit itself. The omission of Korea became a sore point

---

* Eric F. Goldman's celebrated "shocks" thesis poses some problems. Richard M. Freeland has argued that two of the shocks—the Soviet A-bomb and China's fall—had been "anticipated by American officials" and were no real threat to national security, while Hiss was a minor figure who betrayed "no important secrets." It was events *before* 1949, the genesis of Truman's anti-Soviet foreign policies, which so conditioned the public as to deprive it of the proper "perspective" in which to locate these events. Freeland, *The Truman Doctrine and the Origins of McCarthyism: Foreign Policy, Domestic Politics, and Internal Security, 1946–1948* (New York, 1972), pp. 4–5. In my own view, this argument tends to slight the independent development of public concern over communism and internal security. On the other hand, the notion that external events jarred the precarious balance of public comprehension cannot be accepted as a free-floating historical axiom: for the Truman administration (and the foreign-policy elite), it provided a comforting explanation of the drift toward McCarthyism. Richard L. Strout offered in the *Christian Science Monitor* (March 21, 1950) a contemporaneous report of the "growing feeling" in Washington that McCarthyism owed its rise to the "irritation and dismay" occasioned by the loss of China, the Soviet A-bomb, the Hiss case, and other discordant world events. For another critique of the Goldman thesis, see Nelson W. Polsby, "Toward An Explanation of McCarthyism," *Political Studies*, 8 (Oct. 1960): 252–53.

only after the outbreak of war in June, but Republicans immediately seized upon Acheson's indifference toward Taiwan as a further indication of the administration's sellout of the Chinese Nationalists.[24]

In 1950, Acheson emerged as the administration's most vulnerable political target. On January 25, the day of Hiss's sentencing, the Secretary refused to comment to newsmen on matters presently before the courts but, when pressed, invoked his Christian duty to a friend. "I will not turn my back on Alger Hiss," he said, and thus opened his flank to a murderous Republican barrage. The lack of a constant instinct for political survival frequently embroiled Acheson with hostile Congressmen. Nor did the Secretary's impatience with some of his more dogged critics advance the esteem in which Congress held him. (Characteristically, Acheson at a later date denied the contention that he would not "suffer fools gladly"; he had often done so—"if not gladly, at least patiently.") [25]

Conveniently, almost every line of the McCarthyite attack converged on the person of Dean Acheson. His sponsorship of the China White Paper had already angered a number of Republicans. His remarks about Hiss made him the focus as well of doubts about the loyalty of government employees. In the words of Congressman John Jennings, a Southern Democrat, Hiss and Acheson were "two birds of a feather"; so long as Acheson stayed in office, Hiss's influence would permeate the State Department. Styles Bridges inquired whether friendship with Hiss made the Secretary himself a security risk.[26] Through Acheson, the inner citadel of the Truman administration could be breached.

In early 1950, a percussive note of nuclear devastation obscured the sinister, woodwind theme of treason raised by the Hiss case. On January 21, President Truman disclosed that he had instructed the Atomic Energy Commission to launch work on a hydrogen bomb to offset Russia's development of an atomic device. Increasingly, "the bomb" intruded upon the American consciousness. A nation which had not suffered attack within its continental limits since 1814 now debated building bomb shelters. Washington real estate entrepreneurs began advertising properties possessing the virtue of being beyond the range of a nuclear attack on the capital. A representative of the New York Frozen Food Locker Association gave the chilling advice that his product offered "one of the safest places to be in the event of an atomic explosion." One scenario of a nuclear attack on Manhattan provided for digging mass graves in Central Park.[27]

No sooner had news of the H-bomb decision been absorbed than authorities in London announced that scientist Klaus Fuchs had confessed to having spied for the Soviets while working on Anglo-American nuclear research during World War II. Within months the American members of the spy ring to which Fuchs had been linked were arrested. In an unrelated case concluded in March 1950, a jury found Judith Coplon, a Justice Department employee, guilty of having transmitted secrets to her lover, Valentin Gubitchev, who passed them on to his Soviet superiors. When Gubitchev was permitted to return to the Soviet Union, Acheson underwent a further drubbing by his critics. In June a federal grand jury indicted William Remington, a Commerce Department official, for perjury for having denied the Communist affiliations of which he had been accused by Elizabeth Bentley.[28]

Perhaps the jolts of 1949 and early 1950 alone could have caused the reverberations of the McCarthy era, but the force of these events was sharply amplified by the existence of numerous fault lines in the nation's political structure. The mutual reinforcement between these long-term trends and more immediate, accumulating crises explains the depth and virulence of the anticommunist alarmism of the 1950s. Senator McCarthy happened along at a time of maximum frustration on the part of Republicans, who looked back at twenty years of failure and impotence. Since 1933, the Democrats had paraded the benign icons of Franklin D. Roosevelt at every election and succeeded in labeling theirs the party of the common man. The Republicans reflected gloomily that they had not nominated a President since 1928; since 1930, they had wrested control of Congress from the Democrats only once. In 1948 they had, in the current phrase, snatched defeat out of the jaws of victory. Given a fighting chance by few besides himself, President Truman had won the election despite the splintering of his party on the right and the left. Republicans experienced the vexation of knowing that the Democrats could not be beaten even when deserted by the Deep South and the followers of Henry Wallace.[29]

In 1948, the Republicans had made passing reference to the topic of subversion. National Chairman Hugh Scott foretold "the greatest housecleaning . . . since St. Patrick cleaned the snakes out of Ireland.'' "There will not be any Communists in the Government after January 20,'' Dewey pledged; the Republicans, unlike the Democrats, did not "regard Communist activity as a 'red herring.' " Dewey's running mate, Earl Warren, raised the issue with more gusto, criticizing the administration for having "coddled" the Communists. Expounding on a text similar to that which McCarthy would later use, the California Governor lamented that "while we spend billions to halt the spread of the Communist conspiracy abroad, we find this same conspiracy reaching its stealthy fingers to grab the framework of our own free institutions and tear them down.'' [30]

Notwithstanding these examples, the Republicans used the communist issue sparingly in 1948. Both Dewey and Warren hedged their statements on the subject: there would be no witch-hunt; only the disloyal would lose their jobs. In a nationwide radio debate with Harold Stassen on the eve of the Oregon primary, Dewey had argued on both practical and civil-libertarian grounds against outlawing the Communist Party, preferring to keep it "everlastingly out in the open" where it could best be fought. Stassen retorted that this was a "soft policy," but Dewey's primary victory seemed to foreclose that gambit. Later, when a delegation of conservatives called on Dewey to urge him to deal vigorously with the communist issue, he resisted their entreaties. During the fall campaign, he gave not much more attention to the communist issue, broadly construed, than did Truman.[31]

With a characteristic mixture of defensiveness and braggadocio, Truman declaimed from the hustings that his administration alone had found effective means to combat communism. He handicapped his opponents—Republicans, Progressives, and Communists—as an unlikely three-horse parlay destined for nowhere but the political glue factory. The proof of his anticommunism, argued Truman, lay in the Communists' violent hostility toward him. They actually "wanted a Republican victory," he charged, and to achieve it they were "supporting that Third Party" in the hope that it would take votes away from the Democrats. He advised Republicans to "consider well the strange bedfellows the Republican Party has this year." The reason the Communists were so eager for a GOP triumph, Truman explained, was their knowledge that this result would weaken America in the face of communism at home through economic depression and abroad through isolationist foreign policies.[32] In a major address at

Oklahoma City, Truman strenuously defended his anticommunist programs—foreign aid, domestic social and economic gains, deportation of alien subversives, the federal loyalty program, prosecution of Communist leaders, and FBI vigilance. The Republicans had obstructed these measures, failed to produce "any significant information about Communist espionage which the FBI did not already have," and cast "a cloud of suspicion over the most loyal civil service in the world." Far from hurting the Communist Party, the Republicans, said Truman, "have helped it." In Boston he labeled GOP charges of red infiltration "just a plain malicious lie" reminiscent of the Ku Klux Klan's smears against Al Smith in 1928.[33]

The Democrats were quick to nail the banner of anticommunism to the mast. Attorney General Tom Clark rehearsed the administration's achievements—deportations, the loyalty program (which confirmed the fidelity of all but a handful of federal employees), and the prosecution of the twelve Communist Party leaders whose trial was scheduled to begin October 15.* Congress, Clark noted, had dragged its

* The timing of this trial might appear more than coincidental. Freeland argues that earlier proceedings against alien Communists flowed out of the administration's political aims and speculates that the Smith Act indictments were intended to keep the grand jury from reporting on its original topic of inquiry: espionage. This ploy would thus prevent revelation of embarrassing testimony (by Bentley and Chambers) during the campaign. *Truman Doctrine,* pp. 216–19, 239–40, 337–38. This explanation poses difficulties. The purported strategy carried high risks and long odds. Since the star espionage witnesses did go before congressional committees, it was also a failure—unless one argues that the heat would have been greater had the grand jury reported sooner. In addition, preparations for the indictments were not as rushed as Freeland implies. As of early April 1948, the FBI had put together a brief (and this project had begun some time before). Furthermore, U.S. Attorney John F. X. McGohey was at least willing to suggest the wisdom of putting the case before a *new* grand jury.

One element of timing into which politics did enter was the Attorney General's anxiety that the presentation to the jury not be made (or at least not become public) until after the Democratic convention—"to avoid the charge of bringing out indictment [*sic*] merely for political purposes." See McGohey's handwritten "Memo of Conferences on F.B.I. Brief," n.d. [April 8–June 29, 1948], Box 1, McGohey Papers, Truman Library.

Finally, while party strategists anticipated and rhetoricians hailed the coming trial, preliminary motions delayed its start until early November—too late to have much effect. Spingarn, "Memorandum for the SJS White House Assignment File," Sept. 10, 1948, Spingarn Papers, Truman Library; memorandum, Spingarn to George M. Elsey, Oct. 13, 1948, *ibid.*

feet on voting the funds necessary for the loyalty program and failed—for all its talk—to produce its own anticommunist law (save the antilabor Taft-Hartley Act) or to enact the proposals of the Justice Department. In 1946 the Republicans had shrilled about Communists "under every government desk," but, despite Clark's importunings, they had named "not a solitary one." The Democratic National Committee assembled a fifty-four-page brief for party workers documenting the Democrats' stern yet measured vigilance against subversion.[34]

Though Truman dismissed as a "red herring" congressional absorption in the Chambers-Bentley stories, Democratic operatives behind the scenes fretted over the potential damage. George M. Elsey, a White House aide, mused that "spies" had become "a major Republican issue" which was "getting worse, not better." At several meetings, administration officials tried to concert strategies to counteract the congressional hearings and demands for loyalty data. The issue had become delicate enough to prompt the Justice Department to ponder submitting the entire controversy to a prestigious, bipartisan commission. In early September, Stephen J. Spingarn, a Treasury Department officer experienced in loyalty-security matters, went over to the White House to "coordinate" the administration's position on these matters during the campaign.[35]

Good fortune aided the Democrats mightily in 1948. Although Truman's impolitic disparagement of the Hiss sensation prefaced the fall campaign, Whittaker Chambers did not produce the "pumpkin papers" until after the election. In addition, the publicized activities of Communists in the Progressive Party may have served as a "lightning rod" to divert charges of communism away from the Democrats.[36] This circumstance was not wholly accidental. As several historians have noted, the noisiest anticommunists in 1948 were Truman and such liberal supporters as the Americans for Democratic Action (ADA). In his renowned memorandum of election-year strategy, presidential advisor Clark Clifford pointed out that Truman's vigorous anti-Soviet foreign policy might be good politics and that, in order to achieve the "insulation of Henry Wallace," liberals would have to expose the Reds and fellow travelers comprising the "core" of his backing. In March, Truman had disdained the support of "Henry Wallace and his Communists"; on several later occasions he denigrated his left-wing foes. The Research Division of the Democratic National Committee hired Kenneth M. Birkhead to ply his skills as a professional observer of totalitarian groups—both right and left— against the Progressive Party.[37]

Before the campaign had progressed very far, however, it became clear that the communist issue had faded in proportion to the decline in the Progressives' fortunes. The spotty ranks of "Gideon's army" who straggled into the autumn campaign proved less numerous than once anticipated. Both Birkhead and Truman turned their energies to other matters. Polling results revealed that the topic of communism was of low salience to most voters. The 1948 election, its outcome decided by questions of socioeconomic substance, was a "maintaining election" within the framework of issues and party loyalties forged by the New Deal.[38] Some have argued that liberal red-baiting of Wallace in 1948 lit the fuse for the later explosion of Republican-inspired McCarthyism. However, this hypothesis, which credits the public with an extraordinary recall (triggered by later events) of the turgid rhetoric of the campaign, would appear to be vitiated by the evidence of the electorate's ho-hum response to the issue of domestic communism.[39]

From another perspective, 1948 marked a turning point which failed to turn. In the elections since 1936, the Democrats had been losing momentum: the time seemed ripe for the GOP to recapture the White House. Dewey's defeat emboldened conservative Republicans who sought to wage a more hard-hitting battle against the Fair Deal; they listened impatiently to further counsels of moderation. Dewey, declared the Chicago Tribune, "refuses to be deterred by jibes of 'me too,' and will gladly lose the Republican party half a dozen more Presidential elections to prove his point." Many of the conservatives, followers of Taft rather than Dewey, also formed the phalanx of opposition to the bipartisan foreign-policy line which prevailed in 1948. That year's debacle weakened the restraints under which these insurgents operated and tilled the ground for McCarthyism.[40]

Other rumblings within the GOP worked to undermine bipartisanship. Senator Vandenberg, no longer a potential national candidate after the election, exerted diminished influence upon his Republican colleagues. More significantly, his declining health kept him away from the Senate much of the time prior to his death in 1951. In

1949, another spokesman for bipartisanship, John Foster Dulles, lost his briefly-held Senate seat.[41] A further augury of the party's shift toward a more conservative position was the replacement of Hugh Scott, Dewey's appointee as Chairman of the Republican National Committee, by Guy G. Gabrielson.

The 1949 senatorial campaign in New York offered clues as to the direction in which the country's politics were moving. John Foster Dulles plied the "red" issue against his Democratic challenger Herbert Lehman. His adversary, Dulles claimed, had received support from Communists in past campaigns, had been "surrounded" by them while directing UNRRA relief in Eastern Europe after the war, favored Fair Deal schemes which were "chapters out of the Communist book," and limited his opposition to "a daily dozen of anti-Communist words." "I know he is no Communist but I know also that the Communists are in his corner and that he and not I will get the 500,000 Communist [i.e., American Labor Party] votes that last year went to Henry Wallace in this state." Lehman, Dulles charged, played "the old New Deal political game of spanking the 'Commies' and their fellow-travelers in public and coddling them in private." Even Governor Dewey, deserting the "high road" of 1948, asserted that the Communists backed Lehman and sought to "purge" Dulles. Lehman defended the "welfare state" against Dulles's attacks and argued that the Communists, sworn enemies of liberalism, saw in "reactionary republicanism the one best hope of creating that demoralization at home that might destroy all our efforts to hold communism in check abroad." [42] While the 1948 election outcome helped conservative Republicans to wrest control of the GOP from their "liberal" counterparts, the 1949 New York race showed that the latter were capable of capitulation as well as defeat.

By early 1950, themes of subversion and communism in government bade fair to become a major political issue. In January, Senator Taft had attacked the "left-wing group" in the State Department "who obviously have wanted to get rid of Chiang." The conviction of Alger Hiss prompted Senator Styles Bridges to inquire: "How many termites like Hiss are left in the State Department?" Congressman Nixon forecast that Truman would have "further reason to regret his red herring remark." The Republican National Committee and the House and Senate Republican conferences demonstrated an intention to exploit these topics with the issuance on February 6 of their "Statement of Principles," a semiofficial campaign platform which condemned the Democrats for underestimating the communist threat. It deplored "the dangerous degree to which Communists and their fellow travelers have been employed in important Government posts and the fact that information vital to our security has been made available to alien agents and persons of questionable loyalty." The Republicans promised an overhaul of the loyalty program and prompt removal of "all Communists, fellow travelers and Communist sympathizers." [43]

If by 1950 the Republicans seemed bent on throwing restraint aside, the Democrats, too, contributed to the incubation of partisanship and the rise of red-baiting. Harry S. Truman had never been one to stifle his own political combativeness; his astounding 1948 victory engendered a still more cocky assertiveness which did not facilitate working with the opposition party. In December 1948, for instance, rejecting an opportunity to soften his "red herring" remark after further revelations in the Hiss case, Truman defended his initial judgment as "what the people thought" too. When differences arose, Truman was quick to attribute selfish, purely political motives to his opponents, seldom recognizing the applicability of the same charge to his own behavior. During his second term he sometimes took Republican foreign-policy cooperation too much for granted. Senate Democrats struck another blow at foreign-policy harmony by appropriating a seat on the Foreign Relations Committee to which the Republicans thought themselves entitled. Jealous of the prestige and deference accorded to Senator Vandenberg, Tom Connally, the incoming chairman of that committee, occasionally impeded bipartisanship. The appointment of Dean Acheson as Secretary of State in 1949—a choice on which Truman did not consult the Republicans—boded further trouble. With his abrasive manner, lack of support on Capitol Hill, and ties to Alger Hiss, Acheson soon became a prominent target of GOP attacks.[44]

If the decline of bipartisanship signaled the administration's political vulnerability, the looming issue of internal security measurably increased it. Loyalty and security tests had been proliferating for a decade. Starting with the Hatch Act of 1939, various laws and regulations had prohibited federal employment to members of the Communist Party or other groups advocating forcible overthrow of the government. In World War II, the Attorney General, the Civil Service Commission, two interdepartmental committees, the FBI, and other executive agencies had all worked at the problem of winnowing the disloyal from federal jobs. Congress, led by HUAC, had continued to roil the waters, most notably with a 1943 appropriation bill which cut off the salaries of three federal employees singled out as leftists. During the emergency, Congress had also empowered the heads of the armed services to dismiss summarily any official who constituted a "security risk." This "summary discharge" authority was extended in 1946, through the so-called McCarran rider, to the State Department and, subsequently, to other "sensitive" agencies. The gaggle of regulations which emerged from the war resulted in a set of uncoordinated, overlapping programs with disparate standards and in investigative backlogs which clearly called for remedy.[45]

Forces beyond mere administrative desiderata propelled Truman toward the enactment of an expanded government loyalty program. The 1945 *Amerasia* affair and the 1946 Canadian spy revelations accentuated the plausibility of fears that espionage threatened American security. Demands for tightened government loyalty standards had moved the Democrats to authorize an investigation by a subcommittee of the House Civil Service Committee. After a hasty inquiry, on the eve of the 1946 campaign, the two-man Democratic subcommittee majority issued a report urging the President to set up a commission to examine and regularize loyalty standards. Republican Edward Rees of Kansas drafted minority views which asserted that not just "changes in technique or issuance of directives," but an "immediate and thorough housecleaning" was required. (Rees also claimed a primary role for Congress in maintaining the loyalty of the civil service, whereas the Democrats were readier to cede that responsibility to the executive branch.) At the same time, the Justice Department under Attorney General Tom C. Clark was also pressing for a loyalty program.[46]

Moved by this combination of forces, on November 25, 1946, Truman named representatives of six executive agencies to the President's Temporary Commission on Employee Loyalty. Charged with surveying current rules and procedures and with recommending needed changes, the Commission found it difficult to define the scope of the loyalty problem. Though one member suggested that the group's very appointment presupposed the existence of a serious threat, others wanted facts. These, however, were hard to pry out of the agencies involved. D. Milton Ladd, Assistant Director of the FBI, testified vaguely that there were a "substantial number" of disloyal government employees. The Attorney General conceded that the disloyalty problem "was not as serious as it once was" but argued that the presence of any unfaithful public servants was a grave matter. Though the majority of the commission were disposed to assume the existence of a problem demanding remedy, even they resisted making recommendations on the basis of such skimpy data. The group balked at its early reporting date (February 1, 1947) and succeeded in postponing it for twenty days.[47]

Despite occasional misgivings and expressions of caution, the viewpoint of military and naval intelligence and of the Justice Department generally prevailed. Panel members from these agencies held that when national security conflicted with individual liberties, all doubt should be resolved in favor of the former. On February 20, 1947, the Temporary Commission submitted its report, which, with few changes, Truman implemented on March 22 with Executive Order 9835, establishing the federal employee loyalty program. The measure provided for the creation of departmental and regional loyalty boards, a Loyalty Review Board within the Civil Service Commission which had appellate jurisdiction over the lower boards, and a system of loyalty investigations for applicants and employees. The criteria for dismissal of federal jobholders included the existence of "reasonable grounds for belief that the person is disloyal." [48]

Contemporary critics and later historians raised a number of weighty objections to the loyalty program. It so confounded concepts of loyalty and security in the public mind that an employee dismissed as a security risk was daubed inevitably with the stain of disloyalty. Thus, a man too reliant upon the bottle, or having suspicious relatives, or in other ways vulnerable or indiscreet, might be fired on security grounds; the program's workings left the unjustified but nearly certain implication that his allegiance, too, was in question. A suspect could be charged by anonymous accusers whom he was not allowed to confront. "Guilt by association" became an important gauge of disloyalty. Loyalty boards questioned employees on a wide

variety of topics—like race relations—which were unrelated to loyalty. It appeared that thought, not just overt acts, would be penalized,
and the enforcers of governmental purity had rather far-reaching notions of what constituted dangerous ideas. Truman's penchant for ap-
pointing conservatives to the loyalty apparatus in order to outflank
right-wing critics did not ameliorate the situation. Seth W. Richardson, first Chairman of the Loyalty Review Board, warned that the
"first padlock" on disloyal speech might be applied to "the mouths
of teachers and scientists." Queried on the possible dangers of such a
proposal, he responded that "the man who fears that his thinking will
be curbed by a check of loyalty may be thinking things that tend to be
disloyal to his country." [49]

Truman's loyalty program has been condemned for its motivation
as well as its consequences. Noting the Temporary Commission's inability to delineate the extent of the disloyalty problem, its refusal to
propose countermeasures beyond an expansion of the extant program,
and the timing of Executive Order 9835, Richard M. Freeland has
argued that the Truman administration "was only incidentally concerned with national security." Its aim was less to snatch the issue of
internal security from a ham-handed conservative Republican
Congress than to facilitate its campaign for acceptance of a démarche
in its foreign policy. The Executive Order came a mere nine days
after the "Truman Doctrine" address to Congress, to which it
"seemed a fitting sequel." The White House, it is suggested, orches-
trated the timing of its release of the loyalty order so as to counter-
point its request for aid to Greece and Turkey.[50]

A number of contemporaries drew the connection between foreign
and domestic anticommunism. Republicans were quick to underscore
this theme. It was necessary to aid the Greeks, Congressman Charles
Kersten agreed. "However, we should also immediately deal with
Communism in America." In 1950, seeking to determine the reasons
for Senator McCarthy's initial successes, reporter William S. White
observed in retrospect that "fear of communism was, in the first
place, fed by the Administration" to build public support for its
foreign programs. Richard H. Rovere similarly lamented the administration's error in "selling the Marshall plan to Congress almost entirely as a weapon to defeat Communism," for it was "coming home
to roost" in 1950.[51]

Yet to discover the baneful consequences of the overlapping of the drives for internal and external security does not necessarily prove that the administration pursued the first to promote the second. The argument that the loyalty program was enacted in such a way as to facilitate passage of foreign aid remains highly speculative, as does the suggestion that Truman held back the Temporary Commission's report so as to link its release with his call for aid to Greece and Turkey. (If such was his aim, the Washington *Post* obtusely missed the point: its editorial lamented the "unfortunate" coincidence which permitted "an impression" that the loyalty order, issued during a time of rising international tensions, was "somehow related" to the global struggle against communism.) The delay may actually have stemmed, as A. D. Vanech, Chairman of the Temporary Commission stated, from the fact that Truman "wanted more time to consider the report and . . . had several pressing things on his desk which required deferment of his consideration of the report." * The Supreme Court's decision in *Friedman* v. *Schwellenbach* may also have played a role in the timing of Executive Order 9835; four days before publication of the loyalty order, the Court, refusing to review a lower court ruling, let stand a dismissal carried out under the wartime loyalty program (and cleared a path for the new order).[52]

Any hypothesis as to Truman's motives in establishing the Temporary Commission admittedly relies upon conjecture and circumstantial evidence; nonetheless, his desire to preempt the loyalty issue before

* Discounting this explanation, Richard Freeland has asserted that the delay stemmed from no such "careful appraisal." His contention appears to be based on a memo which states obscurely that Vanech "said that the preparation of the implementing Executive Order or Orders was not the reason for the delay. . . ." *Truman Doctrine*, p. 142; Spingarn, "Memorandum for the Loyalty Commission File," Feb. 24, 1947, Vol. II, folder 1, Treasury Department File, Spingarn Papers. This, I would argue, does not refute the statement (in the same document) which is quoted above in the text. It does not show that there was no presidential review of the report—it would be hard for a document dated February 24 to particularize events of the ensuing four weeks. Instead, it may simply mean that the delay was not due to a problem in the mechanics of drafting the order. Furthermore, in those hectic weeks when the Truman Doctrine was germinating, it is quite plausible that "pressing things on his desk" did keep Truman from a careful scrutiny of the report. In addition, it would be remarkable, if Truman had pursued so guileful a strategy, that opponents did not make an issue of it.

the conservative, Republican Congress could seize it probably played a decisive role. (This goal may have prompted the early reporting date set for the commission.) Truman's executive order, said Congressman Adolph Sabath with gleeful overoptimism, "stole the Republican thunder." Representative J. M. Combs, who chaired the subcommittee which had urged the establishment of the President's Temporary Commission, told that group that Congress would accept a good loyalty program from it but, if dissatisfied, would take the initiative itself. Edward Rees, Combs's Republican successor as subcommittee chairman, bore out the latter's prophecy by introducing a bill providing for a more stringent loyalty program whose governing apparatus was to be independent of other executive agencies. The Rees bill was passed by the House in June 1947, but the Senate failed to act on it.[53]

If Truman's loyalty order forestalled competing congressional efforts, it failed to insulate the administration from continued political recriminations. Republicans applauded the executive order but deplored the conditions which prompted it; they also claimed credit for forcing Truman to act. Congressman B. Carroll Reece expressed pleasure that Truman, "however belatedly, has adopted this important part of the program" espoused by the GOP in the recent campaign. Furthermore, the Republicans questioned the President's sincerity, dragged the loyalty issue into the debate on aid to Greece and Turkey, castigated the administration for slowness in implementing the program (before ink on Executive Order 9835 was even dry), and held up funding for it until July. As a preclusive device, the Truman loyalty program achieved marginal success at most.[54]

The Truman administration, as critics have noted, shared responsibility for the ramifying forces of repression which accompanied the cold war. If there was no explicit connection between the launching of the loyalty program and the pursuit of containment abroad, nonetheless administration rhetoric in defense of the one and in advocacy of the other did nothing to diminish public anxieties. Administration spokesmen sometimes offered overblown pictures of the internal communist threat. Secretary of Labor Lewis Schwellenbach, for example, undercut the forces of restraint when he testified before a House committee in March 1947 that the Communist Party should be outlawed. Truman's Attorneys General were given to blowsy rhetoric—their duties frequently included advertising the administration's vigilance before audiences thought to be especially jittery about communism. J. Howard McGrath warned, in a passage much quoted by historians, that Communists were "everywhere—in factories, offices, butcher stores, on street corners, in private businesses." [55]

Historians have criticized Truman, too, for accentuating public fears. In launching the loyalty program the President, according to Barton J. Bernstein, "exaggerated the dangers" posed by disloyal bureaucrats and in his anxiety "seemed also to be promising *absolute* internal security"—a clear impossibility. A single disclosure of subversive activities would validate right-wing charges that government security was lax: Truman had given too large a warranty for his loyalty program and so "contributed to the loss of public confidence and set the scene in which Joseph McCarthy could flourish." Truman has also been accused of heightening tensions by his rhetorical conduct of the cold war. A "self-righteous arrogance" suffused his foreign-policy pronouncements, according to Athan Theoharis; the President verbalized increasingly alarmist appeals to a narrowly conservative, messianic anticommunism. Soon he was describing the cold war as a virtual jihad. America would achieve peace, Truman said, "because we are on the right track, and we will win—because God is with us in that enterprise." [56]

However, the context of these fulsome utterances merits attention. For instance, in assuring his listeners that "God is with us," Truman was claiming not that God was against the Soviets— only that He was for peace. The speech leaves the impression not of Truman as Peter the Hermit preaching a crusade against communism, but of "Give 'em Hell Harry" campaigning for world peace.* Similarly, even the speeches of Attorney General McGrath, for all their anticommunist hyperbole, emphasized the necessity for protecting civil liberties. In

---

* His "one ambition" as President, said Truman, was "to obtain world peace." He would no more flag in that quest than he had in his pursuit of election in 1948. Then he had faced the challenge of convincing Americans that he was "on the right track and for their benefit"; he succeeded and won. "Now we want to convince the world in exactly the same manner that we are on the right track, and we will win—because I think God is with us in that enterprise." *Truman Papers, 1950,* p. 344. Truman's "I think" in the original also adds a note of tentativeness which is missing from critiques of the speech. Cf. Theoharis, "Rhetoric of Politics," p. 213.

the same paragraph as his oft-noted reference to the perils of Red meat shops, McGrath warned against "careless speech, irresponsible labelling of individuals as 'Communists,' character assassination, witchhunts, hysteria" and termed it essential to "remedy the defects of democracy which provide the Communists with ammunition." McGrath also tried—ineptly, perhaps—to temper his frightening message by adding that "the situation is not alarming, not a condition to cause hysteria or panic." *

McGrath's speech alluded, albeit crudely, to a problem of which Truman and others in the administration expressed frequent awareness: the need to balance the competing demands of internal security and individual rights.[57] However, even if there is justification for emphasizing the more strident portions of the rhetoric, the view that the Democrats' cold-war oratory exacerbated national anxieties and thus led to McCarthyism rests on an unproven supposition: that people actually listened to the speeches and weighed their nuances. Language is not without influence, but to attribute so much to Truman's is a risky inference. Evidence that Truman's speeches led to the jelling of an anti-Soviet, anticommunist mood is lacking. It is not clear that Truman shaped public opinion so much as he conformed to it. Even before he took office, 60 percent of the respondents to a Gallup poll suspected the Russians of seeking additional territory after the war (and 51 percent believed they should not have it). In September 1946, 62 percent said their feelings toward the Soviet Union had grown less friendly in the past year; only 2 percent avowed a more friendly attitude. In whatever direction Truman's policies toward the Soviet Union may have erred, only 6 percent of the public in 1947 believed them too harsh; 62 percent found them too soft. As for domestic Communists, 36 percent in 1946 were urg-

---

* McGrath's speech, alarmist despite its plea for restraint, exemplified another trait of the administration's defense of its loyalty program: an elitist tone. (See Theoharis, *Seeds of Repression,* pp. 150–51, 165, 169.) Thus, while warning against vigilantism, McGrath advised citizens to report "pertinent information" to the FBI: internal security was a job for "the expert, not the amateur." Though the *New York Times* (April 20, 1950) called the speech "one of the most vigorous denunciations of Communists to come from a Cabinet member," it highlighted McGrath's message on behalf of moderation. Evidence that the speech stampeded anyone is lacking. Delivered in mid-April, 1950, it was more likely a response to the McCarthy incubus than its progenitor.

ing stringent measures ("Get rid of them, report them, jail them, shoot them") and 16 percent would keep them from public office or "make it hard for them to be active"; 23 percent were willing either to do nothing or merely to be vigilant.[58]

The existence of a tough anticommunist consensus neither justified the repressive consequences of cold-war politics nor nullified the statesman's obligation to maintain his critical faculties; it does, however, outline the limits within which the Truman administration operated. Regardless of the administration's response to the rising concern over loyalty, the Republicans were homing in on that issue. Perhaps it was true that Truman himself let the genie out of the bottle in heeding Senator Vandenberg's advice to "scare hell out of the American people" in order to get his foreign aid programs past the isolationists and economizers of the Eightieth Congress. It is also true that liberals indulged in red-baiting as blatant at times as that of the McCarthyites. Regardless of their own activities, the Democrats were bound to face a mounting barrage of Republican charges of softness on communism, as the 1944 and 1946 elections bore out. Even after Henry Wallace had been forced out of the Cabinet (and before Democrats began to red-bait him), B. Carroll Reece taxed the Democratic Party on grounds that the Wallace influence persisted in its ranks. Congressman John Byrnes of Wisconsin declared that his own party was free of "Russia Firsters, the pinkos, the fellow travellers, the Red Peppers and the Two World Wallaces." Even though West Virginia Congressman Jennings Randolph had pressed Harry Truman to enact a loyalty program, his Republican foe of 1946 dismissed these efforts as "belated." The communist issue was cropping up in local contests as well. In 1945, a Detroit mayoral candidate suffered from accusations that he was "a foxy playboy of Stalin's Gang" and part of a plot to make Detroit communism's "guinea pig city." [59]

At several junctures one can find flaws in the Democratic response to the communist issue and to McCarthyism, but one should first note that the very notion of a "Democratic response" is an uncertain metaphor for a more complex reality. The fact that neither of the two major parties has ever been a particularly cohesive political body heightened their difficulties in elaborating a position on McCarthy—or on most other issues. Traditionally, American parties have consisted of diffuse conglomerations of politicians representing different constituencies and viewpoints. Party unity and discipline have been rarities. During FDR's first term, the Democrats gave unusually solid support to his programs, but the New Deal coalition splintered under the stresses of 1937–1938—the court-packing effort, labor militance, and the Roosevelt recession. Harry Truman had to contend with the same divided party that hampered his predecessor. Truman's liberal proposals, especially in the area of civil rights, completed the alienation of the Southerners from that wing of the party which was anchored in the White House.[60] In league with like-minded Republicans, Southern conservatives managed to block Fair Deal measures which came to a vote; thanks to seniority, they also controlled the switches by which the President's program could easily be sidetracked at the committee level.

From 1937 through the Truman era, power in the Senate followed a pattern of "decentralization," a fact which tended to diminish the role of party leadership.[61] The Democratic Party's fragmented condition reinforced the Senate's passivity in the face of McCarthy's excesses. Southern conservatives and Northern liberals seldom cooperated to shape common programs. Save on foreign-policy issues, the nominal majorities the Democrats enjoyed in the Truman years (except during the Eightieth Congress) were virtually meaningless. Reflective of this division in the party was the unassertiveness of the Democratic Senate leadership, whose modest abilities and initiative made more difficult the marshaling of Democratic ranks against McCarthy. Scott M. Lucas became Majority Leader in 1949; the Southerners, appraising his lukewarm affection for the Fair Deal, could tolerate him. In 1951, Ernest McFarland succeeded Lucas, defeating the more liberal Joseph C. O'Mahoney. The New York *Post* suggested that McFarland resembled "a baseball manager who can't help rooting for the other team." Like Lucas, he was "carrying the Fair Deal flag at half mast." [62]

As the loosely structured American party system permits, the Democrats, while largely united on what measures to take to halt communism abroad and, to a lesser degree, at home, entertained diverse opinions on the meaning of McCarthyism and the response it warranted. At one end of the spectrum, Pat McCarran accepted virtually every McCarthyite premise concerning the nature of the threat of internal subversion. McCarthy could usually count the puissant Nevada

Senator as an ally. Senators James Eastland and Willis Smith, staunch conservatives, perceived a communist menace of equal gravity, but they stopped short of public support of McCarthy. Other Southerners, while they, too, lamented the political unorthodoxy of many New Dealers, generally had confidence in Acheson and his department, backed Truman's foreign policies, and gave little credence to McCarthy's charges. At the party's other extremity were the Northern liberals. Few of them offered much opposition to the loyalty program, the majority agreeing with the conservatives as to its necessity. However, the liberals did muster greater indignation against McCarthy than did their Southern colleagues during most of the Wisconsin Senator's period of influence. Some spoke out vigorously against McCarthy, but a number of others, fearful of his presumed power, remained discreetly silent. Democratic moderates, often holding marginal seats from midwestern or mountain states, were still more cautious. Obviously, to shape a party policy from these materials was comparable to erecting a statue out of gelatin.

The historical trends which increased the Democrats' difficulties in coping with McCarthy facilitated his rise to national prominence by their cognate effect upon the Republican Party. Although the Democrats' inability to contain McCarthyism was rooted in plural causes, one of their problems lay in the weakness of their party as an institution. While the GOP was no stronger a tool for policy-formation, it sufficed for McCarthy's purposes. What he required of his Republican colleagues was tolerance. The desperation of the conservatives, the congressional Republicans, over their party's continued failure to seize national power, played into his hands, just as he, they thought, played into theirs. (Some of the Senator's foes would recall with a shudder that certain German conservative groups had seen in Hitler a pawn who could be used and then discarded.) McCarthy was the product primarily of the rhythms and movements of partisan politics. He emerged as the GOP was shifting toward a new center of gravity. He wielded forcefully a political weapon toward which other Republicans, shelving their scruples after the frustrations of 1948, were moving. McCarthy thus managed to obtain the sufferance, if not the enthusiasm, of many sectors of the Republican Party because he appeared to have fastened upon a winning issue.

McCarthy's dependence upon this altered balance within his own party explained at once his power and the inability of the Democrats to exert much leverage upon his activities. Over the internal affairs of the opposition party, Truman and the Democrats could have little influence. The Democrats committed errors at various stages in the conflict with the Senator from Wisconsin and the political forces he exemplified, but the fact that McCarthy, for five years, enjoyed a privileged sanctuary within his own party goes far to explain the Democrats' failure to neutralize McCarthyism when it emerged.

CHAPTER 2
"A List Of 205 . . ."

IN 1950, Joseph R. McCarthy, not quite forty-two years old, enjoyed membership in the most august legislative body in the world. His political standing was all the more remarkable for the modest surroundings in which he had begun his ascent. McCarthy, as Richard Rovere, one of his biographers, has noted, barely missed being born in a log cabin; the farm which his family worked near Appleton, Wisconsin, provided a sufficiently austere background without it. But McCarthy, early in life, revealed qualities which were to take him to the United States Senate.

His adolescence and the forces which shaped him remain obscure. Poverty may have been the crucible of his throbbing ambition and the doggedness and normlessness which accompanied it. Perhaps Joe's awkward, hulking appearance set him apart, and so germinated the drives which eventually made of him a force-fed extrovert. (His looks, however, were not that unusual; some credited him with a rough-hewn handsomeness later in life. For that matter, Lincoln, too, was ambitious.) There are accounts of a shy, lonely boy, mocked by eight brothers and sisters, seeking refuge in his mother's apron, consoled by her admonition: "Joe, you be somebody. You get ahead."

Whatever the lessons of his youth, McCarthy never felt them worth reporting. In his public rhetoric, there was almost no mention of childhood or family—or anything which preceded his increasingly mythologized military career. Except for his comparisons of the mucky, dirty business of chasing Communists to the skunk-hunting he had done on the farm, McCarthy rarely turned around in later years to see where he had been. While the pasts of those whom McCarthy attacked came back to haunt them, McCarthy's own was outdistanced by the fast-moving Senator.[1]

During McCarthy's rise in the world, frustrations mingled with triumphs which almost parodied Horatio Alger. At the age of fourteen McCarthy quit school. Entering the chicken-breeding business, he began to prosper, but in his nineteenth year disaster struck; he contracted influenza, and while he convalesced, his business fell into ruin. He moved from Grand Chute to Manawa and took a job as manager of a grocery store; he soon acquired a reputation for hard work and gregariousness. Resuming his education, he completed four years of high-school work in a single year thanks to the phenomenal energy and stamina which would characterize later successes. He also got ahead through charm and a sometimes convenient disregard for convention, if not propriety—features which would also recur. One teacher who resisted the McCarthy juggernaut in the classroom finally yielded under the subtler pressures of the dance floor: McCarthy invited her to the school prom. Having passed her course and everyone else's, McCarthy was graduated. He then matriculated at Marquette University, where he received his bachelor's and, in 1935, his law degree.

In law school McCarthy had been attracted to the prospect of a political career. His first law practice, in diminutive Waupaca, was so unlucrative and his poker playing so intensive that he earned more at the card table than at the bar. In 1936 he moved to Shawano and entered a partnership with a more substantial lawyer. A Democrat by inclination and experience, McCarthy took his first crack at politics when he sought the office of district attorney. After a vigorous campaign, he outpolled his Republican opponent but finished well behind the victor, who belonged to the Progressive Party.

Wisconsin politics had been in flux during the 1930s. The Progressive Party, founded in 1934 and led by Philip F. La Follette and Robert M. La Follette, Jr., the sons of "Fighting Bob" La Follette, ruled the state until 1938. The Progressives briefly tapped the votes of those who would support neither the Republican Party, whose conservatism had been reinforced by the Progressives' exodus from its ranks, nor the Democrats, who in Wisconsin were slow to respond to the liberal leadership of FDR. In 1938, a conservative reaction set in. Eventually, Wisconsin's Democratic party would attract many liberal Progressives, but in the short run the Republicans stood to benefit from the decline of the third party. Accordingly, McCarthy began to edge almost imperceptibly toward the GOP.[2]

As a first step, in 1939 he announced his candidacy for judge of Wisconsin's Tenth Circuit Court, a nonpartisan post then held by the respected Judge Edgar V. Werner. He turned Werner's chief asset— long experience on the bench—into a liability. The sixty-six-year-old judge, hoary with age according to McCarthy, deserved a well-earned retirement. In some of his campaign literature, McCarthy portrayed the judge as seventy-three. At times he advanced his opponent's age to eighty-nine and lopped a year off his own for good measure. McCarthy also harvested votes by an energetic house-to-house and farm-to-farm canvass which became a legend in the state. When the ballots were in, he had achieved a startling upset victory. As a jurist, McCarthy made good his promise to clean up the cluttered docket of the Tenth Circuit; he did so chiefly at the expense of due process.

Alert to opportunities for advancing his political career, McCarthy, at the outbreak of World War II, decided to join the glamorous Marine Corps. By his own account, he enlisted as a private and rose through the ranks; actually, he requested and received a commission as first lieutenant. Serving in the Pacific as intelligence officer for an aviation squadron, McCarthy performed competently, but he hungered for other forms of distinction. He logged hours as a volunteer tail-gunner of some of the (usually routine) observation flights assigned to his unit. He enjoyed firing machine guns at coconut trees and once set a record for the number of rounds expended in a single day.

In 1944, friends back in Wisconsin entered McCarthy's name in the Republican senatorial primary (his first open avowal of Republican allegiance). As a serviceman—now a captain—in uniform, he could not lawfully campaign, but in his speeches he offered comments which he *would* have made on the issues had the law permitted. The incumbent, Alexander Wiley, won easily, but McCarthy finished second out of four with a handsome vote. Early in 1945 McCarthy sought another leave from his Marine duties to run for reelection to the circuit court. His request denied, he resigned from the Corps. Once returned to office, he began to lay plans in earnest for the senatorial race the following year.[3]

McCarthy's aspirations led to a confrontation with Robert M. La Follette, Jr. In 1946, the Progressive Party breathed its last; Senator La Follette and most (but not all) of his followers determined to go back to the Republican fold. Welcome they were not. Most Republican leaders, including Thomas E. Coleman, chairman of the state's Republican Voluntary Committee, opposed the return in force of the deserters of twelve years before. McCarthy, also critical of La Follette, promised him a "very rough, but clean fight" for the nomination. To many Republicans, this challenge seemed presumptuous; Coleman's plans to defeat La Follette called for a more established candidate, not a johnny-come-lately like McCarthy. But the young judge worked assiduously, traveling to every corner of the state, pumping hands, visiting local party leaders, lining up delegates, and keeping visible. At the state convention, Coleman and his associates found that McCarthy could not be denied the nomination, and they were reluctantly forced to support him.[4]

During the campaign, McCarthy attacked La Follette on several scores, some of them, such as the charge that La Follette had become a Virginia grandee oblivious to his home state, rather trumped up. But La Follette had neglected political fences, and in 1946 he campaigned only briefly and desultorily. At the same time, the Democratic candidate for Senator, Howard McMurray, pounded La Follette as an isolationist and betrayer of the late FDR. Although La Follette was favored to win, McCarthy gained a narrow victory with 207,935 votes to La Follette's 202,557. In the general election, largely a formality, McCarthy rolled up 62 percent of the vote.[5]

Latter-day foes of the junior Senator would savor a bitter irony in these results. McCarthy, they claimed, had actually received aid in the primary from the Communists, who were bent on defeating La Follette because of his outspoken opposition to Soviet imperialism. Communists occupying strategic positions in the Wisconsin labor movement allegedly managed to poison the wells of La Follette's support among urban workingmen. But while one can document the Communists' hostility to La Follette and instances when they sought to impart their animosity to other unionists, one cannot show a clear causal link between these actions and La Follette's defeat.[6] Numerous other forces were at work. With his mates in the Republican Class of '46, McCarthy benefited from momentary public vexation at the floundering Truman administration. He and others in 1946 also profited electorally from the appeal of their youth and attractive war records. Once in the Senate, they distinguished themselves by vocal opposition to Communists, particularly of the domestic variety, while they often voted against proposals of the Truman administration directed against the foreign threat of communism. On socioeconomic questions, they were unabashed conservatives.*

In 1946, however, the full lineaments of the McCarthy who emerged in 1950 had not yet become clear. During the campaign, he was not the isolationist he would later be labeled: he applauded the Byrnes-Vandenberg foreign policies. Moreover, his candidacy was closely associated with the national ambitions of Harold Stassen and seemed to signify the growth of internationalism in the Republican Party. Indeed, after the election, McCarthy categorized Stalin's recent disarmament proposal as "a great thing and he must be given credit for being sincere about it." Appraising the brash young victor, the Milwaukee *Journal* surmised that he would take a stance in the Senate's "liberal Republican bloc" and called the "McCarthy story" one of the "truly American type." The *Journal* could only reserve judgment on the seamier side of the McCarthy candidacy—his refusal to resign his judgeship when he ran for the Senate (as the state constitution required) and the granting of "quickie" divorces to his political pals.[7]

McCarthy's first three years in the Senate revealed no legislative statecraft; he involved himself chiefly in the projects of several of Washington's lobbyists and fixers. Thus, his efforts to end wartime controls on sugar at the behest of a noted soft-drink bottler earned

---

* Members of the Class of '46 included Harry Cain of Washington, William E. Jenner of Indiana (though he had served part of a term previously), Zales N. Ecton of Montana, and James P. Kem of Missouri. Kem, Cain, and Ecton were beaten in 1952. However, it should also be noted that Ralph E. Flanders, McCarthy's severest Republican critic, and Albert V. Watkins, chairman of the committee which recommended McCarthy's censure, were elected in 1946. Other non-McCarthyites who won in 1946 were Henry Cabot Lodge, Jr. (reelected, having resigned his seat in World War II), Irving Ives, and Edward Thye.

him the title of the "Pepsi-Cola Kid." In 1948 he managed to emasculate a moderate federal housing bill and demonstrate his subservience to certain private housing interests. One of these, the Lustron Corporation, a prefab housing concern which was currently surviving on Reconstruction Finance Corporation (RFC) loans, paid him $10,000 for a short article on private housing which was published over his signature. At $1.43 a word, McCarthy's compensation exceeded the rate at which Winston Churchill, a somewhat more accomplished author, was remunerated for his World War II memoirs. Lustron had a soundly engineered product but suffered under management which was both inept and too busy currying favor with federal authorities. Soon after McCarthy's article appeared, the firm folded.[8]

In 1949, McCarthy became embroiled in a controversy which prefigured some of his later activities: the Malmedy massacre. During the Battle of the Bulge, Nazi stormtroopers had slaughtered in cold blood 150 American prisoners of war. The criminals were later apprehended, made to confess, and brought to trial. In 1949 a subcommittee of the Senate Armed Services Committee investigated charges that the Nazis had been tricked and tortured into confessing. Soon McCarthy entered the picture; he invited himself to subcommittee sessions, where he interrogated witnesses and bullyragged the chairman, Senator Raymond Baldwin of Connecticut, and other members. He took the part of the stormtroopers and (as five years later) attacked the veracity and honor of the Army. His help came from suspect sources. He obtained office and research aid from the protégé of a prominent Nazi sympathizer in Wisconsin; a contact in Germany proved to be a Communist. It has been suggested that McCarthy saw in the affair a chance to obtain publicity on an issue to which his many German-American constituents might be receptive. In any event, he showed a talent for disruption which his colleagues might well have marked. Only Baldwin saw the portent: when he resigned from the Senate to accept a state supreme court position he may have been partly motivated by a desire to avoid further abuse of the sort McCarthy had heaped on him.[9]

McCarthy crossed swords next with the Secretary of the Navy, Francis P. Matthews, over the dismissal of Admiral Louis E. Denfeld as Chief of Naval Operations (CNO). In 1949, the administration had announced Denfeld's reappointment for another two-year term. The Senate had confirmed him, and his commission had been prepared, but in the meantime the Admiral, testifying before a House committee, had criticized the administration's handling of military unification. He feared that it threatened the very existence of the Navy and Marine Corps. Matthews now urged President Truman to replace Denfeld with Admiral Forrest Sherman, who was appointed *ad interim*.

The Navy's watchdogs bayed and McCarthy joined in, tapping the bitterness engendered by the interservice rivalries of the era.* He pounced on ambiguities and discrepancies in Matthews's statements and questioned whether it was even legal to confirm Sherman. Denfeld had not taken the oath of office, but he had received his commission informally and unofficially. Brandishing a copy of it, McCarthy argued that the office of CNO was not vacant—Denfeld occupied it. He repeatedly impugned the abilities of Secretary Matthews, who he alleged "had never sailed in anything larger than a rowboat." He accused Matthews of lying, then redeemed him from that sin only by declaring him incompetent: "the use of the word 'lie' presupposes that the person concerned knew what he was talking about."

It took time to shag the long, foul flies McCarthy batted out, but it was done. His case rested on semantic quibbles, memory lapses by Matthews, and bureaucratic short circuits. The fact remained that Denfeld had never been sworn in for a second term; not even McCarthy disputed Truman's authority to fire him. Senator Millard Tydings, Chairman of the Armed Services Committee, termed it a "sham battle" involving "a pretty small peanut." But with a number of small peanuts McCarthy had led the Senate around in circles for several days. He had shown a capacity for delay, obstruction, and distortion. He had learned to deny that *he* was making value judgments: he was not "interested in making out a case for or against anyone . . . merely presenting facts to the Senate." Having suggested that im-

---

* The Denfeld affair, said McCarthy, was part of a larger problem. "I have just looked over the President's budget, and I see that we are now in the unusual position of having a Marine Corps with practically no Marines and we shall very shortly have a Navy without any ships." McCarthy accused Matthews of being a mere " 'yes' man" unwilling to fight for the Navy's interests. *Cong. Record,* 96 (Jan. 12, 1950): 342, (Jan. 18, 1950); 519.

peachment might be in order, he denied that he had even made charges. It was up to others—the Armed Services Committee—to put the facts together.[10]

McCarthy raised another theme which would recur in his attacks on the State Department: there was a plot by the executive branch to withhold from Congress the information necessary to its proper functioning. He warned of "the complete iron curtain which has been established around the Pentagon." Nor was the Pentagon unique in this respect: McCarthy cited the frustrations of Congress in obtaining data on the loyalty program. Even the imposition of the administration's policy of secrecy was shrouded in secrecy.[11] McCarthy had thus begun to mine a number of veins connected with the mother lode of national security, but he had not yet found the real strike.

By 1950, McCarthy had demonstrated a talent for obstreperous disruption, but no political benefits had accrued. Indeed, his abrasive behavior had closed a number of doors to him. Thus, in 1949 he lost his seat on the Banking and Currency Committee, partly because of GOP election losses but more directly because Senator Burnet R. Maybank told Majority Leader Scott Lucas "that if he wanted me to be chairman (of the committee) not to put McCarthy on it." [12] McCarthy was also losing ground back in Wisconsin. Alarming reports of his past activities were circulating throughout the state; the Madison *Capital-Times* was publishing accounts of the irregularities in his past campaigns and private finances. Miles McMillin of the same paper had instituted a lawsuit on the question of whether McCarthy had violated state law or bar association ethics with his 1946 candidacy.[13] Politicians have survived worse scandals, but not without some compensatory stock in trade by which to reward the patience of their constituents. As of January 1950, the young Senator had no such political property.

The quest for a potent issue reportedly led McCarthy to a significant meeting on January 7, when he dined with Father Edmund A. Walsh, director of the School of Foreign Service at Georgetown University; Professor Charles H. Kraus, who taught political science at Georgetown and worked for McCarthy; and William A. Roberts, a Washington attorney. The three wished to make a more conscientious legislator of McCarthy. On his part, the Senator vented his anxiety over his failure to find an attractive political issue. Roberts suggested that he fight for the St. Lawrence Seaway. McCarthy, unimpressed, countered by asking his companions' views on the feasibility of pushing a modernized version of the Townsend Plan; they thought little of it. Father Walsh then remarked how salient the issue of communism had become. McCarthy, delighted with the idea, began to ponder its possibilities. The three men all tried to impress him with the need for a cautious, informed approach, but McCarthy, even this early did not heed the counsels of restraint; ultimately, when he proved to be a sorcerer's apprentice, all three were forced to disavow him.[14]

Roy Cohn, McCarthy's aide at a later date, has offered the Senator's own purported version of his seizure of the communist issue. In November 1949, three patriots fretting at the inroads of communist subversion went to see McCarthy. Disturbed that an FBI report on this problem, to which they had access, had lain dormant in Pentagon files for two years, they had taken their data to three Republican Senators; but each resisted their entreaties for an offensive against communism. McCarthy carried their material home, became engrossed as he read it overnight, and called one of his mysterious informants at 6:30 A.M. to report that he was "buying the package"— much, says Cohn, as one would buy a used car. McCarthy's authorship of the tale weights the odds against its reliability, and his own testimony is contradictory. Asked in April 1950, how long ago he had discovered communism, he answered: "Two and a half months." [15]

However, there is evidence that McCarthy had moved tentatively toward the communist issue before the celebrated "Dinner at the Colony." The historian Michael J. O'Brien has discovered a remarkable buried instance of McCarthy's use of the topic in November 1949, against political enemies in Wisconsin. In a speech in Madison on November 11 and in a memorandum which he sent to local opinion leaders heralding the talk, McCarthy insinuated that the Madison *Capital-Times*, published by his arch-foe William T. Evjue, was "the red mouthpiece for the Communist Party in Wisconsin." He founded this indictment chiefly on the claim that the city editor of the newspaper, Cedric Parker, was a Communist. McCarthy's enemies were vulnerable: Evjue himself had once called his employee a Communist; Parker was widely assumed to have been, if not a Communist, a fellow-traveler. McCarthy's documentation (much of it from HUAC reports) was incomplete, but it sufficed to garner considerable news-paper coverage. *Time* magazine even picked up the story. As O'Brien has pointed out, the Cedric Parker affair taught McCarthy a lesson in the political utility of the communist issue.[16]

However, even prior to his November 1949 assault on the *Capital-Times,* McCarthy had dabbled in anticommunism. He had made references to his "communistically inclined" opponent in 1946 and in a radio speech had asserted that much of the current "industrial unrest" could be "laid right smack at the door of the communists in the labor movement"; but these had been sporadic kidney punches, not a sustained barrage. In 1947, in his depredations upon public housing, he had labeled one housing project in New York a "breeding ground for Communism." In September 1949, urging the enactment of import quotas upon foreign furs, McCarthy managed to link the most parochial political concern to the campaign against communism. Not only did fur imports undermine American businesses, but since the bulk of the furs came from communist countries, each alien pelt earned dollars which subsidized Soviet spying in the United States.[17]

At other times as well McCarthy, albeit fleetingly, raised the specter of communism. He inserted into the *Congressional Record* of October 19, 1949, material questioning the loyalty of some State Department officials. In arguing against the dismantling of German industrial plants, he suggested that some State Department personnel might be "more sympathetic to certain foreign ideologies than to our own." He went on to quote a news article critical of John Stewart Service, who allegedly had sold out the regime of Chiang Kai-shek. A few moments later, he called attention to an article assailing the State Department's "Two-Faced" foreign policy: while spending billions to halt communism in Europe, it was "playing the Soviet game in the Far East."[18] In Kenosha on November 15, he again adverted to communist penetration of the State Department and to John Stewart Service. He scored America's benighted foreign policy once more in a December 3 speech in Philadelphia; two days later in Milwaukee, he blamed the State Department for the "tremendous pace" at which the nation was losing ground in the cold war. To a Madison audience he explained that he had voted against the reappointment of Leland Olds to the Federal Power Commission "because he is a

Communist." On January 5, 1950, McCarthy mounted another attack on Service and those who had espoused the cause of the Chinese Reds.[19]

The Hiss case greatly impressed McCarthy. Its outcome made it urgent, said McCarthy, that Acheson "either clean the Communists out of the State Department or resign and let President Truman appoint someone who will." On January 25, the Wisconsinite interrupted Senator Karl Mundt's declamation on the meaning of the Hiss case to ask if Mundt had heard Acheson's "fantastic statement" made moments before, when he announced his refusal to turn his back on Hiss. Was the Secretary implying that "he will not turn his back on any other Communists in the State Department . . . ?" Two weeks later, McCarthy again broached the issue of communist infiltration. He read a news article asserting that one of the top communist spies in government—unnamed—was using a Justice of the Supreme Court—also unnamed—as a "front." Since the matter fell outside the jurisdiction of his own committee, McCarthy marked it for the attention of the appropriate panel.[20] Clearly, the issue of communism was percolating through McCarthy's mind well before the Wheeling speech and, indeed, the Colony dinner.

It would be wrong, however, to exaggerate either McCarthy's interest or preparation in anticommunism prior to his Lincoln Day offensive. In the early weeks of 1950, he was searching for an issue that would increase his visibility. He even toyed with Senator Estes Kefauver's eventual concern, the growth of crime, suggesting that the Senate investigate "whether racketeers and gamblers . . . are attempting to control city politics." He continued to dally with the question of old age pensions. Advance publicity for his Wheeling speech mentioned not a word about his credentials, fresh as they were, as an anticommunist. While he had not announced the subject of his address, the Wisconsin Senator, according to the Wheeling *News-Register,* would probably discuss "the controversial Brannan plan, aid to disabled and aged, and other timely topics." The Wheeling *Intelligencer* touted him as "one of Washington's most ardent champions of adequate old age and other pensions and it is quite sure that he will voice his sentiments along these lines" on February 9.[21]

For his speech, McCarthy had hastily assembled a collage of snippets from the utterances of several more established spokesmen for

Republican anticommunism.[22] On arrival, he gave out copies of a "rough draft" of the speech to the press and radio, but then went to his hotel room to work on the text until shortly before the banquet. For the Ohio County Women's Republican Club, McCarthy sketched the harsh, steely outlines of the cold war and the unbridgeable differences in morality and ideology dividing Russia, with its "communist atheism," from the Christian West. And now, the Senator warned, "the chips are down—they are truly down." In 1945, the free world contained 1,625,000,000 souls while communism claimed only 180,000,000. Now the odds had shifted: 800,000,000 people lay under communist subjugation (and others had gone neutralist) while the free world numbered 500,000,000 people.* America had lost ground not as a result of foreign aggression, but "because of the traitorous actions of those who have been treated so well by this nation," who enjoyed "the finest homes, the finest college education, and the finest jobs in Government we can give." This was "glaringly true in the State Department," where "the bright young men who are born with silver spoons in their mouths are the ones who have been worst." McCarthy named John Stewart Service, Mary Jane Keeney, Gustavo Duran, and Harlow Shapley as examples. Tantalizingly, he intimated

> While I cannot take the time to name all of the men in the State Department who have been named as members of the Communist Party and members of a spy ring. I have here in my hand a list of 205 . . . a list of names that were made known to the Secretary of State and who nevertheless are still working and shaping the policy of the State Department.[23]

Or so his opponents claimed he said. McCarthy himself later maintained that he had used the number "fifty-seven" Communists or party loyalists. Neither McCarthy nor his critics were able to docu-

---

* Griffith (*Politics of Fear*, p. 48) notes that McCarthy copied almost verbatim from a speech by Richard Nixon his remarks about the relative strength of the communist and free worlds. McCarthy's rough draft butchered these figures beyond recognition. However, these statistics did not originate with Nixon, but had popped up with some frequency during the early weeks of 1950 in GOP rhetoric. See *Cong. Record,* 96 (Jan. 5, 1950): 90, (Jan. 24, 1950): 847, (Jan. 26, 1950): 1007 (Senator Jenner, Representatives John Lodge and Richard Nixon).

ment their assertions conclusively. The tape recording from which radio station WWVA broadcast the speech was later erased; its precise contents echoed up the Appalachian hollows and were lost. At the request of the State Department, James K. Whitaker, news editor of WWVA, and Paul A. Myers, its program director, signed affidavits that to their recollection McCarthy had spoken of 205 Communists or spies.[24] Frank Desmond, a reporter for the Wheeling *Intelligencer*, filed a story to the same effect, as did the affiliated Wheeling *News-Register*,[25] the Chicago *Tribune* and other papers which picked up the Associated Press account.[26] McCarthy's "rough draft," containing the crucial paragraph and numbers, survived to plague the Senator.[27]

However, other circumstances cast doubt on whether McCarthy said what his enemies claimed. While the script he handed to the media alluded to a "list of 205," McCarthy had pointedly warned that it was only a rough draft, subject to change. Two days after the speech, Herman E. Gieske, editor of the Wheeling *Intelligencer*, wrote an editorial citing McCarthy's charge that "over fifty persons of known Communistic affiliations" infested the State Department. Gieske, who had attended the address, recalled no mention of the number of 205. Skeptical of Desmond's account, he quizzed his reporter; Desmond insisted he had heard 205, but conceded that he had listened to the speech only "in a general way" and admitted that when he composed his piece he had relied on McCarthy's rough draft.[28]

Similarly, the testimony of the two radio station employees contained loopholes. Several members of the audience claimed that James E. Whitaker, who taped the talk, had been too busy timing it and regulating the quality of the transcription to check closely for content; such witnesses themselves recalled either no mention of 205 Reds or at most that there were two numbers, the *lesser* of which (presumably 57) designated known State Department Communists.[29] Nevertheless, the 205 version cannot simply be dismissed. Paul Myers, the program director, insisted that he heard that figure when he replayed the tape and checked it against McCarthy's script. He listened specifically for that number because it was so controversial; however, he could not vouch for the context in which it was used. Whitaker stuck by his original affidavit to the effect that McCarthy had spoken of 205 Communists and, indeed, remembered that the statement had stirred "quite a hub-bub" among the audience.[30]

Never quite sure himself what he had said, McCarthy conceded that he might have used the figure 205, or possibly "over 200," either in the course of his frequent ad-libbing or in a question-and-answer session after the speech. He denied that he had used the language of his rough draft in which he had claimed to possess a list of 205 known Communists. Witnesses confirmed that he had spoken extemporaneously and often wandered from his notes, but McCarthy was not always consistent on this point: on February 20 he read what he professed to be a reasonably accurate rendition of the speech.[31]

From the welter of conflicting (and not always disinterested) testimony, no fully satisfactory account of the speech has emerged. Only possibilities remain. McCarthy may have said 205, or he may have corrected this to 57 as he did in subsequent addresses. He might even have used both figures—either in confusion and inadvertence or perhaps, as he himself conjectured, with 57 as the key number and 205 in a lesser role. In any case, he had no list at all; the figure 205 was a deduction from a four-year-old letter from then–Secretary of State James F. Byrnes to Congressman Adolph Sabath regarding the screening of some 4,000 prospective employees transferred to State from wartime agencies. Byrnes reported that recommendations against further employment had been made in the cases of 285 of these individuals, of whom 79 had been "separated from service." [32]

McCarthy added to the muddle by several alterations of his text in the course of his journey. When his plane put down in Milwaukee, he dodged reporters, but during a stop-over in Denver on February 10 he submitted to an interview. He claimed he had a list of 207 State Department employees whom he now labeled "bad risks"; at the same time, he elaborated, he knew of 57 "card-carrying" Communists in the department. He even offered to display the list—no, wait, it was in his luggage on the plane. In a radio interview the same day in Salt Lake City, McCarthy declared that in Wheeling he had exposed the retention of 57 "card-carrying" Communists in Foggy Bottom. If the Secretary of State wanted their names, he had only to call—but Acheson should first "show his sincerity" by rolling back the President's 1948 order which had rendered the employee loyalty files confidential.[33] On February 11, from Reno, McCarthy dispatched a telegram to the President trumpeting the presence of 57 Communists in the State Department. He challenged Truman to ask Acheson why of the "approximately 300" (i.e., the 285 of the Byrnes letter) certified by the Department's Loyalty Review Board for discharge only about 80 had been dismissed, and then only "after lengthy consultation with Alger Hiss." [34]

As the publicity increased, the hedges McCarthy placed about his original utterances sprouted profusely. To a reporter in Reno, he denied having called "traitors" the four persons he had named. "And you will notice I didn't call them Communists either." He conceded that he "should have had a line in there saying they were specific cases of people with Communistic connections." He had also crossed out the number 205 from his manuscript and substituted 57. Even so, his warning to a Reno Republican gathering about "57 card-carrying members" of the Communist Party elicited gasps and, in some cases, tears from his audience.[35] Then he was off to Las Vegas for another speech on February 13; the next day, at a press conference in Los Angeles, McCarthy restated the conditions on which he would yield his 57 names. He offered his message ("57 active Communists") to the Republican faithful of Huron, South Dakota, grabbed a quick nightcap, and went winging back to Washington by way of Milwaukee and Appleton, having left behind a trail of contradictory news accounts and the seeds of disputes which would rage for years.[36]

One of the mysteries of the McCarthy era is, however, the manner in which these garbled declarations to chicken-and-peas party ceremonial convocations shortly became the stuff of which history is made. Amid the Lincoln Day oratory of such formidable GOP spokesmen as Richard Nixon, Kenneth Wherry, John Bricker, and Guy Gabrielson, news reports of the Wheeling speech were few.[37] While the wire-service dispatches from Wheeling may have alerted reporters to hunt up McCarthy at the Milwaukee and Denver airports, it was his personal challenge to Truman and the official response to his utterances which made his charges newsworthy: the first articles in the *New York Times* and Washington *Post* headlined McCarthy's telegram to the President and carried the State Department's denial of his claims.[38]

Hitting upon the communist issue as it reached full ripeness, McCarthy benefited from good timing. The fall of China, Russia's A-bomb, Hiss, Fuchs, the H-bomb decision—these events could not help but register upon the public consciousness. Equally important, other Republicans had begun in earnest to box the compass of espionage revelations and the administration's laxity in regard to security. Thus, Senator Homer Capehart asserted on February 4 that there were other spies besides Fuchs, "and there will continue to be as long as we have a President who refers to such matters as 'red herrings' and a Secretary of State who refuses to turn his back on the Alger Hisses." On February 14, Karl Mundt charged that for eighteen years the nation had been "run by New Dealers, Fair Dealers, Misdealers and Hiss dealers who have shuttled back and forth between Freedom and Red Fascism like a pendulum on a kukoo clock." The GOP's statement of principles, released on February 6, showed the party's intention to make a major campaign issue of the loyalty program and communist subversion; many Lincoln Day speeches gave testimony of that inclination.[39]

Yet why was it the novice McCarthy who emerged as the leading exponent of anticommunism? Since his potshots were part of a general Republican salvo, the State Department may have accorded him undue prominence simply by singling out his charges. While the numerical specificity of McCarthy's claims made them unusually vulnerable, the State Department's denials seemed only to give the charges greater newsworthiness. The administration's jumpiness in regard to the loyalty-security question may have prompted what one journalist called its "quick reaction." Arthur Krock reported that the Democrats knew the topic had "explosive and destructive potentials" and that Truman, while wanly hopeful that the issue would not damage his party badly in the next election, was scrupulously avoiding any further "red herring" remarks.[40]

For whatever reason, the State Department made McCarthy its target. On February 10, press officer Lincoln White scouted the Wheeling assertions: the Department had identified no Communists in its employ, "and if we find any they will be summarily discharged." The next day, Deputy Undersecretary of State John Peurifoy wired McCarthy to ask for the 205 names. On February 13, Peurifoy told reporters he knew of no Reds in his department. "But if I can find a single one," he assured them, "I will have him fired before sundown." At his February 16 press conference, President Truman exclaimed that there "was not a word of truth in what the Senator said." Scott M. Lucas, the Democratic Majority Leader, stated that if he had made McCarthy's statements, "I would be ashamed of myself for the rest of my life." [41]

Although these remarks by administration spokesmen constituted something of a challenge, McCarthy himself apparently took the initiative which led to the Senate confrontation of February 20 over his charges. The causal linkages at this stage are obscure. McCarthy had pondered his next moves while still flying westward to fill his speaking dates. Having stated the terms for disclosure to the State Department of his 57 names, in Salt Lake City he broached the alternative that he might make them public after conferring with colleagues. In Los Angeles he said he expected to ask Senator Clyde Hoey to convene the Special Investigating Subcommittee to consider his charges. The Wisconsin Senator also retracted his offer to reveal his list of names to the State Department, since that agency would only resort to further efforts at concealment. At a news conference on February 18, McCarthy declared his intention of laying his case before the Senate in a formal speech.[42] Several newspapers had editorialized that McCarthy should "put up or shut up," but it is not clear that either public opinion or pressure from the Democrats forced McCarthy to take his charges to the Senate floor.[43] Given the Republicans' rising interest in the issue McCarthy had tapped, the atmosphere in which he operated was permissive rather than compelling.

Obtaining the floor late in the day on February 20, McCarthy outlined his charges and strove to tidy up the figures which had been quoted in the past ten days. He explained that he had extrapolated the number 205 from Byrnes's 1946 letter; it was the difference—or nearly so—between 285, the number of security risks or undesirables of whom Byrnes had been apprised by a personnel screening board, and 79, the number of these who had been discharged shortly after. Amid much badgering, mostly by Senator Lucas, McCarthy repeated what purported to be his Wheeling speech. The text he read spoke of "57 cases of individuals who would appear to be either card-carrying members or certainly loyal to the Communist Party." His radioactive 57 had a short half-life; no longer would he even certify that they were all card-carrying Communists. McCarthy also noted that the Wheeling and Reno speeches had been recorded, "so there is no question about what I said. I do not believe I mentioned the figure 205. I believe I said 'over 200.' " Some, but not all, of the 57 were among these 205. Lucas gratingly insisted upon the exact language used in Wheeling, noting newspaper references to 205 Communists, but McCarthy stood fast.[44]

McCarthy moved on to a recital of information taken, he said, from the files of 81 State Department employees of questionable loyalty—thus a new figure entered the calculations. It later developed that McCarthy had derived this data from a collection of summaries of 108 loyalty files culled out in 1947 by the staff of the House Appropriations Committee as a sampling of the effectiveness of the State Department loyalty program. First examined by a subcommittee of the House Appropriations Committee, the "108 list" received scrutiny from three other committees and provided ammunition for several speeches.[45] Perhaps fifteen or twenty Congressmen knew of the list when McCarthy came back from his Wheeling junket; he may have acquired the dossiers from one of them or from a committee staff member. On February 20, McCarthy had no names—only a batch of excerpts labeled anonymously by number. Of the 108 individuals (some of them mere applicants for employment in the first place), only 57 remained in the State Department at the time the 108 list was drawn up—hence McCarthy's "57 Communists." [46]

As McCarthy labored through his cases, the few Democrats on the floor continued to snipe at him. Why, queried Herbert H. Lehman, had he not immediately submitted his 57 names to the State Department? Lucas demanded the name of case number 1; McCarthy replied that he preferred to reveal the names in executive session before the appropriate committee, but, if the Senate so desired, he would release the names. When McCarthy reached case number 14, Senator Wherry, the Republican floor leader, suggested the absence of a quorum. (Ten or so were present.) This fact confirmed, Lucas made the unusual demand that the sergeant-at-arms request the presence of the absent Senators. Lucas then moved adjournment, but his parliamentary ploy was defeated, eighteen to sixteen. All eighteen negative votes were cast by Republicans; all sixteen affirmative, by Democrats. A quorum was obtained, and McCarthy continued. Thereupon Senator Brien McMahon, who had hurried back to the floor in evening dress, began to grill McCarthy on whether he was reading only the derogatory information in the files. McCarthy so stipulated, but he questioned the relevance of data on whether a suspect was "good to his wife and children and all that sort of thing." McMahon countered that McCarthy's method, precluding a balanced assessment of the data, smacked of the "star chamber." McCarthy retorted that by this criterion Lucas, who had insisted he name names, was the worst offender.[47]

When McCarthy finally concluded his eighty-one cases, they fell far short of proving Communist infiltration of the State Department. One case, by his own admission, dealt not with a subversive at all, but with a loyal American who did not get a job. Another raised no question "insofar as communistic activities are concerned," but suggested "rather unusual mental aberrations" of which delicacy prevented disclosure. Similarly, case number 77 repeated case number 9, cases 3 and 4 were the same, and four cases got lost in the shuffle. Only later did it become clear that these dossiers were simply warmed-over remains, sampled and forgotten by others.[48]

Despite the evident puncturability of McCarthy's arguments, the Democrats did not riposte effectively. Senator Lucas, leader of the corporal's guard of Democrats present for the entire speech, was primed to the extent that he had clippings of McCarthy's speeches in front of him. As he persisted in interrupting McCarthy, however, he gave the impression of having lost sight of the distinction between rebuttal and harassment. His thrusts lacked finesse. He tried to pin McCarthy down on his "numbers game," but pending evidence obtained from Wheeling (in itself inconclusive), McCarthy's explanation was at least plausible. Moreover, it is unlikely that the proof of inconsistencies in the use of numbers and labels convinced many onlookers, except those already hostle to McCarthy, that he was perpetrating a sham. Similarly, Lucas did not occupy the firmest ground in daring McCarthy to name names. Much subsequent criticism of the Senator from Wisconsin focused on occasions when he did name names. Interjections by other Democrats also failed generally to hit the mark.

Yet if tactics of rebuttal brought few returns, a strategy of silence was little likelier to succeed, for the Republicans were already too aware of the utility of the communist issue. The proceedings of February 20 made clear that McCarthy could count on support from his party. Fellow Republicans aided him with friendly leading questions, ran parliamentary interference, and applauded his efforts. Homer Ferguson, who had apparently brought in his own files on the eighty-one cases, assisted his young colleague through their complexities and did nothing to destroy the fiction that McCarthy was presenting new and arcane data smuggled out of the remotest warrens of Foggy Bottom.[49]

Members of both parties recognized that McCarthy's charges would not soon evaporate. Senator Henry Cabot Lodge, Jr., declared his intention to offer promptly a motion instructing the Foreign Rela-tiions Committee to "take up every single one" of the allegations. Lucas chorused his approval and noted with relish that once under oath before a committee, McCarthy could no longer "hide behind numbers." McCarthy also praised Lodge's suggestion and said that he would gladly give his names to such a panel. Thus, by the end of the February 20 skirmish, both sides had expressed eagerness to place McCarthy's charges before a committee, although there was no agreement as to which one should have jurisdiction.[50]

On February 21, with the unanimous support of the Democratic Conference and Majority Policy Committee and with the grudging approval of Tom Connally, chairman of the committee responsible for the proposed inquiry, Senator Lucas offered Senate Resolution 231:

> *Resolved,* That the Senate Committee on Foreign Relations, or any duly authorized subcommittee thereof, is authorized and directed to conduct a full and complete study and investigation as to whether per-sons who are disloyal to the United States are employed by the Depart-ment of State as charged by the Senator from Wisconsin (Mr. Mc-Carthy).

Several Senators objected to the resolution's narrow purview, urging that the investigation make a broader sweep than just of McCarthy's charges. Ferguson insisted that the probers have access to all relevant loyalty records and, with McCarthy, pleaded for vigorous assertion of the Senate's power of subpoena to this end. Owen Brewster dis-coursed upon the ongoing historical conflict between Congress and the Executive over the extent of their powers to compel or refuse disclosure of such information; he eagerly anticipated a further challenge. Retreating, Lucas yielded to the demand that the investigation not be tied exclusively to McCarthy's present charges. Brewster's adamance on the question of subpoenaing executive records delayed final consideration of Senate Resolution 231 for another day.[51]

On February 22, Ferguson reopened the campaign to widen the scope of the inquiry. He failed in his effort to extend the probe to employees of other agencies which dealt with foreign affairs, but he succeeded in persuading his colleagues that former State Department employees of questioned loyalty should be investigated along with current ones. He offered another amendment which would commit the investigators to exercising the subpoena power to obtain "the complete loyalty and employment files and records" pertinent to each case, thus attacking Truman's 1948 "blackout" order. Lucas accepted this proviso but cautioned that the executive branch had traditionally refused to comply with such demands. He also expressed the hope that McCarthy would be as liberal in sharing his knowledge with the committee as the State Department was expected to be. McCarthy, however, reserved the right, as always, not to reveal the name of any informant because "that man's job would not be worth a tinker's dam." Thus, amended, Senate Resolution 231 received the Senate's approval.[52]

To a remarkable degree the debates of February 20–22 foreshadowed the controversies that would rage from March to July. The Republicans had cautioned against a "whitewash." They had gleefully anticipated the problems raised by the issue of subpoenaing loyalty files. McCarthy had argued that without executive cooperation any investigation would be fruitless; he seized upon the initial reactions of Senator Lucas, President Truman, and the State Department as signs of the partisanship which would frustrate the undertaking. Early in the game, he provided himself with another excuse by warning that the investigation would fail unless access was granted to each loyalty file in its entirety. (Later, he would claim that the files examined by the committee had been "raped.") Yet McCarthy himself refused to make full revelations lest he endanger his informants. He would argue that the final responsibility for full details and for apprehension of the guilty was not his, but the administration's. Other Senators, too, had raised issues which would crop up again. Senator

Wayne Morse introduced the matter of whether the hearings should be open or closed. The question of when and where names should be divulged had also been canvassed in advance, as had fears that the investigation would produce "star chamber" proceedings.

Given the sense of *déjà vu* which permeated the subsequent activities of the subcommittee chaired by Senator Millard Tydings, one might ask what motives prompted the Democrats to authorize the investigation. The question is not fully answerable: public utterances by Democrats were not very revealing and other sorts of evidence are scarce. In addition, "the Democrats" did not arrive at strategic assumptions in any cohesive fashion. Save for the decision on Senate Resolution 231 reached by the Democratic conference, there was no unitary party position on McCarthy; nor, given the diffuseness of American parties, was one likely. The White House, the Senate Democrats, and the State Department responded separately to the McCarthy threat; there was collaboration among these groups, but no tight-knit entente.

Within the State Department, those who dealt with congressional affairs judged that McCarthy's initial accusations boded a long-term problem which would have to be faced—the sooner the better. Soon after McCarthy aired his charges, an informal *ad hoc* committee was created to deal with the ongoing attack.[53] However, some State Department functionaries also saw an opportunity in their predicament: by challenging as weak an adversary as McCarthy, they might scuttle for good the periodic charges that their agency was infested by Communists. Stewart Alsop reported the hope of State Department officials that "McCarthy will get his head so thoroughly washed that neither he nor any of his like-minded colleagues will again use this vote-catching technique." Another interested observer saw in the early stages of the investigation a moral for Republicans: "Don't put your wrong Senator forward." [54] Notwithstanding such sanguine expressions, the State Department generally anticipated gloomy prospects in the ensuing weeks and appeared to have foreseen the dangers posed by McCarthy sooner than did the White House or Senate Democrats. Thus, Jack K. McFall, Undersecretary of State for Congressional Affairs, quickly became convinced that the whole controversy should be turned over to a blue-ribbon commission whose findings could command public confidence.[55]

The Democratic Senators, to the extent their attitudes can be plumbed, took a more opportunistic and less worried view of the uproar. They expressed marked skepticism regarding McCarthy's charges during the early debates. Senator Harley M. Kilgore, in whose state it all began, noted that McCarthy "indicated that he did not know himself, how many of the people he was talking about had worked or do work for the Department of State." [56] The Democrats presumably knew that McCarthy's previous senatorial career gave scant evidence of ability. Aside from Lucas's remark that an investigation would put McCarthy squarely on the spot, Senate Democrats did not reveal their goals very explicitly, but they, too, apparently saw a chance to crush the communist issue by deflating one of its weaker exponents. They could also look back upon a string of politically charged investigations from which, with the notable exception of the Hiss case, they had emerged without great losses. One Democratic Senator recalled how, in such instances, "as the investigation proceeds the headlines get smaller and when the findings are released they command but very little publicity," as had been the fate of Senator Hickenlooper's charges against David Lilienthal and the Atomic Energy Commission.[57] At the same time, of course, the Democratic Policy Committee's decision to launch an inquiry indicated an awareness that the communist issue was a live one, and its precaution in assigning that chore to the Foreign Relations Committee was an effort to keep it out of the hands of more zealous critics of the administration.

Initially, the White House revealed even less of its strategic perceptions than did members of the Senate. Truman had expressed contempt for McCarthy in his brisk dismissals of the uproar. Max Lowenthal, an unofficial presidential advisor whom Truman had asked to help shape the administration's defense against McCarthy, even questioned the wisdom of accrediting the charges by having them investigated. Of all the elements mobilizing against McCarthy, the White House seemed least impressed by him, a fact which made it slow at times to come to the aid of the Democrats on the Tydings Committee as their distress mounted.[58]

In their uncoordinated response to McCarthy, the Democrats were reacting more than they were anticipating. Some, for instance, were unduly influenced by McCarthy's insinuation that he had acquired his data from confidential sources. On July 20, as the investigation was drawing to its bitter close, Senator Lucas asked Tydings a leading question: had not the Democratic Policy Committee drafted Senate Resolution 231 "upon the theory" that McCarthy had "direct information from informants in the State Department—as was said over and over in the speech" of February 20? Tydings concurred. The Democrats appeared to consider such claims the weakest part of McCarthy's story (or, more fearfully, its most menacing nuance). McCarthy, of course, had carefully cultivated the impression that he was revealing smuggled data.[59] The Democrats also erred in giving inordinate emphasis to the discrepancies in McCarthy's various numbers; they thus allowed the fact that he possessed no list at all to be obscured in the debate.

The Senate Democrats moved too hastily to submit McCarthy's charges to investigation. Had they held off, they might have hit upon an alternative. As early as February 23, columnist Marquis Childs and Harold N. Graves, Jr., a reporter for the Providence *Evening Bulletin,* revealed that McCarthy had exhumed his cases out of files dating from the Eightieth Congress; this, one day after the passage of Senate Resolution 231, was news to the White House (and presumably to the Senate as well).[60] Looking back on these events, Senator Tydings himself concluded that his party had acted too quickly, moving to investigate "without asking McCarthy to make out a prima facie case to support his statements." It had been an error to begin the probe "without at least calling McCarthy before the Senate Foreign Relations Committee and ascertaining if he had the facts to justify investigation of his charges." By the time the hackneyed nature of McCarthy's data became known, it was too late to abort the inquiry.[61]

Yet too much caution would have laid the Democrats open to charges of obstruction and concealment. Greater care in handling McCarthy's allegations might have succeeded in taking the Wisconsin Senator out of the limelight, but even that eventuality did not guarantee that the loyalty issue would subside. When McCarthy began his solo improvisation, others in his party were ready to pick up the beat and harmony. Indeed, what is surprising was the willingness of Republican colleagues to let this assertive newcomer take over a stage long occupied by others.

Past experience indicated a possible choice other than that to which the Democrats resorted: if willing to suffer delay, repetition, and invective, they might have weathered McCarthy's tirades on the Senate floor. McCarthy had made a shambles in committee of the Malmedy investigation and would wreak worse havoc in the coming probe. Perhaps the lesson Tydings ought to have learned from serving as the administration's floor general in the Matthews-Denfeld affair was the positive result of his adroitly sidestepping McCarthy's demand for a full-scale investigation. By patient, persistent rebuttal in the Senate chamber, he had managed to overcome McCarthy. But Tydings may have mistakenly interpreted the Matthews episode as an indication instead of McCarthy's limited talent for sustained political infighting.

However, in February 1950, the Democrats operated with sharply limited mobility. The communist issue could not be equated with the Matthews or Malmedy affairs except in the crudest fasion. McCarthy possessed in his anticommunist campaign what he lacked in earlier affrays: an issue to which a sizable portion of his party was strongly committed. Many Republicans had cast off previous restraints, had taken up the theme of internal subversion, and would tolerate, if not support, the excesses of their Wisconsin colleague. To these partisans, McCarthy seemed a willing and promising champion against the Democratic foe. (Senator Bricker reportedly said, "Joe, you're a dirty son of a bitch, but there are times when you've got to have a son of a bitch around, and this is one of them.") It was McCarthy who would take the risks; the potential returns, if speculative, might be vast. When McCarthy was alleged to have said, "wait six months and you'll see the results of what I'm doing," his reference to the elections was clear enough.[62]

Thus, Senate Resolution 231 constituted a recognition that the communist issue would not down easily. Just as the shocks of 1949 had altered the international balance of power, so the McCarthy investigation, like so many congressional inquiries—the creation of the Dies Committee in 1938 is an obvious parallel—signaled the acceleration of a shift in the domestic balance of power. In his campaign against the administration, McCarthy enjoyed the protection of fellow Republicans who appreciated his talent for roughhouse partisanship, and this enfolding embrace secured him from most Democratic counterthrusts. It was chiefly this shift within the Republican Party which rendered perilous every alternative that was open to the Democrats in early 1950.

CHAPTER 3

The Tydings
Investigation

DURING THE TWO WEEKS between the debates of February 20–22, 1950, and the onset of the investigation, principals in both parties were aware, as they arrayed themselves for battle, that McCarthy had launched a general engagement whose political impact could well prove profound. Republicans rubbed their hands in anticipation of the embarrassments lying in store for the administration. They envisioned a confrontation over the question of access to State Department loyalty files which might even lead, as Senator Wherry projected, to the prosecution of Acheson, and possibly even Truman, for contempt of Congress. In the event the President remained obdurate, the GOP could capitalize on charges that he was "covering up." If the files controversy together with Acheson's refusal to turn his back on Alger Hiss did not "constitute an issue," said Senator Ferguson, "then I never saw one." Even the law of averages seemed to favor the GOP, for it would take just one "Hiss case" or a reasonable facsimile, as reporter Richard Strout noted, and McCarthy would have earned his hire.[1]

In the two-week interim, the State Department looked to its defenses. Secretary Acheson and Deputy Undersecretary John Peurifoy both welcomed the investigation publicly and derided the Wisconsin Senator's charges. Acheson commented on the striking similarity be-

tween McCarthy's eighty-one cases and a list of loyalty file summaries made available to Congress two years earlier. The Department
realized, however, that coordinated countermeasures as well as rebuttal were required. After taking preliminary soundings on the Hill,
Jack K. McFall, Assistant Secretary of State for Congressional Relations, could only report ominously that McCarthy appeared to be
highly ambitious and a likely source of trouble for some time. In
order that McFall's office, then engaged in a major effort to improve
the Department's standing with Congress, could avoid being drawn
into the melee to the peril of bipartisanship, the task of framing
departmental responses to McCarthy was given to Peurifoy.[2]

In practice, the day-to-day duties of answering McCarthy, maintaining communications with the White House and congressional allies, and mapping strategy, devolved upon an *ad hoc* group under the
informal chairmanship of Adrian S. Fisher, the Department's Legal
Advisor. In deference to its shifting locus and impromptu qualities,
this small band of anti-McCarthy irregulars labeled itself the "floating crap game" (with apologies to the current hit *Guys and Dolls*).
For the next several months, the Fisher group labored to assemble
McCarthy's myriad statements, cross-reference them, do the research
and field investigation needed to refute them, and publish the Department's replies.[3]

In the Senate, the care with which the members of the subcommittee to investigate McCarthy's charges were selected demonstrated a
sensitivity to political repercussions which equalled that of the State
Department. Tom Connally, Chairman of the Foreign Relations Committee, twice asked Millard E. Tydings to head the subcommittee,
and twice Tydings refused before finally consenting. Connally had
chosen well. A man with twenty-four years in the Senate, Tydings
was Chairman of the Military Affairs Committee and spoke with authority on issues of foreign policy and national defense. The urbane
Senator from Maryland dispatched adversaries in debate with rapier
thrusts. While an important, though far from subservient, ally of the
administration on foreign policy, in domestic matters he was so emphatically conservative that Franklin D. Roosevelt had marked him as
a target for his 1938 "purge." FDR's efforts met thumping defeat,
and twelve years later Tydings seemed "politically unassailable."
The fact that a conservative of Tydings's stripe would step to the ad-

ministration's defense was considered an ill omen for McCarthy.[4] The other Democrats on the subcommittee, Brien McMahon of Connecticut and Theodore F. Green of Rhode Island, were supporters of the administration and had impressive senatorial credentials.*

The two Republicans who joined them, Henry Cabot Lodge, Jr., of Massachusetts and Bourke B. Hickenlooper of Iowa, also were prominent figures in their party. Lodge represented the internationalist eastern wing of the GOP, whose leader was Arthur H. Vandenberg and whose members would rally to the candidacy of Dwight D. Eisenhower in 1952. Hickenlooper's views followed those of midwestern Republicans who were less eager for foreign involvements and acknowledged the leadership of Senator Taft. The Iowan was a natural ally for McCarthy; perhaps aware of this prospect, Connally had tried to get the more internationalist H. Alexander Smith named to the subcommittee instead. However, Senator Smith resisted Connally's blandishments.[5] The divergence of views between Lodge and Hickenlooper was pregnant with significance: it became apparent early in the life of the Tydings Committee that to achieve any nonpartisan stature for its findings, the Democrats had to find areas of agreement with Lodge. Hickenlooper, who took McCarthy's part consistently, was given up for lost.

Notwithstanding these preparations, the White House, the State Department, and the Democrats on the subcommittee did not enter the McCarthy investigation with a coordinated strategy. While the State Department dug in for a long war, Tydings and his Democratic colleagues on the subcommittee—at the outset, at least—appeared to discount McCarthy's case and to exaggerate the ease with which it could be punctured. Truman's tart rejoinders to the charges and the counsels of Max Lowenthal, the President's emissary to the Tydings Committee and the State Department, indicated a White House attitude of dismissal.[6]

---

* McMahon, chairman of the Joint Committee on Atomic Energy, had a reputation for statesmanship in this field. He had been approached at one stage to head the investigation. With Tydings, he shared the major portion of McCarthy's obloquy, while Green bore a lighter burden, perhaps because, of the three, he played the least active role in the investigation. Also, unlike the other two Democrats, he was not up for reelection in 1950. *New York Times,* Feb. 23, 1950; Washington *Post,* Feb. 25, 1950; Minutes, Majority Policy Committee, Feb. 21, 1950, Box 326, Lucas Mss.

Overconfidence soon took its toll. At the first hearing on March 8, the Democrats greeted McCarthy with scornful contempt. Before he could read his opening statement, they harassed him with repeated demands that he answer certain questions immediately. Tydings queried him regarding the identity of the unnamed State Department official who supposedly had doctored the records of the employee described in his case number 14. McCarthy objected: "I will be unable to jump, say, from case 1 to case 72 and back to case 58. As of this time I can assure the chairman that all the information which he wants on case Number 57 will be gotten to him, but I frankly cannot give him that information now, because I haven't arrived at that case this morning." When Tydings persisted, Lodge broke in to ask that McCarthy receive "the courtesy everyone gets, of being able to make his own statement in his own way, and then be subject to questioning." Tydings doggedly pursued the interrogation, McCarthy parried, Lodge and Hickenlooper came to his aid, and the hearing degenerated into partisan wrangling.[7]

In the morning's shambles, McCarthy, by studied repetition, managed so to confuse the proceedings that while Tydings had originally grilled him about case number 14, he was defending a refusal to deal with case number 57 and misled the Democrats into the same faulty reference. When he finally began his statement, it dealt not with the eighty-one cases of February 20, but with certain "additional cases." McCarthy also declared grandly that he would let the subcommittee decide whether the hearings should be open or closed to the public; the liberality of the gesture was somewhat attenuated by the fact that he had released his testimony to the press before the hearing.

On the other hand, the Democrats surely savored the prospect of seeing McCarthy humiliated in public. In fact, the subcommittee had voted unanimously the week before to hold public sessions. Tydings and Hickenlooper were willing, they told H. Alexander Smith, to hold executive sessions, provided McCarthy took the initiative in requesting them; but when Smith suggested such a move to the Wisconsin Senator, his advice was rejected. While McCarthy bore considerable responsibility for the open hearings, the committee could with little difficulty have begun with closed sessions, and its failure to do so was probably a tactical error.[8] In public, McCarthy had the benefit of greater publicity (although, as a man seldom hampered by rules, he might easily have evaded the confidentiality of executive testimony).

The Democrats on the subcommittee hoped, of course, for a quick kill. Tydings importuned McCarthy on case 14 in order to trap him in an inconsistency: the security officer whom McCarthy criticized for negligence in pursuing number 14, an alleged homosexual, was the same person McCarthy praised for prosecution of case number 41. The villain-hero, J. Anthony Panuch, commenting that the man in case 14 had been "railroaded," argued that "McCarthy must be crazy if he's raising that case." The Democrats correctly saw in this parlay a chance to expose fundamental weaknesses in McCarthy's indictment, but they pounced too eagerly and thus exposed themselves to charges of excessive partisanship.[9]

Only at the close of the session did McCarthy manage to name his first target: Dorothy Kenyon, a New York lawyer, sometime judge and delegate to UNESCO, who had no current affiliation with the State Department. Tydings and McMahon did not permit the Senator to read *seriatim* his allegations about Judge Kenyon's associations; after each suspect membership was cited, they carefully recorded the name of the body which had declared the group subversive or listed other members of the group in order to place Miss Kenyon in often distinguished company. This method, which permitted concurrent rebuttal, departed sharply from normal procedure, but was certainly fairer to McCarthy's victims.[10]

The sparring continued the next day. McCarthy now said he could name the principal in case 14, but confessed he had only a suspicion as to the identity of the official who had doctored the file. He also speculated that the subcommittee knew the name they were trying to extract. Senator Green almost gave away the game when he said that the point was not to learn the name but "to find out how accurate the foundation is for your charges." (Green's remark was not so much sinister as late: such an inquiry should have come before public hearings were ever held.) McCarthy argued that the full data lay in the State Department's files and that it was the subcommittee's duty to secure these files—and swiftly, for he had heard rumors that someone was "rifling" them. He ostentatiously refused to identify his State Department informants, for then their "heads would roll." Amid this skirmishing, McCarthy concluded his indictment of Miss Kenyon.[11]

In the first two days of hearings, McCarthy failed to substantiate his charges, but neither did the Democrats succeed in destroying his case. It was partly their fault, for they had acted too high-handedly, and their solicitude for the rights of persons accused by McCarthy had permitted Republicans to accuse them of unfairness. Owen Brewster taxed the Democrats for "filibustering" against McCarthy, for permitting him to use only 7 percent of his time before the panel in actual testimony, and for interrupting him eighty-five times. Tydings's refusal to let McCarthy proceed without hindrance was unusual, as James Reston noted; the *New York Times,* skeptical as it was of McCarthy's charges, editorialized that he "deserved a chance to complete his story." [12]

Impressed, perhaps, by such criticism, the Democrats changed their procedure. Tydings, declaring what the Washington *Post* termed a "truce," announced that McCarthy would be allowed to finish the rest of his statement unimpeded. Another indication that the Democrats were beginning to take McCarthy more seriously was the subcommittee's decision to hire a staff. Ultimately, they appointed as chief counsel Edward P. Morgan, a Washington attorney recommended by Senator Green, who had at one time served as an aide to J. Edgar Hoover and had helped direct the FBI's fight against subversion.[13]

After the hectic first two days, the proceedings settled into a pattern of greater calmness for several weeks. On March 13 and 14, McCarthy was permitted to complete his charges against nine individuals: Mrs. Esther C. Brunauer, a State Department official who handled liaison with UNESCO; her husband Stephen Brunauer of the Navy's Bureau of Ordnance; Haldore Hanson, an official in the Point Four program ("a man with a mission . . . to communize the world"); Owen Lattimore, the Far Eastern specialist, Director of the Page School of Diplomacy at Johns Hopkins, and presently on UN assignment in Afghanistan (allegedly a "pro-Communist"); Gustavo Duran, formerly with the State Department but currently working for the UN; Harlow Shapley and Frederick Schuman, academicians from Harvard and Williams respectively; and John Stewart Service, a previous McCarthy target. Somewhat obliquely, McCarthy hit Ambassador-at-Large Phillip C. Jessup, who had "an unusual affinity" for communist causes.[14]

Observers found scant substance in McCarthy's claims. Shapley and Schuman had never been State Department employees; Lattimore and Kenyon, only marginally so. Far from original, the charges consisted generally of the cullings of earlier denunciations by conservative Republicans. Similarly, the "communist affiliations" McCarthy cited relied heavily upon imagination. Of the twenty-eight organizations listed for Miss Kenyon, only four had been classified as subversive by the Attorney General, and she had broken her ephemeral connections with all but one of them before they were so listed. Not even Hickenlooper found her "disloyal" or "subversive in any way." [15] Kenyon, Mrs. Brunauer, Hanson, Jessup, and Service appeared before the subcommittee to offer rebuttals, usually with convincing eloquence. Phillip Jessup could point to impressive testimonial letters from Generals Eisenhower and Marshall; prestigious members of the New York bar spoke out in behalf of Dorothy Kenyon; Senator William Benton and ex-Senator Joseph Ball vouched for Mrs. Brunauer.[16] Though he garnered considerable publicity, McCarthy had failed to prove any charges of consequence.

Like McCarthy, the subcommittee spun its wheels throughout March, waiting while the White House pondered whether or not to release the State Department loyalty files. McCarthy had argued repeatedly that he could only furnish leads; the burden of proof, he said, lay with the subcommittee, and their duty should lead them directly to the loyalty files of the various government agencies. Yet many administration officials opposed any breach of the 1948 Executive Order which had closed these files. Some recalled, for instance, that by standing firm they had won a similar battle with Congress two years before on the issue of releasing the loyalty dossier of Dr. Edward U. Condon. On the other hand, a number of Democratic Senators, including those on the Tydings Committee, worried about the damage McCarthy was doing and labored to convince the White House to relent.[17]

The administration gave the impression that, given a choice between the impairment of its constitutional prerogatives (as well as harming the reputations of guiltless men) or being subjected to charges of concealment, it would opt for the latter indignity. Majority Leader Lucas had warned on February 22 that the Executive Branch had always rejected demands for confidential records. The President seemingly confirmed Lucas's admonition the next day when he cited Andrew Jackson's advice to Chief Justice John Marshall—the Senators, in this instance, had made their decision, now let them enforce it.[18] Privately, however, Truman was more flexible. At a meeting with the Vice-President, Lucas, Speaker Sam Rayburn, and House Majority Leader John McCormack on February 27, the President agreed that if necessary the Tydings panel might have access to a few files in particularly sensitive cases. Publicly, Truman moderated his stance slightly: on March 2, he said that he would decide the files issue "when we get to it." [19] At bottom, his policy was a waiting game; he would stand pat on the files question until political pressures forced him to shift.

Such pressures came quickly. Democrats in Congress, according to William S. White, counseled Truman "not to remain too adamant lest he hand the Republicans the issue of 'covering up.' " Senator Walter George warned that the administration was courting charges of "whitewash" if it failed to relinquish the files. For several weeks Truman and Tydings sought an accommodation which would permit examination of the loyalty files without breaching their confidentiality. It was suggested that when McCarthy accused specific individuals, the subcommittee could be permitted to go to the State Department and there inspect the appropriate file; this expedient had the advantage of maintaining the policy of refusing to hand the files over physically to Congress.[20] By mid-March, Tydings was sufficiently encouraged by his negotiations to predict that the subcommittee would receive access to the loyalty data within two days, and newspaper accounts commented on the likelihood of a shift in administration policy.[21]

Truman encountered differing views from members of his administration. At first the anti-McCarthy strategists in the State Department resisted initiatives aimed at opening the loyalty files, but shortly they were persuaded, in large part by Senator McMahon, that political realities dictated a more flexible attitude. However, Attorney General J. Howard McGrath, FBI Director J. Edgar Hoover, and Seth W. Richardson, Chairman of the Civil Service Loyalty Review Board, all opposed granting access to the files. The weight of their protests—particularly Hoover's—apparently neutralized the views of the State Department.[22]

Subject to mounting pressure from the Republicans, Senator Tydings, on March 22, wrote the President, the Attorney General, the Secretary of State, and the Chairman of the Loyalty Review Board to request access to the loyalty files. After futile efforts to find a *modus vivendi,* the administration returned its reply: No. On March 27, McGrath and Hoover went before the subcommittee to defend this position. McGrath argued that to reveal the contents of FBI files would set a dangerous precedent, and Hoover warned that this action would imperil his agency's work by compromising its informants and tipping off those who were under surveillance. In his own carefully considered reply to Tydings, the President reiterated these arguments and also pointed out the harm to the reputations of innocent people which might result from publication of unsubstantiated charges. To minimize the anticipated political damage, Truman instructed Seth Richardson to have the Loyalty Review Board reexamine the case of every individual accused by McCarthy. This palliative satisfied no one. Faced with the administration's adamancy, Tydings, in a gesture purely for the record, issued subpoenas to the officers in charge of the desired files.[23]

The President may have been following a tactic of delay in order to assess the impact of McCarthy's onslaught. By the end of March, no clear consensus on its effect had emerged. William S. White found a widespread belief on Capitol Hill that McCarthy's charges were wounding the administration and reported one Democratic solon's lament that "the answers so far have plainly not caught up with the charges." On the other hand Arthur Krock surmised that the Democratic "home team" was far ahead and McCarthy had to come from nine runs behind in the last two innings. The *New York Times*'s not-too-analytical survey of national opinion found much skepticism about McCarthy's allegation. On balance, McCarthy's first testimony had not troubled the administration enough to cause a retreat on the issue of access to loyalty data. It was noted, however, that Truman had not given a categorical "no" answer to the question.[24]

As Truman bided his time, he found that the engagement initiated by McCarthy had broadened: other Republicans were unlimbering for the fall elections. Even before McCarthy's first testimony, Styles Bridges had speculated whether Dean Acheson's refusal to disavow Hiss made the Secretary himself a security risk. On March 10, Senator Wherry declared Acheson unfit for office because of his "bungling of the Gubitchev spy case." Later, he called the Secretary the "idol of left-wing, appease-Russia agitators." Representative Leslie Arends termed the decision to let Gubitchev leave the country "one more example of the Administration's softie attitude towards Communists," and Congressman Frank Fellows found in Acheson a "native talent for stupidity, or worse." On March 27, Bridges asserted that the State Department had "fallen into a condition of degradation unparalleled in the nation's history." Charging that a "master spy" still ran amok, Bridges expostulated, "Stalin is not a superman. He had to have help from inside our ranks." [25] While President Truman, as usual, stood fast behind Acheson, Democratic leaders in Congress stumbled over each other to avoid public support of the Secretary. Scott Lucas, reacting to Acheson's statement about Hiss, had earlier told Truman that he would not defend Acheson if the issue came up on the Senate floor. [26]

To stem the Republican barrage, the administration strove first to reknit two-party cooperation in foreign policy by co-opting two prominent Republicans. First John Sherman Cooper was selected to serve as an aide to Acheson in forthcoming talks with the NATO allies; secondly, John Foster Dulles, the GOP's leading foreign policy spokesman, was appointed to an advisory post in the State Department. Perhaps the most dramatic effort to reforge the bipartisan alliance was Truman's overture to Styles Bridges. The New Hampshire Republican was brought rather abruptly into high-level consultations on foreign policy; then, on the eve of Bridges's projected speech against Acheson, Truman implored him to desist. "The communists," he wrote bluntly, "have never had as much help from all the so-called disloyal people as they have had from these indefensible attacks on Mr. Acheson." [27] These efforts proved ineffectual. Bridges gave his speech despite Truman's entreaty, and, while the Cooper and Dulles appointments were widely praised, some Republicans emphasized that the two did not speak officially for the party. [28]

Given the Democrats' aloofness, the strongest support for Dean Acheson came from the Republican bipartisans. Leverett Saltonstall warned against questioning the Secretary's "integrity or loyalty" and—with particular feeling because of his ancestors' experience in seventeenth-century Salem—decried "witch-hunting." Ralph

Flanders also took pains to "disassociate" himself from the campaign against Acheson.[29] Senator Vandenberg, whose failing health kept him away from the Senate, approached the margins of the McCarthy fracas with a published letter to Marshall Plan administrator Paul Hoffman. In his defense of bipartisan foreign policy, some observers inferred, Vandenberg was also chiding the Republicans who backed McCarthy and took potshots at Acheson. (When asked directly about McCarthy, however, Vandenberg wrote that he did not want to "lecture" his colleagues "from behind the 'iron curtain' " of his convalescence.) The aging statesman Henry Stimson leveled the most vigorous Republican indictment of McCarthy. His letter to the *New York Times* mentioned no names, but his reference was clear. McCarthy was damaging the innocent, obscuring the identity of the guilty, and impairing American prestige abroad. "This man is not trying to get rid of known Communists in the State Department; he is hoping against hope that he will find some." His real motive was "to cast discredit" upon Acheson.[30]

At this stage the Republicans were willing to let McCarthy continue to try his luck yet sufficiently wary to withhold formal, collective assistance. Even as the barrage against Acheson reached its most withering intensity, nowhere could a Republican be found to avow that McCarthy's charges had the official GOP imprimatur. Various Republicans pointed out that support for McCarthy was not a formal party matter.[31] Senator Taft's position was illustrative. The Ohioan had on several occasions offered encouragement to McCarthy, advising him to "keep talking and if one case doesn't work out he should proceed with another." [32] He was also reportedly overheard in an elevator telling McCarthy to "Keep it up, Joe." Yet Taft took care to state that the charges were "not a matter of party policy." [33] He further emphasized that "nobody even knew" McCarthy was going to make his original charges in Wheeling. He had offered McCarthy help after his first efforts, but the Wisconsinite, Taft noted, had operated "completely on his own responsibility since that time." Taft remained caught between his sensibilities, which prompted him to term an early McCarthy performance "perfectly reckless," and his awareness of the partisan utility of the exercise, which led him to defend McCarthy from Democratic attacks.[34]

More moderate, bipartisan Republicans viewed McCarthy with less detachment. The predicament in which H. Alexander Smith found himself revealed the hard political choice they faced. Increasingly troubled by McCarthy, the internationalist Senator from New Jersey first sought unsuccessfully to confine future hearings to executive sessions. Disturbed also by attacks on his friend Phillip Jessup, on Acheson, and on bipartisanship, Smith mulled over an answer to them. On March 24 he upheld Jessup's loyalty, but he hung back from supporting Acheson and current foreign policies until he had taken counsel with other Republicans. Senator Vandenberg warned him that a defense of Acheson would be untimely "because of probabl[e] disclosures about the State Department." Consequently, Smith removed almost every reference to the Secretary from his speech. In his March 27 address, Smith expressed reservations about the drive against Acheson and hoped that the communist probe would be moved behind closed doors. A lively debate ensued, but Smith's remarks, while marking the high level of unease over the McCarthy investigation, produced no procedural changes.[35]

The administration derived no benefit from Republican misgivings about McCarthy. Although the Republican moderates might never have succeeded in turning their party away from McCarthy, Truman's actions—apart from the Cooper and Dulles appointments—gave little encouragement to any such effort. Thus, the President sometimes undercut his own efforts to reintegrate a bipartisan coalition with his caustic replies to Republican tormentors. The most newsworthy outburst came at his March 30 press conference. He first opined that McCarthy was "the greatest asset that the Kremlin has," and then censured those Republicans who were "trying to dig up that old malodorous dead horse called 'isolationism.' " "To try to sabotage the foreign policy of the United States is just as bad in this cold war," he ventured, "as it would be to shoot our soldiers in the back in a hot war." Truman mentioned Senators Bridges and Wherry as McCarthy's colleagues in obstructionism. When the President later called Bridges in to elicit support for bipartisanship, one might wonder at the Senator's receptivity after having been called a foreign policy saboteur. Truman's crack also prompted Senator Taft to counter that the President had "slandered" McCarthy, whereupon

Truman quipped, "Do you think that is possible?" [36] Such exchanges served only to raise the partisan temperature.*

By early April, Truman at least had the solace of no longer being alone in defending Acheson or the State Department. William Benton ended Democratic silence in the Senate chamber with his March 22 speech extolling the Secretary. Five days later, he joined Herbert Lehman and Estes Kefauver in support of Acheson. Senator Connally delivered a justification of administration policy in China and, by inference, of Acheson as well. Senator Lucas added his criticism of the "angry wrangling" over foreign policy and of those who "sought for spies or devils to explain the defeat Nationalist China suffered." Speaker Rayburn pronounced it "unfair for a man in a responsible position to make irresponsible statements," and Vice-President Barkley warned of the threat to freedom posed by those who "sow rumors and suspicion among us." National Party Chairman William F. Boyle, Jr., used his weekly newsletter to twit McCarthy for failing to present any evidence; he called for stout resistance to the attacks on Acheson.[37] Within Congress, however, the Secretary of State still had only a few staunch supporters.

Meanwhile, Acheson worked to patch up his own defenses. Notwithstanding a disdain for many congressional types, he began frequenting Capitol Hill, as did Undersecretary McFall and his aides. Acheson also undertook to sell both the administration's foreign policy and himself through a number of speeches around the country. He had scant patience for such missionary activities, however, as his appearance before the American Society of Newspaper Editors revealed. After explicating the administration's "total diplomacy," Acheson added an eloquent, extemporaneous defense of the loyalty of his lieutenants. The speech was effective enough, but Acheson closed with the comment that it would be the last time he would treat this "filthy business"; in aristocratic fashion, he washed his hands of the matter.[38]

The "floating crap game" shouldered heaviest responsibility for defending the State Department. It churned out point-by-point refutations of the Wisconsin Senator's major pronouncements—a practice

* In any case, the opportunity for establishing political civility was fleeting. In April, Republican diffidence in regard to McCarthy would be eclipsed by the sensationalism of his case against Owen Lattimore.

which entailed extensive research and, consequently, lengthy delays.
For instance, the group put together a detailed refutation of Mc-
Carthy's charges of April 20; its press release for that purpose was
not ready until May 17. Such time lags enabled McCarthy to stay
several steps ahead of the State Department and the facts. The Department suffered additionally from having to abide by the require-
ments of due process, which did not similarly bind McCarthy. Each
accusation against a person automatically set the machinery of the
loyalty program in motion and tied the Department's hands, so that
while McCarthy could always attack, State could not always defend.
Neither Acheson's efforts nor the State Department's intramural activities noticeably tempered the impact of the Wisconsin Senator's
charges.[39]

After flailing about ineffectually in the early weeks of the investigation, McCarthy began in late March to make political headway
again, thanks to his new charges against Owen Lattimore. He had
earlier referred to the scholar as a mere "pro-Communist," but on
March 21 he issued a dire warning about an unnamed "top Russian
spy" who was still at large. In executive session he identified Lattimore as the culprit; Drew Pearson broke the story, and, from remote
Afghanistan, Lattimore replied that the allegation was "pure moon-
shine." Nonetheless, McCarthy declared he would "stand or fall" on
the Lattimore case.[40]

On March 30, McCarthy pleaded his case against Lattimore to the
Senate. It was a strange speech. First he waffled on his previous characterization of the professor, who might better be described as a "bad
policy risk." Then McCarthy termed him a "Soviet agent" and
promised to produce a witness who would confirm that Lattimore had
once belonged to the Communist Party. He rehashed much of the
right-wing criticism of Lattimore which had burgeoned since the end
of World War II.* Backpeddling furiously, McCarthy stated, "I fear
in the case of Lattimore, I may have perhaps placed too much stress
on the question of whether or not he has been an espionage agent."

* Some of McCarthy's data came from Alfred Kohlberg, the New York lace im-
porter who personified the putative "China Lobby." Congressman Walter Judd also
gave him information and took credit for arranging the appearance of McCarthy's
"mystery witness," Louis F. Budenz. Ex-Congressman Charles J. Kersten helped
write the speech, and Freda Utley supplied analyses of Lattimore's writings. Joseph

More importantly, he was the " 'architect' of our far-eastern policy." Gleefully, Republicans cheered McCarthy's assault on the Democrats' Asian policies.[41]

The Lattimore case, somewhat paradoxically, both heartened the Republicans who had begun to fear McCarthy would "fall flat on his face" and convinced the Democrats that he had, in fact, no evidence. But it had become clear that McCarthy could not be wished away, that reinforcements must be committed to the battle, and so pressures grew for a reappraisal of the policy regarding the State Department loyalty files. Barely had the administration enunciated its policy before Truman altered it, apparently on the assumption that McCarthy, particularly in the Lattimore affair, had "gotten himself far out on a limb." In an effort to cut it off, Truman gave the subcommittee limited access to Lattimore's loyalty dossier: on March 24, four members of the Tydings group heard a "summary," prepared by J. Edgar Hoover himself, of the FBI's file on Lattimore. After Lattimore's testimony on April 6, Tydings assured him that all four Senators who had heard the summary agreed it contained no evidence of communist connections or espionage, "so that the FBI file puts you completely, up to this moment, at least, in the clear." [42]

Tydings's announcement, however, did not have the desired éclat. In the first place, Hickenlooper objected that he had not been told of the session in the Attorney General's office, nor had he seen the summary, which was not, in any event, an adequate investigation. Later, having examined the digest, he called it "unwarranted" to say that it cleared Lattimore. Senator Lodge (as at other points in the proceedings) occupied a somewhat equivocal position. On April 3, he had commented that "none of the current charges have been proven" and that the information the subcommittee had seen was "such as to inspire confidence" in the loyalty of McCarthy's targets. Nonetheless, he challenged Tydings's exoneration of Lattimore, declaring that he had reached "no final conclusions" and could not until other witnesses were heard. Meanwhile, he had authorized no one to speak for him.[43]

Keeley, *The China Lobby Man: The Story of Alfred Kohlberg* (New Rochelle, N.Y., 1969), pp. 2–3, 5, 99; copy, Freda Utley to Sen. Taft, April 16, 1950, Bourke B. Hickenlooper MSS., in the Senator's possession; Minneapolis *Tribune,* April 15, 1950; Milwaukee *Journal,* March 31, 1950; see also Griffith, *Politics of Fear,* pp. 76–79.)

The appearance of McCarthy's mystery witness, Louis Budenz, dimmed the luster of Lattimore's medallion of innocence. Budenz, managing editor of the *Daily Worker* until he broke with the Communist Party in 1945, was a leading witness against his former collaborators. He declared that he had been told on high authority in 1944 to "consider Owen Lattimore as a Communist"; also that he had received top-secret "onionskins"—all destroyed, naturally—which listed Lattimore as agent "L" or "XL"; and that Lattimore had belonged to the Communist cell in the Institute of Pacific Relations (IPR) and had peddled the party line which described the Chinese Reds as "agrarian reformers." However, Budenz felt that McCarthy's characterization of the professor as "the top Soviet agent" was "technically not accurate." [44]

Budenz's testimony presented some problems. His "official knowledge" of Lattimore's party membership amounted to hearsay. That he had not mentioned Lattimore to the FBI until only a few days before the hearing, despite countless hours of debriefing since he had left the Party, seemed puzzling. Budenz was also fuzzy about recent contacts with certain McCarthy allies. Had he discussed Lattimore with Alfred Kohlberg? "Not to any great extent; no." Or: "to some extent; yes." [45]

Through April the Lattimore case spun on. Lawrence Kerley, once an FBI agent and currently an employee of the New York *Journal-American*, showed up with John Huber, a former undercover agent who would testify, said Kerley, to having seen Lattimore at a party given by Frederick Vanderbilt Field, a sugar daddy for communist fronts. Huber, when the moment arrived, had vanished—he eventually turned up in New York claiming to have "blacked out." [46] Bella V. Dodd, yet another ex-Communist, testified that Lattimore's writings did not follow the party line and ridiculed Budenz's onionskin story. Earl Browder, the fallen eagle of the Communist Party and a testy, unwilling witness, denied that he had ever extolled Lattimore's efforts to place reds in the IPR, as Budenz had alleged, or that Lattimore was a communist. Frederick Vanderbilt Field, equally balky, said he had never known or assumed any Communist connections on Lattimore's part. Freda Utley, a former Communist, strove through exegesis of Lattimore's writings to prove that he had been a "Judas cow," using the communist line to lead "the other animals to slaughter." [47] None of this testimony proved particularly enlightening.

While the value of the statements of Budenz and Utley remained dubious, the logic of calling in Browder to refute their stories was somewhat comparable, as Senator William Jenner put it, to "sending Baby Face Nelson to investigate John Dillinger." Still, Budenz's recitation, which Republicans found "stronger and more explicit" than they expected, gave strength to the flagging McCarthy show. Ralph Flanders, who had been skeptical, commented of the new development: "I find it disturbing." [48]

Buffeted by these events, Senator Tydings sought once more to convince the President to reverse his stand on the loyalty files. In a memorandum of April 12, Tydings argued that McCarthy and those for whom he ran interference had created an atmosphere of suspicion which not only stymied the administration's domestic program (for which Tydings's solicitude was not notable), but also threatened to undercut its highly successful foreign policies. It was essential to "reestablish the White House and the Truman Administration as the foe of Communism at home as well as abroad." To this end, the Maryland Senator first suggested that the full FBI file on Lattimore, after deletion of the names of the informants and certification by J. Edgar Hoover that its contents were intact, should be shown to the subcommittee. Next the files of McCarthy's eighty-one suspects should be made available. The President should broadcast to the nation his reasons for the turnabout and should articulate a defense of his loyalty-security program. This, Tydings advised, was the only way to deflate the communist issue before the coming election. [49]

Throughout April the question of the files hung fire. The grounds for the subsequent change in policy are not entirely clear, but McCarthy's continuing ability to seize the headlines, confirmed by the Lattimore melodrama, probably operated as the main influence. The polling data available are too scanty to permit precise measurement, but they showed that McCarthy had staying power. A Gallup poll taken in late April and early May found that 39 percent of the respondents thought McCarthy's charges were "a good thing," while 29 percent believed they were "doing harm." (Of the rest, 16 percent had no opinion and 16 percent were unfamiliar with the charges.) The respected Minnesota Poll found that 29 percent thought the charges of communist infiltration of the State Department false, but 41 percent believed them true. [50] Congressional intelligence, while spotty, seemed to indicate that McCarthy had gained strength in recent weeks. His exertions so vexed the Democrats as to command the attention of the Majority Policy Committee at each of its meetings from March 14 through May 2.[51]

In April, McCarthy's allies began directing heavy fire at the Tydings Committee. William Jenner labeled the panel an "interlocking directorate of Whitewash Incorporated." It was sinister, he said, that Seth Richardson of the Loyalty Review Board was a law partner of Tydings's father-in-law, Joseph E. Davies, and everyone knew where Davies, of *Mission to Moscow* fame, stood in regard to the Soviet Union. Richardson and Edward P. Morgan, chief counsel for the Tydings Committee, had both served on the investigation of the Pearl Harbor attack and hence were experienced whitewashers. Senator Wherry added that so far the Tydings investigation had been a "pantomine." [52]

Harry Truman liked to say that those who could not stand the heat should stay out of the kitchen, but he never meant that all four burners and the oven had to be kept on to prove one's political stamina. When he decided to let the subcommittee see the loyalty files after all, he was trying to lower the temperature of a political concoction that was overheating. As long as the files remained closed, McCarthy could exploit doubt. Many were convinced by the Senator's assertion before the American Society of Newspaper Editors that if the contents of the files disproved his charges, the Administration would long since have opened them. In the meantime, he could continue to tell Truman to "put up or shut up." [53]

Whatever its motivation, the change came abruptly. Before the Federal Bar Association on April 24, Truman had patiently reiterated why, despite the current "hue and cry," he would not surrender the files. On May 4, the hue and cry triumphed: Tydings announced that the President would permit the subcommittee to examine the files. The Senator from Maryland explained that he had finally convinced the President that since these same dossiers had been inspected by no less than four committees of the Eightieth Congress, nothing untoward would be revealed and no harmful precedent would result. In addition, the subcommittee "had the advantage of a relationship between its Chairman and the President"; his friendship with Tydings may have induced Truman to grant what he had denied to other committees. More skeptically, Senator Wherry attributed the reversal to Truman's "being 'afraid' to face the people" on his coming tour of the West.[54] McCarthy tried to undercut the impact of the announcement by reissuing his earlier charge that any files which were offered were "phony" and had been "raped." Dismissing this "hocuspocus," Tydings retorted, "we've got everything . . . the whole damn thing." [55]

The subcommittee began perusing the State Department files on May 10. The Senators spent the entire day in the White House Cabinet Room where the files were made available under the terms of Truman's dispensation. In attendance were representatives of the State and Justice Departments and of the President, but counsel for the subcommittee were not permitted in the room—a condition which Senator Lodge protested. The Senators were not to remove any notes from the room, a stipulation which irked Hickenlooper. The solons agreed not to discuss the files publicly before they had reached formal conclusions. Sifting through the "raw" files proved an arduous chore; it took Tydings two days to read through thirteen dossiers. Throughout May and much of June the trips to the White House continued.[56]

Inspection of the files made no impress upon public opinion. Partly because of the restrictions under which the subcommittee worked, visits to the White House soon became routine and attracted little or no attention in the press. Late in May, Lodge and Green absented themselves from this daily round in order to investigate State Department security at its installations in Europe; Hickenlooper had a primary campaign in Iowa. Both Republicans, in fact, soon concluded that nothing would be gained from a thorough examination of the files: Lodge completed only twelve dossiers and Hickenlooper, nine. Lodge objected that, with all the undigested material they contained, the files were not illuminating without interpretive assistance. Hickenlooper complained that the files were incomplete and not worth his time.[57]

Lest the sedate perusal of the files remove the communist issue from the headlines, the Republicans kept the pot boiling with suggestions of new areas of inquiry. Seizing upon the State Dempartment's admission that it had fired ninety-one homosexuals, they kept up a drumfire on the issue of "perverts" in government. There was conjecture that Republicans hoped the Tydings Committee would pursue this subject, but ultimately a subcommittee under Senator Hoey investigated it without pyrotechnics.[58] The question to which Republicans persistently returned was the five-year-old *Amerasia* incident. On April 17, Tydings announced that his group would look into the case despite its peripheral relevance. McCarthy claimed that the investigation would expose important espionage, while Hickenlooper hinted that new evidence would cast this "very mysterious" event in a new light.[59]

Beginning on May 4, the Tydings Committee dealt chiefly with *Amerasia* during most of its remaining intermittent hearings. McCarthy punctuated the day's headlines with the baseless prediction that the witness would reveal that among the stolen *Amerasia* documents had been materials bearing upon the top-secret atom bomb project.[60] Many aspects of the episode did warrant explanation—how, for instance, hundreds of secret documents (about one for every subscriber) had migrated to the office of a shoestring publication. Yet despite the drumbeating, by 1950 *Amerasia* had grown cold and lifeless. However, those Republicans who desired to prolong the subcommittee's deliberations hoped to resuscitate the case. H. Alexander Smith mused resignedly that the "McCarthy investigation . . . may run all Summer." The GOP's offensive in this quarter peaked on June 13, when twenty-one Senators sponsored Homer Capehart's resolution calling for a new investigation of the case by a group other than the Tydings Committee. After Tydings's effort to table the motion was defeated, Vice-President Barkley referred Capehart's resolution to the Judiciary Committee.[61]

On June 15, Republican hopes sagged when a New York federal jury inquiring into the problem of espionage issued a report which found no malfeasance in the government's handling of the *Amerasia* case. Tydings exulted that it would be "difficult for anyone to holler 'whitewash' " at this verdict, and the Democrats were elated. Actually, the vindication was only partial: Senator Hickenlooper checked with the foreman of the defunct grand jury and found that its presentment had been inaccurately reported. While no skulduggery had been uncovered, the grand jury had taken up the case too late in its term to investigate thoroughly and had specifically recommended the impanelment of a new jury to look into the topic. Hickenlooper's revelation had little impact, however. The Democrats on the Judiciary Committee (whose chairman, Pat McCarran, had recently declared that there was "no point in multiplying Congressional investigations of a single subject matter") voted to defer action on the Capehart resolution until the Tydings Committee had reported. The Democrats had succeeded in defusing the *Amerasia* issue.[62]

In May, as the Republicans tried to broaden the range of the hunt for subversion, the bitterness of Democratic attacks upon McCarthy mounted. On May 3, Senators Harley Kilgore and Matthew Neely of West Virginia, Majority Leader Lucas, and others unleashed the pent-up irritation of two months upon the Wisconsin Senator. First Lucas tried to read a statment of Deputy Undersecretary of State Peurifoy seconding Congressman Frank Karsten's recent criticism of McCarthy; Wherry called the Illinois Senator to order for his adverse reflection upon a colleague. Lucas persisted, reviewing McCarthy's hedging on his original utterances and the hoary origins of his eighty-one cases. It was time, he said, "to call a spade a spade." Soon an extended debate erupted over just what McCarthy had said on February 9. Kilgore emphasized that like his constituents, he was perturbed at the charges first voiced in this own bailiwick. He challenged Mc-Carthy to state unequivocally what he had said in Wheeling; he displayed photostats of affidavits by two employees of station WWVA who attested that the Senator had claimed to possess a list of 205 known Communists. Seconding Kilgore, Neely declared that someone—he could not say who—was "lying as deliberately and outrageously as Ananias did just before he was struck dead for his sin." Though Tydings affected a pose of judicial detachment, promising a full account at the appropriate time, other Democrats jumped into the fray.

The Republicans made it a general engagement. Knowland strewed articles about *Amerasia* into the *Record;* Wherry growled that the Tydings Committee should investigate Communists and not Mc-Carthy; with Forrest Donnell he chided the probers for not getting their hands on the loyalty files. McCarthy protested the "silly 'numbers game' " and "bickering over whether there were typographical errors in the rough draft given the radio station." [63] Withal, the Democrats achieved little by the debate. They grilled Mc-Carthy regarding his original utterances, but in a sense the political statute of limitations had run out. Since the Republicans sought to resurrect events several years old, the Democrats were justified in harking back a mere three months, yet their reaction time, compared to McCarthy's, was slow. Their quarry had moved on to other charges.

Behind the altercation of May 3 lay a degree of planning by leaders of the Democratic opposition to McCarthy. Ralph Flanders sized up the debate as "apparently a carefully organized attack," and *Newsweek* reported that during the previous week a strategy meeting involving John Peurifoy, Edward Morgan, and Tydings had taken place at the latter's apartment. It was probably more than coincidental that the administration's change of policy in regard to the loyalty files was announced on the day after the Senate debate.[64]

In any case, further attacks on McCarthy—clearly premeditated—soon followed. On May 9, Senator Benton labeled McCarthy "a very talented propagandist of the Soviet type." "He hits and he runs." Three days later, Dennis Chavez of New Mexico assailed McCarthy's prize witness, Louis Budenz. He noted that the ex-Communist's pronouncements had "an added sanctity" because Budenz had gone through "the forms of conversion to catholicism." "My ancestors," Chavez declaimed, "brought the cross to this hemisphere. Louis Budenz has been using this cross as a club." These two attacks were an outgrowth of the mounting concern of Tydings and others with the damage McCarthy had inflicted. Benton recalled, some years later, a meeting in the office of Leslie Biffle at which Tydings in "great distress" lamented the direction his investigation had taken and "asked us to go after McCarthy." Benton obliged by "hastily" inserting critical references to the Wisconsinite into a speech he had prepared for the next day. Then Chavez, who also attended the meeting, delivered his diatribe.[65] Others joined the chorus of criticism. Hubert Humphrey hit the GOP for its "irresponsible and unsubstantiated attack on the state department," and the Department itself redoubled its efforts at refuting McCarthy during the month. The attacks, however, gained little ground. McCarthy and his allies answered in kind; far from damping the partisan furor over the communist issue, the Democratic counterthrusts appeared to confirm it. By the end of May the Democrats apparently discerned the futility of continued rhetorical duels and turned to new tactics.[66]

Not more partisanship, but less, suggested itself as a remedy. Moderate Republicans grasped this point soonest and made suggestions for procedural reforms. In March, H. Alexander Smith had urged the subcommittee to conduct future hearings in executive session. Ralph Flanders also called for an end to public hearings, which had caused "astonishment and uncertainty in our relations abroad" and impaired State Department morale.[67]

Others ventured a more thoroughgoing cure: referring the controversy to a special bipartisan commission composed of eminent men whose findings could withstand the cavil of party. On March 22, Congressman Richard M. Nixon, scolding both parties for injecting politics into the McCarthy investigation, had called for the establishment of a nonpartisan commission. He warned that "the only party that will gain" from a continued exchange of accusations "is the Communist party." Senator Lodge offered a more detailed plan on April 3: a commission of twelve trained experts, six from each party, four members each to be chosen by the Senate, the House, and the President. The panel was to conduct its investigation in confidence in order to end the "mounting damage . . . inflicted on the position of the United States abroad and on the respect here at home for the justice and efficacy of our institutions." It would tread the sinuous path of truth between the administration's stubborn refusal to admit past errors and the recognition (by Lodge) that none of McCarthy's charges had been proven and innocent men had been smeared.[68]

The Democrats greeted Lodge's proposal coolly. Lucas and Connally saw no reason for "changing the venue" of the inquiry. In view of Lodge's pivotal position on the subcommittee and his centrality to any hope for bipartisan acceptance of its conclusions, the Democrats' dismissal of his overture was cavalier. Presumably, in early April the Democrats may still have been more impressed with McCarthy's failure to find culprits than with their own political vulnerability. Indicative of Tydings's perception of the political situation was the fact that one week after Lodge's initiative, he was privately considering a resolution of censure against McCarthy.[69]

The Republicans gave Lodge's solution a warmer reception. Hickenlooper accepted the idea "in principle," provided the commission could obtain access to the loyalty files; Taft was amenable too, if the panel were not under the President's "domination." McCarthy agreed "wholeheartedly" with the plan. Despite some equivocation, the Republicans showed surprising pliability in the face of what in effect was an attack upon the Taftites who tolerated McCarthy's activities. Perhaps the Republicans entertained views similar to the Democrats' regarding McCarthy's failure to make headway. As late as May, Senator James Kem, an ally of the Wisconsin Senator, feared that McCarthy had "by overstatement weakened his case to the point where he may have destroyed his usefulness." [70]

The Democrats, alarmed for opposite reasons, soon began to make proposals like Lodge's. They grew less self-assured and more concerned that they, not McCarthy, suffered as the hearings continued. On April 23, Tydings conceded that it might have been "much better" to have summoned the FBI into the investigation at the very outset to "run down" the clues; now it was too late. In May, he was advocating creation of a commission to assume jurisdiction over McCarthy's eighty-one cases. With Senator McMahon, he offered this design to the President, on the reported assumption that the subcommittee would split along party lines and thus fail to gain public acceptance of its findings. Such an impasse would damage the Democrats in the coming campaign. As an alternative, Tydings urged the President to appoint "distinguished citizens of national reputation as a special panel of the Richardson Loyalty Board to assist his Subcommittee in its examination of the eighty-one McCarthy loyalty cases." McMahon and he hoped its members would include men of the stature of General Eisenhower, Admiral Chester W. Nimitz, and former Justice Owen D. Roberts. Though Tydings never formally made the proposal public, the newspapers picked it up (sometimes without attributing it directly to him). [71] The commission scheme was at odds with Tydings's more pugnacious request for Democratic attacks on McCarthy. It is unclear whether Tydings had reconsidered the efficacy of the latter strategy or whether he was concurrently pursuing two courses united only by the perception that McCarthy had become dangerous.

The Tydings-McMahon proposal presented the administration with another difficult policy decision. After discussing the idea with others engaged in plotting defenses against McCarthy, presidential assistants Charles S. Murphy and Stephen J. Spingarn recommended against the plan. To appoint a "super-panel" to aid the Loyalty Review

Board, they argued, would be a "reflection" upon that body's admirable exertions; moreover, its reach would be "too limited." Instead of merely relieving the Tydings Committee, they put forward a scheme of broader scope which had received consideration on earlier occasions: the establishment, wholly removed from either the Richardson Board or the Tydings group, of a President's Commission on Internal Security and Individual Rights charged with examining the employee loyalty and security programs in all departments,* as well as existing and proposed legislation regarding internal security.[72]

Tydings, less concerned about details than with the need for action of some sort, continued to urge the establishment of a commission during late May and June. To a Maryland political ally worried about public reaction to the loyalty investigation, Tydings confided his hope "that there may soon be an important announcement which will help to clarify this situation." On June 5, he dodged White House reporters after a meeting with the President during which, it was assumed, the two discussed the commission scheme. On June 14, the Senator informed his subcommittee that the President was "anxious" for them to finish their inspection of the loyalty dossiers; there was "being considered a proposition to appoint a special panel to review these files." He assured the President that the subcommittee would complete its examination by June 26.[73] Others turned to similar proposals. Hubert Humphrey envisioned the creation of a commission on national security, and Elbert D. Thomas of Utah and Irving Ives of New York sponsored a resolution seeking to initiate a system of select committees which could be employed to investigate divisive questions such as the current controversy over the State Department.[74]

* In 1949, the idea of such a commission had resurfaced at a seemingly opportune time: the loyalty program had nearly completed its examination of all incumbent employees and the White House was not then "under fire" on the issue. White House staffers were pressing for a commission in early 1950. On February 22, however, George Elsey recorded that Stephen J. Spingarn and he had decided to defer the matter "in view of the poor circumstances now." Memorandum, Elsey to Clark Clifford, Sept. 19, 1949; memorandum, Charles S. Murphy to the President, draft of Jan. 12, 1950, "Proposal for Presidential Commission . . ."; handwritten memorandum, [Elsey], "Employee Loyalty," Feb. 22, 1950, all in Elsey Papers, Internal Security—Federal Employee Loyalty Program; memorandum, Spingarn to Clifford, May 5, 1949, Spingarn Papers, Chronological File.

Such suggestions could capitalize on a growing Republican impatience with the partisan rancor generated by the McCarthy affair. To this development the "Declaration of Conscience" offered on June 1 by Margaret Chase Smith testified most eloquently. Her six moderate Republican cosigners and she held no brief for the administration's dangerous "complacency to the threat of communism here at home," its refusal to accept criticism, or its ineffective leadership; but neither did they countenance the activities of unnamed Republicans who sought party victory "through the selfish exploitation of fear, bigotry, ignorance, and intolerance." Senator Smith sounded her personal concern over the spread of "'know-nothing, suspect everything' attitudes" and warned that the Senate had become a "forum of hate and character assassination sheltered by the shield of congressional immunity." "We are Republicans," the seven Senators noted. "But we are Americans first." Mrs. Smith's colleagues reacted effusively: several rushed over to clasp her hand, and H. Alexander Smith added his concurrence with the sentiments she had expressed. "Since Senator Smith spoke," Senator Elbert Thomas wrote, "there has been a different spirit around the Senate." [75]

Other Republicans volunteered similar views—the Republican Governors' Conference at White Sulphur Springs became a fiesta of anti-McCarthyism. Governor Earl Warren saw no benefit in "blanket accusations" and thought the laws and Constitution provided ample means to punish misconduct. Asked his reaction to McCarthy, Governor Dewey replied: "mixed." Governors James Duff of Pennsylvania and Alfred Driscoll of New Jersey were similarly critical of the Senator from Wisconsin. Senator Edward Thye of Minnesota, a signer of the "Declaration of Conscience," called upon the GOP to "thresh out a responsible position" on McCarthy. Even Styles Bridges, a McCarthy ally, emphasized that he tried to avoid "McCarthy's technique of making charges." [76]

The Democrats took understandable pleasure in these developments. Tydings elatedly called Mrs. Smith's "Declaration" a piece of "stateswomanship," and the President responded jocularly that he "wouldn't like to make a comment as strong as that about the Republican Party." Complacency and flippancy were uncalled for, however. The Republicans who criticized McCarthy did not represent a majority of the party leadership; moreover, as Mrs. Smith, Bridges, and the Governors made clear, their castigation of McCarthy was no endorsement of the current investigation or of the administration's security policies.[77] The cooperation of such Republicans had still to be earned, not taken for granted.

In the context of these events, Prsident Truman convoked at Blair House on June 22 a crucial meeting of his advisors and congressional leaders to debate the merits of establishing a President's Commission on Internal Security and Individual Rights, or PCISIR, as it was abbreviated. Senators Tydings and McMahon pushed strongly for such a commission and were supported by several presidential aides and by the President's advisor Clark Clifford. Senator Green did not approve of the idea; nor did Attorney General McGrath, who feared it might complicate pending litigation against the leaders of the Communist Party. Vice-President Barkley, Speaker Rayburn, and House Majority Leader McCormack also opposed the PCISIR, although Barkley and Rayburn stressed the element of timing in their objections.[78]

Proponents of the commission noted the popular anxiety over internal security and pointed out that this subject was consuming vast amounts of the energies of legislators and government officials. The Tydings Committee, they warned, would assuredly split along party lines when it made its report. The communist issue would endure to plague Democrats in the coming elections, as it had already done in four primary campaigns. Only a highly prestigious body freed of the trammels of partisanship could allay doubts regarding the administration's loyalty-security program or facilitate the framing of policies in this area.

On the other hand, argued opponents of the PCISIR, creating such a panel would only give McCarthy's charges new life at a time when they were fading from the headlines. They also reasoned that the candidates against whom the red issue had been used were especially vulnerable; that Congress, seeking to adjourn, would balk at taking up so important a topic at this late date; that surely the Tydings Committee's report would silence McCarthy. If the President insisted upon a PCISIR, they hoped he would wait until January 1951, after the elections. These objections apparently carried weight. The President had read to the assemblage a draft message recommending establishment of a PCISIR, but he decided to defer action. Thus, a paradoxical mix of overconfidence and worry resulted in the shelving of the PCISIR plan.[79]

There the matter seemed to end, but the outbreak of war in Korea, heightening fears for the nation's security, intervened to reopen the subject. Administration officials disagreed on the nature of the war's impact upon domestic politics. While some presidential advisors argued that the war was increasing the strength of the forces of repression, making the PCISIR even more timely, others reportedly believed that Korea had "driven McCarthy off the front pages" and rendered the commission superfluous. The administration decided to let events take their course without the guidance of a PCISIR and may thereby have discarded an opportunity to salvage a shard of bipartisanship from the political maelstrom.[80]

As on the question of the PCISIR, the Korean War had a palpable if ill-defined effect on the ending of the proceedings of the Tydings Subcommittee. Many Democratic Senators, according to William S. White, "expected the Administration's strong stand on Korea and Formosa . . . to tend to submerge 'the McCarthy issue.' " Joseph C. Harsch reported that "even Senator McCarthy's stanchest supporters admit wryly that 'his show has been taken off the road.' " The subcommittee had already finished its inspection of the loyalty files; it could withdraw from the *Amerasia* case thanks to the grand jury presentment of June 15 and the loyalty clearance granted (for the sixth time) to John Stewart Service. With its own questioning of Service on June 27, the Tydings Committee heard its last testimony.[81]

On June 28, Tydings pressed for the drafting of a report. He wanted to "take what we have got and present it to the Senate and come to some recommendation that we might all agree upon for a further continuance of this thing"—such as a nonpartisan commission. He would gladly label such findings "imperfect" if so desired, but Hickenlooper objected that to write a report would be an "utterly futile" exercise. He himself could list twenty or thirty individuals he wanted investigated. Lodge also hung back: though he had never served on a more hard-working committee, it had not completed its task. Tydings agreeably implied that the report need only be of an interim sort, but thought the group's work "pretty well concluded." Hickenlooper retorted that it had not even begun. McMahon suggested that the report could be labeled a "working paper," but both Republicans voted against the motion to draft a document under any label. In exasperation McMahon remarked that this was the first committee he had ever seen which could not vote unanimously to have its work summarized in a report. That, Lodge noted with understatement, showed "how controversial this subject is." By themselves, the Democrats, Chief Counsel Morgan, and his staff assembled a report. They met once more with the Republicans, but the effort to patch together a consensus failed. Tydings raised the question of whether McCarthy's charges against Jessup, among his flimsiest, had been disproven. Neither Republican would commit himself to a finding of innocence; each announced he would file a minority report.[82]

In the majority report released on July 17, the three Democrats accused McCarthy of perpetrating "a fraud and a hoax" and "perhaps the most nefarious campaign of half-truths and untruth in the history of this Republic." They found McCarthy's charges either baseless or reheated leftovers from the Eightieth Congress. McCarthy, they asserted, had "deceived" and "misled" the Senate and had used the technique of the "Big Lie." The report exonerated all whom McCarthy accused, though Lattimore, Service, and Kenyon were taxed in varying degrees for indiscretion and Miss Kenyon was cited as an example of the Communists' sinister success in exploiting front organizations.[83]

On July 18, Tydings's submission of the report to the parent Foreign Relations Committee provoked one of that body's stormiest sessions in memory. After much haggling, the Democrats agreed to delete two unfavorable reflections upon Lodge and Hickenlooper (references to their failure to read all the files); not a period would they alter in the indictment of McCarthy. Finally, the committee voted eleven to none to "receive" the report and, by a nine-to-two vote, to "transmit" it to the Senate floor without value judgment upon its contents. "We want to go home by Christmas," Senator Connally explained with a grin.[84]

When Tydings sought to lay the report before the Senate, Wherry first obtained a delay of one day, ostensibly to give Republicans time to read it. Then he convened the Republican Policy Committee to discuss means of toning down the report—but without result. The Policy Committee could only leave it to Senator Taft to announce its concurrence in Lodge's criticisms, expressed in his "Individual Views" (a supplement to the report), and to label the majority report "derogatory and insulting" to McCarthy. Hickenlooper dismissed the investigation as "completely inadequate"; the Democrats had not even had the "courtesy" to show him their findings before giving them to the press. McCarthy exclaimed that the document gave "a green light to the Red fifth column in the United States." [85]

On July 20, the Republicans objected to Tydings's attempt to file the document as a committee report. It was no such thing, for, as Lodge put it, the Foreign Relations Committee had sent it to the floor in no more evaluative a manner than the Post Office Department employed in handling letters. In view of the way the Democrats had drafted the report, some Republicans doubted that it even qualified as a subcommittee report. Wherry raised a point of order on whether it did indeed bear the imprimatur of the Foreign Relations Committee. Vice-President Barkley overruled him, and, when Wherry appealed the ruling, Lucas moved to lay the appeal on the table. Lucas's motion elicited a remarkable roll call: forty-five Senators—all Democrats—voted to table the appeal; thirty-seven—all Republicans— voted against the motion. Next Wherry moved that the report not be printed, but be returned to the Foreign Relations Committee, which was to be instructed either to carry out the express terms of Senate Resolution 231 or to recommend establishment of a bipartisan commission to do so. Barkley again ruled the motion out of order, Wherry again appealed, whereupon Lucas again demanded a vote to table. The vote was forty-six Democratic yeas to thirty-seven Republican nays, and intraparty unanimity prevailed a second time. A similar procedural tug-of-war occurred when Forrest Donnell of Missouri moved to recommit the report: forty-five Democratic votes to table and thirty-five Republicans against. Before debate had even properly begun, the straitjacket of party regularity had been stretched over the Tydings report.

Defeated in parliamentary maneuvering, the Republicans resorted to wide-gauge oratory. Senator Hickenlooper, in lieu of a written dissent, gave a speech arguing that the Tydings Committee had not even begun to discharge its duties, let alone reached a stage where a report was appropriate. He contended that many vital witnesses had not been summoned. Lodge maintained that there were a number of questions as yet unanswered and that in most cases not enough evidence had been gathered to make a determination of guilt or innocence. McCarthy's charges, he admitted,ᵉ had not been proven, but neither had they been refuted.

Finally, Senator Tydings rose to defend the report and his stewardship. Alternately bitter, sarcastic, alarmed, self-righteous, he carefully itemized McCarthy's deceptions. He traced the permutations of McCarthy's charges—from Wheeling to Salt Lake City to Reno to the Senate—and asked to play a recording of McCarthy's words on "one of these occasions." An objection deprived the Senate of a chance to hear a record of McCarthy's radio interview in Salt Lake City, whereupon Tydings, with a talent for mimicry which brought laughter from the galleries, imitated McCarthy's voice in rendering his prior utterances.* Tydings reviewed the shopworn sources of the eighty-one cases, met accusations on various topics, and scattered shot among his critics in the press corps. As for William Jenner, who had once been "so kind . . . to take care of me during my absence," he asserted that "Joe Stalin and the *Daily Worker* and the Senator all vote the same way." Declining to act as "prosecutor," he returned the matter "to the hands and the consciences of the Members of the Senate." 86

The Republicans soon riposted. Irving Ives scolded the Democrats for their provocative report and pointed out that they had not been authorized merely to investigate McCarthy's charges. Lodge, too, criticized the incompleteness of the probe, but when asked by Senator Magnuson if he had uncovered any Communists, he replied, "no; I did not." For the Democrats, this admission summarized the subcommittee's findings, but Lodge thought such questions as who had recruited Alger Hiss into the State Department still demanded answers. Jenner labeled Tydings the administration's "trained seal" for perpetrating "the most scandalous and brazen whitewash of treason-

---

* Some observers assumed Tydings had a recording of the Wheeling speech. He was later charged with trying to convey that false impression. Actually, he meant that he had a recording of the Salt Lake City interview, but confusion arose over which "occasion" he referred to. Milwaukee *Journal,* July 21, 1950; *Christian Science Monitor,* July 21, 1950; Deposition of Millard Tydings in U.S. District Court for the District of Columbia, *McCarthy v. Benton,* Civil Action No. 1335–52, pp. 48–77, copy in Tydings MSS.

able conspiracy in our history." Ferguson accused the Democrats of using the techniques of "Goebbels and Vishinsky." And soon McCarthy was back at the old stand, retailing charges about a State Department Communist whom he designated "X." [87]

As an attempt to adjust a shifting political balance, the Tydings Committee investigation had failed. It did not change many minds. Those initially skeptical of McCarthy's charges remained so; those predisposed in his favor stayed that way; there was no great shift among the uncommitted.* Clearly, the Democrats had committed errors, and these contributed to the rise of McCarthyism and made the task of dispelling its influence more difficult in the future. Yet it is hard to gauge how much of this political slippage was inevitable and, conversely, how much could have been averted.

The Democrats may have made their first blunder in calling for an investigation at all. Tydings later regretted that "we proceeded to investigate without at least calling McCarthy before the Senate Foreign Relations Committee and ascertaining if he had the facts to justify investigation of his charges." After the inquiry had begun and the enfeebled parentage of McCarthy's charges was revealed, Tydings considered going before the Senate to expose the ruse. He was advised, however, that in the aftermath of the Hiss case and remarks about red herrings and unturned backs, the attempt would be characterized as a "cover up." Though journalists had uncovered the origins of McCarthy's claims within a day of the adoption of Senate Resolution 231, McCarthy was suffered to proceed with his "additional" cases and allowed to slide off the hook. By the time the Democrats were fully aware of his first sleight of hand, his charges had proliferated beyond the point of easy control. [88]

In holding open hearings, which afforded McCarthy unlimited publicity, the Democrats may also have erred. The question of who was responsible for public sessions was less important than the fact that the Democrats, though retaining the option of going into executive session, failed to exercise it. There was, of course, merit in their reasoning that those attacked in public testimony had a right to reply

* A July Gallup poll found that 31 percent believed or approved McCarthy's charges, 10 percent gave qualified approval, 20 percent disapproved or disbelieved, 6 percent straddled, 11 percent had no opinion, and 22 percent had not heard of them. *Public Opinion Quarterly*, 14 (Winter 1950–51): 801.

under the same conditions. Moreover, when the probers did take executive testimony, McCarthy was little thwarted, for he managed to hawk his own sensationalized versions of what went on.

The Democrats' overconfidence dictated their tactical responses to McCarthy during the early weeks of his ascendancy. Many participants on the administration side were at first optimistic that the Senator's charges would fizzle like those which Hickenlooper had lodged against the AEC in 1949. The Iowan's one-time target, David E. Lilienthal, suggested that the "McCarthy performance" might "end as the Hick thing did." Since initially McCarthy's abilities were heavily discounted, observers and participants kept the earlier incident in mind as a model.[89] The administration counted on "vigorous defense and counterattack" to end the investigation swiftly. McCarthy did stagger under the early punches, but he demonstrated a capacity to take punishment, stay on his feet, and weave. The Democrats continued to underestimate their adversary throughout March. They dismissed the attacks by the Republican right as attempts to stymie the Fair Deal—an assessment which was accurate, but failed to appreciate the depths of public suspicion regarding governmental security.[90]

The growing support for the creation of a bipartisan commission to investigate government security demonstrated a shift away from such blithe optimism. Republicans had broached the idea first, but before April had ended, the Democrats, chastened perhaps by Budenz's testimony, realized that they were in for a prolonged siege and began to give consideration to the idea. Tydings, trapped in an increasingly stormy investigation, was soon pushing for the establishment of a special panel to relieve his committee of its burden. The scheme enjoyed the favor of some Democrats and of Republican moderates like Thye and Ives, had advocates in the State Department and White House, and received strong endorsements from the press.[91]

A bipartisan commission would not, however, have provided a panacea. For one, there was no agreement among proponents as to the structure or scope of a commission. Tydings and McMahon favored a panel which would function as an adjunct to the Loyalty Review Board and would examine the specific charges before the Tydings subcommittee. White House staffers preferred a group which would go beyond the McCarthy charges and scrutinize the entire federal loyalty-security program. Democratic Congressional leaders wished to avoid any responsibility for a commission, requesting that the President, if he insisted on such a body, take the initiative. However, the Republicans, distrustful of any commission controlled by the Executive, would have objected to such an approach. Thus, Senator Lodge proposed that two-thirds of the members of the special panel be selected by Republican and Democratic congressional leadership. McCarthy and other Republicans had commended Lodge's plan, but later the Wisconsin Senator warned that if the administration set up "a new superloyalty board" without Senate consultation, it would "be merely heaping whitewash upon whitewash." [92] McCarthy, Wherry, and their allies would be hard to win over to any administration scheme; conversely, any proposal which they supported would probably offer scant improvement over the Tydings Committee.

Though numerous difficulties confronted any effort to buck the communist issue up to a commission, the results of simply permitting the Tydings investigation to struggle to its bitter end called for some more imaginative approach. The Democrats' ultimate failure, one which might have been mitigated by a bipartisan commission, was their inability to map out any common ground with the Republican moderates. These Senators were troubled by McCarthy's extravagances, yet out of conviction as well as party loyalty, they could not go along with the Democrats' sharp denunciation of McCarthy nor with what they declared to be an inadequate investigation. In the debates provoked by the Tydings report, not Lodge, nor Flanders, nor Saltonstall, nor Margaret Chase Smith and the other signers of the "Declaration of Conscience," nor any other Republican could be induced to desert his party.

Ralph Flanders exemplified both the Democrats' failure to win over the moderates and the inherent difficulty of that task. He had acknowledged doubts about McCarthy; still, he would not dismiss every charge the Wisconsinite made, he questioned the nation's China policy, and he reasoned that McCarthy "would never have had any influence had it not been for the fact that our late, departed, saint, Franklin Delano Roosevelt, was soft as taffy on the subject of Communism and Uncle Joe." In July, he conceded that the bulk of McCarthy's claims were baseless but argued at the same time that the

Tydings Committee was "very evidently directed toward clearing the State Department and convicting Senator McCarthy." His ultimate solution was to move that the Tydings report be withdrawn from circulation. [93]

In similar conflict, Senator Irving Ives expressed the political dilemma of the Republican moderates. "I am not out of sympathy with what Joe McCarthy is trying to do," he stated, "but with the methods of his attack." Like Flanders, he complained that the Tydings Committee tried "first to get McCarthy, and secondly to whitewash the State Department." On June 6, five days after signing the "Declaration of Conscience," he covered his flank by praising a McCarthy speech (with its usual quota of distortions) for its "constructive approach." On June 19, in further retreat, he stressed that the "Declaration of Conscience" was "not aimed at any one individual." When the Tydings report was brought in, he added his voice to the opposition. Another "Declaration" signer, George Aiken of Vermont, while critical of McCarthy, thought his charges "would have been given much less credence if it were not for the way the Tydings Committee has conducted the inquiry." H. Alexander Smith held that while McCarthy had "done much harm by his wild charges," Tydings and McMahon had forfeited confidence by having been "defensive of the Administration and against McCarthy." [94] The Democrats failed to depolarize the communist issue and thus provided no assistance to these Republicans who were caught between the duties of conscience and the devoirs of party.

From these might-have-beens two tactical possibilities suggest themselves. First, a more disciplined, thought-out, researched approach in February and March might have sidetracked McCarthy. "My mistake," Senator Tydings later lamented, "was in allowing him to wander all over the map, out of Senatorial courtesy, instead of holding his feet to the fire." Secondly, once an early squelch proved impossible, it might have been worth the risks to try the commission experiment. It remains the final irony of the Tydings investigation that the Democrats' majority report and Lodge's individual views, differing in so much, concurred in the desirability of such a step. [95]

Although a bad outcome presupposes the likelihood of faulty performance, the Democrats actually had little room in which to maneuver. The Republicans charged that the Democrats used extreme language in the Tydings report, yet if McCarthy had in fact perpetrated a "fraud and a hoax," what other terms described his misdeed? For the Democrats to curb their indignation and desist from angry rebuttal would require superhuman restraint. A bipartisan commission might have been one way to decompress the communist issue, but the history of such blue-ribbon panels has demonstrated that their findings, if politically unpalatable, can be easily discounted.

Democratic efforts to court wavering Republicans faced severe difficulties in any event. Though the GOP moderates stood at the political fulcrum, they did not occupy the moral center of the universe: considerations of party loyalty and a practical awareness of the rising political issue of anticommunism prompted them to acquiesce in much of McCarthy's behavior or to oppose it equivocally and indirectly. It is questionable whether the moderates could have shifted the balance within the Republican Party which enabled McCarthy to flourish and it was not always certain that they wished to try. The Democrats may have failed to exercise fully the leverage available to them, but their control over the internal equilibrium of the Republican Party was, in any case, limited.

Moreover, the "shocks" of 1949 and early 1950 had already charged an atmosphere receptive to McCarthyism. Concurrently with the Tydings investigation, other damaging events produced further political ionization. On March 7, the day before the Tydings panel heard its first testimony, Judith Coplon, a Justice Department employee, was convicted of passing documents to a Soviet agent. In ensuing months the spy ring with which Klaus Fuchs had been connected began to unravel in a series of widely publicized arrests. Harry Gold was taken into custody in May. On June 16, David Greenglass was arrested—the same day the New York grand jury handed down its findings regarding the *Amerasia* case, which the Democrats hoped would allay the espionage scare. On July 17, the day the Tydings Committee labeled McCarthy's charges a fraud and a hoax, FBI agents burst into the apartment of a New York City family as its members were watching television; next to its coverage of the Tydings report, the *New York Times* ran stories about the arrest of Julius Rosenberg.*

* In June, Alfred D. Slack, connected with the same espionage group, was arrested and William Remington was indicted for perjury for denying that he had been a

The Korean War also put the Democrats on the defensive. Their hope that Truman's prompt response to the North Korean invasion would vindicate the State Department was mistaken. The war may have facilitated ending the hearings of the Tydings Committee, but the anticipated wave of national unity which was to engulf McCarthy and his charges failed to materialize. As Americans first read of such new points on their defense perimeter as Taejon and the Uijongbu Road, McCarthy was momentarily eclipsed from the headlines, but soon he was crowding back in. Korea seemed crudely to reinforce what Republicans had said all along. "If our far eastern policy was not betrayed," asked columnist George Sokolsky in criticizing the Tydings probe, "why are we fighting in Korea?" "Today," McCarthy wrote to the President, "American boys lie dead in the mud of Korean valleys" because aid to Korea, like the loyalty program, had been "sabotaged." Tydings noted sadly that the Democrats' refutation of McCarthy's charges made no impression "against this background of grave national concern." [96]

An awareness of the obstacles confronting the Democrats must temper any criticism of their response to McCarthy. Given the growing salience of the communist issue, perhaps even if the Senator from Wisconsin had been deflated early, others might have emerged to exploit current anxieties; McCarthy's was not the only red-baiting of the 1950 Lincoln Day weekend. Having failed to find a way to avoid the "McCarthy problem," the Democrats were content to score points against their foe. Unfortunately, they were not sufficiently alert to the fact that McCarthy was soon dictating the rules, moving the targets, and reporting the scores of the contest to the public.

Communist. Meanwhile, since February Senator Fulbright had been investigating "influence peddling" in the Reconstruction Finance Corporation and Senator Kefauver's crime probe was getting under way—developments which further weakened the Democrats (*New York Times,* March 8, June 17, July 18, 1950).

CHAPTER 4

On The Track Of The "Commiecrat" Party

DURING THE FIRST MONTHS of Senator McCarthy's new-found eminence, both parties maneuvered and countermarched while keeping one eye on the November 1950 elections; it was widely anticipated that McCarthy's charges would have severe impact on them. McCarthy's singular success in appropriating the communist issue as his own added a new variable to the political equation. After February 1950, many politicians who made anticommunist appeals to the electorate—even those who had seized the issue long before the Wisconsin Senator discovered it—saw their efforts picked over for indications of the strength or weakness of an entity known as "McCarthyism." Their opponents contributed to this phenomenon by their hasty application of that label.

Ironically, but not surprisingly, the first purveyors of McCarthyism in 1950 were Southern Democrats; the earliest test of the communist issue, coming while McCarthy was busy battling with the Tydings

This chapter is adapted from Robert Griffith and Athan Theoharis, eds., *The Specter: Original Essays on the Cold War and the Origins of McCarthyism*, copyright © 1974 Franklin Watts, Inc.

committee, was the Florida Democratic senatorial primary contest between Senator Claude Pepper and Congressman George Smathers. Pepper had long been a bellwether of the New Deal left. In 1944 he had spearheaded the losing effort to keep Henry A. Wallace on the ticket. At the end of World War II, Pepper had opposed what he considered the Truman administration's unduly anti-Soviet foreign policy. He pleaded his case before gatherings sponsored by such groups as the American Slav Congress, which were later characterized as subversive. As the cold war deepened, Pepper retreated from this exposed position, yet in 1948 he made a quixotic attempt to replace Truman as presidential nominee. Ordinarily this maneuver would not have endeared him to organization Democrats, but the effect was blunted by the disenchantment with Truman which was rife in the South. Moreover, Florida's Democratic Party was less a political organization than a shifting congeries of personal followings. As V. O. Key wrote, it was "every man for himself." [1]

Observing that maxim, George Smathers, though once a Pepper protégé, assailed Pepper as an extreme leftist, tied him to the unpopular Fair Deal and to anything that smacked of "socialism," and reminded Floridians of Pepper's previous soft line toward the Soviet Union. "He likes Joe," said Smathers, referring to Pepper's 1945 interview with Stalin, "and Joe likes him." The challenger called for Florida's deliverance from "the spiraling spiderweb of the red network." [2] Emphasizing Pepper's past ties to groups of roseate coloration, Smathers tried to name one Communist front organization per day with which his rival had been connected. He called Pepper "an apologist for Stalin" and "an associate of fellow-travelers." Smathers's supporters issued a pamphlet entitled "The Red Record of Senator Claude Pepper," which itemized all the charges against Pepper and pictured him in the company of Paul Robeson, the black supporter of radical causes. [3]

Smathers also emphasized the issue of race, on which Pepper, for a Southerner, entertained unusually temperate views. The Congressman persistently linked his opponent with proposals to create a Fair Employment Practices Committee (FEPC); he also attacked the efforts being made to register Florida blacks to vote. Even obscurantist vocabulary reportedly served Smathers when he addressed rural audiences: he allegedly expressed shock that Pepper's sister had gone off to the city to become a "thespian" and asked his listeners if they knew that Pepper had practiced "celibacy" before his marriage.[4]

Smathers's aggressive campaign placed Pepper on the defensive. "If they can't make a black out of me," the Senator lamented, "they want to make me a Red." He had constantly to reiterate his opposition to FEPC and his devotion to traditional Southern approaches to race relations. With a mocking portrayal of his opponent's claims, Pepper tried to burlesque the matter of his earlier foreign policy views. Turning up his coat collar, Pepper would sidle across the stage and whisper: "Joe? This is Claude. Got some secrets for ya." [5]

Pepper's exertions were to no avail, for on May 2, Smathers defeated him easily, 387,215 votes to 319,754. The results demonstrated general opposition to the Truman administration and a strong conservative tide, but the race issue was particularly damaging. Pepper lost white votes because of it, and the turnout in black precincts (which gave him 90 percent of their vote) did not offset these desertions. The impact of the red issue is harder to determine. Smathers played it up and observers emphasized its salience. One scholarly account of the Florida primary labels Pepper "one of the early victims of . . . McCarthyism." Pepper himself likened Smathers's tactics to those of "that poison-purveying, headline-hunting Republican senator from Wisconsin, Joseph McCarthy." [6]

However, McCarthyism played a secondary role in the Florida primary. The issue of race upstaged it frequently, and the conservative voting trend revealed in 1950 tended to absorb it along with such related themes as the "socialism" of Pepper and the Fair Deal. Pepper himself concluded "that what they really beat us on was the race issue," which was "the one weapon they had for taking away the little fellow from us." [7] Smathers had in fact cut deeply into the lower-class support on which Pepper had relied in the past, particularly in northern Florida, the section most receptive to Pepper's stand on economic issues but most susceptible to racist fears. Smathers's more conservative economic views won the allegiance elsewhere of upper-income voters, undercutting the considerable appeal which Pepper had always generated as an active, can-do servant of such constituents.[8] Many of Florida's growing colony of Republicans crossed into the Democratic primary to vote for Smathers.[9] Pepper's position on national health insurance also earned him the bitter op-

position of Florida's doctors. (The medical profession, alarmed by
Truman's health insurance proposals, intervened in a number of campaigns against liberals in 1950.) [10] Yet, although Pepper's loss resulted from plural causes, and McCarthyism was not the chief of
them, some observers exaggerated the impact of Smathers's red-baiting. [11]

Pepper's defeat struck home to politicians in North Carolina,
where a comparable primary contest pitted the liberal Senator Frank
P. Graham against the conservative Willis Smith. Graham, the noted
former president of the University of North Carolina, who epitomized
Southern liberalism, had been appointed to a Senate vacancy in 1949.
His opponent Smith was a prominent corporation lawyer who had
served as president of the American Bar Association.* As Smathers
did in Florida, Smith depicted himself as the more conservative candidate and stressed his opposition to FEPC, socialized medicine, the
Brannan Plan, deficit spending, communism, and "all the ideologies
foreign to the American form of government." Like Pepper, Graham
had to respond somewhat defensively: he too opposed all these. [12]

The Smith campaign also hit hard at Graham's racial views. Smith
charged that while Graham now said he opposed FEPC, three years
earlier, when he served on the President's Committee on Civil
Rights, he had advocated such a proposal. Actually, Graham explained, he had inserted into the committee's report a dissent against
a compulsory FEPC. [13] Smith backers played other variations on the
race theme. They publicized the fact that Graham had chosen a black
as second alternate for an appointment to the U.S. Military Academy;
handbills with the young man's picture appeared across the state. [14]
Graham's opponents also circulated spurious handbills signed by
"Walter Wite" of the "National Society for the Advancement of
Colored People" and urging votes for Graham. [15]

Notwithstanding the virulence of these racist appeals, prior to the
May 27 primary, the Smith campaign placed much more emphasis
upon Graham's supposed radicalism, socialism, and links to communism. Smith called Graham a " 'leftwing' Senator who prefers the
socialistic policies advocated by Norman Thomas." Smith's allies

* Two lesser candidates were ex-Senator Robert ("Ouah Bob") Reynolds, a noted
isolationist and xenophobe, and Ora Boyd, whose platform proposed that rape and
"other crimes against white women" be punished by lynching.

ran advertisements playing up Graham's alleged associations with Communist front organizations, notably the Southern Conference on Human Welfare, which, it was recalled, had sponsored unsegregated public meetings for Henry A.. Wallace. One ad stated, "We don't accuse Dr. Graham of being a Communist." However, it went on, he had belonged to eighteen groups cited as Communist fronts by HUAC.[16]

Graham's legion of admirers, who viewed him as "a homespun saint," resented these charges. Jonathan Daniels, Democratic National Committeeman and publisher of the Raleigh *News and Observer,* exclaimed that North Carolinians "have never had a chance to vote for a finer, cleaner, more Christian and more patriotic Democrat than Frank Graham." He was a gentle soul, who, when coach of a baseball team, had instructed his boys not to bunt against an opposing pitcher because the latter had an injured leg.[17] Graham himself was startled by the ferocity of the campaign. Surely, he commented, a man who had been reviled by Andrei Gromyko and the Communist press on account of his work as a UN mediator could not be much of a procommunist. One of his supporters remarked: "If Stalin or Molotov could cast a ballot on May 27, it would be cast for some other candidate, not for Frank Graham." [18]

Minus these two voters, North Carolina gave Graham a 53,000 plurality over Smith.* Graham's impressive total fell short of an absolute majority, however, so that Smith could ask for a runoff election. Now Graham was at the mercy of events, and they were not kind to him. Smith deferred his decision until June 7; his announcement that he would seek a runoff came two days after the Supreme Court jolted the South's segregated education system in the *McLaurin* and *Sweatt* cases. In addition, liberal Democrats had stimulated a sharp Senate debate over FEPC, which served as a further irritant. The "black" issue was becoming more salient than the "red" issue.[19]

While the Smith forces did not neglect Graham's leftist associations and "socialism" in the second primary, they redoubled their attention to the race question. Smith noted the "bloc voting" by blacks

* Graham received 303,605 votes and 49.1 percent of the total vote; Smith received 250,842 votes. Reynolds and Boyd received 58,759 and 5,932 votes respectively, some few of which might otherwise have gone to Graham.

on his opponent's behalf; at the same time he expressed the pious hope that unscrupulous politicians would not make race an issue in the campaign. A handbill put out by anonymous Smith supporters asked Tarheel workingmen: "Did You Know Over 28 Percent of the Population of North Carolina Is Colored?" Luridly it described what FEPC might do to white jobholders. More circulars portraying Leroy Jones, the black alternate to West Point, appeared. Another throw-away connected Graham with a conspiracy to destroy the Southern way of life and raised the specter of miscegenation. "Frank Graham favors mingling of the races," asserted yet another handbill.[20]

Against this barrage, Graham reiterated that he had consistently opposed a compulsory FEPC and approved traditional North Carolina solutions for the race problem, while his headquarters strove to play down the black support he was receiving. But even when Graham took with him on the campaign trail the white he had appointed to West Point, some onlookers remained convinced that he was trying to deceive them. The closing racial "blitz" took its toll: many Graham supporters were intimidated into silence or inaction. On June 24, Smith won by a margin of 18,000 votes. Graham's vote total had declined by less than one percent, but Smith had caught him by scoring an 11.3 percent gain over his showing in the first primary.[21]

Most observers considered the race issue decisive. Jonathan Daniels failed to see how anyone "would question the fact that this racial feeling was the one single factor in the second primary." The "Red business," he was certain, had taken a back seat to the "black issue" in the second campaign. Graham's campaign manager concluded similarly that the Senator had been "knocked out by a veritable tidal wave of racial hate and prejudice" among lower- and middle-class voters.[22] In his analysis of the campaign, Samuel Lubell also emphasized the force of racism, but added that in some middle-class areas economic conservatism also worked against Graham. In the first primary Graham had fared well in the highly agricultural eastern counties, which contained the largest proportions of blacks in the state, but eighteen counties which he had originally carried switched to Smith in the runoff due to the race issue. Graham improved his vote only in the western part of the state, which had a low percentage of black population.[23] Another analysis of the election by Taylor McMillan confirmed the importance of the race issue; McMillan found a high correlation (0.71) between the percentage of black population of a county and its tendency to switch to Smith in June.[24] In both Florida and North Carolina, a racist appeal coupled with an emerging conservative voting trend had proven effective. While the precise impact of McCarthy-like rhetoric cannot be measured, in both states politicians perceived its likely potency. Although the coin of anticommunism was not as valuable as racism in Southern campaigns, it was clearly negotiable.

The communist issue also colored the California primary. Conservative Democratic opponents of the liberal Congresswoman Helen Gahagan Douglas, who sought her party's senatorial nomination, termed her soft on communism and supported her rival E. Manchester Boddy. Mrs. Douglas was accused of having aligned herself with the "notorious New York radical" Vito Marcantonio on votes affecting national security. She was belabored for voting against HUAC appropriations, and the outgoing Senator Sheridan Downey charged that her nay on aid to Greece and Turkey "gave comfort to the Soviet tyranny." Boddy warned voters to thwart the efforts of a "small, subversive clique of 'red hots' " to capture the state's Democratic Party. Mrs. Douglas won the primary, but during the autumn, dissident conservatives continued to flay her for an inadequate appreciation of the communist menace.[25]

In the Idaho senatorial primary, candidates of both parties criticized Senator Glen Taylor for communist propensities. Taylor, a foe of Truman's foreign policies who had run with Wallace as a Progressive in 1948, was unusually vulnerable to such charges, which he had encountered before. After his party bolt, regular Democrats, never his enthusiastic supporters, were eager to dump him. Ex-Senator D. Worth Clark, his principal Democratic opponent, frequently labeled him a "dupe" of the Communists. The several Republican senatorial hopefuls, led by Herman Welker, pitched their campaigns in a similar key. The hostile (Boise) *Idaho Daily Statesman* published installments from "The Red Record of Senator Claude Pepper," noting with relish all the references to Taylor; the newspaper called Taylor the Soviet Union's leading spokesman in the Senate. Barnstorming in his customary singing cowboy fashion, Taylor tried to strike back at his enemies' "smear techniques," but on August 8, he was narrowly defeated by Clark.[26]

Senator Taylor—like other contestants in 1950—found his political fortunes enmeshed with the grim reports of battle from Korea. The Korean War accentuated all the anxieties that came under the heading of "communism" and altered political strategies in both parties. Republicans supported Truman's intervention in Korea but almost as promptly began to blame the war on the administration. "Truman's war" loomed sharply as an issue in the elections. Senator Mundt reported that "most everybody down here feels that the Korean War has given a tremendous impetus to Republican prospects this fall." Soon Senator Taft and other Republicans were calling for Acheson's resignation. Senator Wherry, no newcomer to Acheson-baiting, stated in August that "the blood of our boys in Korea is on his shoulders, and no one else." [27] McCarthy, too, heaped blame upon Truman, Acheson, and the State Department for Asian developments. "The Korea deathtrap" could be laid, he asserted, at "the doors of the Kremlin and those who sabotaged rearming, including Acheson and the President, if you please." [28] Even the ordinarily temperate Republicans on the Senate Foreign Relations Committee accused Acheson and Truman of "inviting" the North Korean invasion. Bipartisan foreign policy was finally dead—again—much in the fashion of Little Nell. Korea would play a prominent role in the campaign: it would enable the more fastidious to talk about and around the communist issue, yet not associate themselves too intimately with McCarthy.[29]

Despite such rumblings, many Democrats chose to accentuate the positive effects of the crisis, assuming that the war would breed national unity and that Truman's prompt response to aggression would squash charges of softness on communism. Such intuition influenced the decision to foreclose the Tydings investigation and to defer creation of a President's Commission on Internal Security and Individual Rights.[30] Thus, at the outset, many prominent Democrats gambled on the possibility that the Korean situation would work to their advantage.

It was a losing bet. Korea redoubled the cold war pressures and anxieties on which McCarthy thrived. While it was true that Korea momentarily removed McCarthy from the headlines, before summer's end a full-scale red scare had come into being. It was fueled by such events as the arrest of Julius Rosenberg in July and his arraign-

ment (with his wife) in August, followed shortly by the arrest of
Morton Sobell; a month later, Alfred Dean Slack pleaded guilty to
charges of spying for the Russians during World War II. Counting
ten such spy arrests since early February, Republican National Chairman Gabrielson asked, "Does this look like a 'red herring'?" [31]

Americans responded rapidly to threats real and imaginary. In July
the city of Birmingham warned all Communists or those who volun-
tarily associated with them to leave town within forty-eight hours; in
August a similar ordinance passed in Macon, Georgia. McKeesport,
Pennsylvania, handled its red peril by decreeing that all Communists
must register with the authorities. When a man arrived to register
under such a law in the town of New Rochelle, police were nonplussed to discover that he was a Republican, not a Communist. He
had thought the law required registration by "commuters." Freedom
House, the prestigious organization in New York which tried to strike
a balance between national security and civil liberties, came out in
favor of outlawing the Communist Party. With Americans dying in
Korea, a Freedom House manifesto argued, it was absurd to permit a
"Russian party" to remain on the ballot. [32]

Other opinion-shapers also succumbed to a crisis mentality. In
August, the NBC network and General Foods Corporation announced
that actress Jean Muir had been dropped from the "Henry Aldrich
Family" show to be aired in September. The sponsor declined to
present "controversial personalities," in which category Miss Muir
fell because she had been listed as a member of four Communist front
organizations in the recently published book *Red Channels*. Soon
other entertainers so listed came under fire. In Omaha, an American
Legion official objected to a local playhouse production of *Born Yesterday;* its author, Garson Kanin, was named in the book. Irene
Wicker, television's "Singing Lady," lost her sponsor for the same
reason. Gypsy Rose Lee, about whom there ought to have been little
new to uncover, was criticized for her alleged associations. A Hollywood studio cancelled production of a movie based on Longfellow's
Hiawatha lest it be construed as communist peace propaganda. [33]

A similar anxiety seeped into government activities. A Brooklyn
judge, for instance, gave jail sentences of six to twelve months to
five people for the crime of having painted "Peace" signs in Prospect
Park. While the judge did not call the culprits fellow travelers, he did

assert that "when you see a bird that has the characteristics of a duck and associates with ducks, then it is reasonable to assume that it is a duck." Motivated in part by the Korean emergency, federal officials requested revocation of bail in the cases of Harry Bridges and the Communist "eleven" and asked that the passport of singer Paul Robeson be lifted. When the Polish liner *Batory* entered New York harbor, customs officials subjected it to a four-hour search to make sure that it was not carrying an atom bomb. Pressures for undiscriminating opposition to communism finally cracked the Democrats' resistance to the extension of economic aid to Franco; they grudgingly accepted an amendment to an ECA appropriation calling for a $62 million loan to Spain. In August, Navy Secretary Francis Matthews suggested the possibility of a preventive nuclear war to preserve peace: "It would win for us a proud and popular title—we would become the first aggressors for peace." [34]

Congress, taking note of the link between communism in Korea and communism at home, proceeded to write it into legislation. On August 9, it voted to legalize the death penalty for espionage in peacetime as well as war. It extended to several new departments the authority by which the head of a government agency could summarily discharge security risks. But the Korean atmosphere moved Congress to action far broader than this and led ultimately to the Internal Security Act of 1950, a distillation of a number of antisubversive proposals including, most notably, the Mundt-Nixon bill of the Eightieth Congress, which had expired in the Senate in 1948. A similar bill, opposed by the Truman administration, languished in committee in the Senate during 1950; however, the Korean crisis unblocked the jam. Congress no longer debated whether antisubversive legislation was to be voted, but what kind. Senator Pat McCarran argued the need to "fortify the home front even as we are today fortifying our boys on the battlefield of Korea." [35]

Aware of the direction of opinion, the White House acted to head off unduly repressive legislation, its task complicated by the fact that elements within the Justice Department had often given encouragement to the drive for harsh antisubversive measures.[36] To bring the security mania under control, Stephen Spingarn again urged establishment of a President's Commission on Internal Security and Individual Rights. Fearing that Congress might pass the Mundt-

Ferguson-Johnston bill (S. 2311), which would require Communist action and front organizations to register with the Attorney General, Spingarn suggested that the President assume leadership in the internal-security field to prevent such a disaster. "Since it is difficult to beat something with nothing," Spingarn advocated a presidential message to Congress stressing the federal government's ability to handle emergencies under extant law and recommending less drastic measures than those before Congress.[37]

On August 8, Truman sent to Congress a message on internal security. He asked for a tightening of existing espionage and foreign agent registration laws and authorization for the Attorney General to "exercise supervision" over deportable aliens. But he warned that the legislation Congress was currently considering would drive "the real conspirators" underground while it endangered basic American freedoms. Though some liberals thought the message extreme, it fell far short of what most Congressmen now deemed necessary. House Minority Leader Joe Martin asserted that it was not even "a step in the right direction." Senator Wherry said that it would treat "Communist revolutionaries with kid gloves" and "betray our American boys who are fighting in Korea." [38] As the liberals were mobilizing ineffectually, Senator Pat McCarran on August 17 brought in from the Judiciary Committee an omnibus bill which included the stringent Mundt-Ferguson proposals.[39]

Liberal Democrats who believed that Truman's program provided insufficient counterweight to the McCarran measure offered their own substitute. Senator Harley Kilgore, aided by Paul Douglas and others, authored a proviso which empowered the Attorney General to confine potential spies or saboteurs in special detention camps during a national emergency. The Kilgore substitute, supporters argued, was an antisubversive bill with teeth. Thus, Hubert Humphrey derided the McCarran offering as a "cream-puff special" and Lucas termed it a "milk-and-water measure" while McCarran, incongruously, struck back by declaring the liberals' bill "not workable under any of the accepted standards of Americanism" and a violation of the Fifth, Sixth, and possibly Thirteenth Amendments. Majority Leader Lucas offered the Kilgore proposal as a substitute for McCarran's. When that maneuver failed, he suddenly moved to tack the "concentration camp" bill, as critics called it, on to the McCarran omnibus, confounding defenders of both plans. This piggyback measure was narrowly defeated, but after Lucas rounded up votes and McCarran added procedural safeguards, the hybrid law was approved by a vote of 70 to 7.[40]

To no one's surprise, Truman returned a stinging veto on September 22. The Internal Security bill would not hurt the Communists, he insisted; it would help them. Requiring Communist organizations to register was "about as practical as requiring thieves to register with the sheriff," and applying that provision to front organizations smacked of the Alien and Sedition Acts. The law made "a mockery of the Bill of Rights" and put the government "into the business of thought control." [41] (It is charged that Truman, lacking a firm commitment to civil liberties, grounded his veto not on civil-libertarian, but on practical arguments. Most of the veto message argues that the law would not work, but it also contains several passages defending American freedoms. Moreover, Truman's long-held intention to veto the measure appeared to be based on the threats it posed to freedom. "What you have been saying on the subject of civil liberties during the last fifteen months," wrote the executive secretary of the ACLU, "is in a class by itself.") [42]

Despite Truman's urgent appeal, Congress overrode the veto. Facing a bitter campaign in which his previous obstruction of such bills had become an election issue, Lucas so voted because, he said, "the American people are anxious to have an anti-Communist bill placed on the statute books." [43] Other Democrats, though troubled of conscience, felt compelled to follow suit. Thus the McCarran bill presented an unpleasant but recurrent choice for liberals: whether or not to try to outflank conservatives and McCarthyites with an end run on the issue of antisubversive legislation.[44]

Contrary to expectations, the fight over the McCarran Act had only secondary impact upon the advancing campaign. Some opponents of the bill, such as Congressman Andrew Biemiller and Congresswoman Helen Gahagan Douglas, had to defend their votes and Lucas was accused of foot-dragging, but their stands on the McCarran Act did not suffice to explain their defeats in November.[45] Just one senatorial incumbent who voted against the Internal Security Act faced reelection in 1950—Herbert Lehman. His opponent alluded only fleetingly to the law, and Lehman assumed the offensive himself, labeling the measure "sinister and more dangerous than any law since the Alien or Sedition Act of 1798." Though observers predicted that the issue would cost Lehman some votes, his convincing success at the polls argued that in this one case at least opposition to the law had proven no liability.[46] (However, not all Democrats hailed from strongholds of urban liberalism like New York.) Conversely, those who supported the McCarran omnibus in the hope that it would confer immunity on the communist issue were to be disappointed. Republicans could still charge, as did Senator Wherry, that "Administration forces" had opposed the original bill.[47]

Moreover, the Republicans found too many other weak points on the Korea-Communism front into which they could rain fire. Throughout the summer the perilous position of the UN troops in Korea enabled Republicans to blame the administration for having hamstrung the military and virtually invited North Korean aggression. Acheson's National Press Club speech of the preceding January received further exegesis and Republicans, including McCarthy, charged the State Department with having held up military aid voted for Korea. Briefly, Acheson enjoyed the small comfort of sharing the obloquy with Defense Secretary Louis Johnson, who became increasingly vulnerable as American troops clung grudgingly to the Pusan perimeter. Johnson's resignation on September 12 left Acheson alone once again with his enemies; two of them, Senators Capehart and Wherry, objected that "the wrong man resigned." Democrats rejoiced at the appointment of General George C. Marshall to succeed Johnson, and one Republican, expressing the feelings of others, noted ruefully that Marshall was "a tin god." In the increasingly partisan atmosphere, even the General was open to attack. McCarthy, who had in April denigrated Marshall's tenure in the State Department ("a pathetic thing"), now cautioned that he "should not be confirmed unless and until he convinces the Senate that he has learned the facts of life about communism." [48]

As the seeming political potency of anticommunism grew, the Democrats abandoned the optimistic assumptions of June and perceived the need for countermeasures. The Democratic National Committee published a " 'Bible' to answer some McCarthy charges" which praised the State Department's personnel and its security program. The Committee's Nationalities Division strove to fend off GOP "mudslinging" among various ethnic groups regarding Communist infiltration of government, Yalta, and Korea. Party spokesmen continued to employ the argument that the far Right and Left played into each other's hands, whereas it was the Democrats whom the Communists feared most. This was so, argued Attorney General McGrath, because of the Democrats' "skillful dynamic foreign and domestic policies." "Who is fighting the Communists anyhow?" asked Senator Clinton Anderson. "Can it be the people who talk about spy rings in the State Department and then vote against appropriations for military aid?" [49] To defend against Republican accusations of softness on communism, the Democrats cited chiefly the administration's effective, internationalist, anticommunist foreign policies—in contrast to the GOP's "isolationism." Vice-President Barkley asked: "Are you going to tell Stalin and the Kremlin that the American people are not behind the Truman Administration?" Senator Warren Magnuson warned that Republican congressional leaders would "march us down that road to isolationism again." If the Democratic campaign had any unifying theme, it was opposition to isolationism, an issue which had since 1940 become, like the Depression issue, a staple in Democratic electioneering. [50]

However, given the centrifugal tendencies inherent in off-year congressional elections, the national Democratic campaign remained amorphous; issues and emphases varied from state to state according to local circumstance. President Truman had hoped to provide some direction, perhaps by barnstorming during the autumn, but the Korean crisis kept him "practically caged" in Washington. He contented himself with a single partisan speech on November 4, which encapsulated the points Democratic orators had been making in the preceeding weeks. He, too, distinguished between his administration's foreign policy and GOP "isolationism," which he declared "one of the main issues in this election." The McCarthyite claim that the Democrats were "communistic," said Truman, was "the craziest idea of all." His party had "done more to defeat communism in this country" than anyone else—it had "saved free enterprise," prosecuted Communist leaders, and built up the might of the free world. The Republicans had shown themselves "willing . . . to undermine their own Government at a time of great international peril" through their irresponsible charges. The emerging "victory" in Korea, Truman boasted, was "the greatest step toward world peace that has been taken in my lifetime." [51]

On balance, however, the Korean War helped the Republicans: it provided a topic less to be argued than simply mentioned. For a few giddy weeks after the Inchon landing and the Pusan breakout in September, as UN troops pressed toward the Yalu, Democratic sermons about standing up to world communism rang true. "If President Truman blundered in Korea," Alben Barkley exulted, "he certainly blundered us into a great victory." Then in late October and November, a massive Red Chinese counterattack routed United Nations armies. On the eve of the election Harold Stassen could announce that the past week had brought the heaviest casualties of the war. As speculation mounted that Korea might have to be evacuated, Democratic arguments about enlightened internationalism and sober anticommunism versus Republican isolationism circulated at a discount. By January, 66 percent of the respondents to a poll felt American troops should pull out of Korea, while only 25 percent were willing to stay in; a growing number (50 percent) thought the original commitment had been a mistake. [52] Korea probably had a more encompassing (and damaging) effect upon the elections than the narrow issue of communism-in-government associated with McCarthy.

However, "McCarthyism" so defined did figure in a number of contests, although the emphasis varied in each campaign, as did McCarthy's personal influence. In the California Senate race, Congressman Richard Nixon, the Republican nominee, made anticommunism his principal theme. The Democratic primary had already implanted it in the campaign's rhetoric, and during the autumn, conservative Democrats continued to link Helen Douglas to "the Communist Party-liner," Marcantonio. Nixon leaned heavily upon the support of the anti-Douglas Democrats and, aside from refighting the Hiss case, had little to add to their exertions. He claimed to voice the views of those who recognized "that all Americans must stand together" against communism just as most Republicans and Democrats in Congress united on national security matters; in contrast, his opponent ran with "the left wing clique" which voted against such measures. "Mrs. Douglas," he declared, "has not denied that she has voted with the man she calls a Communist party liner" more often than any other Representative. "We stopped counting when

those votes totaled 354.'' Although he scored Mrs. Douglas's hostility to HUAC, Nixon concentrated more heavily upon her association
with Democratic foreign-policy "blunders." He challenged her to
state "whether she subscribes to the Acheson-Lattimore policy" in
Asia or that of General MacArthur; he characterized her as "committed to the State Department policy of appeasement toward Communism in the Far East." [53]

If the campaign surged too frequently around the effigy of "Communism," it was partly the fault of the Douglas forces. They conceded the salience of the issue, for instance, when they sponsored
speeches designed to belittle Nixon's role in the Hiss case and to sell
Mrs. Douglas as the more redoubtable anticommunist. They acknowledged the legitimacy of the Marcantonio roll call comparison in
using it against Nixon. Nixonites replied with the so-called "pink
sheets," which detailed hundreds of alleged parallels between Mrs.
Douglas's votes and Marcantonio's. Mrs. Douglas lambasted her adversary's use of "smears" and warned that "McCarthyism has come
to California." (She also referred to Nixon and his backers as
"young men in dark shirts.") Nixon sought to avoid the label of
"McCarthyism," pointing out that he had had no connection with the
McCarthy investigation and that he had advocated a nonpartisan commission to look into his colleague's charges.[54]

Despite the vast Democratic edge in registration figures and the
considerable help she received from the national administration, Mrs.
Douglas lost the election by nearly 700,000 votes. Though the weak
challenge offered by her running mate James Roosevelt against the
popular incumbent, Governor Warren, also hurt her, it was chiefly
with his vigorous anticommunism that Nixon carried the day. He had
used some methods that could be called "McCarthyism," but it
would be imprecise to label him a McCarthyite; while there were and
would continue to be parallels, Nixon had seized upon the communist
issue earlier, could point to more concrete achievements, and usually
demonstrated greater restraint than McCarthy. The California campaign would have assumed its ultimate outline even in the absence of
a Joe McCarthy. The Wisconsinite's one speech in California, despite
its rhetorical extremism ("Ask the basket-cases if they agree that
Acheson is an 'outstanding American' ''), had no effect on the con-

test and was not welcomed by Nixon, who preferred "home talent." [55]

Charges of communist leanings had considerable influence upon the defeat of Senator Elbert D. Thomas of Utah. The Republican candidate, Wallace Bennett, promised to show that Thomas was the "darlin[g] of several un-American organizations," but handbills originating outside the state attacked Thomas more mordantly. The most flagrant of these, the *United States Senate News,* falsely accused Thomas of having presided with Paul Robeson at a communist-oriented fund-raising dinner. It was headlined "Thomas Philosophy Wins Red Approval" and reprinted quotations taken out of context from a book by Thomas. Posted late in the campaign, the tabloid, according to one student of the contest, "startled and shocked" Utah voters.[56] Even before its appearance, the Democrats had become sensitive to the damage done by the communist issue: the several national party luminaries who campaigned for Thomas assailed the Republicans for questioning the Senator's loyalty. Red-baiting was probably the critical factor in Thomas's defeat.[57]

Republicans plied the communist issue in other western states. In Idaho, Herman Welker continued to avow his muscular anticommunism; his identification with the issue may have helped him beat his Democratic opponent, D. Worth Clark (who, in offering postelection congratulations, urged the victor to "continue his fight against Communism in all its forms"). Clark himself was not, however, vulnerable to charges of communism.[58] In Washington, the GOP senatorial candidate, W. Walter Williams, railed that Senator Magnuson had once sponsored a rally of Communists and fellow-travelers, but Magnuson quashed the charge by explaining that his name had been used without permission. Williams also tried, unsuccessfully, to link Magnuson's voting record with those of Senators Pepper and Taylor; but more typically, Williams labeled his foe a "spender." In any case, Magnuson achieved reelection by a comfortable margin.[59]

The "red" issue tinted, but did not shape, the campaign in Colorado, where Republican Senator Eugene Millikin accused his challenger, John Carroll, of "coddling Communists." Millikin hit the Truman administration's "appeasement and encouragement of Communism at home" and made mention of Yalta, the loss of

China, and Communists in the State Department. A rightist agitator issued a pamphlet charging that Carroll "plays piggy-back with Stalin's pals," but the author had no connection with the Millikin campaign. The communist issue, only a secondary weapon in Millikin's arsenal, did not account for his victory.[60]

In several races the impact of McCarthyism was diluted by either more general or more local issues. Hickenlooper of Iowa sought to reap benefits from his pro-McCarthy stand as a member of the Tydings committee, but farm policy was a more decisive factor in his reelection.[61] In Oklahoma, the Reverend "Bill" Alexander charged that A. S. "Mike" Monroney, his Democratic senatorial rival, "went East and turned left" while serving in Congress and found Monroney's opposition to communism lukewarm. Monroney retorted that Alexander, in attacking the administration's Korean policy, was "unknowingly repeating the Communist Party line." More often, however, Monroney spoke as a defender of the New Deal, while Alexander campaigned more as an evangelist (calling it time to "return some Christian principles to Washington") than as a McCarthyite.[62]

The communist issue also emerged in several eastern states. John Fine, the GOP gubernatorial aspirant in Pennsylvania, attacked the Truman administration for hiring those who "flirted with Communism" and accused his opponent, Richardson Dilworth, of courting the votes of "pinks" and subversives. Dilworth responded that it was "political machines" like his foe's which actually bred communism. Fine, he said, was ducking the real issues: "All he wants to talk about is Joe Stalin." Senator Francis Myers joined in to charge that the Republicans were "using Communist tactics and techniques." Myers based his reelection appeal upon his experience and seniority and strongly defended the Korean police action against the claim of his opponent, Republican Governor James Duff, that the war was "unnecessary." Duff declaimed against the Fair Deal's extravagance and "socialistic experiments," the Yalta accords, and the nation's unpreparedness for Korea. He asserted that the Democrats had failed to "appreciate the danger" posed by Russia's rapid rise to world power, but he spent little time on the issue of domestic communism. Duff's popularity as Governor and the Korean debacle greatly outweighed the issue of communist subversion in his victory over Myers.[63]

In Ohio, too, the "pure" issue of communist infiltration was a secondary ingredient of the Republican campaign. Organized labor supplied the muscle behind the effort to unseat Senator Taft, and Republicans reciprocated by denouncing "labor bosses." Taftites maintained that Joseph T. Ferguson, the Democratic candidate, was a mere puppet of the CIO Political Action Committee. Taft stigmatized the CIO-PAC as "the Socialist Party in this country, and although it has gotten rid of most of its Communists, it still uses Communist techniques." He harangued Ohio workingmen regarding the communist origins of the CIO, the socialist programs pushed by its minions, and the "lie and smear campaign" against him. He denounced the socialism and the "strange pro-Red sympathy" of the administration. Communist aggression in Korea, he asserted, had followed hard upon its statements that America would not defend the area. "We practically invited them," he exclaimed.[64]

Ferguson's ineptness muddled the issues in Ohio. (A popular epigram summarized his foreign-policy views as "Beat Michigan.") Ferguson could not "see how any red-blooded loyal American" could support his foe. Dosing Taft with his own medicine, Ferguson condemned the use of "communistic tactics in branding labor union leaders and union members as Communists" and demanded that Taft explain a recently republished photograph picturing the Senator together with one-time Communist notable Earl Browder. Ferguson also noted the congruence between Taft's voting record and that of the ever-unpopular Marcantonio. In November, Taft swamped Ferguson; if the campaign had any central meaning, it indicated broad resentment, even among workingmen, of the much-bruited strong-arm tactics of labor. Taft's anticommunist rhetoric served chiefly to orchestrate this theme and differed in liturgy from McCarthy's, which seldom emphasized a nexus between communism and labor.[65]

A similar contest developed in Michigan between Governor G. Mennen Williams and his Republican challenger Harry F. Kelly. Kelly said Williams was "dominated" by "labor bosses" and such "splinter groups" as Americans for Democratic Action (ADA) and the CIO-PAC. "It is a short jump," he reasoned, "from the methods used by the Americans for Democratic Action to capture control of the Democratic Party to the teaching of un-American philosophies in our schools." "None of us," Kelly boasted of his own party, "has any secret ambitions to change the American way of life into some other strange way of life." Williams answered Kelly in several ways. Having worked to purge a suspected Communist from his own party's ticket, he could lay some claim to active anticommunism. On the ADA, of which he was a founder, he equivocated, now praising its leaders (innocence by association), now minimizing his involvement with it. More hyperbolically, he accused Reds and Republicans of ganging up on him. "Everywhere when the chips are down," he warned, "Communists team up with the extreme right in an effort to defeat those who follow the middle course." The GOP campaign nearly turned the trick, but, after trailing in the preliminary count, Williams squeezed out a thousand-vote margin of victory in a total vote of almost 1,900,000.[66] As in Ohio, Republican red-baiting did not depend particularly upon McCarthy's formulations of the creed, stressing instead a more antilabor theme.

The states where the Senator from Wisconsin actively stumped provide a somewhat more precise gauge of the political force of McCarthyism. In his home state, McCarthy electioneered strenuously, and his influence etched itself sharply on several contests. Initially, some Wisconsin Republicans had been reticent in supporting McCarthy's anticommunist crusade, but such views were in the minority; during the campaign, party workers welcomed his assistance, and he drew the largest crowds of any Republican orator.[67]

The pressures of the campaign dictated a united front. Thus, Senator Alexander Wiley, seeking reelection, had avoided outright expressions of approval of McCarthy during the spring, had defended Philip Jessup's reputation, and had hastened to congratulate Senator Smith for her "Declaration of Conscience." Yet Wiley had to tread carefully lest he alienate McCarthy or his followers. In late March he opined that McCarthy had "pretty well documented his case" and hotly objected to attempts to smear McCarthy. By autumn he had suppressed much of his ambivalence as he echoed McCarthy's indictment of American foreign policy and was gladdened by his colleague's aid. Thomas Fairchild, Wiley's opponent, and other Democrats criticized Wiley's affinity for McCarthyism on the tactical assumption that votes were thereby to be gained.[68] Wiley countered that McCarthy was not the issue, that the junior Senator's "technique" and "personal affairs" were irrelevant. He charged that McCarthy's discoveries had been whitewashed and blamed the Democrats for "seventeen years of coddling Communists." On another occasion, he announced that "Joe didn't find anything new, but he took all of the things we knew before" and "alerted this country to the danger of Communist penetration." [69]

Walter J. Kohler, Jr., the Republican gubernatorial candidate, balanced his rhetoric more precariously: his public appearance with McCarthy must not, he cautioned, be construed as an endorsement of the Senator. Since the Democrats had not uncovered the truth—such as it might be—behind McCarthy's charges, he was "suspending judgment" until Joe got a fair hearing. For good measure, Kohler declared that he had not "the slightest doubt that there are thousands of Communists in key places of the government. The case of Alger Hiss proves that." Other Republicans hastened to campaign as more enthusiastic McCarthyites. Charles Kersten, who had done legwork for McCarthy in Washington earlier in the year, all but welcomed his foe's charges of McCarthyism. In a neighboring district, congressional candidate John C. Brophy backed McCarthy but believed the Senator had not gone far enough.[70]

In November, all of these Republicans but Brophy emerged victorious. Outwardly, the results appeared to be a mandate for McCarthyism, but some astute observers expressed reservations. They noted that the Democrats, though in no immediate danger of winning, had shown strength out of character for a party which not long before had comprised Roosevelt every fourth year and unelectable patronage seekers the other three. The organizational effort which younger Democrats, many of them former La Follette Progressives, had pumped into the party since World War II had begun to bear dividends. The Democratic gubernatorial aspirant had made a 2 percent gain over his showing in 1948, when Truman led the ticket and carried the state. Fairchild, with 46 percent of the vote, had provided the sharpest challenge by any Democratic senatorial nominee in recent years. While they lost ground in Milwaukee (perhaps because that city's large Polish population was responsive to the communist issue), the Democrats improved upon their 1948 performance in twenty-three other counties. The Democratic vote dropped off in forty-three counties, but the Republican vote declined in sixty.[71]

No precise measurements exist to determine exactly how McCarthy's unique style may have altered the traditional, though eroding, Republican strength upon which Wiley drew, but apparently McCarthy's direct intervention brought him little help. Robert Fleming, a reporter for the Milwaukee *Journal,* found that McCarthy "did not pull votes" in the cities where he spoke: relative to 1948, the Republican vote increased in six of these cities but fell off in nine. A hometown effect may explain Republican gains in two cities in which McCarthy and Kohler had their residences. McCarthy's well-publicized invasion of Democratic South Milwaukee, heavily populated by Polish-Americans, did not elect the McCarthyite running for Congress there, nor did it help Wiley appreciably. The 1950 election may provide evidence for the contention that McCarthyism's "impact on the political and cultural life of the state was not particularly great." [72] A formidable but not omnipotent force in Wisconsin, it was of greater moment in national than in state politics.

McCarthy also took a keen interest in the Illinois contest between Senator Scott Lucas and ex-Congressman Everett Dirksen. Dirksen hit hard at the Democrats for tolerating communistic infiltration of the federal government. A Republican victory would inform Stalin "that there will be a housecleaning of his sympathizers and party liners such as this country has never seen before," Dirksen promised.[73] In a Chicago address, McCarthy declared Lucas guilty with Tydings and McMahon of whitewashing the State Department. A vote for Dirksen, he exclaimed, would be a "prayer for America" as well as a "vote against Dean Acheson" and the "commicrat party." [74]

While he was defensive about his maneuvering in regard to the McCarran Act, Lucas counterattacked primarily on the issue of foreign policy, labeling his rival a "fumbling, confused isolationist" aligned with Colonel Robert R. McCormick's Chicago *Tribune.* He capitalized on Dirksen's about-face on the Marshall Plan, which the erstwhile Congressman had once supported but now repudiated as money poured down a "rathole." In October, as UN forces pinched the North Koreans back across the 38th parallel, Lucas hailed Truman's Korean policy as "a great victory." After Red Chinese armies stemmed the advance, Dirksen asked: "where is this peace?" of which the Democrats had bragged.[75]

Dirksen's triumph owed less to "isolationist" or McCarthyite appeals than to the issue of crime. Senator Estes Kefauver's special investigating committee had held hearings in Chicago during the autumn which implicated, among others, a Chicago police captain, who
thereupon became noted as "the world's richest cop." Since that en-
trepreneur was slated on the Democratic ticket, Lucas suffered; the
votes in Cook County needed to offset Dirksen's downstate strength
were not forthcoming. Despite the fact that his support for the Fair
Deal had been lukewarm at best, the Majority Leader was chalked up
as the foremost casualty suffered by the administration.[76]

In Indiana, McCarthy's intervention was irrelevant. His speech in
Indianapolis had little effect on the race between Senator Homer
Capehart and Alex Campbell, the Democrat. Aided by his colleague
William Jenner, Capehart compounded a splenetic mixture of isolationism and anticommunism; he charged that "we are still appeasing
Russia," termed Acheson "Quisling-like," but at the same time
expressed willingness to give up Berlin to the Russians. He called his
opponent a "Truman stooge" and a member of the President's "red
herring brigade." Campbell was unusually resilient to red-baiting
since, as an Assistant Attorney General, he had helped to prosecute
Alger Hiss. (The Republicans were quick to denigrate both Campbell's and the Justice Department's role in the case.) Campbell
likened Capehart to McCarthy in his use of "unwarranted smears"
and asserted that both Indiana Senators had "voted consistently"
with Vito Marcantonio. To the Republican charge that current prosperity grew out of "the warfare state," Campbell retorted that the
phrase originated in the *Daily Worker*. The Indiana campaign encompassed issues broader than communist subversion: Capehart attacked
the whole thrust of New Deal–Fair Deal liberalism ("idiotic experiments with all kinds of isms") and Democratic foreign policies ("a
third terrible war in 33 years"). Campbell was unable to neutralize
the conservative discontent at work in the Hoosier state.[77]

If unnecessary in Indiana, McCarthy's efforts proved insufficient in
Missouri, where Senator Forrest Donnell faced a strong challenge
from Thomas C. Hennings, Jr. Hennings warned of the threat to
freedom posed by McCarthyism and stoutly upheld Truman's veto of
the McCarran Act. Conducting a temperate campaign, Donnell did
not espouse McCarthyism, but the Wisconsinite rectified that oversight with a speech in Jefferson City in which he repeated his charges

against the State Department and what he had taken to calling the "Commiecrat" Party. Alluding to anti-McCarthy advertisements placed at Hennings's instruction in the local papers, McCarthy declared that while the Young Communists had used such devices against him, this marked the first time Democrats had done so. Unimpressed, Missourians elected Hennings by a substantial margin, making Donnell the only GOP Senator to lose his seat in 1950.[78]

In Connecticut, McCarthy also failed to realize his aims as a political spoiler. His three appearances in the state had little *éclat*. Since the local Republican organization had no desire to sponsor McCarthy, a nonparty group invited him. When he spoke in New Haven, only one GOP candidate, Senator McMahon's foe, graced the platform. On two other occasions, he regaled small audiences.[79] McCarthy was unable to sway voters in "the Land of Steady Habits." Though McCarthy assailed him for his role on the Tydings committee, McMahon won reelection easily. While Governor Chester Bowles was defeated,* Senator William Benton, another McCarthy target, won a narrow victory. Relative to 1944, McMahon did lose support in some counties with high concentrations of Catholics; the communist issue and McCarthy's agitation may have accounted for this decline, but the effect was negligible.[80]

In the aftermath of the elections, McCarthy received credit for many of the critical losses suffered by the Democrats. His colleagues believed, according to William S. White, that he "beat" Tydings and "contributed a heavy part, if not perhaps the decisive part" to Lucas's downfall, that Herman Welker "owed much" to him, and that Wallace Bennett was "at least unconsciously and unwittingly a beneficiary" of his. Doris Fleeson wrote that fellow senators scored "an assist" for McCarthy in the defeats of Graham and Pepper. "In every contest where it was a major factor," Marquis Childs reported, "McCarthyism won." Drew Pearson averred that "the main issue contributing to Truman's setback" was McCarthy's attack.[81]

McCarthy was strikingly successful in identifying himself with militant anticommunism and its political dividends. "Above all,"

---

* Bowles was charged with "socialism" and "softness" on communism, and his rival John D. Lodge, in a televised speech, alternated a photograph of Bowles with pictures of Marx, Lenin, and Stalin; but McCarthy did not attack the Governor personally.

one political scientist concluded, "the 1950 election was a spring-board" for McCarthy as a party figure. He had been the most sought-after Republican campaign speaker in the nation.[82] After 1950, his allies and he made frequent reference to his electoral might. Herman Welker remarked that but for McCarthy some seven Senators, including himself, would not be holding forth in the upper house. Senator Brewster interpreted the election as a "triumph" for McCarthy's charges.[83]

Unquestionably the communist issue did trouble American voters in 1950. Not confined to races for the House and Senate, the question arose in the contest for secretary of state of Indiana, attorney general of California, lieutenant governor of Pennsylvania, and in many local races. The 1950 campaign witnessed unusual amount of scurrility, distortion, and red-baiting. It appeared at times that every Democrat in Washington voted with Marcantonio (which solidarity did not save the Manhattan radical from the Republican-Democratic-Liberal coalition that finally knocked him out of Congress). So many Democrats seemingly shared the banquet platform with Paul Robeson that that worthy must never have enjoyed a meal in domestic solitude. If not even Robert Taft, steady helmsman of the right, could resist the photographic embrace of Earl Browder, the latter's allure must have surpassed that of Homer's sirens. The McCarthyism prevalent in the campaign produced, in the view of one onlooker, a "panic in the streets." [84]

The effects of the communist issue, ranging as they did from considerable to marginal, could not be gainsaid; still, too many observers failed to distinguish method from mandate, and the impact of McCarthyism was consequently overstated. The Wisconsinite was not exclusively responsible for the outpouring of anticommunist appeals in 1950 or for the accompanying underhanded tactics. Because the label "McCarthyism" seemed apposite and was too facilely employed, McCarthy received excessive credit for the political trend. The venerable theme of "socialism," for instance, long antedated McCarthy's rise in national politics. Furthermore, a number of Republicans had discovered the threat of subversion in government well before he did. Others emphasized the nexus between communism and labor, a theme with which McCarthy seldom dealt. The issue of Korea gave color to some of McCarthy's extravagant claims, but it also enveloped and superseded them. It was a measure of McCarthy's genius for publicity that he managed to attach his name to all these trends in partisan warfare.

These concerns would have developed in any event as critical campaign issues. The GOP had been feeling its way toward the communist issue early in the year, as attested by the number of other Republicans who emphasized loyalty-security questions in their Lincoln Day oratory. The Florida and North Carolina campaigns presented the phenomenon of McCarthyism without McCarthy. The red-baiting which flourished in Colorado, Utah, and California did not depend on McCarthy or his bill of particulars; the cold war and the frustrations of American conservatives sufficed to produce not only McCarthy, but other practitioners of anticommunism as well.

In some ways it was a typical off-year campaign, lacking the central direction of a national candidate for president who might emphasize themes of unity rather than conflict. The election occurred at the juncture of a number of forces which fertilized the soil both for McCarthy and for anticommunist rhetoric—the cold war, Korea, Hiss, and Fuchs. It also coincided with the maturing of the talents and methods necessary for such tactics: the rise of politics by public relations and mass advertising.[85] The more lurid examples of campaign literature employed against liberals in 1950 were linked to "McCarthyism," but the Wisconsin Senator had not invented this genre. For instance, John T. Flynn's anti–New Deal pamphlet, *The Road Ahead,* had first appeared in 1949; this polemic against socialism enjoyed great vogue in several 1950 campaigns, while other authors produced more extremist tracts for use in Florida, North Carolina, Utah, and other states.[86]

The election results did not reveal quite the grassroots appeal which friend and foe attributed to McCarthy. Though McCarthyites won, so did more classic conservatives like Taft and Millikin— without their bumptious colleague's aid. Liberal Republicans also scored victories. Governors Dewey and Warren, Senators George Aiken and Charles Tobey, no friends of McCarthy, were reelected; James Duff, likewise critical of the Wisconsinite, won a Senate seat. The successes of the moderates balanced the triumphs of the conservatives.[87] Furthermore, Republicans generally had scored a less than famous victory: their gains of five Senate and twenty-eight House seats conferred control of neither chamber and represented smaller midterm increments than the GOP had achieved in 1946, 1942, or 1938. The Democrats could console themselves with the fact that their losses were only slightly more than half the average loss in the last three midterm battles.[88]

In another respect, political pulse-takers exaggerated the spell which the communist issue cast over the electorate. Opposition to the Internal Security Act of 1950 was less than the political suicide which observers predicted. Of twenty-one Democratic Congressmen who voted against the bill, only five lost (two in quests for Senate seats); conversely, of the twenty-eight Democratic Representatives beaten in November, twenty-three had supported the measure. While the Mc-Carran Act may have taken its toll on the candidacies of Scott Lucas and Helen Gahagan Douglas, Karl Mundt's prophecy that Truman's veto of the measure would provide "the best political issue in more than a decade" proved unduly sanguine.[89]

On balance, a closer examination of the 1950 results ought to have tempered the optimism of the McCarthyites and the despondency of their foes,[90] but both groups chose to interpret the election as a mandate for McCarthy and guided subsequent actions according to their heightened perception of his political power. For his opponents, the problem lay in the fact that apprehension soon outstripped reality. The problem was partly one of semantics, but more than choice of words was at fault. Too many observers assumed a single-issue orientation in campaigns which turned on plural concerns and ignored the ambiguous cases for the dramatic. They tended to fix upon the most clear-cut instance of McCarthy's involvement: the defeat of Millard Tydings. In Maryland McCarthy most firmly established his style and weight as a political freebooter; in that election his critics found fullest confirmation of their fears.

CHAPTER 5
Footloose In Maryland

IN 1950, Millard E. Tydings was one of the most powerful members of both the United States Senate and the Senate's "inner club." He enjoyed wide respect among his colleagues and was rated by *Time* magazine among the ten "most valuable" Senators. Sharp of wit and tongue, he could bury his verbal rapier to the hilt in the hide of an opponent in debate. A rising politician in Maryland even before he returned from World War I as a much-decorated veteran, he won election to the U.S. House of Representatives and, in 1926, to the Senate. His successful quest for renomination in 1938 in the face of efforts by the Roosevelt administration to purge him demonstrated his political invincibility. In 1944, he won again, running well ahead of the Roosevelt ticket.[1]

Tydings seemed a cinch for reelection in 1950; gamblers gave one-to-ten odds in his favor early in the year. A member of the Foreign Relations Committee and the Joint Committee on Atomic Energy and chairman of the Armed Services Committee, he had the stature of a national statesman. As he began sparring with Senator McCarthy, he was concurrently gaining considerable attention for his proposals for international disarmament talks. Rumors—planted by foes as well as friends—had it that Tydings might be in line for a place on the national ticket in 1952.[2] A man so unassailable politically, who possessed such impeccable credentials as a no-nonsense conservative, became a natural choice to head the subcommittee investigating Mc-

Carthy's charges. Tydings, despite his initial reluctance, accepted the task. It proved far more perplexing than he anticipated.

At the outset, Tydings and the other two Democrats on the sub-committee overconfidently assumed that McCarthy's accusations would be dispersed in the first rush. After the tumultuous opening hearings, they realized that McCarthy required more than perfunctory treatment and so they settled down to a long siege. One can only conjecture at their vexation as they observed the manner in which Mc-Carthy unwrapped the discarded remains of earlier investigations, weaved his way from case to case with never a scintilla of hard proof for his ever-changing charges, yet managed to escape destruction. Before long McCarthy began to accuse the Democrats, particularly Tydings and McMahon, of hampering the investigation, seeking to cover up, and treating his victims with kid gloves. He referred often to the "Tydings-McMahon" or "Lucas-Tydings-McMahon white-wash clique" and angrily prepared to carry the feud into his enemies' home ground.

Tydings soon saw that McCarthy was drawing blood. His arguments in favor of opening up the State Department loyalty files had hinged upon the political damage McCarthy was inflicting, as had his advocacy of the creation of a bipartisan commission to look into the charges. But Tydings, complacent about his position in Maryland, perceived more slowly that McCarthy also posed a threat to his own political fortunes. He ought to have known better. On domestic issues he could dissociate himself from the Truman administration,* but the chief issues of 1950 clustered about defense and foreign policies, for which Tydings could not, and generally did not, disavow responsibility. In fact, he traded heavily upon his duties in these areas, not realizing that he thereby placed himself at the very coordinates of the barrage McCarthy and other Republicans laid down.[3] Tydings also suffered a unique disadvantage in that, with his constituency draped sprawlingly about the District of Columbia, what for other colleagues

---

* Tydings's conservatism was less obvious under Truman, however, than it had been under Roosevelt. According to one account, he had followed a "middle of the road course" which avoided either outright opposition or partiality to Truman's domestic program. Baltimore *Evening Sun,* July 10, 1950. While Tydings's foes attacked him as Truman's "errand boy" and for his connections with Fair Deal "socialism," they offered no evidence.

was national news became local news for Marylanders. Hostile media centered in Washington such as the Washington *Times-Herald* and the radio broadcasts of Fulton Lewis, Jr., reached out in Maryland, and McCarthy himself could penetrate the heart of the enemy's country with an hour's drive.

In addition, treacherous long-term voting trends coursed beneath the surface of Maryland politics. The growth of the suburbs of Baltimore and Washington had infused the traditionally Democratic electorate of the Free State with a growing number of Republicans. Since 1936, the Republican vote had climbed steadily. Tydings might do well among such constituents (as he had previously) by presenting himself as the more conservative candidate. He had swept up Maryland's conservative vote when he ran against the liberal David Lewis in the 1938 primary; but no one thus far had attacked the areas of his greatest political strength, either the conservative suburban vote or the Eastern Shore, where politics were carried on in traditional Southern ways.

Other political shifts compounded Tydings's predicament. In Baltimore City, Tydings had always counted on the organization vote, but here, too, erosion had occurred. The urban wing of Maryland Democrats leaned toward the New and Fair Deals; how long it could straddle both New Deal liberalism and Tydings's conservatism was a matter of some doubt. Tydings also failed to attract support from blacks, heavily concentrated in Baltimore, who resented his pro-Southern stand on civil rights. Western Maryland customarily produced a large Republican turnout; but the voters of this region of railroads and mines had no particular liking for Tydings's stand-pat position on domestic matters, so that here his conservatism operated as a liability. Finally, Maryland's large Catholic population, located chiefly in Baltimore, had always supported Tydings before, but might prove a volatile element in a campaign that stressed the issue of communism.[4]

Tydings created additional handicaps for himself; he had neglected fence-mending and pork-dispensing and had grown away from his constituents to become more and more that phenomenon known as the "Washington Senator." As one reporter commented, "Global statesmen have to be elected at home and there are spots in Maryland where the Senator's popularity is said to have suffered." A Baltimore

Democratic district leader remarked to the Republican senatorial campaign manager that when Tydings came to him during the campaign to jolly him, he resented it, for Tydings had neither spoken to him for seven years nor answered any of his letters.[5]

Maryland's Democratic Party was also riven by factionalism precisely when Tydings needed united support. The incumbent Governor, W. Preston Lane, had made enemies as a result of the adoption of a state sales tax during his administration. In 1950, a bloody primary fight developed between Lane and George P. Mahoney. This feud required a delicate balancing act of Tydings. Never close to Lane, he still had to avoid the embrace of the Mahoney forces, who were not loathe to create at least the impression of such an alignment.[6]

Well before the campaign began, signs of weakness in his home base reached the senior Senator from Maryland. After the first two hearings on McCarthy's charges, for instance, a respected attorney and prominent organizational activist from Baltimore paid a visit to Tydings's office, having been delegated by his associates to check up on how the probe was being conducted. If press reports of an attempted "whitewash" were true, the visitor warned, those who had backed Tydings in the past would be "very much disgusted" and would "change their vote to elsewhere." From a powerful Democratic leader in Baltimore came the worried advice that the investigation had people murmuring in an unprecedented fashion.[7]

As McCarthy's charges were disseminated, more or less organized support for them began cropping up in Maryland. The executive secretary of a group calling itself the Republican Activities Committee of Maryland wrote to Tydings taxing him for letting his subcommittee apply a "white-wash brush to dirty blotches." [8] Another organization, the Maryland Committee for Representative Government, also reproved Tydings for his handling of the investigation.[9] A Catholic group, the Maryland Action Guild, seasoned its frothing anticommunism with vitriolic condemnation of Tydings. The rise of criticism "in conservative circles, normally the haunt of the Senator's most ardent worshippers," was noted by a Maryland political reporter.[10] Seemingly unperturbed, Tydings delayed until July 8 the announcement that he would run again.[11]

In his campaign for renomination, Tydings did not have an open field. One rival, former Congressman John A. Meyer, received the support of Maryland's AFL and CIO. Despite his laborite orientation, Meyer condemned Tydings not for his conservatism, but for the "complete whitewash" he made of the McCarthy investigation.[12] Hugh M. Monaghan II, a Baltimore attorney, attacked Tydings as bitterly as had McCarthy. Monaghan asserted that Tydings's attitude as Chairman of the Armed Services Committee "was in large part the cause of our unpreparedness" for the Korean War. He quoted a statement by Tydings—unfortunately dated one week before the war's outbreak—calling for talks with the Russians and said that Neville Chamberlain's achievements, compared to Tydings's record, were "positively brilliant." The Tydings report, Monaghan argued in McCarthyesque language, "has given the green light to Stalin's agents in this country." Monaghan even challenged the two Democratic candidates for Governor to declare their positions on the Senator's candidacy; he would not "support any candidate for State office who is not willing to put his conviction against communism into practice sufficiently to repudiate Senator Tydings' candidacy." [13]

Since the Republican senatorial aspirants agreed that the Tydings investigation was the prime issue, bipartisanship prevailed in the primary campaign. Before he dropped out of the race, Herman L. Mills, the Republican mayor of Hagerstown, chided Tydings for his "willful attempt to excuse, cover up, whitewash, or protect governmental policies harmful to the nation." A more redoubtable candidate, General D. John Markey, raised the same themes, charging that Tydings had "changed 180 degrees on the Red issue" and confidently predicting that the people would turn against the Senator. Markey, who had narrowly missed defeating Tydings's colleague Senator Herbert O'Conor in 1946, loomed as the strongest GOP candidate. A third Republican, John Marshall Butler, concentrated even more heavily than Markey on the "whitewash" issue. Butler, a respected Baltimore lawyer, was a lightly regarded latecomer to politics; while he enjoyed the support of much of the Republican organization in Maryland (such as it was), Markey remained the favorite. To counteract this disadvantage, Butler's campaign headquarters strove to radiate an aura of optimism and to concentrate on the counties which Markey was neglecting. Maryland's unit vote system, a sort of miniature electoral college, dictated this strategy, for a candidate who carried enough electoral districts might win the nomination even if his opponent gained a larger total popular vote.[14]

In July, Butler began to receive crucial outside help. First, on the recommendation of Mrs. Ruth McCormick ("Bazy") Miller, publisher of the Washington *Times-Herald,* friends of Butler contacted Jon M. Jonkel, a Chicago public relations man experienced in political warfare. Jonkel agreed to serve as campaign manager. While his formal title was obscure, Jonkel enjoyed such unquestioned authority that the Senate subcommittee which investigated the Maryland election declared it "a matter of the campaign manager and the campaign headquarters directing candidate Butler rather than candidate Butler directing the campaign manager and campaign headquarters." [15]

Nourishing a desire for revenge, Senator McCarthy also entered the campaign. In July, Butler and a lieutenant sat down with McCarthy and his staff to map strategy. McCarthy placed all his material on the now-concluding Tydings investigation at Butler's disposal.[16] Eventually, McCarthy would provide much more: speeches, financial help, assistance in producing campaign literature, and logistical support. In the meantime, Butler fashioned his campaign closely after McCarthy's charges. He berated Tydings for "the thoroughly disgraceful manner in which he whitewashed the State Department employee loyalty investigation" as well as for his stewardship of the Senate Armed Services Committee. The Tydings report he labeled a "blotch on the integrity of Maryland." During the primary campaign, both Butler and Markey concentrated their fire on Tydings while ignoring each other.[17]

As his opponents sharpened their knives, Tydings had ample indication that the State Department investigation had impaired his prestige. According to Senator A. Willis Robertson, many Democrats had at first hoped that the Tydings probe would quash the McCarthy charges for good, but the result had been the opposite: the "prevailing impression in the Nation" placed the onus of "whitewash" upon the subcommittee.[18] On June 8, before announcing his candidacy, Tydings sent out a set of questionnaires to Maryland Democratic Party leaders asking them to wet their fingers to the wind in regard to his prospects and to the issues stirring the electorate. Of the eighty-six forms returned, thirty mentioned McCarthy' charges, the investigation, or related topics (such as Owen Lattimore) as salient issues. Three of the respondents thought the McCarthy brouhaha had helped Tydings, and three dismissed it as harmless, but twenty-three believed that McCarthy and the investigation had done varying amounts of damage. (One man felt the issue might have either a positive or negative effect.) Thus, 77 percent of those who alluded to McCarthy as a factor in the campaign and 28 percent of all respondents thought the McCarthy investigation had a negative impact on Tydings's candidacy. Several of these Democratic leaders noted the erosion of support for Tydings among conservatives—including some Republicans—who normally were an important source of the Senator's strength.[19] This intelligence came in before the Tydings subcommittee's report occasioned outbursts of partisanship which further poisoned the atmosphere. Senator O'Conor confirmed the more direful predictions. At a celebration on the Eastern Shore, O'Conor huddled with local Democrats who advised that Tydings was in "critcal" shape in that region.[20]

Tydings maintained a complacent attitude toward these ill omens. "Just you wait," he told O'Conor, "fifteen days after I start my campaign, all this opposition will disappear." Although he announced his candidacy on July 8, his campaign remained dormant a good month after that. In mid-August, he had yet to deliver a speech; pleading the press of business in Washington, he asked, "Why should I?" When he became active, Tydings did not at first set out to rebut the charges of his opponents, but instead emphasized his value as a man with power and seniority on whom the responsibilities of the nation's defense and foreign policy weighed heavily.[21]

Soon, however, he decided to "meet squarely the intensive campaign of falsehood, mudslinging and political propaganda" in a major radio and television speech on August 31. Scouting the rumor spread by Fulton Lewis, Jr., that his reward for serving as the administration's lackey would be the post of Ambassador to the Court of St. James's, Tydings invoked his reputation for independence, which had prompted the 1938 effort to purge him. The "whitewashing" charges, he dismissed as "ridiculous." Tydings refuted McCarthy's claims point by point and exposed McCarthy's "numbers game," his backtracking and failure to repeat charges without senatorial immunity. While Tydings held "no brief for the State Department, or anyone in it," or for Owen Lattimore, he had been assigned the specific chore of finding whether there were any Communists in the State Department, had investigated as best he could, and found none.[22]

The "whitewash" charges continued to take their toll, however, according to a number of Tydings supporters. Early in September, Tydings sent out a second batch of questionnaires. Of the fifty-seven forms returned, forty-nine, or 85 percent of them (as compared to 35 percent in the first poll), mentioned McCarthy, the subcommittee investigation, or related topics as a (and generally *the*) troubling issue locally. While one man made bold to suggest that the communist issue had helped Tydings and two thought the speech of August 31 had repaired much of the damage, the remainder of the forty-nine responses noted varying degrees of disaffection. Ninety-four percent of those who perceived McCarthy's charges as an issue thought they had had a harmful impact, while 81 percent of the entire sample reached this conclusion. The McCarthy investigation, as gauged by Democratic Party functionaries, had become the chief issue in the Senate race, and to many of them the outlook appeared dismal.[23]

A thumping primary victory might dispel some of the pessimism and, on September 18, Tydings thought he had scored such a triumph when he amassed 172,572 votes to 40,015 votes for Meyer and 47,718 for Monaghan. In the Republican primary, General Markey polled 27,939 votes to 21,700 for John Marshall Butler; however, the unit system accorded more unit votes and hence the nomination to Butler. Similarly, in the Democratic gubernatorial primary George Mahoney, with 191,193 votes, outpolled Governor Lane, who had 173,611 votes, but the unit system gave Lane a majority of unit votes at the upcoming convention. Theodore R. McKeldin, a popular liberal Republican and former mayor of Baltimore, received the Republican nomination for Governor and threatened to win numerous Democratic votes in the general election. Senator Tydings exulted that the results of the primary had defused the "whitewash" charges. As the Korean situation improved, Tydings could also take pleasure in the fact that his management of the Armed Services Committee now seemed above reproach.[24]

Such optimism may have been premature, however, for Tydings's primary victory, viewed from another perspective, revealed a "substantial undercurrent" against him. Neither Democratic challenger had been widely known, so that their showing evinced either residual unhappiness with Tydings or specific dissatisfaction with his conduct of the loyalty investigation, the principal issue of both Democratic rivals. Republican strategists noted also that some 120,000 Democrats who had troubled to mark their ballots in the gubernatorial contest did not register a choice in the senatorial primary—and they interpreted the abstention as a protest against Tydings.* Jonkel, Butler's chief adviser, cited this statistic as demonstrating that Butler had all but won the election before the autumn campaign began.[25]

After the primary, the quarrel over the gubernatorial nomination immobilized the Democrats for two weeks or more. When Mahoney asked for recounts in several counties and lauched a court test of the unit system, an impasse threatened. Senator Tydings worked discreetly to reconcile the Lane and Mahoney forces, and he helped engineer Mahoney's withdrawal at the Democratic convention on October 2. Even so, a number of bitter-end Mahoney supporters moved bag and baggage (and file and mailing list) into the McKeldin-Butler camp. In the interest of party solidarity, John Meyer endorsed Senator Tydings, but Hugh Monaghan, despite hints to that effect, refused to make the same gesture. During the interim, the Democrats lost precious time.[26]

In the general election campaign, Butler received considerable help from sources outside the state, notably from McCarthy and his allies. After his initial proffer of assistance, McCarthy had limited his direct intervention to one public appearance prior to the primary. On September 15, he addressed an Americanism rally in Baltimore sponsored as a nonpartisan event by several Catholic, veterans, and citizens groups. While the rally's moderator remarked pointedly that the speech might have profound repercussions on the campaign, McCarthy affected a pose above politics. He did not mention Tydings by name, but instead presented a now-standard indictment of Acheson, Lattimore, Service, and company. Opponents of McCarthy, armed with materials from their own out-of-state sources, passed out reprints of a recent Madison *Capital-Times* editorial summarizing McCarthy's financial troubles. McCarthy, apparently nonplussed, alluded to the "communistic party line views" of the writer of the editorial, who was William T. Evjue.[27]

---

* The validity of this interpretation is conjectural, however. One could equally argue that the gubernatorial fight and the sales tax simply generated more voter interest. Also, the senatorial campaign was not a close enough contest to stir up much voter concern.

This aid from a liberal like Evjue to the conservative Tydings presented something of a paradox, but one which, in the face of a common enemy, became understandable.[28] Other liberals also supported the incumbent, however improbable that situation would have been before McCarthy rattled the political structure of Maryland. Tydings thus received advice and assistance from a local veterans' group which took its cues from the American Veterans Committee, an early opponent of the Wisconsin Senator. Already incensed by McCarthy's performance in the Malmedy investigation, the AVC had in June urged McCarthy's removal from the Senate. Now, some of its members supplied Tydings with data on the Malmedy incident for possible use in the campaign.[29] Tydings even obtained the backing of a local chapter of the Americans for Democratic Action.[30] Grudgingly, some elements of organized labor also swung in behind him. A member of the Democratic State Central Committee for Frederick County assured the Senator that his efforts against McCarthy would bring him votes in that locale which he had not had since the liberal Davey Lewis ran against him in 1938.[31]

In neither magnitude nor effectiveness did such accretions of liberal strength balance the growing involvement of Senator McCarthy in the campaign. A week after the primary, he dropped in on Butler and renewed his offer of assistance. He helped launch the Republican campaign with a speech on September 23 in Hyattsville, in which he scored Senators Lucas, Tydings, and McMahon as "men of little minds" and protectors of Communists. On October 30, his address to the Young Republican Club of the District of Columbia, broadcast over several Maryland radio stations, carried his gibes at Acheson, the "commiecrat Party" and the "whitewash committee" or "Tydings-McMahon combine." [32]

Butler adopted a line which, if not coinciding exactly with McCarthy's, paralleled it closely. Where McCarthy made pointed accusations, Butler sought to suggest or to nurture suspicion. Jonkel labeled this tactic exploiting the "big doubt." In his first act as campaign director, Jonkel had taken an informal sampling of public opinion and found that nearly 70 percent of those interviewed simply did not know whether Tydings had conducted a whitewash or not. Jonkel did not essay the unmanageable task of proving conclusively that Tydings had concealed subversion. He advised that the campaign

" 'not get into the business of proving whether or not it was a white-wash, let's stay in the business that a doubt does exist.' " Candidate Butler even raised this theme explicitly, declaring that "the whole investigation had left doubts and wonderment in the minds of a great many people" Communism, Jonkel noted, gave the Republicans the same sort of issue, one which did not require much disputation, as the Democrats had once possessed in the "Hoover apple." [33]

Butler worked strenuously to associate Tydings with the Truman regime. He referred frequently to the "Truman-Tydings combine" and warned, absurdly in view of his opponent's voting record, against following the "Truman-Tydings line of socialization of medicine, agriculture and industry." [34] Tydings responded that he had vigorously advocated economy in government, opposed the administration on such questions as the Internal Security Act and the Brannan Plan, and was emphatically not a "Me Too" man. When he struck at the "shabby device of linking my name with that of the President" and disavowed support of socialized anything, Butler whipsawed him by charging "an all-time low in ingratitude and indecency. . . . If he can't stick behind his own party when the going gets rough, who is he going to stick with?" In short, Tydings was hung both for a loyalist and for a rebel. [35]

Butler threw himself into the normal round of oyster eating, rallies, and ceremonial speeches which Maryland demands of its politicians. He coordinated his campaign with that of the more popular McKeldin, and the two candidates traveled about in the same "caravan." This, as the Senate committee which investigated the election later stated, was the "front street" campaign. However, a few of Butler's supporters also carried on a campaign whose more noisome aspects were "back street" in character. Butler, who rarely set foot in his own headquarters, was unaware of some of the details of this "back street" operation conducted under Jonkel's loose supervision. [36] Some "back street" activities bore the heavy impress of McCarthy and his confederates. Jean Kerr, an employee of McCarthy (and later his wife) played a significant role in arranging a $5,000 contribution to Butler from Alvin Bentley, a former State Department employee and a McCarthy sympathizer. In connection with McCarthy's office, a Mr. and Mrs. Robert E. Lee organized and helped financing for an ambitious Butler postcard project. Various McCarthy supporters contributed money, among them Alfred Kohlberg, putative head of the "China Lobby," Senator Owen Brewster, Clint Murchison, the Texas oil tycoon, and other bankrollers of right-wing political causes. Miss Kerr culled research materials from McCarthy's files for Butler and remained in close contact with Butler headquarters throughout the campaign. Other McCarthy staff members lent assistance, and the distinction between voluntary, off-hours help and "company time" was at best murky.[37]

Aid to Butler from McCarthy allies also included the warm editorial support of the Washington *Times-Herald,* recently purchased by Robert R. McCormick of the Chicago *Tribune* and published by his niece, Ruth McCormick Miller. In addition, Butler benefited from several harsh attacks upon his rival by the radio commentator Fulton Lewis, Jr., over the Mutual network (which was 19 percent owned by the Chicago *Tribune*).[38] Colonel McCormick, at the bidding of "Bazy" Miller, offered the services of Roscoe Simmons, a *Tribune* columnist, family factotum, and prominent black Republican politician, who electioneered for Butler among Maryland's black population. Mrs. Miller also made sizeable monetary contributions plus personal loans to her protégés, Jonkel and Simmons.

The notorious campaign tabloid "From the Record" owed its genesis to much the same group. At McCarthy's behest, Mrs. Miller lent her facilities and her employees' time to the production, at an abnormally low cost, of this pamphlet. Much of the material for the tabloid came from McCarthy's office; it was supplemented chiefly with reprints from the *Times-Herald*. Frank Smith, chief editorial writer for the *Times-Herald* and later Senator Butler's administrative assistant, composed the tabloid; assistant managing editor Garvin Tankersley helped on layout; McCarthy's staff did legwork and research.[39]

Circulated the weekend before election day, "From the Record" gathered together all the strands of McCarthyism which enfolded the Maryland Senate race. Its lead headline blared: "Senator Tydings Promised Probe, But Gave Whitewash Instead." An article from the *Times-Herald* followed. Another story alleged that Tydings's Armed Services Committee "held up" arms voted for South Korea—all save the $200 in baling wire to which McCarthy so constantly adverted; an excerpt from a McCarthy speech embellished this charge. Insinuatingly, the tabloid pointed out that the Senator and his wife had sponsored a public forum, a fund-raising device for Bryn Mawr College, at which Owen Lattimore had spoken and for which Alger Hiss had also served as sponsor. (That Mrs. Tydings was a Bryn Mawr alumna, that the sponsorship was monetary and *pro forma*, and that Tydings did not attend the lectures—these facts the tabloid omitted.) Along with quotations from hostile editorials and from senatorial critics of the Tydings probe, the tabloid reprinted McCarthy's tale that the loyalty files examined by the Tydings committee had been rifled. One page, which headlined Tydings's claim that there was not "a single pro-Communist in the State Dept.," carried pictures of Lattimore, Jessup, Acheson, Service, Haldore Hanson, William Remington, and Gustavo Duran. Remington, while subsequently convicted of perjury for denying his Communist affiliations, had served in the Commerce Department, not State. The other photographs permitted further inaccurate inferences.

In a year of scurrilous campaigning, no episode horrified critical onlookers more than the deceptive "composite" picture (so captioned) of Tydings and Earl Browder. It showed Browder thoughtfully stroking his chin while a pensive Millard Tydings leaned toward him, presumably absorbing the outcast commissar's every word. When Browder, according to the commentary, was "cajoled into saying Owen Lattimore and others accused of disloyalty were not Communists," Tydings answered "O, thank you sir." Garvin Tankersley had fabricated the composite from a recent photograph of Browder and a picture out of the morgue which showed Tydings listening to election returns in 1938, the circumstance accounting for his rapt expression.[40]

As these events were being shaped, Senator Tydings—once again—reacted tardily to the forces gathered against him. Resorting to traditional campaigning techniques, he embarked upon a statewide tour with other candidates, showing the colors at numerous Maryland crossroads and hamlets. In Garrett County a rampaging steer sent him scrambling over a fence; on the same day, he suffered the indignity of being momentarily confused with Warren G. Harding by an elderly, hard-of-hearing voter.[41]

At first Tydings generally played down the issues which had been raised against him in the primary, having decided that, barring a change in the effectiveness of his opponents' campaign, his conduct

of the investigation required no further defense.[42] Instead, he emphasized his experience, seniority, and grave burdens in the realm of
defense and foreign policies. "I hear all the secret information on
atomic weapons," he boasted. Like other Democrats in 1950, he
made an issue of the Republicans' "narrow isolationism" versus the
reasoned anticommunist policies of the Democrats.[43] He advised
Democrats to "forget petty things" and to concentrate on the main
question: American survival and the prevention of World War III.
Offering the intelligence that "we still have been unable to make
peace in many places," Tydings declared that the best answer to
would-be aggressors was to maintain a strong America.[44] Such high-
flying rhetoric failed to convey the conscientious concern Tydings
had recently given to the problems of nuclear disarmament and So-
viet-American relations; ideas of international import do not translate
well into the *patois* of the hustings.*

In the latter part of October, Tydings decided to respond more directly to the Republicans' "smear campaign." [45] He was sensitized,
perhaps, by the hostile radio broadcasts of Fulton Lewis, Jr., who in
October stepped up his assaults on the Senator's "whitewash" of the
McCarthy investigation. On October 18 Tydings objected that Lewis
had inserted blatantly partisan appeals into an allegedly nonpartisan
format and demanded equal time to reply. On October 20, Tydings
delivered his rebuttal. When several minutes of his rejoinder were
lost due to technical failures, Tydings protested, arguing that he
deserved another program anyway as compensation for Lewis's two
recent attacks.[46] He received a second hearing, but Lewis ultimately
had the last word, and the squabble added to neither the dignity nor
the effectiveness of Tydings's campaign.[47]

Tydings sought to turn the outside intervention of Lewis and others
to his advantage. He stigmatized the McCormick press for its isolationism and its meddling in Maryland politics. He cited 1938 to illustrate the short shrift Free Staters gave to efforts at external dictation.

---

* Further emphasis on his views on these subjects might only have hurt Tydings; his
opinions portended a "softer" line than that pursued by the Truman administration,
which found itself somewhat embarrassed by these suggestions. See Coral Bell, *Negotiation from Strength: A Study in the Politics of Power* (New York, 1963), p. 8.
Tydings had been attacked during the primary campaign for his call for negotiations
with the Soviet Union.

Seeking to stop vote leakage on the whitewash issue, Tydings summoned support from other politicians. Eyeing the Catholic vote in particular, he importuned Senator O'Conor to make several speeches defending his handling of McCarthy's charges, despite O'Conor's misgiving that he, rather than Tydings, should be so heavily featured in these late appeals. George Mahoney and other Maryland politicians also took up Tydings defense. On November 3, Tydings himself lashed out at his opponents' "carefully planned and executed campaign of propaganda, founded upon the technique of character assassination." [48]

The appearance of "From the Record" stimulated Tydings's most vehement self-defense. Taking to radio and television on November 5, Tydings displayed the tabloid and called it a "new all-time low" in the Republicans' "false, malicious and vicious smear campaign." Indignantly he exposed its "outright falsehoods," innuendoes, and "faked photographs." On the eve of the election Tydings broadcast another denunciation of the "malicious and false attacks" on him. Butler replied that he had delicately not brought out the "kind of information that is available about the Senator's long, long political career that could have been in questionable taste." Dismissing complaints about the tabloid as "whining," he accused Tydings of having "tried to smear me by claiming he had been smeared." [49]

On this dignified note, Marylanders proceeded to the polls on November 7. The early returns from Baltimore showed Butler in the lead. Tydings held out in the hope that the counties, always a source of strength, would turn the tide, but the outstate returns only added to Butler's lead. The final results gave Butler 326,291 votes to 283,180 for Tydings. McKeldin swamped Governor Lane by a still larger margin, 369,807 to 275,842. [50]

With unanimity, observers attributed Tydings's defeat substantially to the issue of the loyalty investigation and McCarthy's charges. One Maryland political reporter declared that "McCarthyism alone would have been sufficient" to defeat Tydings. His inability to "argue away the accusations of 'whitewash' " constituted the "most plausible explanation" of the upset, according to another journalist. William S. White found a "consensus" among Senators that McCarthy defeated Tydings. [51] Other elements, it was true, also played a role in the decision. Tydings, as some election postmortems noted, had suffered grievously from his association with Governor Lane, whose sponsorship of the sales tax and primary fight with Mahoney had damaged the Democrats. Conversely, Butler profited by his firm grasp on the coattails of Theodore R. McKeldin. Tydings was hurt also by the worsening Korean situation, and the issue was exacerbated by his chairmanship of the Armed Services Committee.[52] To these liabilities Tydings added others of his own: he had grown aloof from the rank and file; there had been, in Edward F. Ryan's words, a "loss of personal appeal" and the "little irritations" accumulated over four terms in office.[53] But it was McCarthy and the "whitewash" issue which consumed most printer's ink.

Ironically, while most hostility to Tydings presumably mounted on the right side of the political spectrum, one sizeable defection came from voters to Tydings's left. Though Tydings had never, because of his views on civil rights, been popular among Maryland's blacks, he had managed, thanks to the potency of the Democratic organization, to obtain a substantial share of Baltimore's black vote in 1944. In 1950, however, his opponent carried the vote in Baltimore's black precincts—in one by 85 percent. Tydings's losses in Baltimore City, according to one reporter, came "notably in areas where the Negro vote is strongest." [54] Jonkel and Roscoe Simmons had carefully cultivated the black vote; Butler headquarters turned out a pamphlet, "Back to Good Old Dixie," which criticized Tydings's record on civil rights.

Black opposition to Tydings stemmed from civil rights issues, not from the question of communism; this single-issue emphasis prompted the Baltimore *Afro-American* to oppose Tydings, whom it labeled a virtual Dixiecrat. It reported that his defeat "was not interpreted so much as support of McCarthy's Reds in the government charges, but as a protest at the denial of civil rights on the part of the Lane 'machine.' " A few blacks did make a perverse sort of connection between civil rights and internal security in one instance. The *Afro-American,* which complained that the State Department had employed a double standard when it lifted the passport of black celebrity Paul Robeson, commented: "If Mr. Secretary Acheson, were more active in keeping Russian agents out of this country and out of the State Department, we could applaud his action." While adopting quasi-McCarthyite premises in this case, the *Afro-American* on other occasions attacked the listing of several black entertainers in *Red Channels* and opposed the McCarran Act. The Free State's Democrats, Tydings included, forfeited black votes because of the civil rights views. "There should be no mourning" over the defeat of Tydings, one reporter concluded.[55]

Politicians were much more concerned with the impact of Maryland's Catholic vote than with the black vote. They heavily credited McCarthy's influence with swinging votes of his coreligionists away from Tydings. Several colleagues accosted Senator O'Conor to express their chagrin on this score; O'Conor argued, however, that the statistics failed to show distinctly any Catholic defection. Thus, Tydings had gone down by 25,000 in the counties outside Baltimore, which contained low Catholic concentrations. Of the nine counties on the Eastern Shore, where Catholics were especially sparse, although Tydings had carried seven of them, his total majority had declined from 16,404 votes in 1944 to only 4,345 votes in 1950. O'Conor related that Tydings had, unlike 1944, lost Frederick, Allegany, Charles, Garrett, and Washington counties, none of which boasted many Catholic voters.* While Catholics in Baltimore, O'Conor admitted, unquestionably voted heavily against Tydings, the *Catholic Review,* the weekly publication of the archdioceses of Washington and Baltimore, termed the Catholic vote "the easy answer" to decipher the results, but "the wrong one." The *Review* asserted that only an "unusual and weighty departure" could explain Tydings's defeat, and that was the "whitewash" issue, which obliterated religion as a factor in the vote.[56]

Yet from another perspective, the statistics may reveal more of a "Catholic vote" than O'Conor was willing to concede. It was true that Tydings lost ground on the Eastern Shore in comparison to his 1944 showing: his share of the vote declined by 10.6 percent (from 63.7 percent to 53.1). But this drop did not match the *statewide* decline in Tydings's vote, which was 15.7 percent; Tydings's vote actually fell off comparatively little in these nine counties of lowest Catholicity.[57] Similar attention to the *falling off* of support for Tydings (rather than the vote itself) also casts doubt upon the conclusions

---

* Among the weaknesses of this analysis is the fact that Charles County, while cited as a county where Catholics were not "that numerous," had a population of which 41.5 percent were Catholics—the most Catholic county in the state.

of the *Catholic Review*.* Moreover, the political analyst Louis H. Bean, examining three contiguous groupings of counties, found a positive correlation between the index of Catholic population and the decline in Tydings's share of the two-party vote between 1944 and 1950. Within each of three contiguous groups of counties under examination by Bean, the higher the Catholic percentage, the greater the decline in Tydings's vote.[58] (On the other hand, if the counties are examined *en bloc,* not as regional groupings, Catholicism does not correlate significantly county by county with sentiment against Tydings.) [59]

The analysis is complicated by another long-term trend: since 1938, when Maryland gave a much higher percentage of its vote to the Democrats than did the rest of the nation, the disparity between Maryland and the voting trend elsewhere had narrowed. By 1950, the Free State had reached a position just about commensurate with the rest of the country's voting habits. Tydings was particularly reliant upon the Democratic "organization" vote in 1950, but that vote had shown signs of erosion. Tydings, then, had to fight a twelve-year riptide against Maryland's Democratic Party.

Granting this fact and even suggesting the absence of any strong "Catholic factor" in 1950, it remains likely that the McCarthy issue operated as the primary cause of Tydings's undoing.[60] The crude polls of local Democratic leaders which were taken in Tydings's behalf during the campaign confirm the growing salience of this issue. Of the numerous campaigns of 1950 upon which McCarthy was supposed to have had electoral impact, Maryland demonstrated most unequivocally that he did exercise some influence upon the voting results.

Initially, Tydings laid his defeat to plural causes. He blamed it on the national Republican trend and the weakness of the state Demo-

---

* E.g., it is noted that heavily Catholic St. Mary's County did not turn as sharply against Tydings as did low-Catholic Carroll, Prince George, Anne Arundel, and Garrett. If one merely compares Tydings's share of the total vote in these counties, it is true that he fared better in St. Mary's (49.7%) than in the others (41.6%, 42.8%, 41.2%, 35.5%). However, a comparison of the decline in Tydings's share of the vote from 1944 to 1950 shows that his losses in St. Mary's exceeded his losses in Carroll and Garrett. Still, it is true that not just Catholics turned against Tydings; and Catholicism may not have been the decisive factor.

cratic ticket, the vulnerability of the Truman administration, Korea, "the smear campaign used against me, and so on." His explanation to the Chairman of the Democratic National Committee gave roughly equal weight to "the smear campaign of 'whitewash' " and Governor Lane's unpopularity. In an interview, he emphasized the lack of unity among Democrats; while McCarthy's personal influence, he said, was nil, McCarthyite issues and "propaganda" bore some weight.[61] Gradually,Tydings placed more stress upon his opponents' misdeeds, some of which came to his attention only after election day. He disliked losing "through fraud or deceit," he said, and lamented that "the mountain of lies and propaganda was too high for us to climb over." [62]

In late November and December, his growing knowledge of the more sordid aspects of the Butler campaign fed Tydings's bitterness. He learned about outside influences acting through his opponents, about the shaping of some of Butler's propaganda (notably "From the Record"), about financial irregularities in Butler's campaign, and about the "midnight ride" on which subordinates of Senator McCarthy had taken a Baltimore printer, William Fedder, who had done business with Butler headquarters. The Privileges and Elections Subcommittee of the Committee on Rules, under Chairman Guy Gillette, began a preliminary investigation in November. On December 15, Tydings lodged a complaint with Gillette, "submitting certain facts and occurrences . . . wherein my opponent wilfully and deliberately printed and used false and deceiving statements." Although Tydings said he believed that a candidate by or for whom such materials were used "should be barred" from the Senate, he stopped short of a formal contest of Butler's right to a seat. While Tydings welcomed the possibility that the Gillette Subcommittee might itself take that initiative, the subcommittee, according to its chairman, saw at the time "no basis for recommending action." [63]

Other Democrats declined to dismiss the case so lightly. Senator Clinton P. Anderson raised the issue in the Senate Democratic caucus. "In times like this," he argued, "we are entitled to something better than picture-faking in a campaign." While he was disturbed by literature circulated in several states, in Maryland the candidate's responsibility for such objectionable material seemed clearest. At the Democratic caucus on January 2, 1951, Anderson lectured his colleagues on the significance of the Maryland contest. He asked Senator Richard Russell, the distinguished Georgia conservative, what canards might follow him after he took over the chairmanship of the Armed Services Committee from Tydings; he warned Senator Connally of a movement afoot in Texas to smear him as a procommunist because he failed to oppose Dean Acheson; he raised the question, apropos of the composite photo, of what similar photographic magic might be applied to a picture he once saw of a prominent Senator skinny-dipping on a Pacific atoll.[64]

These arguments struck home to even the crustiest, most secure Southerners. Although Gillette reiterated that there were no firm grounds for denying Butler his seat, Senator Walter George moved that a resolution be offered to seat him "without prejudice"—either to Butler or to future Senate action. If subsequent investigation warranted, Butler could then, the Democrats argued, be removed by a simple majority rather than a two-thirds vote. Though the Republicans disputed the Democrats' interpretation of this maneuver, they did not oppose the motion when the new Majority Leader Ernst McFarland offered it on the opening day of the Eighty-first Congress, and Butler took his oath without prejudice.[65]

After the new year, the Privileges and Elections Subcommittee, which had been conducting a rather sporadic investigation of the Maryland election, had its membership reconstituted. Chairman Gillette was joined by four new members—Republicans Margaret Chase Smith and Robert Hendrickson, and Democrats Thomas C. Hennings and A. S. "Mike" Monroney. Senators Smith and Monroney were set to work on the Maryland investigation. When the two, neither of whom were lawyers, called for help, the subcommittee decided to pursue the investigation in earnest, and Gillette established a special hearings subcommittee comprising all the members of the subcommittee but himself.[66] Initially the deck appeared stacked against McCarthy, for Senator Smith had drafted the "Declaration of Conscience" and Hendrickson had signed it, while Hennings had won his Senate campaign over McCarthy's opposition and Monroney had triumphed despite charges of leftism.

However, various influences operated to curb the investigators' taste for the hunt. Both Republicans were aware of a responsibility to protect their own party. Hendrickson, who came to hold Butler in

high regard, stated the GOP's case aggressively in questioning anti-
Butler witnesses. Both Hendrickson and Smith were sensitive to the
destructive potential of McCarthy's animosity. McCarthy had even
managed to "bump" Senator Smith from her seat on the Permanent
Investigations Subcommittee of the Government Operations Committee. Chairman Gillette, who always trod softly in McCarthy's vicin-
ity, omitted himself from the hearings subcommittee and seldom be-
stirred himself or his colleagues to aggressive action.[67]

All four Senators performed their duties with fairness, dispatch,
and competence, but once again, as in the case of the Tydings Subcommittee, it proved impossible to alter competing prejudices or to
resolve the issues at hand. In part the difficulty may have originated
from the questions themselves: "the truth" sometimes remained a
fugitive commodity in the Maryland probe. Moreover, the investigation uncovered few wrongs which could be pursued by due process of
law and dealt perforce with sins whose exact level of immorality was
subject to dispute. More importantly, the inquiry demonstrated the inherent frailty of the committee as an institution; no degree of impartiality by the subcommittee members could entirely dissipate the partisan atmosphere which gathered around the investigation. The
subcommittee's role as factfinder carried with it the implication that
wrongs had been done and thus prejudiced many Republicans against
the entire enterprise.

The very staffing of the Privileges and Elections Subcommittee
became embroiled in the animosities which precipitated the probe.
Ralph Becker, the associate counsel, whose appointment had been
inspired by the Senate Republican Policy Committee, had once
headed the national Young Republican organization. His law partner,
who had played a peripheral role in the Maryland contest, was also
drawn into the proceedings. During the hearings Becker sought to
confute testimony which impugned Butler or his associates, made
himself available to Butler's advisors and others implicated in the
Butler campaign, and, before the hearings had begun, attended a
briefing session with a number of these principals and with representatives of the Republican Party.[68] Becker did nothing unethical by
Capitol Hill standards; his involvement simply demonstrated the impossibility of factoring partisanship out of the equation.

The Democrats could lay no better claim to the mantle of impartiality. Partisan imputations were inevitable, but in some instances, such as the hiring of Louis H. Fried by the subcommittee, they could have been avoided. Fried's chief claim to the position was a recommendation from Tydings, hardly a disinterested onlooker. As a friend of William Fedder, the Baltimore printer allegedly taken for a "midnight ride," Fried had passed the story on to interested persons; ultimately, Fried and Fedder gained entree to Senator Tydings. As an afterthought, Tydings asked Fried if he would like a job as investigator for the Privileges and Elections Subcommittee, which was looking for such employees. Fried accepted.[69]

Charges of partiality and wrongdoing counterpointed the progress of the investigation. Becker accused Fried of having helped Fedder prepare his opening statement to the subcommittee. Fried in turn claimed that Becker had leaked secret data to witnesses he was assisting. In the midst of the hearings, the subcommittee retreated into executive session to consider this crossfire of acrimony. It resolved the immediate crisis with a vote of confidence in its entire staff, but the vote could not allay all misgivings. Soon afterward, Fried was dropped from the payroll, ostensibly as an economy measure.[70]

Several hostile Republicans sought to throttle the investigation in its crib. After the first hearings, freshman Senator Herman Welker, a McCarthy ally, bellowed at Tydings's effort to "crucify" Butler. Welker sniffed that the literature of which Tydings, the "Whitewash King," complained would not be out of place at a "Sunday School picnic." Hugh Butler seconded him with the assertion that if the people of Maryland elected whomever they wished in a legal manner, "we have no right to reject him because we do not like the color of his hair or his demeanor here." With uncharacteristic vigor Gillette guaranteed the fairness of the Monroney subcommittee, but a week later Senators William Knowland and James Kem rejoined that the RFC and mink coat scandals and the 1946 Kansas City elections provided a more fertile area for investigation than Maryland. Republican floor leader Kenneth Wherry asked Vice-President Barkley to use his influence to curtail the investigation. When the attempt failed, Welker and Butler placed the issue before the Republican Policy Committee, but that body failed to hit upon a suitable policy.[71] The Republicans had little to fear, however, for the Maryland investigation presented distinctly limited prospects for action against any of the principals. Virtually no one, save possibly Tydings, resolutely contemplated the removal of John Marshall Butler; the latter claimed privately to have sufficient pledges from Democrats to insure against "serious trouble" if the issue ever came to a vote on the Senate floor.[72]

At the first subcommittee hearing, before Tydings could begin to make his case, Senator Butler claimed the floor on a point of personal privilege. If charges were to be preferred, he wanted a bill of particulars; he expected to be informed of what witnesses were summoned; and he insisted on the right of reply. He doubted that grounds existed for further proceedings by the subcommittee, since the proper state authorities had duly certified his election and no one had lodged a complaint against him under Maryland law. More coyly, he claimed that he had "no personal knowledge" of violations of the Federal Corrupt Practices Act. He was not, admittedly, an "expert in political procedures"; nor could he exercise control over the many zealous amateurs who might have committed "technical" violations. Angered that the committee would allow Tydings to "blacken the name and reputation of Maryland," he demanded either the preferment of specific charges or a full exoneration and an end to the probe. When the subcommittee refused to accept the latter limitation upon its jurisdiction, the new Senator from Maryland departed, leaving the field to his predecessor.[73]

Tydings reaffirmed that he was not contesting Butler's seat—that was the subcommittee's responsibility. (While he subsequently filed formal charges with the Secretary of the Senate, he himself did not seek to supplant Butler.) [74] Tydings felt compelled to "disclose certain scandalous, scurrilous, libelous, and unlawful practices" employed in the campaign. Bitterly excoriating those responsible for "From the Record," Tydings itemized its innuendoes and falsehoods. How, he wondered, would his distinguished colleagues on the Armed Services Committee react to the slur that the "Tydings Group Held Up Arms"? He noted that a "front organization of so-called 'Young Democrats for Butler' " had sponsored the tabloid, but Butler headquarters had paid for it, circulated it, derived what benefits it brought, and refused to disavow it. Tydings dwelt at length upon the "composite" picture, a case, he said, "where the evil intentions and wicked designs of the conspirators who assembled this lying pamphlet were caught redhanded.'' Tydings asserted that the Washington *Times-Herald* had printed the tabloid at roughly half its true cost.

Tydings detailed other examples of outside interference in the campaign, including the activities of Roscoe Simmons and the intervention of Fulton Lewis, Jr. Both Lewis' broadcasts and "From the Record,'' he suggested, might fall under the libel provisions of the District of Columbia code. He also claimed knowledge of financial irregularities: Butler's campaign manager had spent moneys which were not listed on the official report of expenditures; individuals, including Butler himself, had illegally assumed responsibility for political expenses in excess of $5,000. He previewed William Fedder's story of being taken, in Tydings's words, for a "midnight ride . . . Chicago gangland style'' by three men, of whom two were from McCarthy's office. Tydings charged that Butler and his headquarters knew of all these instances of "moral squalor." [75]

After Tydings, the subcommittee heard William Fedder, the printer whose testimony revealed the complex casualness of Butler's campaign financing. Fedder had had at one point some $18,000 owing to him for printing, mailing, and distribution work; with the money barely trickling in, Fedder, holding bales of literature in his plant the week before the election, began to apply pressure: no money, no goods. At this juncture Butler drafted a letter guaranteeing payment for all services rendered; he assumed a financial obligation beyond what the law permitted. Shortly, as money came in from various sources, Jonkel endorsed whole checks over to Fedder (and to other importunate creditors) rather than first sending such contributions to the campaign treasurer as required by law. Fedder also received checks and cash from Jean Kerr of McCarthy's staff—again, money which never passed through the hands of Butler's treasurer.

The most dramatic feature of Fedder's testimony dealt with the midnight ride. In the closing preelection rush Fedder had agreed to arrange for the addressing and inscribing of a number of Butler picture postcards. These, which he had jobbed out to various women, he was to collect and turn over to members of McCarthy's staff for mailing, but the task proved too ambitious for the short time left. Late on Sunday, November 5, Fedder's wife received two allegedly abusive and frightening phone calls from Ewell Moore (of Mc-

Carthy's staff) and George Nilles, who had come to pick up the cards; when Fedder met Moore and Nilles, he lied to placate them, saying he had already mailed a large batch of cards—contrary to previous orders. After Donald Surine, another McCarthy employee, arrived, Fedder repeated the story, which Surine ascertained and Fedder admitted to be false. At this point, Fedder testified, the three men grew menacing. Surine asked the printer to hand over Butler's letter of guarantee, allegedly threatening him with a "McCarthy investigation," among other things, if he refused. The three forced Fedder into a car, drove around to several houses to pick up completed cards, then stopped at a restaurant where Surine began drafting a statement by which Fedder was to disavow any further financial claims in connection with the postcard project. Returning to Fedder's house, the three men let Fedder go in to retrieve a check he had received as advance payment on the cards. He surrendered it to Surine; finally, the last cards were mailed, and Fedder was released at about six in the morning, after signing the statement which Surine had written.[76]

Later, Surine, Moore, and Nilles testified that Fedder's charges of having been virtually abducted, held under duress, threatened, or forced to sign the statement were false. Fedder, they said, had lied from the outset about mailing the cards; the "ride" had constituted nothing more than voluntary completion of a business transaction. Their warranted suspicions regarding Fedder's financial shenanigans, which they claimed he had discussed expansively with them, had prompted Surine to compose the statement, which Fedder had corrected in his own hand and willingly signed.[77] If Fedder was in physical danger, why had he not called for help at any time at the restaurant or at various homes? Why had he not phoned the police when he was alone inside his own home or even after his release? Fedder could not supply wholly satisfactory answers, nor resolve other flaws and inconsistencies in his testimony. To this day the exact circumstances of the "midnight ride" remain obscure, but Senator Hendrickson surmised with some justification that the ride's "awfulness" was open to some doubt.[78]

Partly because of all the confusion surrounding Fedder's account, critics of the campaign had to concentrate less on the activities of

McCarthy's agents than on those of Butler's associates. The campaign manager, Jon M. Jonkel, testified volubly about his role, providing extensive information regarding his public-relations approach to politics and revealing how by his efforts Butler became a commodity to be merchandised much like any other product. Jonkel, having discovered that almost no one had even heard of his candidate, strove simply to get Butler's name before the public as often as he could. For instance, in the closing days of the campaign, radio audiences were bombarded with "Be for Butler" jingles reminiscent of Bromo-Seltzer ads and with other "P.R." gimmicks.[79]

The financing of these high-powered tactics led Jonkel to grief. The radio stations would not broadcast the Butler spots without money in hand. In such cases, or when other creditors were laying siege, Jonkel, intent only upon pursuing the campaign, endorsed over to such claimants any checks that were handy. Since the official treasurer, Cornelius P. Mundy, was seldom available when needed, Jonkel resorted to this irregular method of payment, which he labeled "short-circuiting." He thought he had sent Mundy letters outlining the transactions, but Mundy disclaimed any knowledge of them and would surely have protested vehemently, he testified, had he known. When, in February, hints of financial aberrations began to seep out, Senator Butler's legal advisor counseled Jonkel to search his memory for instances of unreported expenditures. Mundy refused to take responsibility for Jonkel's belated recollections, so Jonkel had the unpleasant duty of executing the "supplementary" financial report, whose tardiness was a violation of the Maryland Corrupt Practices Act.[80] State officials took note, and a grand jury indicted Jonkel. In June, Jonkel pleaded guilty and was fined $3,000. He suffered alone.[81]

Jonkel's technique of exploiting the "area of doubt" regarding Tydings proved more disturbing than these financial errata. His method was far more surgically deft than that of other Butler enthusiasts or of McCarthy and his coterie. Unlike the fabricators of the tabloid, Jonkel would never say—or have Butler, whose every speech he wrote, say—that Tydings had held up arms for Korea. He preferred to pose open-ended questions leading toward similar conclusions. He would ask: "You are a father, you are a mother, do you believe that we are well organized here? Do you feel that you know for sure that there are no Communists or Communist influence in the top levels of our Government?'' [82]

As for "From the Record," while its umbilical cord led back to his office, Jonkel explained that it had never been a headquarters project. After a number of Butler supporters, including McCarthy, had urged a much more hard-hitting assault, Jonkel finally decided to let them "throw the book" at Tydings, although he felt the tabloid unnecessary. Jonkel and the subcommittee quibbled over whether that project had been launched because he had said yes or because he had not said no, but the subcommittee failed to view the slapdash functioning of the Butler command as any extenuation. Jonkel, and above him Butler, bore responsibility for all the less lovely aspects of the campaign. [83]

On April 11 the subcommittee heard its last testimony. Two major participants in the campaign had been noticeable by their absence from the hearing room. After his initial complaint, Senator Butler had not returned to exercise his privilege of rebuttal. Senator McCarthy never appeared. He received an invitation, but he declined it. He did not refuse to come; he merely disclaimed any desire to appear, but said he "would be glad to do so if . . . any of the members of the committee or counsel have any questions." The subcommittee allowed McCarthy's punt to roll out of bounds. [84] His nonacceptance of their invitation constituted no great loss, since his testimony would in all likelihood merely have emphasized his contention, expressed in the "Individual Views" on the election which he had printed, that the real issue in Maryland had been Tydings's whitewash of the State Department. [85]

Between the end of the hearings and the issuance of the report, more than three months elapsed. The delay may have resulted partly from the distractions of other business, perhaps the upcoming investigation of the Ohio senatorial campaign. The untimely decision of chief counsel Edward McDermott to return to his law practice further hobbled the probers. When the House of Representatives refused to exempt from the conflict-of-interest statutes the subcommittee's first choice as McDermott's replacement, the Senators remained without adequate legal assistance. Noting that Hendrickson and he were the only lawyers on the panel, Hennings advised Gillette that they did not intend to "go into the law libraries and do the research." [86]

All this while the four Senators found it no easier to ascertain the delicate balance between righteousness and party loyalty. Too harsh a report might force one or both Republicans to dissent, spotlighting party differences, repeating the unfortunate experience of the Tydings Committee, and putting the investigation back where it started. In June the Republican Committee on Committees offered an eloquent case for caution by placing Senator McCarthy on the parent Rules Committee. (The death of Senator Vandenberg and the appointment of a Democrat to his seat had deprived the Republicans of two committee posts and forced a reshuffling of assignments. McCarthy, who lost his position on the Appropriations Committee, was recompensed with a seat on the Rules Committee.) Innocent though the circumstances, the subcommittee members could not have viewed McCarthy's presence on the Rules Committee with indifference.[87] Chairman Gillette required little persuasion to move with superabundant caution.

Senator Monroney and the subcommittee staff set to work on the report; the result was unsatisfactory. Responding to Monroney's plea for help, Senator Smith and her assistant drafted a report. The subcommittee began deliberations which proved inconclusive, and patience began to fray. Late in June, Gillette brought matters to a head by threatening to resign as Chairman of the subcommittee. Reportedly, he was "embarrassed" and in "personal discomfort" over the handling of the Maryland investigation. Expressing pique of his own, Hennings complained that the subcommittee lacked legal counsel. Hendrickson, who had tried to persuade Gillette not to resign, warned the following week that he would tender either his own resignation or an individual report unless the group completed its work swiftly. Service on the subcommittee was rapidly losing its allure. Senator Smith also informed the panel that she would submit her own report if the subcommittee failed to agree on one. Eventually, with Gillette mollified and full-time counsel obtained, the report was assembled. On August 2, the four Senators plus Gillette gave it the official approval of the Privileges and Elections Subcommittee.[88]

In its report, the subcommittee declined to recommend Butler's unseating: no binding precedent existed, and Gillette and his colleagues did not think "an example should be made" of Butler. To prescribe campaign standards and hold him accountable to them smacked of "enacting a law and applying it retroactively." The report strongly, if vaguely, urged the framing of rules to govern election contests in future cases. With a meaningful glance at McCarthy, it added that the "question of unseating a Senator for acts committed in a senatorial election should not be limited to candidates in such elections." Furthermore, rules should be adopted to fix a political claimant's precise responsibility for the actions of subordinates. The report also recommended a reappraisal of the campaign spending limits of the Corrupt Practices Act, an investigation of the "extent powerful national groups or combination [sic] of forces under cover of anonymity are invading State elections," and sanctions against the use of "defamatory literature"—particularly composite pictures.[89] These noble suggestions received a minimum of serious attention, however.

The report's enduring significance rested on those passages which viewed the "back street" campaign with alarm. The subcommittee took note of the numerous financial irregularities on Butler's side, but the accounts were so muddled that the Senators frankly threw up their hands on the question of whether Butler's spending exceeded legal limits and referred the problem to the Justice Department. The report also dwelt at length on the literature published by Butler's supporters, especially "From the Record." Such conduct, the subcommittee believed, tended "to destroy not only the character of the candidate who is its target, but also eats away like acid at the very fabric of American life." The loose rein Butler kept on his assistants did not, his colleagues admonished, absolve him of moral accountability for misdeeds on his behalf.

The subcommittee did find extenuating circumstances in the fact that many of the more sordid phases of the campaign, especially the tabloid, traced their origins to "outside influences." Senator McCarthy, the report declared with understatement, was "actively interested" in the contest. Left hanging were such questions as whether the *Times-Herald* had in fact printed the tabloid at less than cost or what had really transpired during the midnight ride. The subcommittee transmitted its report to the Justice Department and asked for a determination if any of the facts set forth merited prosecution.[90]

The Maryland Report punished no past deeds and offered only vague promises that the prevention of future recurrences would be studied. While the subcommittee members left no doubt about their distaste for McCarthy's activities, they couched their emotions in the language of senatorial courtesy. The document implied far more than it directly avowed. Historians have made much of the apparent connection between the halfheartedness of the report's recommendations for action and its unanimous approval by the subcommittee. Actually, the prospect of disciplinary action against any of the principals had been discounted for some time; in mid-July, Hendrickson had been certain that Butler would be "completely exonerated." [91] The Maryland Report, in sum, administered nothing beyond a slap on the wrist to McCarthy and Butler.

Yet it was a slap felt by each. When the report went up to the Rules Committee on August 3, bitter debate ensued. McCarthy, beside himself with anger, sought to suppress the report pending further study, but he was defeated by an eight to five vote. The Rules Committee deferred final action but released its findings to the press. "As long as puny politicians try to encourage other puny politicians to ignore or whitewash Communist influences in our government," McCarthy snarled, "America will remain in grave danger." He had anticipated the behavior of Senators Smith and Hendrickson on the basis of the "Declaration of Conscience," but he was "surprised that the Democrats have not learned that the American people just do not like whitewash." Hendrickson retorted that this "hasty estimate" might well validate previous criticisms of McCarthy's conduct.[92]

On August 8, the Rules Committee resumed consideration of the report. The row continued, but except for agreeing to tone down a reference to Jean Kerr's connection with the tabloid, the authors refused to retreat. The committee voted nine to three to approve the subcommittee's determinations. Jenner and Wherry joined McCarthy in opposition; Smith and Hendrickson voted with the Democrats. Not even McCarthy's ally Wherry condoned every feature of his activities in Maryland, and the Nebraskan apparently agreed with the subcommittee's recommendation for standards for future election conduct. McCarthy took violent exception, fearing that it would be inferred that Wherry considered McCarthy's behavior so bad that, if such standards were enforced retroactively, grounds for his expulsion would exist. Nor could he concur in Wherry's expression of thanks for the subcommittee's good work, which, he claimed, retailed smears little different from those in the Tydings report.[93] His colleagues' formal disapproval of his conduct stirred McCarthy to wrath and may even have prompted him to take action to reclaim the initiative: on August 8 he threatened to reveal the names of twenty-nine alleged loyalty risks still working in the State Department. Less significant than the charges—which were not new—was the timing. On August 9, he made good his threat. While he garnered considerable news coverage, it did not black out the Maryland report.[94]

On August 20, when Senator Carl Hayden brought in the Maryland report, Wherry rose to criticize it and clarify his own position. Like McCarthy, he believed the hearings subcommittee had unfairly restricted its inquiry to the Republicans' activities in the campaign and to the complaints of Tydings alone, although he did not make clear just what Democratic sins merited scrutiny. He also thought the subcommittee should not have based its broad-gauged recommendations upon so limited an investigation—a single campaign in one state, and a relatively mild one at that. If Butler's campaign had been so scandalous, why did the subcommittee "clear" him? Wherry was backtracking from his position of the day before, as Senator Margaret Chase Smith brought out when she got him to agree that he had earlier told her the report was a "whale of a job." [95]

McCarthy had his "Individual Views" printed with the subcommittee's report, but for good measure he also read them to the Senate. When he reiterated that Senators Hendrickson and Smith had prejudged the issues, both replied vigorously. It was rather late, thought Mrs. Smith, for McCarthy to question her qualifications to serve on the investigation. "Opposition to communism," she added, was not "the exclusive possession of Senator McCarthy. Nor does differing with him on tactics automatically make one a Communist or protector of communism." Defiantly she reinserted her "Declaration of Conscience" into the record and twitted McCarthy with the fact that no other Senator had signed his individual views—a minority report, apparently, of one.[96]

However mild its recommendations for punitive action, the Maryland verdict had stung McCarthy. It had gained the support or at least the sufferance of a broad spectrum of his colleagues: the only formal vote, in the Rules Committee, had not produced a strictly party-line result, and partisanship on the Senate floor was narrowly circumscribed. Every member of the Gillette Subcommittee had approved the findings, and that, said Hendrickson, was the "remarkable fact" of the episode.[97] A consensus had been constructed on the simple, if indeterminate, issue of decency, and McCarthy had been found wanting. Here lay the strength of the Maryland report as a tool—and a lesson—for McCarthy's opponents.

At the same time it posed a dilemma: bipartisanship could be purchased, but only with a willingness to make bland findings of fact, qualified indictments, and feeble recommendations for action. Failing this, party lines might have been drawn as tightly as they had been a year before over the Tydings Committee findings. As a result of these political exigencies, the Maryland investigation did not tangibly impair McCarthy's power.

Still, McCarthy's ethics had been questioned publicly by a Senate subcommittee, and that was a rare enough occurrence. More remotely, the Maryland report had weightier consequences: Senator Benton based his resolution calling for an investigation looking to McCarthy's expulsion upon this document and thus triggered another probe by the Gillette subcommittee. The Wisconsin Senator's contumacy toward that group would become a ground for his censure in 1954. In that distant sense, the judgment was part of an important chain of events.

More immediately, however, it was not much more than a single gesture—unconnected with the more peripheral attacks made upon McCarthy by other Senators, with the concurrent rhetorical offensive of the Truman administration, or with the quixotic efforts of his very few persistent adversaries. While some observers perceived the cluster of events attending the issuance of the Maryland report as a coordinated offensive against McCarthy, such was not the case. Most of the impact of the Maryland judgment was swiftly dissipated.

CHAPTER 6
The Marine And
The Artilleryman

IN THE WAKE of the 1950 elections, an increasing share of the burden of opposing Senator McCarthy fell to the executive branch. Most Senate Democrats, contemplating no action against McCarthy beyond the Maryland election probe, gladly sat back to permit the White House to take primary responsibility for challenging him. If the Senate displayed little relish for confronting McCarthy, there was scant reason, based on previous performance, to anticipate much greater results from the activities of the Executive. The President and his staff had always entertained a lively distaste for the Wisconsin Senator, but somehow their attitude, when translated into action, had produced policies of halting uncertainty. The White House's responses to McCarthy in 1950 had often appeared out of phase with events.

In part the administration's difficulties resulted from the President's initial tendency to underestimate McCarthy's capacity for damage. Generally, Truman had dismissed the Wisconsin Senator with flippant remarks—"the Kremlin's greatest asset"—which smacked of partisanship and failed to allay the concern which McCarthy had tapped. During the spring of 1950, Truman had considered McCarthy more evil than dangerous. However great a scoundrel he might think the Senator, he did not at first treat him as a major peril. To Truman,

McCarthy was simply another Republican fish swimming in a school of red herrings. These suppositions partially explained the administration's indecisiveness in handling the State Department loyalty files question and the proposal to create a Commission on Internal Security and Individual Rights. Similarly, Truman assumed that criticisms of the loyalty program arose from Republican political ambitions; the surmise, though more than a little accurate, prevented the administration from working out effective countermeasures against the anticommunist crusades of its adversaries.

Truman came to the realization—apparently during the summer of 1950—that McCarthy was not just one more Republican troublemaker. The growing congressional insistence upon stringent internal security legislation and the general anxiety prompted by the Korean War demonstrated that the administration's troubles flowed from deeper springs. Dismayed by the security frenzy yet powerless to deflate it, Truman at times fell into an attitude of philosophical acceptance. Even before the panic-producing reports from Korea, Truman revealed his thoughts to Vice-President Barkley, to whom he recounted a fable of Aesop "that might apply to some of your bad boys." Once upon a time a dog so misbehaved that its master put a "clog" on its neck to stop it from biting his neighbors, whereupon the dog foolishly thought it a badge not of shame, but of honor. "Men often mistake notoriety for fame, and would rather be remarked for their vices and follies than not be noticed at all." Aesop's moral, said Truman, "seems to describe certain ballyhoo artists we both know." [1]

Gradually, Truman perceived that his troubles were not merely the consequence of antics by "bad boys" and "ballyhoo artists." Something deeper was bothering Americans. At the height of the clamor for internal security legislation, Truman distributed to political allies and influential citizens a document which attempted to explain the current malaise.[2] The paper, "A Study of 'Witch Hunting' and Hysteria in the United States," summarized past outbreaks of political psychosis such as the Salem witch trials, the Federalists' Alien and Sedition Acts, the Know-Nothing tumult, the anti-German vigilantism of World War I, and the subsequent Red Scare. The paper described witch-hunting as a periodically recurring phenomenon, of which the McCarthy uproar was yet another manifestation. ("History is filled with examples of temporary mob excitement. . . .'') The analysis conveyed the optimistic assumption that this too would pass: ''in the long run reason has prevailed.'' [3] As Truman declared in a contemporaneous message to Congress, thanks to ''the strong faith and common sense of our people . . . we have never for long been misled by the hysterical cries of those who would suppress our constitutional freedoms.'' [4]

The passage of the McCarran Act and the Democratic reversals in the 1950 elections prompted the White House to concert countermeasures, but after November the administration confronted a situation less susceptible to remedy than it had faced three or six months earlier. Both the elections and the retreat of UN armies in Korea emboldened the opponents of bipartisanship to renew their attacks on current foreign policies. In December 1950, Herbert Hoover and Joseph P. Kennedy launched the rhetorical duel which came to be called the ''Great Debate'' with their pleas for a ''Fortress America'' approach to national defense; after Truman announced plans to move four divisions to Europe, Senators Taft, Wherry, and others broadened the assault in January 1951. The debate stretched on into early April; soon after it the dismissal of General MacArthur occasioned more fireworks. [5]

Nerved by the outcome of the 1950 elections, a number of Republicans began once again to cry for the ouster of Secretary of State Acheson and to mount a general offensive against the administration's Asian policies. Acheson, said Senator George Malone, had taken a prominent role in forcing the resignation of Secretary of Defense Louis Johnson and his replacement by General Marshall. The latter, having been ''Acheson's front-man in building up the Communist victory in China,'' would be ''complacent'' toward other red initiatives. With a distrustful eye to the future, Wherry, Bricker, and McCarthy charged Acheson with conspiring to remove General MacArthur from his command; James P. Kem and Styles Bridges suggested impeachment of the secretary. And if the ''treasonable farce'' of refusing the aid of Chiang's Nationalist forces in Korea continued, exclaimed McCarthy, then Congress should ''stand up and be counted and immediately impeach'' Truman. ''Why Mr. President,'' he asked, ''do you follow the orders of your Secretary of State, who feels that only the sons of American mothers should fight and die?'' [6]

Many Senate Democrats quailed before the blustery political gale. While they did not join the public demands of James Eastland and Pat McCarran that Acheson resign, many of them reluctantly concluded that the Secretary had become an insupportable political burden. In November, Clyde Hoey of North Carolina urged that Truman replace Acheson with a man who "would command the complete confidence of the American people." Lester Hunt argued that Truman would be wise to accept Acheson's resignation fairly soon because "the attacks on him have so undermined him . . . that his usefulness . . . is questionable." [7]

Speculation regarding the likelihood of Acheson's departure appeared in the press with the frequency of weather reports: the outlook was universally stormy.[8] Walter Lippmann intoned weighty advice for "the new Secretary of State," while Drew Pearson knowingly predicted that Acheson would quit within sixty days. The Gallup poll seemed to confirm Acheson's fate: while 21 percent thought Acheson should stay in office, 31 percent felt he should go. Yet the beleaguered Secretary seemed almost to enjoy needlessly twitting his foes. When Senator Taft issued a call after the election for a "reexamination" of U.S. foreign policy, Acheson likened the "re-examinists" to the farmer who pulled up his crop every morning to see if it had grown during the night.[9]

While McCarthyite Republicans led the pack in pursuit of Acheson, impatience with the Secretary was growing in all sectors of the GOP. Significantly, it was Senator Irving Ives, a moderate internationalist, who proposed that the Republicans frame a party position regarding Acheson. To the Republican senatorial caucus Ives offered a resolution which would put the group on record in favor of Acheson's dismissal, but his timing proved inauspicious. Other Republicans questioned the wisdom of such a divisive maneuver at a time when world events, notably the Red Chinese incursion in Korea, placed a premium on national unity. Governor Dewey, of Ives's home state, objected to the "get-Acheson" drive. The deepening crisis prompted Ives and his colleagues to reconsider for a time, but the hesitation soon passed; as Acheson left for important NATO talks in Brussels, the Republicans in Congress came out for his replacement.[10]

Considering their postelection gloom, the Democrats responded to these blows with unusual alacrity. President Truman, after what

James Reston described as "a relatively silent summer and a neutral autumn," stepped vigorously to Acheson's defense. Senator Hoey found the President privately "very stubborn about this matter." Truman had never flagged in his support for his lieutenant, but he had for some time avoided public expressions of it. "How our position in the world would be improved by the retirement of Dean Acheson from public life is beyond me," he now snapped querulously at his press conference. He clinched the argument by asserting that if communism, save the mark, were ever to triumph, "Dean Acheson would be one of the first, if not the first, to be shot by the enemies of liberty and Christianity." [11]

The crisis of confidence through which Acheson passed proved grave enough to elicit renewed efforts in his behalf by the members of the "floating crap game," the group first mobilized to answer McCarthy's early attacks. Now it concentrated upon enlisting support for the Secretary on Capitol Hill, trying to stir Democrats to defend Acheson on the floor of Congress. [12] Probably less due to these efforts than to the unity forced upon them by the Republican assault, Democratic Senators began to accord Acheson some help. James Murray responded sharply to Walter Lippmann's past-tense references to the Secretary; John Sparkman concurred with the President's contention that no one "could have done more to oppose communism" than Acheson; Robert Kerr, in a column for home-state consumption, berated the Republicans for their untimely attacks. When Senate Republicans brought up a resolution insisting that the administration divulge full details of recent discussions between Truman, Acheson, and British Prime Minister Clement Attlee, the Democrats mustered near unanimity in defeating the measure. J. William Fulbright inveighed against the "character assassination" and even cantankerous Kenneth McKellar accused the Republicans of "helping the Russians." [13]

For the moment, Acheson was safe. In February, Senator Clinton P. Anderson could write that "the Republican agitation against Acheson has died down terrifically these last few weeks." But the Secretary was not home free. The firing of General MacArthur again prompted Republican sachems to demand his scalp. Democratic leaders on Capitol Hill reportedly renewed their pleas that Truman jettison Acheson; the question of his removal, said one columnist, was "not whether but when." [14] Yet Acheson survived and during the autumn even enjoyed a brief recrudescence of respect, if not popularity, as a result of his masterful handling of the Japanese Peace Treaty conference and other diplomatic negotiations. "Don't tell me that man is soft toward communism," one housewife wrote her Senator after watching Acheson on television. "I saw him shove a microphone down the Russians' throat." Even Senator Knowland, a longtime critic, had to concede that the Secretary was "superb" at San Francisco. As Acheson's position improved, the usually anonymous Democratic Senators who served as weathervanes began to swivel in a direction more favorable to him, and Drew Pearson even prophesied that the Secretary would complete his term. [15]

In a sense the battle of Foggy Bottom remained a standoff. With redoubtable firmness, Truman refused to yield: Acheson stayed the route. Yet he remained an easy mark for Republican attacks; some even theorized that the Republicans pulled their punches, hoping to keep Acheson in office for target practice during the 1952 campaign. Few thought that he was a political asset to his party or that his foreign policies enjoyed much support. Even at the peak of Acheson's "popularity," 56 percent of the respondents to a Gallup poll agreed with Senator Taft that the Korean police action was an "utterly useless war." [16] Moreover, Acheson's troubles may have had a larger significance. Forced to demonstrate their obdurate anticommunism, the Secretary and the Truman administration may have so rigidified their position as to prevent diplomatic solutions to a number of problems of the cold war. [17]

If Truman could claim a draw in the tug-of-war over Acheson, he fared worse on the issue of subversion in government. The Republicans, among them Hickenlooper and Senator-elect Butler, construed the 1950 elections as a mandate for more investigations of the sort McCarthy had triggered. The Wisconsinite himself announced his plan to go after Communists in not only the State Department but also Commerce, Agriculture, and the Bureau of the Budget. [18] Voicing his fear that the administration was attempting to sabotage the McCarran Act, Homer Ferguson called for an investigation of the enforcement of that law. Moved by a similar mistrust, a number of Senators also impeded confirmation of Truman's nominees to the Subversive Activities Control Board created under the statute. Concurrently, other solons advocated the establishment of a body paralleling the House Committee on Un-American Activities, or alternatively, a joint House-Senate committee to scrutinize such doings.[19]

Spearheading the anticommunist drive, the Senate Judiciary Committee, a conservative and antiadministration panel, obtained authorization in January 1951 to set up an Internal Security Subcommittee. Senator Pat McCarran of Nevada, a Democrat hostile to the administration, chaired both the parent committee and its offspring. McCarthy termed the new body "an excellent idea" and promised to "cooperate 1000 percent" with it. He attended its meetings, passed on tips, lavished praise upon its members, and played a preliminary role in the subcommittee's melodramatic seizure of the dead archives of the Institute of Pacific Relations, then stored in a barn in Lee, Massachusetts. (The files, whose existence was no secret, had been carefully examined by the FBI the year before; nonetheless, the McCarran Committee had them brought to Washington under armed convoy amid predictions of "sensational" revelations.) As the McCarran Committee began to review allegations he had made the year before, McCarthy could look forward to many months of effortless publicity and corroboration.[20]

So congenial were McCarthy's relations with the Internal Security Subcommittee that he once even contemplated asking that group to serve as a tribunal to judge a new set of charges he was elaborating. McCarran, however, expressed only wan enthusiasm for the proposition: he sought to avoid having his sub-committee labeled a carbon copy of McCarthyism. While no less flinty a red-baiter than McCarthy, the Nevadan did proceed with more finesse and attention to the amenities of due process than his Republican ally. Though grilling witnesses for minute details sometimes a decade old and then bludgeoning them with contrary documentation often wrenched out of context might leave something to be desired in the way of fairness, still the McCarran panel did its investigative spadework more meticulously than McCarthy ever did.

At the same time, the Internal Security Subcommittee had no more success than McCarthy in pinning overt acts upon the subjects of its scrutiny. McCarran strong-armed the Justice Department into obtaining the indictment of Owen Lattimore on perjury charges arising from minor vagaries of his testimony (the date, for instance, of his 1939 luncheon with the Soviet Ambassador) and from tendentious generalities such as the claim that the professor had lied in denying he had followed the Communist line. The fact that the case was eventually thrown out of court marks the limits of the McCarran Committee's attainments. Against its many victims, the Internal Security Subcommittee could chalk up few convictions.[21]

The McCarran Committee did, however, increase the rebound velocity of McCarthy's charges. Allegations issuing from it forced many officials to go once again through the loyalty-security mill. Several State Department employees were caught between the upper millstone of the McCarran Subcommittee and the nether stone of the Loyalty Review Board. As men singled out for attack by the McCarthy-McCarran bloc resigned or were dismissed, the Wisconsin Senator received due credit for having—at the very least—started the whole process. Members of the subcommittee also accepted such McCarthyite theses as the claim, in Willis Smith's words, that Owen Lattimore "unquestionably was of great assistance to the Communist advancement in the world, or at least in the Far East." [22] These and other developments such as the sentencing of atom spy Harry Gold, the perjury conviction of William Remington, and the defection of British scientist Bruno Pontecorvo to the Soviet Union kept the broth of anticommunism simmering and made effective countermeasures by the Democrats more difficult.

As its congressional foes rushed to assert their claims to the internal security issue, the Truman administration moved at last to regain the initiative: its method was to establish a President's Commission on Internal Security and Individual Rights. The idea, which had received consideration since 1948, had attracted growing interest after McCarthy's advent. Following the dissolution of his subcommittee in July 1950, Senator Tydings had argued that it would be "forehanded" to set up such a body before others went ahead to launch what might become "an inquisition rather than a constructive matter." [23] In September, several liberals had strongly urged Truman to accompany his veto of the McCarran bill with an order establishing such a panel, and early drafts of the veto message had contained that provision.[24] After the election, Tydings declared that if his earlier advice had been heeded, "it not only would have made a difference to me in my campaign but would have helped others who suffered in some degree from the same tactics.[25] Francis Biddle, a former Attorney General and currently national chairman of the Americans for Democratic Action, encouraged Truman to create a Commission on Internal Security and Individual Rights because "the country needs reassurance that its public servants are loyal." The Washington *Post,* an early proponent of the idea, found its prescience confirmed by the "influential part" played by McCarthyism in the election.[26] Moved by such considerations and the vigorous advocacy of several of his aides, Truman took up the proposal once more.[27]

In November 1950, the White House immersed itself in preparations for the project. Truman first offered the chairmanship of the commission to Herbert Hoover, declaring his hope that an authoritative inquiry into the charges of Communist infiltration would "restore the confidence of the people in the organization of the Government" and "help the Foreign Policy situation very much." Hoover doubted, however, that "any consequential card-carrying communists" not known to the FBI remained in the government; moreover, the public suspected the presence not of Communists *per se* but rather of officials "whose attitudes are such that they have disastrously advised on policies in relation to Communist Russia." To achieve the results Truman sought, the investigation would have to be broader in scope than the President envisioned, would require the stamp of Congress as well as the Executive, yet at the same time would duplicate congressional inquiries. Regretfully, Hoover declined. His decision provided an ominous warning of Republican attitudes toward the project.[28]

Truman turned ultimately to retired Admiral Chester W. Nimitz, who accepted the chairmanship. On January 23, 1951, Truman announced creation of the President's Commission on Internal Security and Individual Rights (PCISIR), which he instructed to "seek the wisest balance that can be struck between security and freedom." Its task encompassed a broad scrutiny of all the nation's laws and programs against espionage and subversive activities. By his moderating role as a regent during the recent University of California loyalty-oath controversy, Nimitz had attained a reputation for level-headed awareness of civil liberties.[29] Several other members of the PCISIR offered further encouragement in this direction, particularly Anna Lord Strauss, commission vice-chairman, who had been president of the

League of Women Voters, and William E. Leahy, a prominent District of Columbia attorney and civic leader of liberal views. Two clergymen, Reverend Emmett M. Walsh, Coadjutant Bishop of Youngstown, and Reverend Karl Morgan Block, Episcopal Bishop of California, also served on the commission. Russell Leffingwell, a J. P. Morgan partner and former Assistant Secretary of the Treasury, and Harvey S. Firestone represented finance and industry, and former Republican Senator John A. Danaher seemed likely to be able to neutralize conservative misgivings.[30] It was an impressive but not an all-star lineup, however; several more notable nominees apparently declined to serve on the commission.[31]

Moreover, as the panel's leading historian has written, the members of the PCISIR placed greater emphasis on security than on liberty; this circumstance might have caused the PCISIR to fall short of its supporters' expectations if it had ever completed its assignment. Russell Leffingwell, for example, believed that "employee tenure and civil rights generally have to be subordinated to the right of the nation to defend itself against Russia." The "many deplorable things that are happening—call it witch-hunting or hysteria, or whatever . . . will continue to happen until the people are reassured that the country is safely guarded against spies and traitors and saboteurs, and against the ventriloquists who preach and teach with the voice of Moscow."[32]

Its mandate also posed a considerable challenge for the PCISIR. Truman had sincerely asked the Commission to make an inquiry both exhaustive and independent and had invited suggestions for reforms in the loyalty-security program; but at the same time, he had little doubt as to the outcome of such an undertaking. With perhaps unintentional candor, he wrote Admiral Nimitz that if the PCISIR could "investigate thoroughly and completely the actions that have been taken and the results that have been attained the confidence of the country could be restored." "We believe the Government loyalty program has worked pretty well," stated an outline for the President's use at the first meeting of the Commission. "The Commission will probably find ways in which it could be improved and should try to do so." Adjustments would be tolerated, but as Truman planned it, the PCISIR was to ratify more than amend. One presidential aide captured the administration's aims in his comment on a discussion of the optimum size for the Commission: "We don't want 'efficiency'—we want a group that has public appeal [and] can sell the country." [33] However, the administration's enemies in Congress were unlikely to allow such a political gambit to go unchecked.

Notwithstanding these handicaps, the Commission received the applause of civil libertarians, who swiftly adopted it as their own. Spokesmen for the American Civil Liberties Union, the American Jewish Committee, the Federation of American Scientists, and the fledgling Ford Foundation offered their congratulations to the President and, in some cases, their help.[34] Some commission members, in turn, welcomed the cooperation of the Ford Foundation.[35] Had the more conservative commissioners made their inclinations felt, countervailing liberal forces were not too far away.

As well as its friends, its enemies attested to an expansive view of the PCISIR's potential. Conservatives with a stake in the communist issue, as their unenthusiastic responses made clear, saw that the Nimitz Commission boded them no good. Senator Ferguson attacked the PCISIR as an attempt to undercut the McCarran subcommittee; he charged that Truman meant to "cloak the subject with confusion in the hope that nothing effective will be done about security risks in the Government." The Nimitz panel, thought Senator Hickenlooper, would be "compounding evils already in existence." Columnist George Sokolsky asserted that the very idea for the Commission had first been broached by Communists and fellow travelers and that Nimitz was to serve as a mere figurehead. McCarran stated archly that he "would not entertain the thought" that the Nimitz group had been created as a rival to his own subcommittee. Predictably, authors and advocates of the McCarran Act looked dimly upon the creation of a forum for criticism of their handiwork. Commissioner Danaher reported that "several Senators are definitely miffed over the President's having appointed our Commission at a time when that very [Judiciary] Committee had already passed a sweeping resolution for an investigation into the same general field." [36]

Rather than avow such self-interested motives, opponents of the PCISIR made use of a legal snare. Before the lawyers and businessmen nominated to the Commission could serve, they needed to be exempted from the conflict-of-interest statutes; otherwise they would be forbidden to have any business dealings with the federal government for some time after completion of their official duties. Appropriate legislation cleared the House of Representatives in March but ran into trouble when it went to the Senate Judiciary Committee. Chairman McCarran was at first reassuring, but his colleagues and he professed to have serious doubts. The exemptions were referred to a special subcommittee composed of Willis Smith, Herbert O'Conor, and Homer Ferguson, all members of the Internal Security Subcommittee, in whose hands the measure was as good as dead. They stood firmly against what McCarran called the "piecemeal destruction" of the conflict-of-interest laws.[37]

Had the Nimitz Commission been willing to bargain, it might have achieved a *modus vivendi*. At its inception, the PCISIR had mutually plighted "cooperation" with the Internal Security Subcommittee; McCarran strongly hinted that to effectuate the alliance the Commission would have to grant his subcommittee access to departmental loyalty files. In short, the Senators were again trying to breach executive confidentiality. The Commission would not fall for this "squeeze play," as Nimitz termed it.[38]

On April 30, the Judiciary Committee voted down the exemptions and so torpedoed the Admiral and his mates. The commission members submitted resignations in May, but Truman sat on them, hoping that the Senators might yield. He implored McCarran to reconsider, but the Navadan could not be moved.[39] Congressman Francis A. Walter tried to put through the exemptions as a rider to another measure; when that ploy failed, the fate of the PCISIR was sealed.[40] Truman toyed with the idea of revamping the commission with members—fewer, perhaps—who were not vulnerable to the conflict-of-interest statutes, but this avenue led nowhere.* [41] Another expedient—asking Congress to establish a nonpartisan commission independent of both the Executive and Congress—was also rejected.[42] Others canvassed the possibility of having the Nimitz Commission's functions taken over by one of the foundations then interesting themselves in the problems of loyalty and security, but that suggestion too

* The Russell amendment, which held the Commission to a January 23, 1952, reporting date (unless a new executive order was issued), posed a further complication. Also, the vast amount of work projected for the Commission would have extended its labors far into the election year and embroiled its findings in the campaign—an additional disincentive.

came to naught.[43] In July Truman, impatient at the failure to activate the PCISIR, assigned one of its tasks, an examination of the government's security programs, to the National Security Council. (An Interdepartmental Committee on Internal Security submitted a report in 1952, after receipt of which Truman asked the Civil Service Commission to map a plan to merge the loyalty, security, and suitability programs into one. No reforms were forthcoming during his administration, however.) [44] After further efforts at resuscitation failed to lift the Nimitz Commission from its comatose state, death notices were published in October 1951, amid much public lamentation. McCarran commented that the "bomb" the President had hurled at the Internal Security Subcommittee had turned out to be "a dud." [45]

Whether the time had ever been ripe for the PCISIR is questionable, but Truman chose the worst possible moment to launch the project. Once the elections had shown the ostensible power of the communist issue, the President would find it hard to outflank the conservatives of both parties who raced to stake out their claims to the territory. He had become a victim of circumstances. Before the elections, the passage of the McCarran Act, and the divisive Tydings report, administration forces might have overridden right-wing opposition to a PCISIR, but even then several of Truman's own congressional leaders opposed the scheme. At best, an early attempt to establish a Commission would have carried the endorsement of several important Senators then wrestling with the communist issue: Tydings, McMahon, Lodge, and possibly Hickenlooper.

Before its demise the Nimitz Commission participated peripherally in the significant administration decision to change the loyalty criterion under Executive Order 9835. Hiram Bingham, the new chairman of the Loyalty Review Board (as well as his predecessor Seth W. Richardson and the Chairman of the Civil Service Commission Robert W. Ramspeck) had asked for a revision which would permit dismissal of an employee when there was "reasonable doubt" as to his loyalty—in contrast to the original obligation to demonstrate "reasonable grounds" to doubt his allegiance. The new standard would obviate the need for evidence indicating *present* disloyalty; it also placed a heavier burden of proof upon the suspect and a lighter one upon the loyalty board. This redefinition—actually a reversion to the formula employed during World War II—would, it was hoped, firm up the administration's loyalty program against attack.

In particular, the alteration was put forward to prevent the recurrence of any more nettlesome cases such as that of William Remington. Accused of Communist Party membership and espionage, Remington had been dismissed from the Commerce Department by a regional loyalty board but then cleared under the old standard by the Loyalty Review Board. In 1951 he was convicted of perjury for having denied that he had once been a party member or transmitted secret documents to the Communists. The case greatly embarrassed the loyalty program and created pressures for the more stringent "reasonable doubt" formula. Truman was eager to have the PCISIR pass on the standard, but the Commission, stymied, could not make a formal recommendation. Informally, however, all but one of its members approved the change. Unwilling to await the improbable eventuality that the PCISIR might be able to take up its duties, Truman on April 28 decreed the new loyalty criterion without the Commission's concurrence.[46]

Truman had failed in his effort to wrest the initiative from the Senate conservatives and red-hunters; they had beaten back his effort to defuse the loyalty issue, thus denying him the chance, as former Senator Danaher put it, to "exculpate" himself on that score. Distantly at least, the shift in the loyalty standard also marked a triumph for critics of the program. While members of the administration itself (if Bingham fits that category) had pushed for the change, Republicans could claim that they had supplied the necessary impetus. Before Executive Order 9835 was amended, Senator Ferguson had introduced a bill to that effect.[47]

Under the new standard, hundreds of loyalty cases decided on the "reasonable grounds" criterion were reopened. Several State Department officials cleared under reasonable grounds were dismissed on the basis of reasonable doubt. To some critics it seemed that the administration, by sacrificing individual liberties to national security, had upset the very balance which the Nimitz Commission was to seek. The aggressiveness of Hiram Bingham, the new chairman of the Loyalty Review Board, resulted in a further loss of control over the loyalty program by the administration. Under Bingham, the Board expanded the number of its "post-audits" of decisions by the departmental loyalty boards, examining not only cases in which the defendant had been dismissed, but also—going beyond the intent of Executive Order 9835—those in which the employee had been cleared. (In 1955, the Supreme Court ruled that the Loyalty Review Board had exceeded its authority in the latter procedure.) [48]

One might think that the loyalty program, headed first by Seth Richardson, an Assistant Attorney General under Hoover, and later by the former Republican Senator Bingham, would be proof against right-wing criticism. The administration had such tactical considerations in mind when it made the appointments. "They wanted an old-fashioned conservative Republican," Bingham recalled. "They told me so." [49] However, if Truman thought he would disarm his adversaries by staffing the program with such men, he was mistaken. To many members of the GOP, Richardson was a renegade. His administration of the loyalty program became suspect when his board cleared William Remington. Consequently, when Richardson was nominated to head the Subversive Activities Control Board (SACB) set up under the Internal Security Act, McCarran and his allies forestalled his confirmation. Ill and *persona non grata* on Capitol Hill, Richardson resigned in June 1951. The McCarranites similarly blocked the nomination of Charles La Follette, a liberal, to the SACB. None of this expedited the work of that body, which had been conceived, according to its progenitors, to counter deadly perils; but McCarran and his confederates were unmoved. Having raised a strident alarm in September 1950, the Senator from Nevada in May 1951 somewhat perversely advised Truman (in the course of garroting the Nimitz Commission) that he believed the loyalty program "basically sound." [50]

Throughout 1951 and 1952, McCarran's Internal Security Subcommittee harassed a number of men whom McCarthy had previously attacked. As the committee investigated the Institute of Pacific Relations, Owen Lattimore, John Stewart Service, John Carter Vincent, John Paton Davies, and others associated with the past decade's China policy came under scrutiny. Allegations against these men in turn provided tinder for new proceedings in the loyalty program—new indications of smoke and, according to McCarthyites, further evidence of fire. A dismissal implied vindication for McCarthy; a clearance, not proof of loyalty, but of malfeasance on the part of members of the State Department loyalty board.

Partly responsible himself for some of the problems encountered in the nation's pursuit of the disloyal, Truman expressed concern from time to time that the system had gotten out of hand. After a session with Francis Biddle and other representatives of the ADA, who criticized aspects of the loyalty program, Truman acknowledged that he was "very much disturbed with the action of some of these [loyalty] boards" and wanted to "find some way to put a stop to their un-American activities." Similarly, in his request for a study of federal security programs, he admonished that "one of the highest obligations of the Government" was to insure that individual rights "are protected in its own operations." No reforms took place, however, during the remainder of Truman's term of office. The leverage for change lay—if anywhere—not with the administration, but with its foes.[51]

The functioning of the loyalty program enabled McCarthy to profit from the momentum of events. Under Bingham's activist leadership and with the new "reasonable doubt" criterion, the dragon's teeth of charges sown by McCarthy in 1950 began to sprout in 1951 and 1952. Did the State Department dismiss an employee or even, as required when loyalty or security proceedings were instituted, suspend him? That became further grist for McCarthy. The Senator benefited, for example, from an echo effect when Mrs. Esther C. Brunauer of the State Department and her husband Stephen Brunauer of the Navy Department fell under renewed scrutiny. Both had received loyalty clearances prior to 1950; both had been McCarthy's targets. On April 10, 1951, the Navy suspended Brunauer pending a security investigation; this action triggered the simultaneous removal of Mrs. Brunauer from her duties. In June, convinced of the Navy's intent to dismiss him, Stephen Brunauer resigned. Anticipating more understanding treatment, Mrs. Brunauer stuck to her guns. The department board affirmed her loyalty, but in June 1952, she was severed from the Department as a security risk.[52]

Other McCarthy targets—some sooner, and some later—fell prey to the increasingly rigorous loyalty-security program. John Paton Davies, Jr., the veteran China expert, was suspended as a possible security risk in June 1951. He was cleared, reinvestigated, and cleared again in December, with the Loyalty Review Board concurring. Davies, however, still had to endure the hazing of the McCarran committee, which assailed his reporting from China, insinuated that he had tried to infiltrate the CIA with Communists, and tried unsuccessfully to have him indicted for perjury.[53] O. Edmund Clubb, Jr., the Director of the Office of Chinese Affairs, who was suspended with Davies in June 1951, fared less well. Recommended for dismissal on security grounds, he appealed the ruling. After referring the case to former Ambassador Nathaniel P. Davis for advice, Acheson cleared Clubb. Reassigned to the Division of Historical Research, Clubb chose instead to retire from the Foreign Service. Members of Congress grumbled ineffectually about revoking Clubb's pension, and McCarthy used the affair to cast further aspersions upon the State Department.[54]

Before the Clubb and Davies cases reached their denouements, McCarthy cited them to demonstrate not the vigilance of the State Department but its laxness. If these two had been suspended, why, he demanded, had not John Carter Vincent and Philip Jessup received the same treatment? Vincent soon was running the gantlet between the McCarran Subcommittee and the Loyalty Review Board. First slated to become Ambassador to Costa Rica, Vincent was sent instead to Tangier as diplomatic agent, a post which did not require Senate confirmation and thus avoided a row. Meanwhile, Louis Budenz made the claim that, as a party functionary, he had seen "official" party reports characterizing Vincent as a Communist. After some two years in and out of loyalty-security channels, Vincent was declared a loyalty risk. Acheson created a special panel headed by retired Judge Learned Hand to give further advisory consideration to the Loyalty Review Board's decision, but when John Foster Dulles took office, he decided to make his own finding. He dismissed Vincent for neither loyalty nor security reasons, but for substandard reporting and advice from wartime China.[55]

Still another McCarthy target, John Stewart Service, notwithstanding six prior clearances, was adjudged a loyalty risk by the Loyalty Review Board in December 1951, largely because of his involvement in the *Amerasia* affair. On hearing the news McCarthy, reviewing his previous charges against Service, exulted, "Good, good, good." Service retained the last word: in 1957 the Supreme Court ruled that he had been improperly dismissed, on the (narrow) grounds that the Secretary of State had not abided by established procedures.[56]

In each of these cases, McCarthy's gains were modest. To be sure, every story of a dismissal, resignation, or reinstatement carried an acknowledgement of his initial charges, but these ricochets seldom scored the bullseye of publicity wich McCarthy had enjoyed in 1950. What is remarkable about McCarthy's *éclat* during 1951 and 1952 was the long periods of page-seven articles and the rarity of front-page stories. He tried mightily to recapture the headlines. He impugned the loyalty of men close to the President—Chairman of the Council of Economic Advisors Leon D. Keyserling (and his wife), presidential aides David D. Lloyd and Philleo Nash—but while these outbursts created momentary static, their force was soon dissipated.[57]

In 1950, McCarthy, with auspicious timing, had capitalized on the rising discontent over Democratic foreign policy, particularly in regard to Asia. But the very developments which swept him into prominence were now, in 1951, growing beyond his grasp, often outstripping him, and only with difficulty could he keep pace. McCarthy exploited the Korean stalemate in numerous speeches, but anxieties over Asia had become so general that at times they threatened to engulf him. While there were still victories to be won, often the Wisconsin Senator had to share the publicity. The stage had become crowded: McCarthy's soliloquys on the subjects of the Asian "betrayal" or disloyalty and misfeasance in high places were often obscured by the chanting of an ever-larger chorus.

If McCarthy seemed to have slipped since the halcyon days of 1950, why did he remain a dangerous presence? In part the answer lay in his genius for publicity, for obtaining maximum mileage from the flimsiest piece of news. Better than any, McCarthy knew the fourth estate, its weaknesses, its pressure points and reactive nerves. He was master of what Daniel Boorstin has labeled the "pseudo-event," news which is not news. He could threaten or promise to issue charges, make them or back off as he chose, or announce ominously that new, arcane evidence was being gathered, and then move on to some wholly unrelated topic. It all made the papers. Because he was a Senator—and a prominent one—reporters never ignored him, and so pseudo-events and non-stories continued to cascade into print.[58]

The press itself, apart from any talents of McCarthy's, gave the Senator unintentional assistance. To a peculiar degree, McCarthy flourished as a product of his media exposure, even when it was hostile to him. He thrived on what one veteran of the era called the

"phobofilia" of the press—its self-defeating fascination with its enemies. "The newspaper and radio commentators play into his hands
by publicizing all he says and does," wrote Senator Hoey, "and
nothing could please him more." The impression of power operated
as power itself. "McCarthy has, indeed, almost won his fight,"
Hubert Humphrey argued, "for both the anti and pro-McCarthyites
are able to carry about 80% of the news columns of the press and a
sizeable portion of the radio time." "Through his enormous publicity
channels," Senator Hunt lamented, McCarthy could "turn the tables
and make anyone who criticizes him appear to be favorable to Communism." [59]

McCarthy's journalistic foes knew that something was amiss. One
group, alert to his success "in baiting liberals and in commanding
provocative headlines," asked: "How can liberals and the press restrain themselves from falling into McCarthy's publicity traps?" [60]
When *Editor and Publisher* castigated McCarthy for his attempt to
launch an advertising boycott of *Time* Magazine, the Washington
Post warned that "this may seem to be giving Senator McCarthy's
theatrical threat more seriousness than it deserves." [61] The canons of
their profession required journalists to report what the Wisconsin
Senator said, but forced them in the process to confront the frustrating realization that they were accurately reiterating falsehoods. The
press served, "in a sense, as irresponsible executors of his decrees,
inflicting punishment by publicity upon the innocent," commented
the Washington *Post*. To break out of that bind required "something
more than objectivity," but the solution remained elusive. The journalist Alan Barth argued that his confreres should counter those who
played them for "suckers" by "relentless checking and double-
checking" and then publication of the real truth at the same time that
the charges were printed. [62] Such an antidote was easier to prescribe
than to administer. The "sheer physical difficulties raised by daily
publication" operated against continually balanced treatment of Mc-
Carthy stories, Philip L. Graham, publisher of the Washington *Post,*
pointed out. "And even in stories, like the McCarthy story, I confess
that I am fearful of our using our power unfairly when we try to print
the 'whole truth' instead of merely being 'objective.' " The fourth
estate never discovered a satisfactory formula for covering McCarthy.
Owning up to the vulnerability of the press to the McCarthy method,

the *New York Times* could only shrug that "the remedy lies with the reader." [63]

The Truman administration encountered problems similar to those of the mass media in its second major effort to subdue its Wisconsin tormentor: a rhetorical offensive. During the summer of 1951, the President struck back at McCarthy and McCarthyism with a series of speeches emphasizing the trustworthiness of the bulk of federal employees, the effectiveness of his own loyalty program, and the harm being done to American liberty by the purveyors of hysteria. Some administration officials resisted a strategy of oratorical confrontation. Press Secretary Joseph Short, for instance, suggested to Truman that constantly replying to McCarthy was unwise, and asked authorization to tell the State Department to "lay off." However, presidential aide George M. Elsey expressed the more prevalent White House view that "a forceful, indirect rebuttal to McCarthy's lies and reckless charges is necessary. The 'be quiet and he will go away' approach was tried and it did not work." [64] While there is little direct evidence of advance planning or coordination underpinning this counterattack, many journalists were certain that it constituted a premeditated campaign.

Truman opened the barrage on July 28 with an address criticizing the "doubters and defeatists" who sought to "stir up trouble and suspicion between people and their Government" and used "the big lie for personal publicity and partisan advantage, heedless of the damage they do to the country." To illustrate the nation's plight, Truman cited an incident in Madison, Wisconsin, on the Fourth of July, when a reporter tried to get passers-by to sign a petition consisting of passages from the Declaration of Independence and the Bill of Rights; of 112 people solicited, 111 refused to sign out of fear that it was some kind of subversive document. [65]

On August 14, in a speech to an American Legion gathering, Truman again unlimbered his guns, maintaining that "real Americanism" differed distinctly from what its self-styled "chief defenders" said it was. Real Americans did not "create fear and suspicion among us by the use of slander, unproved accusations, and just plain lies." Nor did they seek to convince us that "our Government is riddled with communism and corruption" or to make us "so hysterical that no one will stand up to them for fear of being called a

Communist.'' While vigilance against subversion was essential, Truman warned that ''when even one American—who had done nothing wrong—is forced by fear to shut his mind and close his mouth, then all Americans are in peril.'' In September, Truman sent a letter to the American Chemical Society cautioning that American freedom was under sharp attack and that ''liberty can be endangered by the 'right' as well as by the 'left.' '' In a speech to the National Association of Postmasters he categorized aspersions upon the loyalty of federal employees as ''contemptible.'' He urged the AFL to beware of those who used the communist menace ''as a screen for their attacks on the very foundations of our civil liberties.'' [66]

Other administration leaders took up the cry. Before the Veterans of Foreign Wars, Secretary of Labor Maurice J. Tobin scored the practice of ''irresponsible slander from the privileged sanctuary of the Senate of the United States.'' [67] Navy Secretary Dan A. Kimball expressed his concern over assaults upon ''public servants of the highest integrity and selfless devotion to the American cause.'' Any future candidate who adopted the tactics of the anti-Tydings campaign in Maryland, Attorney General McGrath advised sternly, should be disqualified from office. The U.S. Commissioner of Education, Earl J. McGrath, called for care lest ''in our excessive zeal in defending ourselves against the subversive doctrines of the Communists we unconsciously adopt their most repugnant totalitarian practices.'' [68] Dean Acheson denounced the ''reckless and heedless attacks'' upon State Department employees, while General Conrad Snow, Chairman of the Department's Loyalty-Security Board, declared the Wisconsin Senator's accusations ''baseless and disproved.'' According to Secretary of the Interior Oscar Chapman, such charges as McCarthy's threatened the nation with a ''mental straitjacket'' of conformity. [69]

Party officials also reflected the new militancy. In several instances, they took note of McCarthy's campaign against Tydings, balancing fears with a resolve to prevent any recurrence. William M. Boyle, Jr., citing the Maryland campaign, accused the GOP of launching the 1952 campaign on a ''level of moral squalor,'' and his successor as Chairman of the Democratic National Committee, Frank McKinney, claimed that some Republicans saw in the ''campaign of lies and vilification against Millard Tydings'' a ''blueprint'' for

1952.[70] Twice in the autumn Truman conferred with Wisconsin Democratic Party leaders, who emerged from the meetings to tell of his eagerness to see McCarthy beaten—an expression of sentiment McCarthy termed the "understatement of the year." [71]

All these developments, it was speculated, formed part of a concerted drive against the Wisconsin Senator.[72] Moreover, this Democratic opposition seemed to many onlookers to be having some effect. "Is McCarthy Slipping?" queried one journalist. Commenting that McCarthy's admirers had never seen their St. George "quite so deep in dragons before," Eric Sevareid reported that the Senator was "losing momentum." Several reports intimated that Truman and the Democratic National Committee had mastered their fear of McCarthy's popular appeal and had decided that a direct assault upon him would yield large dividends.[73] A number of observers reasoned that the series of attacks heralded a determination to make the Senator and his tactics a major issue in the 1952 campaign. William S. White wrote that Truman had concluded that a "general and all-out counteroffensive" might bring about McCarthy's "political destruction," while Arthur Krock, on the basis of these thrusts at McCarthy and the concurrent stout defense of Acheson, proclaimed a shift in administration tactics from "Fabian" to "Napoleonic." [74]

These rhetorical blasts undoubtedly hit McCarthy at a low point. Since the spring, in fact, things had not gone well for him. MacArthur's dismissal had preempted the headlines; during the ensuing investigation McCarthy's more august colleagues on the Foreign Relations and Armed Services Committees had held the limelight. Although his reference to the President as a son of a bitch who must have fired MacArthur while under the influence of "bourbon and benedictine" achieved brief notoriety, the Senator soon began to fade from public view. His speech in April on the MacArthur episode, a pastiche of clippings and time-worn critiques of Acheson, Drew Pearson, Lattimore, and others, made little impression. A desperation born of his current insignificance may have prompted McCarthy's attack of June 14 upon General George C. Marshall, whom he implicated in "a conspiracy . . . so immense as to dwarf any previous such venture in the history of man." [75]

Many Republicans as well as Democrats experienced wordless revulsion at the assault on Marshall; this widely shared distaste may have encouraged the more militant mood of the Democrats in the next several months. By July, Kenneth Hechler of the White House was advising Senator Robert Kerr, about to engage in a debate with Senator Wherry, to "[p]ut him on the spot about whether or not the Republican leadership condones Senator McCarthy's smear tactics." McCarthy's popularity had slipped: an August Gallup poll found that 13 percent of its respondents held favorable views of him while 22 percent were unfavorably impressed—a sizeable drop in appeal in the year since the Tydings report.[76]

While no polls, unfortunately, exist to gauge the impact of the administration's offensive, these efforts in themselves appear to have had little to do with McCarthy's partial fall from grace; it is possible they even assisted him. Some Democrats, while agreeing that attacks on McCarthy were warranted, feared lest they by "overdone" and merely serve to "magnify his position." A number of politicians, of course, gave this advice to rationalize a lack of nerve. Nonetheless, such counsels of caution (if not cowardice) had a certain validity during the summer of 1951. At a time when McCarthy's engines of publicity were beginning to labor,* it may have been dubious strategy to single him out for attention.[77]

Moreover, the Senator from Wisconsin showed ingenuity in meeting each administration blow with a counterblast—sometimes several. After Truman's first thrust, he replied that the President had "tried to slander" those citizens of his state who had refused to sign the trumped-up petition circulated by a Madison *Capital-Times* reporter, whose paper published editorials "aping or paralleling those in the Communist *Daily Worker.*" Truman's American Legion address provided McCarthy a still better chance to counterpunch. Admitting that the speech did not mention him by name, McCarthy nevertheless termed it "an extremely vicious smear attack" and demanded equal time from the four major radio networks to answer it. Then he milked not one but three separate publicity items from the

---

* The August Gallup poll showed a decline in public recognition: whereas a year before, 22 percent had not known who McCarthy was, in 1951, 30 percent were unfamiliar with him. "Left alone," argued conservative columnist Frank Kent, McCarthy would "sink into obscurity. But violent attacks on him not only would revive interest in him but solidify and strengthen his following." Baltimore *Sun,* Sept. 9, 1951, clipping in Tydings MSS.

exchange. ABC carried his rebuttal on August 22, NBC and CBS broadcast a later speech, and Mutual put him on an interview program. He also reaped public exposure after Secretary Tobin censured him before the Veterans of Foreign Wars: by inviting him to reply, the VFW gave the Senator the last word.[78]

Still, as the administration barrage rose in intensity, McCarthy's lines did seem a bit ragged. Some observers declared him to be in full retreat, and McCarthy himself acknowledged that the Democrats were going "all-out" to discredit him before the 1952 elections. Although the Senator welcomed a confrontation over the issue of "McCarthyism," the Democrats could find encouragement in the fact that his stature within his own party had tumbled. Most notably, Senator Taft took exception to McCarthy's "extreme attack" on Marshall and his practice of overstating his case.[79] Coupled with criticisms of McCarthyism by other Republicans and reports from Wisconsin that Governor Kohler might run against him in the senatorial primary, the Taft statement bespoke considerable Republican disenchantment with McCarthy.[80]

There is, however, no evidence that Democratic oratory prompted the growing GOP impatience; if anything, it probably made Republicans readier to close ranks than to break with their burdensome colleague. The Truman administration lacked the ability to speak as an authoritative source on questions of political morality. At a time when the public had little faith in the administration, surely hardened Republican leaders would give little credence to the utterances of Truman and his associates. (In November Truman reached the nadir of his public appeal: a Gallup poll found that only 23 percent approved of the way he performed his duties, while 58 percent disapproved.)[81] Perhaps the administration's rhetorical offensive did achieve the more limited objective of bucking up the party faithful— or stemming the discouragement which might have ensued if McCarthy's attacks had gone unanswered. If bravado produced few apparent dividends, timidity in the year before a presidential election offered the administration no better prospect. There was something to be said for simply holding the line.

McCarthy's partial eclipse resulted less from the Democrats' activities than from his own blunders, such as the Marshall speech, from the shift of attention to other related but transcending issues, notably

MacArthur, and from the fact that he had run low on charges—one of the occupational hazards of red-baiting. After the Tydings investigation McCarthy rarely could do more than piece together tired repetitions of earlier accusations, minor embellishments, or spurious revelations of ephemeral interest. He remained a celebrity but was now reduced more often to riding remote circuits to address this banquet, to receive that Americanism award from some veterans' or citizens' group.* He could still rustle up reporters for his latest pronouncement, but after mid-1950, for long periods, he was patrolling the more obscure marches of the communist issue. Others—especially the McCarran Committee—with the best good will frequently jostled him away from the front lines.

McCarthy lacked a permanent rostrum of his own from which to keep himself in the forefront of anticommunism. He had singular bad luck in his efforts to secure such an institutional niche. In January 1951, he obtained a seat on the Appropriations Committee and its subcommittee which dealt with the State Department. However, Senator Vandenberg's death in April and his replacement by a Democrat deprived McCarthy of that assignment. (He regained it in 1952.) His claim to a position on the Republican Policy Committee proved unavailing. It became fashionable to explain McCarthy's capacity for mayhem by the fact that he enjoyed congressional immunity. Yet this constitutional buttress probably explains his persistence as a national figure in 1951–1952 less well than what Robert Griffith has labeled his "political immunity"—his timely seizure of the interrelated questions of subversion and Far East foreign policy.[82] Paradoxically, however, the Korean War, even as it contributed to McCarthy's political durability, circumscribed his influence as well. While political "inflation" may have undercut the value of the issues McCarthy exploited, they still remained a negotiable property.

Nevertheless, in the last two years of the Truman regime Mc-

---

* McCarthy was no longer sought after by such groups as the American Society of Newspaper Editors, and, surprisingly, he never addressed the American Legion's national convention. That he filled a speaking date before the Hager family reunion in Ramage, West Virginia, was indicative of the marginality of his fame. Daniel F. Whiteford, "The American Legion and McCarthyism," *Continuum*, 6 (Autumn 1968); 327; Washington *Post*, Sept. 10, 1951; cf. Harper, *Politics of Loyalty*, p. 217.

Carthy's power was as remarkable for its limitations as for its de-
structiveness. He remained a menace, but commonly his opponents,
having previously erred at times by underestimating his power, now
exaggerated his individual potential for damage. They failed to realize that the communist issue had become firmly rooted in a matrix
created less by McCarthy than by other politicians of both the Republican and Democratic right. McCarthy often had—and needed—help
from others to wreak his fullest havoc. The continuing harassment of
such men as Lattimore, Vincent, and Davies owed less to McCarthy
than to the zeal of the McCarran panel. Similarly, the dismissals of
State Department officials caught up in the loyalty-security program
resulted only distantly from McCarthy's own charges: the system was
inertially guided. The momentum of decisions (whether dismissals or
clearances), appeals, and official rebuttals served inescapably to keep
the Wisconsin Senator's name in the news. Similarly, by 1951, as the
hard fact of Korea settled into the public consciousness, the Asian
policies which had helped to germinate McCarthyism also obstructed
any move to uproot it.

   In its pursuit of McCarthy, the administration made a number of
missteps unrelated to these limiting circumstances. Truman, for instance, saw the problem chiefly as a political issue to be met on the
hustings—an assumption which, if analytically sound, was therapeu-
tically valueless. By 1951 the administration did not possess sufficient credibility to convince broad sectors of the electorate in debate. It had seldom articulated its foreign policies with more than
moderate success, and its pronouncements circulated at an increasing
discount as the Korean stalemate dragged on. Beset by one political
contretemps after another (including revelations of corruption), the
administration was too weak to strike blows of more than momentary
effect. There remains a strong possibility that by 1951–1952, under
the cumulative weight of these developments, not even perfect conceptualization of the challenge posed by McCarthyism or execution
of countermeasures could have altered the administration's plight
very significantly.

   Notwithstanding his reputation as a partisan scrapper, Truman exercised his combative instincts only sporadically against McCarthy.
His reticence may have been prompted by his awareness of the limited duration of America's previous outbreaks of political hysteria

("we recovered from all of them") and by his confidence that history, however ponderously, was moving in the direction of sanity.[83] Whatever the reason, he made only halting use of the leverage available to the executive branch against the Wisconsin Senator. In contrast, Huey Long, before his death in 1935, had come under attack from several quarters—all under the coordination of the White House. President Roosevelt had denied all patronage to the Louisiana Kingfish; the Treasury had instituted tax procedings against Long's lieutenants and was moving against Huey himself at the time of his assassination. McCarthy was not Huey Long, of course. For the administration this meant, among other things, that since McCarthy normally received no patronage, none could be taken away. Although some of his followers in Wisconsin (as well as he) had tax difficulties, unlike Long he was not hostage to a bloated personal apparatus riddled with corruption. There was not much of a McCarthy "machine" to dismantle.[84]

Furthermore, any attempt to "get" McCarthy personally ran the risk of being interpreted as spiteful retaliation against a man who had found a Democratic sore point; such an effort would only serve to validate McCarthy's accusations. Additionally, as is so often the case with charges of congressional malfeasance, the porousness of the applicable laws and elusiveness of the accused combined not only to render conviction unlikely but to discourage prosecution. Moreover, the administration had to fight a widely held belief that the best solution to the McCarthy problem could be provided by his constituents in the 1952 election.[85]

The administration's unwillingness or inability to coordinate its anti-McCarthy operations with those occasionally carried on by Democratic Senators constituted a more serious failing. Yet many conservative Senate Democrats, foes of the administration, would not have done its bidding under virtually any circumstances; at the same time, the liberals who were willing to work against McCarthy lacked influence upon the rest of their colleagues. A considerable part of the problem lay in the Senate's own incapacity for action and in the fragmented condition of the Democratic Party. On the other hand, the executive branch did not respond energetically to the few initiatives of its supporters on Capitol Hill and launched few attempts at cooperative measures of its own. Some administration officials realized that a successful anti-McCarthy front had to be anchored in the Senate. The State Department proposed, along these lines, that Vice-President Barkley take the floor to deliver a strong sermon against Mc-Carthyism.[86] Barkley did not pursue the suggestion.

During its final two years, the administration could mount no effective opposition to McCarthy. At the same time, however, McCarthy himself could no longer carry on sustained campaigns, but had instead to lie in wait to pounce when the Democrats made a mistake. This fact was a measure of the Democrats' weakness, but also of McCarthy's. No less than they, he too was a prisoner of circumstance, often reacting more to events than shaping them. McCarthyism had passed its epidemic stage, but so enfeebled had the Truman administration become that the Senator came to resemble a low-grade infection, not acute enough to kill the patient, but too persistent to be overcome.

CHAPTER 7

The Corporal's Guard

IN THE SENATE, opposition to Senator McCarthy confronted a frustrating paradox: those willing to take on the Republicans' leading red-baiter lacked the power to make their defiance effective, while those with the institutional strength to thwart him usually lacked the will. In all, the number of Democrats who offered resistance to McCarthy in the last two years of the Truman administration was small. Characterizing McCarthy's Senate opponents as either "militants" or "critical," Frank J. Kendrick found only four militants and one critical during 1951, and in 1952 only two of the former and five of the latter.[1] Because his taxonomy stressed confrontations on the Senate floor, Kendrick slightly understated the opposition to McCarthy and neglected more covert forms of influence. Nonetheless, by any classification, McCarthy's foes never amounted to more than a corporal's guard. Such checks as they placed in front of McCarthy during these two years often rested on narrow grounds—typically, the dignity of the Senate, its institutions and members. Ultimately, McCarthy's violation of Senate norms would bring his downfall, but in the meantime, his colleagues were slow to outrage, sporadic in resistance.

Fear goes far to explain the dearth of Senate volunteers. Few Democrats could view the carnage of the 1950 elections with equanimity. The outcome in Maryland "sent a chill down the spine of old line politicians," according to two reporters. "The ghost of Senator Tydings floats over the Senate," observed another onlooker.[2] Never long on subtlety, McCarthy himself offered blunt reminders to any who missed the point. He urged critics at one stormy hearing to abate their hostility; "otherwise it is reminiscent of another committee [Tydings's] before which I appeared some time ago." Once during rocky going in the Senate chamber, he warned the Democrats that Senator Lucas, who had crossed him, "is no longer a Member of the Senate," and Tydings, who had done likewise, "is no longer with us." When a colleague asked impatiently for some substance in the charges McCarthy had raised, Senator William Langer riposted that he could find it in the recent elections.[3] Yet fear, if generally a deterrent to action against McCarthy, sometimes precipitated it. A feeling of "there but for the grace of God go I" raised by the defeat of Tydings led Democrats, including powerful Southerners, to urge an investigation of the Butler campaign.

In any case, resistance to McCarthy was often not so much lacking as it was futile. Senate opposition to McCarthy totaled less than the modest sum of its parts. It proceeded by makeshift and happenstance, normally required some unusual outrage (like the Maryland campaign) to activate it, and seldom progressed much beyond the immediate crisis. McCarthy's excesses occasionally goaded his fellow Senators into some sort of lumbering collective response, but after a few anguished outbursts, they customarily reverted to passivity.

The divided condition of the Democratic Party reinforced the dormancy of the Senate in its response to McCarthy. Except on foreign-policy issues, there was scant cooperation between Southern conservatives and Northern liberals. It was not that the Democrats disagreed with each other publicly over McCarthy—in the few instances when votes were counted, party unanimity prevailed. The problem lay in the fact that not many roll calls on McCarthy were taken: the Democrats acted in unison when the issue was thrust upon them, but they rarely concurred on whether—or how—they themselves should seize the initiative in the "McCarthy problem."

Southern Democrats displayed particular caution in their dealings with the Senator from Wisconsin. Understandably, they did not hark to cues by the Administration to beat back the McCarthy onslaught. Their relations with Truman had become so frayed in the last years of his term that, except on such paramount issues as the Korean War and MacArthur's dismissal, he could depend upon their apathy or opposition. On many questions, they found the ideological position of the conservative Republicans more congenial than that of the administration. While there never was an articulated party program against McCarthy, had Truman put one forward, the Southern conservatives would on the whole have responded indifferently. His party and theirs were the same in name only.

Notwithstanding their unwillingness to tangle with McCarthy, very few Democratic conservatives believed his charges, and fewer still had any respect for him. In varying degrees they defended the Tydings Committee against criticism. Tydings "did a good job," according to Clyde Hoey of North Carolina. Though Hoey assumed that in the past the State Department had been "too lax in dealing with the pinks, subversives and communists," he believed that since 1947 "a determined effort" had been made to oust them; thus, he argued, "practically everyone of the persons named by Senator McCarthy have [sic] not been in the employ of the State Department for several years." Even Willis Smith of North Carolina, who as a member of the Internal Security Subcommittee harbored deep suspicions about Owen Lattimore and the Institute of Pacific Relations, had reservations about the Senator from Wisconsin. "Whether or not Senator McCarthy can or will prove any of his charges, I cannot at this time tell. But, I would prefer to see the proof accompany the charge to the end that no innocent person shall be falsely accused." [4]

While Southerners generally discounted McCarthy's veracity, they rarely translated disbelief into opposition. Their feelings about their colleague, though cool, were outweighed by their strategic perception of their role in the Upper Chamber. Some avoided overt opposition to McCarthy because such activity did not comport with their view of proper senatorial behavior. Members of the Senate's "Inner Club," as William S. White has styled it, prized the grandiloquent courtesies traditional to the upper house. Naively, perhaps, Senators assumed "that every member is a gentleman in a gentleman's world." [5]

At the same time, members (Northern and Southern) of the Senate Establishment tolerated a modicum of demagoguery by their peers provided it did not overly disturb the proprieties of the world's greatest deliberative body. This sufferance operated to McCarthy's advantage. In the first place, few of his colleagues desired to combat him at the pitch of invective which the task made inevitable. As Lester

Hunt, the Wyoming moderate, said, "it would be necessary to fight on his level which means getting down in the gutter and that we refuse to do." Furthermore, Rule XIX demanded that "no Senator shall speak disparagingly of another Senator . . . and most of us like to live up to the rules." "Veteran Democrats" declared privately that to tussle with McCarthy was to risk "a loss of stature." "He who plays with a pup gets licked in the face." [6]

Southern Democrats had an additional problem to mull as they considered McCarthy's antics: in disciplining a colleague, they did not wish to establish a precedent that would return to haunt them. Throughout the McCarthy era, this *caveat* made a number of Senators hesitant to move against the junior Senator from Wisconsin. The Southerners, ever sensitive to the role of the filibuster in the battle against civil rights legislation, frequently invoked the Senate's time-honored freedom of debate, although they were aware it could be misused by others. "Our free speech leads to a great many excesses," Senator Hoey conceded, "and yet probably the benefits are greater than the adverse results." [7]

Generally, Southerners stayed aloof from the McCarthy problem not simply because of fear or loathing, but because he seldom became a particularly salient issue for them. Their distaste for his posturings was to a considerable extent cancelled out by their lack of enthusiasm for defending the administration. Nor did the issues of civil liberties or "character assassination," which McCarthy's activities raised, strike very close to home. When McCarthy did intrude into their world, as in his defeat of Tydings, or if he assaulted a member of the "Club" or disregarded procedural niceties, then in surprise and anger they might strike back. Their remoteness from the McCarthy problem sometimes shielded the Southerners from firsthand knowledge of their colleague's behavior. Senator J. William Fulbright's initial encounter with McCarthy did not come until the autumn of 1951. He told William Benton he "hadn't imagined that the man could be as bad as he turned out to be." [8]

Fear and not insouciance probably served as the chief obstacle to action on the part of Northern Democrats. It was a common assumption recorded by Richard Rovere that "just about everyone" in the Senate was "scared stiff" of McCarthy. The "timidity" of his fellow Senators, wrote two reporters, encouraged him to greater excesses. McCarthy came to be "feared by his colleagues more than Huey Long ever was." When the Senate declined to confirm the nomination of one of McCarthy's prime targets, it was scored as a "triumph of cowardice." "The so-called liberals," lamented the Madison *Capital-Times,* "are doing nothing" to check the Wisconsinite; with other members of the Upper House, they "sat frozen in their seats." McCarthy, playing heavily upon the fear of his colleagues, must have sensed that it was there, and the silence of an entire panoply or liberal heroes also testified to its presence. The names of John F. Kennedy, Paul Douglas, and other famous liberals do not often appear in the chronicle of opposition to McCarthy.[9]

However, the argument that fear immobilized such men possesses more plausibility than proof. Liberals often employed it to explain why their paladins failed to challenge McCarthy. Perhaps in their own cold-war persuasion the Senate Democrats, liberals included, shared more of the anticommunist premises of the Right than they were willing to admit or able to perceive. Senators rationalized their disinclination to cross McCarthy not only on the ground that "you don't get into a contest with a skunk," but also, as "T.R.B." reported, with statements that "after all, there was Alger Hiss." Paul Douglas (not noted for a lack of courage), while disapproving McCarthy's methods, had to concede that "we have had some Alger Hisses in government." "We were handicapped," he later recalled, "by the fact that many of the men who McCarthy singled out were implicated to some extent." The Democrats had always to contend with the possibility that another Hiss case might materialize, but such anticipations did not alone explain their defensive posture in the early 1950s. Two critical biographers of Hubert Humphrey concluded that, though ready enough to don the baldric of anticommunism in order to protect himself from red-baiting, he had a fear of communist conspiracy which was genuine. Humphrey wrote of his conviction that "many liberals in this country have failed to face up to this issue." "Aggressive communism" was a major threat, he believed, "and liberals should be in the forefront of the fight against it, not in the rear." [10]

Often Democrats felt compelled to flex the muscles of their anticommunism for all to see. "One may talk about concentration camps" or "a police state," Senator Lucas exclaimed during debate over the McCarran Act, "but when we are dealing with a Communist group . . . there is nothing too drastic." Democrats also criticized McCarthy, in William Benton's words, as a "Joseph-come-lately" to the battle against communism which their party had been waging for years.[11] Notwithstanding such fulsome rhetoric, the circle closes with a return to the "fear" explanation; for while one cannot prove the presence of fright save by inference, neither can one argue—except by assumption—that the source of the Democrats' anticommunist posturing was pure ideology uncontaminated by fear. Bravado is often the offspring of timorousness.

Despite the restrictions under which senatorial opposition to Mc-Carthy labored, occasional victories were won: the Anna Rosenberg confirmation fight illustrated how those ordinarily not found among McCarthy's adversaries could offer an *ad hoc,* successful, but limited rebuff to their fractious colleague. After General Marshall hand-picked Mrs. Rosenberg to be his Assistant Secretary of Defense, a covey of the nation's more noisome anti-Semites, joined by several professional red-baiters, erupted in full cry. The campaign against the distinguished manpower expert and public-relations counsel hit high gear when Fulton Lewis, Jr., insinuated that she had once belonged to the subversive John Reed Club. Through a set of byzantine liaisons materialized a witness, Ralph De Sola, a former Communist who promised to testify to this effect. De Sola, it developed, was sponsored by Benjamin H. Freedman, who had been referred to him by the veteran Communist-hunter, J. B. Matthews. Freedman went to Washington to tout his witness, first to the virulent racist and anti-Semite, Representative John Rankin, then to Congressman Ed Gossett of Texas, ultimately to Senators Lyndon Johnson and Richard Russell of the Armed Services Committee. The plot thickened as Don Surine of McCarthy's office and Edward Nellor of Fulton Lewis's staff paid a call on Freedman in New York, carrying *bona fides* from a sinister source, the notorious anti-Semitic agitator Gerald L. K. Smith. McCarthy's involvement was secondhand, but his demurrer on the nomination sufficed to induce the Armed Services Committee, which had approved the nomination, to reopen hearings.[12]

Rapidly, the conspiracy unraveled. De Sola positively identified Anna Rosenberg and swore he had attended meetings with her in the 1930s. But then a series of witnesses who De Sola claimed would corroborate his story flatly repudiated it. Freedman himself gave muddled testimony; he subsequently pelted the subcommittee with explanatory memoranda and later, in disgust, he said, flushed pertinent documents down the toilet. Finally, the FBI tracked down another Anna Rosenberg in California who admitted having belonged to the John Reed Club. (At one point there were forty-six Anna Rosenbergs in the New York phone book.) Russell's committee voted unanimously to confirm Mrs. Rosenberg, and each member hastened to certify her integrity. A grand jury looked into the tawdry cabal, summoned De Sola, Surine, and others to testify, but declined to hand down indictments.[13]

Having long since extricated himself personally from the affair, McCarthy escaped serious consequences, notwithstanding the fact that his office had been a staging area for the intrigue. The members of the Armed Services subcommittee dismissed all the ugly canards whispered against Mrs. Rosenberg, but, as Robert Griffith has pointed out, the mere fact that these outpourings received a serious hearing indicated the degradation which had befallen American public life. The momentary setback failed to check McCarthy, who voted to confirm Mrs. Rosenberg—however sheepishly the record does not state. As on other occasions, he simply moved on to new pursuits, and the episode was allowed to slip into oblivion.[14]

Most of McCarthy's colleagues habitually sought to avoid confrontation with him, a fact substantiated by their response to the President's selection of Ambassador-at-Large Philip C. Jessup to be representative to the General Assembly of the United Nations in September 1951. Well aware of McCarthy's earlier attacks on Jessup, the Democrats greeted the nomination coolly. Seeking to avoid a donnybrook with the Wisconsin Senator and his confederates, several Democratic leaders, including Senator Connally, the Vice President, Majority Leader McFarland, and Speaker Rayburn, advised against the naming of Jessup. Connally feared the appointment would "stir up trouble and open wounds that were in the process of healing," for Jessup was "one of the casualties of the political calumny" of the last two years. Despite audible rumbling from the GOP presaging a major fight, Truman stood firm.[15]

McCarthy argued his case against Jessup before a special subcommittee of the Foreign Relations Committee chaired by Senator John

Sparkman, Alabama Democrat. Flourishing a set of "documents" encased in lurid pink folders, he struggled for two days to demonstrate Jessup's "great affinity for Communist causes." His evidence, most of it over a year old, had not improved with age; he still tortured significance out of the fact, for instance, that excerpts from a letter to the *New York Times* which Jessup had coauthored had been reprinted by a group later declared subversive. With the exception of Senator Owen Brewster, the subcommittee members made clear that they were not buying McCarthy's shopworn goods. Sparkman and especially J. William Fulbright skirmished frequently with their contrary witness. When McCarthy cautioned after one flimsy indictment that one must wait to weigh the data in their totality, Fulbright observed that "a number of zeros doesn't make it amount to one if you put them all together." After McCarthy attainted Jessup with one of his wife's associations, Fulbright inquired puckishly whether his colleague was not being too exacting upon husbands. When McCarthy admonished that "men of little minds" were trying to make communism into a political issue, Fulbright asked: "You would not do anything like that; would you?" [16] So taxing was the Democratic rebuttal that observers marked it as further evidence of the Democrats' growing willingness to speak out against McCarthy.[17]

The hearings might have been a losing bout for McCarthy had not an unexpected partner, Harold Stassen, tagged him and jumped into the fray. Stassen's testimony shifted the focus of the hearings from Jessup's associations to the diplomat's involvement in Asian policy. Stassen labored to implicate Jessup in a "world-wide pattern of action" initiated by Asia hands who, having consigned Chiang Kai-shek to defeat, were now operating to throw Nehru's India to the Communists. To tie Jessup to the foundering junk of Nationalist China, Stassen cited a conversation he had had with the late Arthur Vandenberg in which the Senator recalled a February 1949 White House meeting at which Acheson and Jessup had urged an abrupt termination of aid to Chiang. It developed that Jessup, busy on UN business, could not have attended the session. No matter, Stassen argued; since Jessup had been in Washington not long before the meeting and had conferred with Acheson, he *must* have been involved in the abortive démarche. Stassen next claimed that in October 1949 he had attended a State Department round-table conference at which Jessup presided benignly over an attempt by those who advocated recognition of Red China and other procommunist moves to carry the debate and alter U.S. policy. When Stassen had objected to him about the "ten-point program" of this "prevailing group" (of which Owen Lattimore was coleader), Jessup replied that the "greater logic" lay with their position. However, records of the meeting failed to bear out the allegations of the graying former boy Governor.[18]

Despite the lack of evidence, the nomination was doomed. Stassen's willingness to backstop McCarthy indicated the GOP's inclination to merchandise doubts about the administration's Asian policies. Indeed, the Republicans—especially Brewster—gave every semblance of seeking to broaden the proceedings into a reprise of the MacArthur hearings, and Stassen came to a hearing equipped with maps showing the progress of the Chinese civil war. The Democrats had no stomach for another Asian autopsy. "Frankly," said Senator Hoey, "I have been somewhat troubled about this nomination . . . although I do not follow at all the McCarthy charges." [19]

The rejection of the nomination came as no surprise. As anticipated, Sparkman and Fulbright voted for the nomination, and Ferguson against. The key votes, both negative, came from Senators Guy M. Gillette and H. Alexander Smith. Gillette, a Democratic moderate from Iowa, had persistently desired to avoid controversy with McCarthy, but his committee assignments (Rules and now Foreign Relations) precluded such tranquility. As tension over the Jessup nomination mounted, Gillette caved in. Praising the diplomat lavishly, he found little evidence of Jessup's involvement in China policy and believed McCarthy had given a "warped and distorted picture"; but since Jessup lacked public "confidence," Gillette voted against him.[20]

More pivotal was the vote of Smith, who expressed "absolute confidence" in the "integrity, ability and loyalty" of his old friend Jessup, but could not get around the fact that the nominee was "the symbol of a group attitude toward Asia" which had brought disaster to China. The New Jersey Republican believed that "somebody, somewhere, somehow had to take a stand for what he believed to be right with regard to our Far Eastern policy"; but as for "yielding to McCarthyism," that, said Smith, was "furthest from my thought." [21] After the subcommittee vote, through bipartisan prearrangement the Foreign Relations Committee killed the nomination by declining to act upon it. Had a division been taken, Jessup would probably have been approved by one vote, but the Democrats declined to face the violent floor fight which was sure to follow. Harold Ickes, the "Old Curmudgeon," encapsulated the verdict as "Not Guilty—You're Fired." [22]

Although his own influence had proven less than decisive, McCarthy could claim some credit for the outcome, which he labeled "a great day for America and a bad day for the Communists." But while McCarthy had initiated the engagement, most observers agreed that Stassen had had more to do with its outcome. [23] McCarthy had not come off well in his appearance before the Sparkman panel, but the larger forces which defeated Jessup gave McCarthy, because of his success in identifying himself with the now-standard scenario of "betrayal" in high places and "sell-out" in Asia, a measure of political security.

However, the blanket which protected could also smother. The issues which McCarthy had appropriated were not his exclusive property. During the MacArthur controversy in the spring of 1951, other men, other events crowded him off the front page. At such times McCarthy pressed harder than normally and in several instances exceeded the boundaries of acceptable senatorial behavior. His charges against twenty-six State Department employees caused H. Alexander Smith to surmise that he was "trying to get the headlines ahead of the McCarran Committee. There are too many 'smears' without foundation." Subtly and sometimes imperceptibly, these episodes eroded his position, leaving McCarthy temporarily vulnerable.

The supreme example was McCarthy's attack on General George C. Marshall of June 14, 1951. The speech, placing a highly conspiratorial construction on the nation's military and foreign policies of the preceding decade, made a less than convincing case against the man whom Harry Truman styled the "greatest living American." To have shied some muck upon the Olympian Marshall would have constituted a significant Republican coup, given the suprapolitical prestige the General's presence lent to the Truman administration, but generally members of both parties greeted McCarthy's effort with a hush of revulsion. [24]

Republicans were quick to disassociate themselves. After Robert Hendrickson had innocently agreed with a colleague that McCarthy's was an "important" speech, he felt compelled to explain his remark: he had not meant "to applaud in any manner" the oration, with which he generally disagreed, but merely to "point to the lack of attendance." After McCarthy sent a copy of the address to John Foster Dulles, advising him to read it, the covering letter was marked "not acknowledged" and a brusque annotation (apparently by Dulles) declared the speech "destroyed." Senator Ralph Flanders confided that the Marshall assault "did Senator McCarthy more harm than good." Senators Duff, Morse, and Saltonstall were reported "scarcely . . . concealing their concern"; and Bob Taft refused to condone the attack.[25]

At first the Democrats, either stunned or cautious, kept silent about the Marshall speech and only gradually aroused themselves to froth at its enormity. By the 1952 campaign, it had become a staple in their larder of criticisms of McCarthy, but during 1951 they made little public reference to the episode. The Democrats mulled the possibility of answering the attack or of applying sanctions, such as the silent treatment, but nothing materialized from these mutterings.[26]

However, the Marshall speech did mark the commencement of a three-and-a-half-month period during which Democrats, among them several who had not previously been drawn into the fray, publicly expressed displeasure with their Wisconsin colleague. On August 9, when McCarthy named twenty-six alleged State Department security risks, the few Democrats who had not conspicuously absented themselves from the chamber gave the speech a surprisingly hostile reception. Majority Leader McFarland, who had not troubled much with McCarthy before, heatedly castigated him: "I have sat on the floor of the Senate and heard men charged, by innuendo and inference, with disloyalty, and even with high crimes and misdemeanors, without any substantial evidence." To sow distrust in this fashion served the Kremlin's purpose "just as effectively as one of their paid agents." Next Senator Lehman decried McCarthy's "character assassination" and avowed that Jessup, for one, "deserved much better . . . than the shabby and dastardly treatment" accorded him. Senator Wherry jumped up to invoke Rule XIX against this reflection upon a colleague, to which Lehman responded: "I withdraw the word 'dastardly' and I substitute . . . 'cowardly.' " [27]

While most often the Democrats found themselves in a position of reacting to some McCarthy outrage, occasionally a few Senators seized the initiative. For example, on February 1, 1951, William Benton criticized the Republicans for giving McCarthy a seat on the Appropriations Committee and the subcommittee charged with handling the State Department's budget. Benton begged GOP leaders to reconsider this invitation to McCarthy to serve as "his own kangaroo court" for the department of which he was an "implacable and . . . irresponsible enemy." He summarized McCarthy's method with the slogan: "If you can't make one libel stick, try another, and then try another." Herman Welker accused Benton of violating Senate rules with this personal reference, and Edward Thye and Kenneth Wherry defended the committee assignment as a normal result of the seniority system and as a sovereign undertaking of the Republican Committee on Committees. Revealing a trace, perhaps, of touchiness, Hugh Butler, chairman of the latter group, offered to confer with Benton on the issue. Although Benton claimed to have achieved "one major objective"—making Republicans "take full responsibility for him [McCarthy] and his appointment"—his gambit brought no apparent gains to the Democratic side.[28]

When Harley Kilgore chose on February 12 to mark sardonically the first anniversary of McCarthy's Wheeling speech, his exertions proved equally unavailing. The past year had witnessed "a river of words" from which a "fog of confusion" had risen, yet McCarthy had not uncovered a single culprit—let alone seven, or fifty-seven, or 205. The time had come for the Wisconsin Senator to produce the names of the guilty. Kilgore received assistance from other Democrats. Olin Johnston threw out leading questions, Herbert Lehman commiserated with the "patriotic and loyal Americans" whose reputations McCarthy had heedlessly blackened, and Hubert Humphrey warned that McCarthy's onslaught had been "very unfortunate morally" and had loosed a "psychosis of fear" upon the land. But as the Democrats concluded, the Republican right trotted out its own totems. William Langer recalled how Klaus Fuchs, "the known Communist," gave secrets to Russia. "I say shame on a party . . . which would defend that kind of thing." Hugh Butler rattled the bones of the Tydings Committee, to whose records he referred the incredulous Kilgore.[29] Rhetorically, the skirmish was a standoff; strategically, the Democrats achieved nothing.

A number of concerned Democrats who did not ordinarily partici-
pate in such oratorical melees groped for an alternative approach.
Several legislators began in 1951 to seek structural remedies for the
general problems of which McCarthy was only the supreme exemplar. Congressional committee procedures had long disturbed
those interested in civil liberties. In the Eightieth and Eighty-first
Congresses, Senator Lucas had proposed reforms of committee
usages; hearings had been held, but his resolution got "lost in the
shuffle" in 1950. In January 1951, Senator Paul Douglas suggested
that any citizen defamed before a committee be granted redress by
being permitted to file a statement of rebuttal as part of the permanent
record, to testify in his own behalf, to summon corroborative witnesses, and to cross-examine his accusers. Douglas would also end
the practice of issuing reports or statements which did not carry the
approval of a majority of the committee.[30]

In August 1951, on behalf of nine other Democrats and eight
Republicans, Estes Kefauver offered a resolution which made similar
concessions to individuals maligned before investigating committees.
It also proposed that anyone whose activities a committee planned to
scrutinize be so apprised in advance and that any anticipated charges
be examined first in executive session, to be made public only after a
majority of the committee approved. The resolution was referred to
committee, where it expired. Kefauver offered similar proposals over
the next several years.[31]

Such devices thrust only indirectly at McCarthy. While he had
committed some of the sins which Douglas, Kefauver, and their allies
hoped to halt—notably the unauthorized release of information gathered in executive sessions—nonetheless, at this stage of his career, he
did not rely nearly as heavily on the institutional weapons which congressional committees afforded as he would when the Republicans
controlled Congress. During the Truman administration, it was others
who abused the investigative prerogative. As committee reforms related to McCarthy, they were at this point more predictive than reme-
dial.

Concerned Senators looked for other sorts of institutional restraints
to limit the damage done by McCarthy or his imitators. Both Kefauver and Lester Hunt urged that safeguards be provided for individuals unfairly attacked in speeches on the Senate floor. Agitated by the

pummeling Anna Rosenberg had received at her confirmation hearings, Hunt proposed that the law be changed to permit a person libeled in the course of congressional activities to sue the government just as if one of its trucks had collided with his car. Senator Kefauver sympathized with Hunt's objectives, but he saw no reason to make innocent taxpayers pay for damages inflicted by careless legislators. Instead, on August 24, 1951, the same day he proposed committee reforms, he sponsored with Tobey, Hunt, and Mrs. Smith a resolution to require that a congressman, whenever feasible, give advance notice to any citizen about whom he intended to make derogatory remarks on the floor of Congress. That individual would then be allowed to file a rebuttal to be read into the record. To dramatize the problem, Kefauver cited McCarthy's recent listing of twenty-six State Department security risks. Even the Senator from Wisconsin, Kefauver noted, had declared that he would be sorry if some of them were innocent and were hurt by the notoriety. Regret would not suffice, however.[32]

Kefauver's proposals fell into the legislative hopper at a time of rising dismay over all forms of congressional conduct. Senator Douglas and others such as Senator Benton were expressing chagrin at the low level of ethics adhered to by some of their colleagues. Significantly, when Douglas's Labor subcommittee criticized the ethical standards of government officials, it urged a set of guarantees similar to Kefauver's proposal to guard against slander by lawmakers. A substantial segment of the Senate demonstrated support for the broad-gauge objectives of various reform programs. Among the cosigners of Kefauver's committee reforms were Herbert O'Conor, a conservative Democrat, and the Republican moderates Irving Ives, Charles Tobey, Frank Carlson, Margaret Chase Smith, and Alexander Wiley. However, the fact that so many Republicans, including several who were quite diffident about challenging McCarthy, cosponsored the bill illustrates how tenuous was the connection between committee reforms and McCarthyism. Even McCarthy could play the game: with Harry Cain he had assumed a civil-libertarian stance in a debate over whether two unwilling witnesses at Kefauver's crime hearings should be cited for contempt. It was precisely the omnium-gatherum nature of the issue which Kefauver was trying to tap; these problems, he argued, "concern all of us, regardless of party, or whether we might call ourselves liberals, or middle-of-the-roaders, or conservatives." [33]

To the extent that Kefauver was correct, he was proposing a very dilute opposition to McCarthyism; his colleagues could offer support without committing themselves on the real issue. Thus, Senator Wiley denied that his cosponsorship was a condemnation of his junior colleague. "This has nothing to do with Senator McCarthy," he cautioned. "Love everybody, that's my motto." [34] Significntly, Wiley (and all other Republicans but Tobey and Mrs. Smith) declined to sign the accompanying resolution dealing with defamatory speech; few Senators of either party wanted to stick their necks out by implicitly labeling as slanderous the activities for which McCarthy was noted. Moreover, given McCarthy's disregard for ground rules, further procedural codification was not going to bring him to heel.

The various reform proposals did constitute a sort of fever chart for the ravages of McCarthyism. A small band of Democrats and moderate Republicans continued to offer such bills during the Eighty-second Congress and more of them in 1953; 1954 brought a strong freshet of them and a realization by conservative Republicans that McCarthy had to be reined in. But 1954 was a long way from 1951. Before then, it would be impossible to legislate against McCarthyism by indirection; afterwards, it would be beside the point.

Neither the rhetorical outbursts against McCarthy nor the efforts to tighten Senate rules brought results. The miscellaneous Democratic initiatives of 1951 and 1952, particularly the verbal assaults, lacked coordination. If such challenges had the plausible purpose of flushing out McCarthy, the better to hit him, they did not achieve that objective. Moreover, these efforts sometimes worked at cross purposes. Thus, Senator Kilgore complained chiefly that McCarthy had failed to name names, yet when he did precisely that, Senators Lehman and McFarland pounced on him. Granting that McCarthy lacked proof for the latter set of accusations and merited a rebuke, the two episodes nonethless show how improvised and unsustained was the opposition of Senate Democrats in 1951 and 1952. The exertions of Senator William Benton constituted the one great exception.

In Benton, the Senator from Wisconsin had roused a formidable adversary. Before appointment to the Senate, Benton had already traversed careers enough for several men. During the twenties he had

scaled the heights of Madison Avenue, helping to found the firm of
Benton and Bowles in 1929. The agency prospered, even in the
Depression, as it pioneered in such fields as the sponsorship of soap
operas (e.g., "Portia Faces Life") and consumer-product surveys
(one established Benton as "the world's greatest authority on the
sanitary napkin"). In 1936, Benton gave it all up, resigning to join
Robert M. Hutchins as vice-president and general troubleshooter at
the University of Chicago. Virtually as an aside, he also acquired a
controlling interest in the Encyclopaedia Britannica Corporation and
in Muzak. Voluble, a gusher of ideas, Benton possessed such energy
that one associate quipped, "Bill, you'll never get an ulcer, but you
sure are a carrier."

In 1945, public service beckoned: Benton became Assistant Secretary of State, taking charge, appropriately, of the Department's ex-
panding overseas information programs. He assisted at the founding
of UNESCO and served as midwife, if not father, to the Voice of
America. In 1949, his former partner Chester Bowles, now Governor
of Connecticut, selected him to fill the seat of Raymond Baldwin,
who was retiring from the Senate.

In some ways Benton was ideally fitted to take on the Senator from
Wisconsin. From Madison Avenue to academe, through the prestigious Committee for Economic Development and the State Department, Benton was fiber and bone, but not temperament, of the eastern liberal establishment (and even had some attachments to its
midwestern conservative counterpart). While these ties made him a
conspicuous mark for McCarthyite attacks, they also gave him prominent friends and a security buffered by wealth which made him less
vulnerable to McCarthy's wrath.[35]

Yet Benton's background also made for weaknesses in the coming
battle. His status as a political amateur, while it immunized him from
the fears which assailed so many colleagues, also left him short of influence in the Senate "Club" and of savvy in the way affairs were
managed in the Upper House. He suffered impatience, justified but
fruitless, at the slow ways and rhythms of the Senate. A nonstop
broker and merchandiser of ideas, Benton had a hard time curbing his
exuberance as a Senate freshman.

As a rookie, Benton had raised his voice against McCarthy. In
March 1950, he had defended Acheson and Jessup; in May he had

joined in the Democrats' brief oratorical counteroffensive against Mc-
Carthy. In November he won election to the last two years of Ray
Baldwin's term after a campaign in which he claimed to have "faced
up to the McCarthy issue in every speech." With a bare 1,100-vote
victory margin, he declared brashly from the White House portico
that the results showed McCarthyism was "through as a national
issue." [36] On the way past Arlington Cemetery, he probably
whistled.

After the election, Benton began to pay greater attention to the Mc-
Carthy problem. Millard Tydings's defeat "saddened and indeed terrified" him. He gave increasing thought to what tactics McCarthy's
foes ought to use. Having delivered his own attack upon the assignment of McCarthy to the Appropriations Committee, Benton also
commended the "pounding and hammering" Senator Kilgore administered on the anniversary of the Wheeling speech. "We can't
win out here by turning ourselves into punching bags," he said.[37]

Only after examining the Maryland Election Report did Benton
resolve to launch a personal crusade against the Wisconsin Senator.
A member of the Rules Committee, Benton received an advance copy
of the proposed report on August 3, 1951. He read it over the weekend, and his dismay deepened. Sensing his colleagues' inclination to
let the matter drop, Benton determined that this promising opening
should not be lost. With his assistant John Howe, he drafted a resolution based on the Maryland Report. After only the barest efforts to
untangle procedural underbrush and none at all to gather support for
his initiative, on August 6, Benton introduced his resolution. Taking
note first of the concern over the recent "cribbing" scandal at West
Point, he argued that the Senate should be at least as chary of its own
reputation, which McCarthy had deeply tarnished. In consequence,
Benton asked that the Privileges and Elections Subcommittee investigate the contents of the Maryland Report and any other possible
misdeeds with a view toward recommending McCarthy's expulsion.
In the meantime, he suggested, the Wisconsinite's only honorable
course lay in voluntary resignation; failing that, he ought at least to
withdraw from Senate business until his fate was decided.[38]

Members of the Privileges and Elections Subcommittee and the
parent Rules Committee greeted Benton's proposal inhospitably. The
Maryland probe had exhausted their zeal for confrontation with the

Wisconsin Senator; some observers even feared that the resolution might derail the Maryland Report, which had not yet been approved by the Rules Committee.[39] Margaret Chase Smith thought Benton's move "unfortunate," because it disregarded an understanding that the recommendations in the Maryland Report were not to be retroactively applied. Hendrickson considered the resolution "untimely" and Senator Wherry agreed, adding that the maneuver was inspired by the desire to "take the heat off" party chairman William M. Boyle, Jr. (who was currently embroiled in scandal over "influence peddling").[40] When Guy Gillette, the chairman of the Privileges and Elections group, who had already shown himself adroit at ducking trouble with McCarthy, announced that he had no plans for action on Benton's resolution, its burial seemed imminent.[41]

Outside the Rules Committee, the Benton resolve stirred even less enthusiasm. Senators, even those who disliked McCarthy, emphasized that the precedents for expelling a member were sketchy at best. Benton's timing, too, was questioned: with McCarthy facing an election in 1952, it seemed wiser to let his constituents decide his fate.[42] Some Democrats dismissed Benton's effort as futile. Willis Smith, who occupied a seat next to Benton, thought "he got himself in a fight unnecessarily" and told him "he was making a mistake because there was no chance whatever of [expelling McCarthy] since it would take a two-thirds vote and there were more than enough Republicans to prevent it." [43] Some Senators feared the possible portents. Though he reserved final judgment, J. William Fulbright considered Benton's challenge "a very drastic step" and, if successful, a "dangerous precedent." [44] Still others were just plain hostile. In the heyday of the bipartisan conservative coalition, liberal defenders of the administration at best received scant shrift. As a talkative, assertive tyro, Benton commanded no loyalty from the Senate's gray heads. One Senator commented that the McCarthy-Benton feud might result in "an ideal double murder." [45]

Among Republicans, even those hostile to McCarthy, Benton received a frosty reception. Taking note of Benton's "blast" and the Maryland Report, H. Alexander Smith termed it "all most undignified and unfortunate." Benton's old friend Ralph Flanders had drafted his own "resolution aimed at 'McCarthyism' " some weeks earlier and kept it in readiness; nonetheless, Flanders was "sorry indeed" about Benton's attack, because McCarthy, who had been "rapidly fading from the public scene," was now "in the limelight again." Even when his wife implored him to help Benton, Flanders kept silent.[46]

Benton had little idea of what he had gotten himself into. "This David doesn't have a slingshot," one columnist noted. Aware that "the political response" had been "practically nil," Benton realized that he needed a crash course in the way things got done in the Upper Chamber. He reminded Senator Clinton Anderson of his account of "the background of those poker games at the Wardman Park" and requested "that same kind of discussion to help me understand why my political support is so tragically lacking on this McCarthy issue." Slowly he made headway against the inertia. His assistant John Howe met with Ernest McFarland's staff. The Majority Leader's aides threw cold water on the likelihood of McCarthy's ouster, urging an attempt to censure him instead. Alerted to the "complications . . . in terms of party policy," Benton "suggested," according to Senator Hennings, "that he would be happy to see his resolution somewhat modified." [47]

Meanwhile, prodding party leaders and the executive branch, Benton "insisted that Bill Boyle put a man on the job, and that the Department of Justice move in." Boyle promised to talk to the President and detailed Charles Van Devander of the Democratic National Committee to assist Benton.[48] The Senator from Connecticut also initiated a rather fruitless correspondence with Attorney General McGrath aimed at showing that if McCarthy had the information he claimed regarding Reds in government and failed to present it to the proper legal authorities, he was "derelict" in his duties.[49] Generally, however, Benton had to proceed largely on his own without assistance from party leaders. Where, he asked in retrospect, "were Les Biffle and all the others? Where was the Democratic National Committee?" Given this "complete and abysmal lack of guidance for a freshman Senator," it was "amazing that the so-called two party system can hang together as it does." [50]

By the end of August Benton got a promise from Senator Gillette to hold hearings on Senate Resolution 187, but the Iowan soon began to hedge, and the subcommittee's squeamishness made questionable whether the commitment would ever be honored.[51] The skeptics failed to reckon, however, with McCarthy's growing penchant for provoking his colleagues. His Marshall speech had rankled; he had goaded McFarland to wrath with his charges of August 10; ten days later, in his rebuttal to the Maryland Report, he stirred Hendrickson and Mrs. Smith to anger with his insinuation that they had been biased investigators. His colleagues also pricked up their ears at reports that McCarthy, in Georgia, had hinted that some of them had Communists on their staffs.[52]

McCarthy committed his ultimate folly when he offended members of the Privileges and Elections Subcommittee as they addressed themselves to Benton's resolution. On September 18, he made public a letter advising Senator Hennings to withdraw from the subcommittee. Hennings's participation was inappropriate, said McCarthy, because a law partner of his had served as defense counsel for a prominent Communist, and Hennings himself was retained by the St. Louis *Post-Dispatch,* which opposed "my anti-Communist fight along the same lines followed by *The Daily Worker."* While not intending to imply that Hennings was "sympathetic" to communism, McCarthy confessed he had "no way of knowing whether you receive a percentage of the general income in your office which would put you on the payroll of the *Daily Worker."* Outraged, Hennings challenged his assailant to hear his reply in the Senate "even if it requires your temporary absence from inventing smears and lies about others." The Missouri Senator dealt swiftly with the specific allegations and invoked the issue of the dignity of the Senate and its established committees. He termed McCarthy's letter "an affront to the honor of the Senate" which "impugns the integrity of one of the Senate's committees." [53]

The episode helped to shift Senate opinion against McCarthy. Unlike Benton, Hennings was a member of the Senate establishment, the "inner club." It was one thing for McCarthy to go after Benton or a vulnerable bureaucrat; quite another to attack Hennings, who had close ties with conservative Southern Democrats. The latter reacted angrily to McCarthy's assault. "Tom is one of us," declared an anonymous, prestigious Southerner to reporter William S. White.[54] McCarthy's indiscretion provided a rare if fleeting and narrowly based opportunity to muster sentiment against him.

McCarthy's overstepping of Senate norms prompted members of

the Gillette subcommitee to repress momentarily their disinclination to consider Benton's resolution and, in that sense, had an enduring impact. On September 24 the subcommittee voted unanimously to let Benton testify. Margaret Chase Smith also euchred the Wisconsin Senator by asking the Rules Committee to determine the propriety, which McCarthy had questioned, of her participation in the inquiry. The committee unanimously termed her "well qualified" to serve, and the ruling confirmed Senator Henrickson in his intention to remain on the subcommittee too. In asking for a vote of confidence, Senator Smith had found a ploy which would serve other McCarthy adversaries well. Such a gambit did little but vindicate the principals against the suspicion that they were still beating their wives, but it had its uses. McCarthy received another rebuff when the subcommittee rejected his demand that he be permitted to cross-examine Benton and that the latter testify under oath.[55]

On September 28, Benton presented a lengthy ten-point indictment of McCarthy. He strove first to allay conservative, Senate "Club" misgivings about his resolution. His research showed "ample precedent" for a motion to expel; moreover, he intended no assault upon congressional immunity or freedom of speech. He charged that McCarthy had "lied" and "practiced deception" upon his colleagues in six instances: when on February 20, 1950, he gave a doctored version of his Wheeling speech; when he claimed that he had been involuntarily forced to name names publicly; when he attacked Marshall; when he promised to repeat his charges without the shield of senatorial immunity; when he displayed (June 6, 1950) what he falsely termed an "FBI· chart"; when he declared a willingness to give eighty-one names which he did not possess. Benton also found McCarthy guilty of unethical conduct in taking money from Lustron, in propagating "deliberate falsehood" in the Maryland campaign, in manhandling his colleagues in the Malmedy affair, and in employing men whose base behavior paralleled his own. If the "prima facie case" of perjury anent the Wheeling speech stood up in court, Benton conceded, then his resolution was "academic" since "a Senator in jail, for all practical purposes, has been expelled." McCarthy's acceptance of a fee from Lustron, he argued, showed him to be "a Senator apart from the rest of the Senate." And if McCarthy really believed his "towering lie" about Marshall, the subcommittee might examine the one precedent for an "expulsion proceeding against a Senator thought to be of unsound mind." [56]

It was an impressive performance. One of Benton's attorneys called it the "most libelous statement" he had ever read. On October 9, the Privileges and Elections Subcommittee voted unanimously to order its staff to investigate Benton's charges and to submit findings by November 1 as to whether further action was warranted.[57] However, in the first of a train of maddening delays encountered by Benton, the preliminary report was not ready until mid-January. During the intervening months, four or five staff members looked into Benton's charges—a chore which led them to Wisconsin, Wheeling, and back through McCarthy's voluminious public record.[58]

Benton himself was partly responsible for any inertia. After testifying in September, he left the subcommittee largely alone, save to suggest the addition of certain aspects of McCarthy's pre-Senate career to its probe and to call the bizarre Charles Davis affair to its attention. (Davis, a McCarthy hireling, had spied on John Carter Vincent, U.S. Minister to Switzerland, and tried to frame him with a forged telegram; Davis was convicted of "political espionage" by the Swiss.) The decision not to pester the Gillette group was "a matter of deliberate policy," which Benton came to regret. Given another chance, he speculated, he would have been "far more aggressive" and "would hammer away, after perhaps a thirty-day grace period . . . with daily, weekly speeches." What hindsight condemned may, however, have been the most feasible course. Benton's unobtrusiveness with regard to the Gillette panel did at least earn him some gratitude: John Moore, chief counsel of the subcommittee, pronounced Benton's restraint "admirable." [59] A more aggressive strategy would have risked taxing an already grudging commitment to action.

Moreover, Benton and his aides did not fully reckon with the obstructive capacity of their foe. McCarthy had first discounted Benton as "the hero of every Communist and crook in and out of Government." In the State Department, Benton had "worked hand in glove with the crimson clique." McCarthy intended to ignore the vaporings of "Connecticut's mental midget." [60] When Gillette invited McCarthy to reply to the charges, he responded: "Frankly, Guy, I . . . do not intend to even read, much less answer, Benton's smear attack," whose like could "be found in the *Daily Worker* almost any day of the week." "If Benton had any intelligence," McCarthy added, "he'd be a very dangerous man and I'd have to do something about him." [61]

In late November, the Wisconsin Senator reversed himself and began making personal assaults upon the committee in an attempt to immobilize it. He first charged that the investigation was a "dishonest" effort to defeat him at the polls, that the probers "should be paid by the Democratic National Committee," and that the subcommittee should mark well the fate of Tydings. On December 6, he accused the Gillette group of "stealing" public funds. He charged it with exceeding its jurisdiction by loosing "a horde of investigators hired . . . at a cost of tens of thousands of dollars of taxpayers' money . . . to dig up on McCarthy material covering periods of time long before he was even old enough to be a candidate." A day later he demanded the names and salaries of the investigators, their instructions and mandate. On December 19, he termed each subcommittee member "just as dishonest as though he or she picked the pockets of the taxpayers." His missiles were aimed chiefly at mild Guy Gillette. [62]

One of McCarthy's bombs bore a delayed-action fuse. On December 27, Daniel Buckley, a lawyer employed for seven weeks as a subcommittee investigator, trumpeted in a press release that he had been fired for refusing to abet the "insidious campaign" to "discredit and destroy any man who fights Communist subversion." He claimed he had found evidence which "demolished" the perjury case involving McCarthy's Wheeling speech, but that the chief investigator refused to accept such findings. Gillette deflated these allegations, explaining that Buckley had been dismissed (with two others) in a normal reduction in force. During the weeks before his heated charges, Buckley had, it developed, been in close contact with McCarthy's office, where some suspected his accusation had been drafted. [63]

If McCarthy guessed that the subcommittee's activities boded him no good, he was right, for on January 18 the investigators submitted an ominous "preliminary report." Given the Gillette group's reputation for timid temporizing, the report indicted McCarthy's behavior with remarkable vigor. The staff recommended against hearings on two of Benton's ten "cases" (those concerning the Marshall speech and the promise to forego congressional immunity) because the proof would be too fugitive; hearings on the Maryland election, Malmedy, and McCarthy's aide Surine were "contraindicated" since the charges were already "substantiated." For five cases, hearings were suggested: McCarthy's Wheeling speech (though the *"prima facie* case" for perjury was "weakened" by contrary testimony), Lustron, responsibility for naming names in public, false claims regarding the "81 list," and the behavior of McCarthy's agent Charles Davis. In addition, the sleuths had uncovered peculiarities in McCarthy's 1944 campaign finances; they urged investigation of his tax returns, bank and brokerage accounts; and they scored his attacks on the subcommittee and his "misleading presentation" in the Jessup hearings. If these recommendations were pursued, both the committee and McCarthy would have their work cut out for them.[64]

At this key juncture, the Gillette panel was thrown into turmoil by the defection of Margaret Chase Smith. At first, it was understood that both Senator Hendrickson and she had asked to transfer, Hendrickson to the Library of Congress Subcommittee and Mrs. Smith to the Rules Subcommittee. Since Everett Dirksen and Herman Welker, staunch McCarthy allies, would presumably fill the resultant vacancies, disaster beckoned. Benton likened the rumored switch to "changing the jury half way through a trial," and even the unassertive Gillette promised "vehemently" to protest the change.[65]

The Democrats applied heavy pressure to convince the two fainthearted Republicans to stay put. Hendrickson began to reconsider—conceivably, as a colleague suggested, he had not really requested a new assignment. At the very least, however, Hendrickson would not have protested such a transfer. Declaring that his sole intent was to "promote harmony," Hendrickson "offered to make any shift" that would expedite matters. Finally, the New Jerseyan, "impressed," he said, by Gillette's argument that a change might be "misunderstood," asked to stay on the Privileges and Elections Subcommittee.[66]

Mrs. Smith proved more resistant. The Democrats offered to relinquish a seat or two of their own to permit her to retain both her old and her new post, but she ducked this volley and lobbed back her own offering: let the Benton resolution be assigned to her new subcommittee, to a special subcommittee to consist of the original membership of the Gillette group, or to the entire Rules Committee.[67] She was not running out on the investigation, she claimed, but merely accepting a more challenging assignment. However, Senator Hayden remarked that the Rules Subcommittee had not met in years. When these halfhearted efforts at accommodation collapsed, the Rules Committee had no choice but to honor Mrs. Smith's wishes. Welker supplanted her on the subcommittee, a switch Monroney called "catastrophic." After extracting a pledge that nothing would be done while he was away, Welker departed on an extended speaking tour.[68]

The prospects for action diminished. Time, the most precious commodity at this point, oozed away. Gillette, who had borne the brunt of McCarthy's assaults, was reported less eager than ever to pursue the investigation, and one observer compared the fighting fettle of the subcommittee to that of a "sodality circle." [69] The subcommittee, Benton noted glumly, "cannot be accused of overriding enthusiasm." Nor could the party high command. To the less than zealous Majority Leader McFarland, Benton argued: "Somebody had to do this job." With a hint of reproach, he added, "it is a lot easier for a group of people to corner a skunk and kill him than for one man to do it." [70]

Slowly, however, the subcommittee shook off McCarthy's attacks and even mounted a counteroffensive. Once again the Wisconsinite's efforts at intimidation overreached and ended by provoking indignation and even activism on the part of his intended targets. Senator Monroney had first called McCarthy's bluff in December, when he "invited" his colleague to offer a resolution to discharge the subcommittee of its duties. This parliamentary device would permit the Senate to record its opinion of the propriety of the investigation and of McCarthy's diatribes against the probers. McCarthy did not respond to the dare. Faced with continuing harassment, Monroney, now the driving force on the subcommittee, returned to this strategy in February 1952. On March 5 the subcommittee agreed to seek a Senate mandate for its actions, a procedure which the Rules Committee ratified. The sponsors of the plan hoped to pull the subcommittee off dead center and also force McCarthy to put up or shut up. They invited him to offer the motion, giving him one month to do so, following which Carl Hayden, Chairman of the Rules Committee, would introduce it. After McCarthy balked, Hayden offered the discharge motion on April 8.[71]

On April 10, when the issue was joined, McCarthy and his allies succeeded in confounding the debate until no one was sure any more exactly what the question was. The Wisconsinite struck preemptively with a resolution (Senate Resolution 304) to investigate the affairs of his prime adversary. He charged that Benton, while in the State Department, had "hired or retained" employees named (mostly by McCarthy) as "Communists, fellow travelers, or dupes of the Kremlin," shielded loyalty risks, purchased products of his own Encyclopedia Britannica Corporation, used tax dollars to send "lewd and licentious" materials abroad through the U.S. information program, and failed to report a $600 donation as part of his campaign funds.[72]

Next Hayden launched debate on the discharge resolution, terming it a test of both the "proper jurisdiction" of the subcommittee and the Senate's "confidence" in that body. McCarthy, like the defenders of the Gillette panel, urged the motion's defeat, but he denied having confidence in a group which had investigated him "practically from birth until death." He then disrupted the proceedings with an attack on Darrell St. Claire, clerk of the Rules Committee, whom he accused of having leaked the investigators' preliminary report to "the leftwing press." Well-placed Democrats denied and condemned his baseless charge, and even Hubert Humphrey, not a frequent participant in debates about McCarthy, declared the continual calumny "sickening." When Senator Hickenlooper, bemused by the verbal carpetbeating, inquired what all the fuss was about, Mrs. Smith asked curtly whether he "was ever accused of being a thief?" The real question, insisted Monroney, concerned McCarthy's efforts "to smear and discredit a committee of the United States Senate."

The vote, after all the wrangling, was anticlimactic, as sixty Senators, agreeing to disagree on the resolution's meaning, voted against discharge, with no dissenters. "So, brethren, dwell together in unity," Senator Dirksen added puckishly. The subcommittee had won partial vindication, but it was a victory without peace or immediate benefit. Moreover, McCarthy's Senate Resolution 304 portended trouble. Still, limited gains constituted an improvement. As Benton's administrative assistant noted, the discharge strategy posed an issue "more likely to get the support of the Southerners . . . than the issue of the merits of the case, or of the political implications," and it might "galvanize the subcommittee" into holding hearings on Senate Resolution 187.[73]

In May the subcommittee did go ahead with hearings, but Gillette had little appetite for them and moved skittishly. He sought to resign his chairmanship at about this time, but Hayden dissuaded him. There was reason to be nervous: McCarthy reportedly had the habit of sidling up, putting an arm about his shoulders, and whispering of his plans to come into Iowa to beat him in the next campaign.[74] That Gillette summoned as his first witness Edward Milne, a reporter for the Providence papers, demonstrated the Iowan's jumpiness. Milne had no evidence; what Gillette sought—futilely—was the source for two of the newsman's stories which, based on the still-confidential "preliminary report" on Senate Resolution 187, had speculated on the future course of the probe. McCarthy had charged the subcommittee with complicity in leaking this information, and Gillette was looking for sheep to cast to the wolves.[75]

At length, the subcommittee took up Benton's case number 2— Lustron. The choice was revealing of Senate priorities: McCarthy's alleged perjury did not faze most lawmakers, but his peculations, as Monroney had consistently argued, would strike a responsive chord. A series of witnesses from the defunct company traced the now-familiar path by which McCarthy found monetary reward as an author—or better, since various government officials and a professional writer had done most of the work, as a literary subcontractor.[76] Little new material was unearthed, and McCarthy almost turned the proceedings into a farce. He expressed with a smirk and with typical distortion his regret that the "star witness" could not testify because he was in an "institution for the criminally insane." [77] One witness, before his testimony, published a press release lamenting his ill-treatment by the subcommittee and that group's persecution of McCarthy. The statement, it turned out, had been typed in McCarthy's office.[78]

The hearings extended little beyond Lustron. Counsel Moore made occasional reference to irregularities in McCarthy's banking and investment transactions, but the two Republicans reined him in sharply. The subcommittee heard testimony from Russell Arundel, a McCarthy crony and cosigner of one of the Senator's promissory notes, but publicly probed no further into McCarthy's finances.[79]

The momentum of early May soon dissipated. A meeting to consider further initiatives was postponed for a week, then put off again.[80] Gillette was happy to avoid any hint of haste. In April he had predicted that the investigation might not be concluded before the election, a prospect which had transparent significance, and the other committeemen chose not to press him. He did not want the subcommittee to do anything that would affect a colleague's campaign, and this disinclination retarded progress. It also cut at the heart of Senator Benton's project, for the Senator from Connecticut had realized that, failing all else, a report which would damage McCarthy in his home state was his best hope.[81]

By a series of spoiling operations, McCarthy soon captured the initiative. There was, first, his two-million-dollar libel suit against Benton, which the latter had invited in March by waiving congressional immunity on his original ten-point indictment. To paraphrase von Clausewitz, trials, to McCarthy, were politics carried on by other means. Benton concurred: "We are dealing with a political problem"; the fight was "not in court" but "with the voters of Connecticut." He considered it worth the stiff lawyers' fees, the inconvenience, and the hectoring if he could prove his charges in court.[82]

The suit proved inconclusive. Amid elaborate legal posturing, extravagant charges by McCarthy, and attempts by both Senators to politicize the pretrial hearings (Benton even thought of getting Winston Churchill to testify), the preliminary hearings stretched into autumn.[83] As the presidential campaign heated up, Judge Matthew McGuire of the Federal District Court for the District of Columbia took a legal point under advisement, assuring the litigants that he would reserve decision "for some little time"—until after the election.* After Benton's defeat in November, the suit became moot—at least in the political sense. Immobility prevailed until 1954, when McCarthy's lawyers suddenly agreed to drop the case. McCarthy claimed that since he could not find a single soul who believed Benton's charges, he could never prove damages. Friends of Benton's launched a newspaper campaign to gather signatures of "Believers"

---

* A three-day flap when the Republicans tried to capitalize on the inadvertent consequences of General Walter Bedell Smith's testimony may have prompted this caution. Smith, Director of the CIA, said he operated on the assumption that Communists had penetrated his agency—meaning to show his concern rather than his certainty. *New York Times*, Sept. 30–Oct. 2, 1952.

in the charges; 14,000 responded. It was a nice, but politically post-humous vindication.[84]

Under McCarthy's prodding, the Gillette committee consented to hear his countertestimony against Benton on July 3. Benton's friends on the subcommittee knew Senate Resolution 304 was a "cheap maneuver" but wanted to be able "to say they gave McCarthy his inning." The Senator from Wisconsin listed seven so-called procommunists Benton "harbored" in the State Department—the names culled from earlier lists. He charged Benton with acting as a "smearhead" for the Communist Party line. Benton, who testified later in the day, rebutted the particulars and declared them a perfect illustration of his charge that McCarthy was an inveterate perjuror. The tackiest questioning Benton faced dealt with his failure to report as a campaign contribution $600 given him by a banker, Walter Cosgriff, for the purpose of reprinting certain Benton speeches on government reorganization. Benton had not considered it a campaign gift; legally, it was not, though one might argue that the reprints benefited his campaign. In any event, Benton had candidly aired the episode long before McCarthy chanced upon it.[85]

After July 3, with elections approaching, the Senators dispersed. The subcommittee staff, instructed to seek "additional evidence," assumed the main burden; where once this circumstance had augured well for McCarthy's foes, not so any longer. Chief Counsel Moore was reportedly "terrified" by McCarthy. By the end of the summer, Hayden, unhappy with Moore's performance, shifted him to the parent Rules Committee.[86] Meanwhile, McCarthy again showed his uncanny ability to tamper with the subcommittee through its employees. Wellford H. Ware, a New Jersey lawyer appointed at Hendrickson's behest, was probing into Benton's financial dealings pursuant to Senate Resolution 304. Benton feared no "embarrassment," but he was disturbed that Ware was in close contact with McCarthy's office and was working with Don Surine, which meant that McCarthy had entree into his adversary's confidential affairs. "There couldn't be a better example anywhere to illustrate why experienced politicians don't get mixed up with fellows like McCarthy." [87]

In September, the subcommittee unraveled at the seams. On September 8, Jack Poorbaugh, a committee employee closely linked to Ware, resigned in protest against "the committee's failure to use its

investigatory power in pursuing the Benton case" and the "lack of
equality" between the two cases. Later that day, on the eve of the
Wisconsin primary, Senator Welker also quit the committee, declaring it was "unfair and was being used for a political vehicle by the
Democratic Party." [88]

Under the crush of these events and, perhaps, McCarthy's victory
(to which the timing of the two resignations may have had a more
than coincidental relationship), Gillette's waning resistance collapsed. At a meeting with the subcommittee Democrats in early September, Hayden had failed to budge the Iowan from his inactivity.
On September 10, Gillette wrote Hayden that he could delay his resignation no longer. (It did not become public until September 26.)
Beset by criticism from "columnists and adherents" of both Benton
and McCarthy, Gillette withdrew "in the best interests of the Subcommittee." [89] Monroney, Hennings, and Hendrickson were immersed in various projects which removed them from Washington,
and the subcommittee also lacked a chief counsel. The staff had
amassed revealing data on McCarthy's finances, but there was no
chance to publish it before the election; it remained locked in Senator
Hayden's office. [90] In November, McCarthy's reelection and Benton's
defeat made action still less likely.

Carl Hayden, however, had not given up. When Gillette resigned,
Hayden pressed Hennings to assume the chairmanship of the subcommittee and to push on with the investigation. He saw to the hiring of
a chief counsel, Paul J. Cotter, and of other staff members, who
began to poke deeper into such areas as McCarthy's speculations in
soybean futures. But after the elections, new problems arose.
Monroney went off to Europe, leaving the committee shorthanded
once again. Hennings, sometimes indecisive without guidance from
his colleagues, was "distressed" at this development, and Benton
had doubts about "how aggressively he will proceed." No more encouraging, Hendrickson, the sole remaining Republican, responded
to Benton's prodding with the excuse that "we are . . . a 'lame
duck' corporation." [91]

Finally, Hayden took matters into his own hands; he sought and
obtained the resignation of Monroney and appointed himself to the
subcommittee so that the investigation could proceed. He followed
Gillette's suggestion that the subcommittee's membership revert to

three, its normal complement prior to 1951.* Hayden's intervention was one of the pivotal, perhaps even heroic steps in the entire affair and, given the fact that his previous behavior had not marked him as an anti-McCarthy zealot, one of the most surprising developments as well. Perhaps his true feelings had simply been masked by his natural taciturnity. A vote could always be accounted for, he had once advised Benton, "but you can never explain a speech." [92]

Still, there were pitfalls. The reconstituted subcommittee, unsure how to proceed, invited both principals to testify, knowing that McCarthy would refuse. Senator Hayden was willing to subpoena McCarthy, but Hennings and Hendrickson, doubtful of the subcommittee's power to enforce a subpoena, were reluctant; and so McCarthy received mere "invitations" to appear.[93] McCarthy stayed assiduously unavailable: hunting in Wisconsin, fishing (according to one report)—it was even rumored that he would go to England to dodge a subpoena if necessary. He notified the subcommittee that he would gladly supply any desired information, but he declined to testify. When Hennings challenged him to answer six questions about his finances, McCarthy replied unresponsively and belligerently.[94]

Thus rebuffed, the subcommittee proceeded to put together a report. A vigorously anti-McCarthy draft was ready before Christmas. However, the subcommittee faced sudden collapse when Chairman Hennings disappeared for a week, allegedly on a "bender," and missed a critical meeting on December 20. Benton searched desperately for him. After Drew Pearson, a personal friend, had taken him in hand, Hennings finally showed up at a meeting on December 28. But now the beleaguered Hendrickson failed to attend. Reached in New Jersey, he agreed to review the draft report at home. Two days elapsed with Hendrickson under simultaneous siege from Hennings and Hayden, who entreated him to approve the report, and from Republicans, who implored him to reject it. McCarthy phoned, then flew to New Jersey to expostulate with him. Hendrickson returned to

---

* During the censure fight in 1954, McCarthy's allies would argue that the subcommittee had not been properly constituted after this point. However, Charles Watkins, the Senate Parliamentarian, had advised that while the subcommittee still consisted legally of five members, three of them could represent a working majority. Unsigned memorandum [Grace Johnson], Nov. 17, 1952, "Composition of Subcomittee on Privileges and Elections," Folder 4, Box 120, Hayden MSS.

Washington on January 1; by 7 P.M. the three Senators had ham-
mered out an agreement on the report, but Hendrickson went along
only on condition that it not be published until 4 P.M. on January
2—too late in the waning hours of the Eighty-second Congress for
action. The Democratic caucus was scheduled for the morning of
January 2, before the report was to be released. The special crew kept
on duty at the Government Printing Office on New Year's Day had
the report printed on the last day of the Congress and of Democratic
control. [95]

Without Hendrickson's approval, the report would have lacked authority; what concessions Hennings and Hayden made to obtain it,
other than on timing, are not precisely known. Hendrickson claimed
to have exacted none: to his knowledge the "conclusions and recommendations" prepared by the subcommittee staff, which he checked
over in galley, were not "changed in one particle." He even denied
having delayed issuance of the report. [96] The Democrats, walking on
eggs to assure Hendrickson's signature, had a different impression.
Hayden and Hennings, according to Senator Clinton Anderson,
"were having a terrific time" securing a unanimous report; so delicate was the balance that they discouraged efforts even to have the
Democratic caucus reconvene over the report lest "that very announcement" make Hendrickson balk at signing. [97] Benton recalled
that the New Jerseyan "flatly refused to sign the report unless something was said adverse to me." Asked by Hennings if he was willing
to suffer a mild reprimand in the matter of the Cosgriff donation,
Benton acceded as the price for Hendrickson's signature. When he
subsequently reminded Hendrickson of the episode, however, the latter "bridled" at the implication that he had demanded changes in the
report, claiming merely to have "insisted that the report stick wholly
to the facts." [98]

The H-H-H Report, so called after its authors, leveled a qualified,
elliptical indictment at the Senator from Wisconsin. It consisted of
some fifty pages of chronology and partly digested findings, followed
by 330 pages of documents, a potpourri of cancelled checks, bank-
ledger entries, anguished correspondence about under-collateralized
loans, and other evidence of tangled finances. The report termed the
Lustron fee "highly improper, to say the least" and pondered
whether McCarthy had "collected funds for his anti-communist fight

which he had possibly diverted to his own use." (At least one such contribution seems to have been channeled into soybean futures—a rather indirect means of fighting communism. It was also conjectured that some of the moneys might have gone to pay McCarthy's income tax.) The report suggested that McCarthy had employed family and friends to obscure the sources of funds diverted to campaign expenses and speculations. His dealings with the Appleton State Bank, the report noted, caused that institution to violate federal and state law. Reiterating Hennings's six questions of November 21, 1952, the authors of the document explained that definitive answers were impossible because McCarthy had rejected six separate invitations to testify. In fact, the subcommittee emphasized McCarthy's contumacy as heavily as his parlous economic undertakings, concluding that he "deliberately set out to block any investigation" and showed "disdain and contempt" for the Senate and its subcommittee. With somewhat hollow ominousness, the report intoned that "the record should speak for itself"; the Benton resolution raised an issue which thrust "to the very core" of the Senate's "authority, integrity and . . . respect." The subcommittee, however, made no recommendation for action.[99]

There remained a thin chance that the H-H-H Report would prompt an eleventh-hour move against McCarthy. Carl Hayden headed off proposals to have the Democrats caucus for a second time as contrary to his understanding with Senator Hendrickson. However, he did seek support for a motion to have McCarthy "stand aside" pending further inquiry when he was called to take the oath of office on January 3. After contacting a number of colleagues, Hayden found the prospects hopeless. As another gambit, he considered introducing a resolution asking unanimous consent to permit McCarthy to answer a question: "In view of the present political division in the Senate," would he "agree to take the oath of office without prejudice to himself or to the Senate" until the Rules Committee resolved any question of his right to a seat? Hayden and Hennings conferred with Lyndon Johnson, the incoming Minority Leader, and the three apparently agreed that "it would be better to let the full Rules Committee consider the report," which it had not yet formally received.[100] Consequently, when the Eighty-third Congress convened, as McCarthy swung down the aisle to be sworn in, there was a "special hush," but nothing more. He gleefully clapped Hayden on the back, was briefly distracted as courtly Alben Barkley chose that moment to kiss Margaret Chase Smith's hand, then took the oath for his second term.[101]

McCarthy's adversaries gnashed their teeth at the seeming spine-lessness. Many Senate Democrats, however, perceiving their party's self-interest somewhat timidly, found several reasons not to contest the issue. The risks were high and the rewards uncertain. In the first place, McCarthy and other Republicans had threatened to reciprocate any challenge by blocking the seating of Dennis Chavez, whose elec-tion was disputed.[102] (Ultimately, the New Mexico Democrat's seat was contested anyway.) McCarthy, labeling the H-H-H Report "a new low in dishonesty and smear," even dared the Democrats to fight. "They'll take one of the worst beatings you ever saw." The Democrats surmised that he would win any vote with near-unanimous Republican backing and would seize upon the result as a "vindica-tion." The matter was particularly delicate in view of the narrow forty-eight to forty-seven Republican majority. (Wayne Morse, an In-dependent, was the ninety-sixth member.) This precarious margin im-pelled the GOP to close ranks behind McCarthy. The Republicans had—and would assert—control. "The truth simply is that we did not have the votes," Senator Hennings lamented.[103]

Other circumstances operated against a showdown. Some Demo-crats rationalized that a fight over McCarthy would divert them from a greater concern: an attempt to tighten the rules against filibustering. Others were hesitant to move against a man whose constituents had returned him to office. "There is," wrote Senator Humphrey, "a definite reluctance . . . on the part of many Senators to reverse the judgment of the electorate." A number expressed satisfaction that the Wisconsinite had now become a Republican problem; during the Eisenhower administration, this formulation became a frequent re-frain of Democrats seeking to justify their unwillingness to engage in confrontations with McCarthy.[104]

The subcommittee was not quite through with McCarthy: Hennings sent the report to the Justice Department, the Bureau of Internal Rev-enue, and the FDIC, thus bypassing the Rules Committee, to which the report would normally go next. "I don't say it was illegal," Senator William Jenner commented, "but I'm far from sure it was proper." Hennings acted shrewdly inasmuch as the Rules Committee, under GOP control, pigeonholed the H-H-H Report. Jenner shortly fired all but one of the staff members who had worked on the investigation.[105] It was probably more than coincidence that the report became unavailable soon after the new Congress began. Only 2,500 copies had been printed; by February, Senator Hunt found them to be "scarcer than hen's teeth." [106] Benton encouraged President Truman to take public notice of the report, but the Democrats were inclined to leave the burr on the seat for the incoming Republicans. The latter showed understandably little zeal for pursuing the matter. After a decent interval, Attorney General Herbert Brownell wrote Jenner that his department saw no basis for further action.[107] Senate Resolution 187 had come to naught.

Benton's drive to oust McCarthy from the Senate had labored under severe handicaps. It departed radically from the pattern of sensibilities, precedents, and folkways which characterized the Senate. Though he came to know much about his adversary, Benton learned less about the institutional framework in which both of them operated. The "Club" mystique has no doubt been exaggerated; nonetheless, a brash neophyte and talkative liberal like Benton was ill-placed to function effectively in the Senate of the early 1950s. His persistence did not endear him to colleagues. "Yes, thank goodness," Senator Hendrickson confided, "Mr. Benton is now out of our hair for a while." [108]

Benton's failure stemmed from an inability either to make his campaign the business of his own party or to broaden it into an issue transcending party lines. He suffered the disadvantages of both partisanship and bipartisanship but enjoyed none of the assets. Conservatives in his own party discounted him, and even some liberals found it hard to work with him.[109] Nor could Benton convince any significant number of Republicans that the justifications for an attack upon McCarthy's influence outweighed the potential damage their party might sustain as a result. Consequently, only when McCarthy committed an unusually outrageous breach of Senate decorum would his colleagues object and thereby register backhanded support of Benton. More commonly, Benton's crusade was dismissed as one side of a personal "feud" between the two Senators.[110]

The exigencies of electoral politics also worked against Benton.

Though launched auspiciously during a hiatus in McCarthy's prestige, the enterprise dragged on until the approach of the 1952 elections made the Democrats more leery than ever about tackling Mc-
Carthy and alerted Republicans once more to his political
serviceability. Given the biennial rhythm of elections and the trep-
idations of his colleagues, Benton could have hit upon no timing ideally suited to his project.

In the usual fashion of documents concerning McCarthy, the report
of the Privileges and Elections Subcommittee lived on in a marginal
way, resurfacing in 1954, when it provided the grounds for censure.
The primary basis of that disciplinary move was McCarthy's contempt in declining the subcommittee's invitations to testify and his
abuse of its members—particularly Hendrickson, whom he labeled
"a living miracle in that he is without question the only man in the
world who has lived so long with neither brains nor guts." [111] By a
circuitous route, then, Benton's efforts had led to showdown. Somewhat grudgingly, his friend Ralph Flanders, author of the censure motion, conceded that "your preliminary work made my final success
possible." [112]

During the Eighty-second Congress, Senate opposition to Mc-
Carthy remained a cluster of possibilities wrapped in unlikelihoods.
Hindsight may indicate numerous errors, missed turns, wasted energy, and lack of coordination. Some of the rhetorical broadsides, for
instance, miscarried. "One cannot deal with McCarthy on the invective level," noted a shrewd observer of the scene. Debate and denunciation did no good and often served merely to "inflate" Mc-
Carthy. [113] Efforts at procedural reform cut rather obliquely at the
Senator. Much righteous senatorial wrath bubbled up, then subsided
without effect. Perhaps Benton erred in not pressing the Gillette Subcommittee harder during the autumn of 1951, when Senate irritation
with McCarthy was at a peak. Greater cooperation, too, from the administration might have moved events along at a swifter pace.

At this stage, however, tactics were usually beside the point—none
could have brought the Senate to do that which most of its members
refused to undertake. Too many Democrats who realized the damage
McCarthy was doing were afraid to act. Others, mostly Southerners,
though somewhat less frightened, were not sufficiently disturbed by
the Wisconsin Senator to act. Eventually McCarthy's repeated tram-

pling upon the dignity of the Senate would provoke reaction, but that would require more outrages and more time. The need, as John Howe observed, was to mobilize the "decent conservatives" against Mc-Carthy, but, as Benton suggested, his resolution had come "two years before the timing was right." [114]

There comes a point when speculation and criticism of method become academic; the historian is left with the fact that, with some few exceptions, month by month during the Eighty-second Congress it was William Benton who offered what sustained opposition Mc-Carthy was to encounter. The magnitude of any failure of Benton's diminishes in comparison to that of most of his colleagues.

CHAPTER 8

"Alger . . . I Mean Adlai"

THE 1952 ELECTION ought to have marked a high point of Joe Mc-Carthy's influence. In recent years, Republicans had raised a persistent litany on the subject of Alger Hiss, William Remington, the fall of China, Yalta, and nuclear espionage and tied it together with the refrain that the Democrats had blundered into a needless war in Korea. Given the Republicans' hunger for victory after twenty years in opposition, it would be natural for them to take up the theme of communist subversion, which McCarthy had made his own, and to link it to the several issues with which it blended. The Wisconsin Senator himself was eager to add his oratorical touches to the occasion. He had his own reelection to seek, but the contest did not prevent him from carrying his crusade into other states. No aspirant for the Republican presidential nomination could ignore the topic with which McCarthy had identified himself. Of each candidate Mc-Carthy would demand his price—usually in the form of a waffling tolerance of his activities—and all would pay.

McCarthyism struck to the very heart of the Republican moral and political dilemma, but while the Senator from Wisconsin had a pronounced impact upon the campaign, he did not have a profound one. Similarly, the communist issue played a significant but not a paramount role in the election. Paradoxically, it was raised in so many forms and by so many candidates that McCarthy sometimes found his equity in it diluted. Moreover, the subject of domestic subversion often remained subsidiary to such issues as the Korean War, frustrations engendered by "containment," corruption in Washington, and swollen federal spending.

Within Democratic ranks, the election produced unusual resolve to meet the McCarthy threat boldly. Many of the party's leading figures, anesthetized by caution if not paralyzed by fear, had not gone out of their way to challenge McCarthy in the months after his rise to national prominence. During the campaign, however, to a remarkable degree they were willing to speak out against McCarthy, the "ism" named after him, and the Republicans' refusal to repudiate him. While Truman and members of the executive branch had challenged McCarthy earlier, other party principals now showed a surprising readiness to make him an election issue.

By 1952, McCarthy had attained an assertive presence in Republican politics. He was a fixture in the newspapers, and his name had become a columnist's byword. Still, his influence had its limits. Though always a major consideration in GOP planning and an object of much conjecture, he was nonetheless in some ways a marginal party figure. His histrionics had settled into a groove of cloying melodrama. In February 1952, for example, he returned to Wheeling, scene of his first triumph, to attack Leon Keyserling of the President's Council of Economic Advisors ("a man with Red leanings"). "See this bag I am packing," he confided to well-wishers on his departure. "It's loaded with dynamite and I have photostatic copies of evidence that would make some people blush with shame—or go to jail." With a plea to local clergymen to "pray for me and the cause for which I am devoted," he was off to Tulsa and another one-night stand. Much had happened in the past two years, but little had changed.[1]

The 1952 election and the importance ascribed to the communist issue held out for McCarthy the prospect of greater exposure on the national stage than was afforded by his pursuit of government functionaries or his feuds with various adversaries. Recalling the Wisconsin Senator's role in the 1950 campaign, members of both parties—with differing emotions—anticipated his active participation in the 1952 contest. He began warming up for the campaign in 1951, when he expressed the pious hope that the voters would have a chance prior to the conventions "to tell the politicians of both parties that they are sick of Communists in Government running our foreign policy." A good presidential candidate, he suggested, would be one who saw that "Communists and incompetents" in government were the main issue. Concluding that General MacArthur best filled that prescription as well as the nation's need for a "get tough" foreign policy in the Teddy Roosevelt tradition, McCarthy contributed marginally to the futile effort to inflate the MacArthur candidacy. This allegiance imposed a somewhat passive role upon McCarthy, but during the 1952 presidential primaries—particularly Wisconsin's—he enjoyed a certain éclat as a little man who wasn't there, but who affected the proceedings nonetheless.[2]

The Wisconsin contest produced a tangled snarl of alliances and rivalries worthy of the Thirty Years' War. The state Republican organization, marshaled by Tom Coleman, leader of the Republican Voluntary Committee, supported Robert Taft. (Both McCarthy and Coleman had deserted their 1948 choice, Harold Stassen, whose quadrennial hopes were beginning to show mildew.) Governor Earl Warren of California was also entered in the primary, and much of his backing came from former Wisconsin Progressives led by Philip La Follette, whose attempted return to politics further complicated the situation. (In 1948, La Follette had tried to reinsert himself into Wisconsin politics at the head of a curious coalition of ex-Progressives and conservative Republicans pledged to the candidacy of General MacArthur.) In these complex maneuverings, the Warren slate served as a halfway house for advocates of General Dwight D. Eisenhower, who was not yet an active candidate.[3]

Observers watched carefully to see how each leader addressed himself to the "McCarthy issue." Warren, who had previously expressed distaste for McCarthy, remained noncommittal while in Wisconsin, declining, he said, to be a "carpetbagger." Harold Stassen, a sometime McCarthy ally, also avoided comment on the Senator. (After his defeat in the primary, however, he criticized his former associate's "wild-swinging recklessness.")[4]

Senator Taft had long maintained an on-again-off-again attitude toward McCarthy, in which the counsels of expedience had warred with his sensibilities. Relations between the two had been outwardly close enough in early 1951 to spawn rumors that McCarthy would be Attorney General in a Taft cabinet. That summer, Taft rationalized that McCarthy's charges had not hurt the GOP, but he performed a seven-league straddle to the effect that "the Republicans haven't endorsed them—except those they agree with." Later he described McCarthy's methods as "perfectly reckless." Moderate Republican organs of opinion such as *Life* and *Collier's* objected to the alliance with McCarthy and may have prompted Taft's attempt to put some distance between himself and the Wisconsinite. In October 1951, he expressed doubt that "McCarthyism" would be a significant campaign issue, questioned McCarthy's "extreme attack" on General Marshall, and declared, "I don't think one who overstates his case helps his own case." [5]

Taft's retreat evoked knowing glances from the liberals and some grumblings from conservatives. McCarthy refused to accredit the remarks until Taft confirmed them: "I just don't think Bob Taft will join the camp-following elements in campaigning against me." Three months later in Wisconsin, Taft adjusted his course to the prevailing winds. McCarthy's investigation, he argued, was "fully justified." Though not the first to search for Communists in the State Department, McCarthy had "dramatized" the issue and "done a great service to the American people." [6] Joylessly, but inevitably, the Senator from Ohio, pursuing a strategy which called for cultivation of right-wing support rather than moderate "mugwump" votes, edged closer to McCarthy. [7]

General Eisenhower, in contrast, was expected to appeal to moderate Republicans and independents who disliked McCarthy. His supposed aloofness from McCarthy was one of several mellow characteristics which, the General's backers argued, made him a winner in contrast to the "Can't Win" Taft. [8] Ike had expressed himself on few political issues, but he had made some utterances which seemed to show that he was no McCarthyite. He had defended Philip Jessup from an early McCarthy attack; as president of Columbia University, he had recorded his opposition to red-baiting and seemed to have some zest for the Bill of Rights. Liberal Republicans saw him as a counterweight to their party's right wing and as a man who could curb McCarthy. Paul Hoffman, one of Eisenhower's staunchest supporters, declared his candidate to be opposed to McCarthyism and a

leader who would dispel the "present atmosphere of fear and hate."
Visitors to the General's NATO headquarters reported his strong
dislike of "witch hunts." [9]

On his return from Europe, Eisenhower, albeit haltingly, began to
carry out the role in which his adherents had cast him. In his home-
coming press conference in Abilene, he criticized McCarthy
obliquely. "No one," he averred, "could be more determined than I
that any kind of communistic, subversive or pinkish influence be
uprooted" from government, but it could be done with "competent
leadership with the kind of agency we have now . . . without be-
smirching the reputation of any innocent man, or condemning by
loose association." Asked whether he would back McCarthy, the
candidate refused to "indulge in any kind of personalities." For the
moment his disclaimer satisfied anti-McCarthyites. Eisenhower continued to strike a position of balanced generality during the preconvention campaign. In Dallas on June 22, he reaffirmed his intention
of eliminating communist influence from the federal service, but he
would not resort to character "assassination." [10]

The Republican convention in July reflected at every turn the control over party machinery exercised by the supporters of Senator Taft.
General MacArthur keynoted the assembly—a choice which highlighted the Asia-first, fundamentalist preferences of many Taftites.*
McCarthy's speech on the third day of the festivities revealed his
position in the Republican galaxy. In terms which had become hackneyed, he defended his lumberjack style of fighting Communists, dismissing "the Acheson-Lattimore method of hitting them with a per-
fumed silk handkerchief"; as visual aids his aficionados displayed
red-herring-shaped placards inscribed with the names "Hiss," "Lattimore," and "Acheson." It marked the convention's "lowpoint,"
according to the *New York Times,* which added optimistically: "From

---

* There was some conservative sentiment for MacArthur (predicated on the hope of a
Taft-Eisenhower deadlock) and some dissatisfaction with Taft's failure to see the
doom awaiting his own ambitions and with his refusal to throw his support to
MacArthur. H. L. Hunt to MacArthur, July 4, 5, 9, 1952; George Creel to Mac-
Arthur, Feb. 14, 1952; Creel to Col. Bunker, May 24, 1952; Brig. Gen. H. E.
Eastwood to MacArthur, July 11, 1952, all in VIP File, MacArthur Papers; Creel to
Herbert Hoover, Dec. 11, 1951; Karl Mundt to Creel, Feb. 22, 29, 1952; copy,
Mundt to H. L. Hunt, March 11, 1952, all in Box 4, Creel MSS.

now on the course must certainly be upward." [11] Eisenhower's nomination, the liberals and moderates hoped, would put to rout the Taft
supporters and troglodyte Republicans of the McCarthy-MacArthur
wing and thus restore the GOP to its accustomed dignity.

Yet, while Eisenhower had triumphed in Chicago, he would eventually have to do business with the sulking conservatives. Taft's
backers were wary of the party's standard bearer. Senator Andrew
Schoeppel expressed privately his "serious misgivings," and Hugh
Butler could only console him: "You can bet your bottom dollar
Andy that you, John Bricker and Bob Taft, with maybe a few others
will run things in the senate, regardless of who is president." Taft
himself concluded ruefully during the next two months that Eisenhower seemed "to be following almost exactly the Dewey pattern." [12]

Strong forces operated, however, to push Ike toward reconciliation
with the right. Whatever his own views, the Republican candidate
would campaign on a party platform charging that the Democrats had
"shielded traitors," appeased communism at home, and blocked congressional investigations with the "false cry of 'red herring' " and by
concealment of loyalty data. Eisenhower's preconvention utterances
had shown at least a moderate sensitivity to the communist issue, and
the selection of Senator Richard M. Nixon as his running mate was a
clear indicator that communism would figure prominently in GOP
rhetoric. [13] Eisenhower praised the Californian's "special talent" for
ferreting out subversives, and Governor Frank Barrett exclaimed that
"no one had done more to put the fear of God into those who would
betray their county." Nixon himself predicted that "communism at
home and abroad" would be a major campaign issue. The Republicans, it was conjectured, would make much of the fact that the Democratic candidate Adlai Stevenson had submitted a deposition vouching for Alger Hiss's good character. Before the campaign began in
earnest, the GOP determined to stress the formula K_1C_2, which stood
for "Korea, Communism and Corruption." [14]

As the election approached, the Democrats, in contrast to their earlier diffidence, had begun to confront directly the issues posed by
McCarthy. The spate of anti-McCarthy speeches launched by the
President in August 1951 revealed an awareness that the communist
uproar demanded a vigorous defense. Observers construed Truman's

pugnacity as a reflection of his belief that McCarthyism could be made to rebound against the Republicans. A group within the Democratic National Committee supported this view. At the same time, a certain fearfulness underlay the strategy: the President and other party spokesmen warned Democrats to anticipate a campaign of "lies and smears" like that perpetrated in Maryland.[15]

Even after Truman, who had taken the strongest line against McCarthy, announced that he would not seek reelection, the Democrats maintained their belligerence toward the Wisconsinite. Most of the party's presidential aspirants recognized McCarthy as a salient issue and an evil. W. Averell Harriman accused the Republican Senator of having introduced "the beginnings of a Fascist movement" into American politics and of doing "more harm to our country than any other individual." Senator Robert E. Kerr ticked off the names of anti-Eisenhower obstructionists who would continue in control of the GOP despite Ike's nomination; as for McCarthy, he commented disparagingly: "This speaks for itself." Even Richard Russell, the paragon of Dixie conservatism, lashed out at "the hucksters of hysteria who play upon the emotions and passions of men and would curb our liberties in the name of fighting communism." [16] Senator Estes Kefauver, the first and most active candidate for the nomination, persistently attacked McCarthyism, labeling it "one of the greatest threats to our nation today," a dangerous amalgam of "character assassination and smear techniques." [17] Governor Adlai Stevenson, not an avowed candidate until the eve of the balloting, was less frequently in the public eye; nonetheless, liberals were reassured by his recorded opposition to McCarthyism. That practice, he had ventured, "has now become the trade-mark of a new breed of political demagogue." In December 1951, he blamed McCarthyism for "the paralysis of initiative, the discouragement and intimidation that followed in its wake and inhibits [sic] the bold, imaginative thought and discussion that is the anvil of policy." [18]

If the Democrats seemed to have donned sword and buckler against McCarthy, the Republicans, notwithstanding their interest in the communist issue, approached the fall campaign with a hint of some ambivalence toward the Wisconsin Senator. The journalist William S. White caused a minor sensation with his story that Nixon would not endorse McCarthy on his forthcoming trip to Wisconsin and might even "inferentially attack" the Senator, whose methods he reportedly deplored. White's article prompted quick phone calls to Denver followed by a clarification from Eisenhower headquarters. Nixon next allowed that Ike and he would back McCarthy. "I want to make it clear," he added, that in so doing "neither I nor General Eisenhower will endorse the views or the methods of Republican candidates which happen to be different from our own." Nixon completed his intricate maneuver by stating: "To the extent that the American people have been convinced that so-called 'McCarthyism' means smear, unfair charges, charges not based on fact, to that extent whoever has to carry the McCarthy issue will have a liability on his back." In any case, he said, the issue had been created by Truman through his failure to deal effectively with the communist problem.[19]

McCarthy, meanwhile, was concerning himself chiefly with his own senatorial primary and with his health. After undergoing surgery in July, he spent over a month recuperating, and only in the week before the September 13 primary did he return to the hustings. He could afford some confidence, since major GOP opposition had not materialized. The only realistic prospect for depriving him of the nomination had lain in the murky intentions of Governor Walter Kohler, who for some time had questioned McCarthy's methods. Throughout the autumn of 1951, Kohler let slip comments that he had definitely not ruled out seeking a Senate seat (in the face of McCarthy's efforts to implant the contrary impression). "I have never said I will not run against McCarthy," he declared in October.[20] Many Wisconsin Democrats surmised that Kohler offered the likeliest chance for defeating McCarthy, and leaders of the State Federation of Labor tried to woo him into the race. Kohler remained aloof, however, and in January 1952 announced that he would seek reelection as governor.[21]

Into this vacuum stepped Leonard Schmitt, an attorney and political maverick from Merrill. Schmitt hoped that an all-out assault on McCarthy's record would attract support from former Wisconsin Progressives and from Democrats, who, under Wisconsin's open primary law, could cross over to vote in the Republican contest. Although McCarthy had the backing of the party apparatus, Schmitt electioneered gamely. For money and exposure, he resorted to the tactic of radio-television "talkathons," some lasting over twenty-four hours, during which he answered questions from all comers. Content at first to let others fill his speaking engagements, McCarthy was worried enough by Schmitt's challenge to break his convalescence a week before the primary with a major address in a Milwaukee suburb.[22] His concern was superfluous; on September 9 he whipped Schmitt by a better than 2½-to-1 margin. His 538,000 votes exceeded by 120,000 the total balloting of his combined opposition in both parties.

The outcome ended a lengthy debate among Wisconsin Democrats as to the best means of defeating McCarthy. Some had argued that their party should unite on a single candidate to avoid a primary contest in order to provide two cracks at McCarthy—the first in the GOP primary—and to conserve energies for the general election. The strategy fell apart. Henry Reuss, one of the young Democrats working to revitalize the party in Wisconsin, had jumped into the race in November 1951. After Reuss had seemingly failed to gain much momentum, Thomas Fairchild announced his candidacy in July 1952. The popular scion of an old political family in the state, Fairchild had been elected attorney general on the Democratic ticket in 1948, an event of some magnitude in Republican Wisconsin. He won a narrow victory over Reuss in the primary.[23] The Democrats could add together the anti-McCarthy vote in both parties, adjust for the fact that the Republican primary had given off more sparks (and attracted 83 percent of the voters), and factor in the knowledge that their party always gained votes between the primary and the general election. With a strong dose of optimism, they could foresee a close race.[24] Less sanguine were those who noted that McCarthy had run extremely well in Democratic precincts, as in heavily Polish South Milwaukee. There had been a Democratic crossover, but the migrants had apparently voted for rather than against McCarthy. Len Schmitt could only conclude sadly that Wisconsinites were "voting against Stalin." [25]

The primary had impact at least as profound outside as inside Wisconsin. The size of McCarthy's vote indicated that his appeal and the weight of the communist issue were considerable. His partisans began to exert themselves to get Eisenhower and his entourage to take a less equivocal attitude. It was time, Senator Mundt suggested, "that the so-called 'McCarthy issue' should be settled." At the same

time, the Democrats had stepped up their attacks on "Mc-
Carthyism." Adlai Stevenson had recently called on his middle-of-
the-road opponent to dismiss his "middle-of-the-gutter" advisors and
had derided Ike's enforced fellowship with the "slanderers" of his
patron General George Marshall.[26]

Eisenhower had tried to maintain his distance from McCarthy. At
his Denver press conference in August, he pledged to campaign for
the entire party ticket, including, tacitly, McCarthy, but he refused to
give "blanket support to anyone who holds views . . . that would
violate my conception of what is decent, right, just and fair." Confronting the aspersions hurled at Marshall, he declared that if his old
chief "was not a perfect example of patriotism and a loyal servant of
the United States, I never saw one." [27]

In groping between loyalty to principle and commitment to party,
Eisenhower would stumble down many brambled byways. The first
unpleasant turn came in Indiana, where Senator William Jenner, who
had termed Marshall "a living lie," sought reelection in a difficult
contest. The General, lecturing to his listeners that the GOP did not
conduct "purges," endorsed Jenner. During the festivities, the Senator leaped over to grasp Ike's hand and raised it aloft in triumph. "I
felt dirty from the touch of the man," Eisenhower told a staff
member afterwards.[28] The pattern and the trauma appeared likely to
be repeated in Wisconsin. The Democrats duly publicized the prospect. Vice-presidential candidate John Sparkman expressed wonder at
Ike's "sad plight" in having to endorse Jenner and, presumably, Mc-
Carthy. Stevenson cited the episode in arguing that the GOP campaign slogan ought to be: "Throw the rascals in." [29]

Republican conservatives awaited still-stronger support for their
confreres. The Indiana Republican state chairman grumbled that the
endorsement of Jenner had only been "lukewarm"; McCarthy's
allies began to agitate for a similar sign of approval. Senator Hickenlooper, the Eisenhower staff learned, was "sore about the McCarthy
situation and thinks that McCarthy should have had the same blanket
treatment as Jenner." [30] Ike had replied with a brisk "no comment"
when he was asked, immediately after the Wisconsin primary,
whether he would urge McCarthy's reelection. He had told his staff
to omit Wisconsin entirely from his itinerary; after he found his instructions had been disregarded, he hit upon the idea of using a

speech scheduled for Milwaukee as a vehicle for praise of General Marshall.[31]

The conservatives and party professionals made swift inroads upon the idealism of their standard-bearer and the amateurs who surrounded him. Senator Frank Carlson, a top Eisenhower lieutenant, announced that McCarthy would be invited to campaign for the ticket in other states; the thumping primary victory apparently prompted increased respect from GOP campaign leaders. Moreover, McCarthy's home state, which had gone for Truman in 1948, possessed closely contested electoral votes which were of strategic importance to Republican hopes. The state party had been badly rent by Eisenhower's victory over Taft, a situation which made it unwise to make further enemies (or neutrals). Arthur Summerfield, Chairman of the Republican National Committee, and Tom Coleman, formerly Taft's chief campaign aide, kept pressure on the candidate for a pro-McCarthy position. Conferring with Eisenhower in September, Governor Kohler emphasized that the Democrats were making an issue of "McCarthyism" and advised the General to bring the debate back to the real question: communist infiltration.[32]

The crosscurrents swirled more rapidly as Eisenhower edged across the heartland of the Chicago *Tribune*. On October 2, the eve of his visit to Wisconsin, as the candidate's train lay over in Peoria, McCarthy, Kohler, and Wisconsin's national committeeman, Henry Ringling, flew down from Madison. The General first spoke— secretly—with McCarthy; according to the Senator, they did not discuss the contents of the upcoming Milwaukee speech. Eisenhower had determined that during the first whistle stop in Wisconsin he would clarify his views regarding McCarthy's methods and his own idea about fighting communism. The next morning, as Eisenhower recalled it, he had a "somewhat strained interview" with McCarthy. When Ike stated his intentions, the Senator warned that the audience "will boo you." Bridling, the General declared that the prospect did not deter him.[33]

At Green Bay, Eisenhower asked his listeners to back the entire GOP ticket. McCarthy, waiting nervously, smiled broadly. His elation was short-lived, however, for Eisenhower next stated that his "differences" with the Senator were "well known." They disagreed not over the goal of "ridding this government of incompetents, the dishonest and above all the subversive and disloyal," but over "method." The culprits could be ousted, Ike claimed, "while we preserve the right of trial by jury and the principle that people are innocent until proven guilty." McCarthy shook his head disapprovingly at these remarks. In McCarthy's home town of Appleton, the next stop, Eisenhower again plumped for the whole Republican slate, made no specific reference to McCarthy, and implied that one way to defeat communism was to enact social-welfare legislation. At Neenah-Menasha, he endorsed the GOP ticket in even vaguer terms. Nevertheless, the day's excursion brought relief to a number of worried Wisconsin Republicans.[34]

Milwaukee, where Ike was to speak that night, presented the ultimate test. On the trip south from Lake Winnebago, Governor Kohler discussed with Sherman Adams the contents of the evening's speech. The latest draft, it was widely known, included a paragraph declaring General Marshall to be imbued with "singular selflessness and the profoundest patriotism" and criticized intimations to the contrary as a "sobering lesson of the way freedom must *not* defend itself." Kohler argued that the paragraph was out of context and inopportune for the time and place. He persuaded Adams and General Wilton B. Persons that it should be omitted; Eisenhower concurred, remarking that the passage merely reiterated what he had already said in Denver.[35]

After several more alterations were made, the resultant speech obscured more than it delineated the differences between Eisenhower and McCarthy; it appeared to be an attempt by the General to envelop the Senator's supporters and to appropriate the communist issue for the national ticket. "He has met the enemy," the New York *Post* headlined, "and he is theirs." Eisenhower ran through the old, well-rummaged stock—"agrarian reformers," "red herrings"—and went far toward accepting the McCarthyite premise of Democratic "treason." As earlier in the day, the cheering was strongest when Ike seemed to agree with McCarthy and weakest when he tried to distinguish his stand from the Senator's. The days's trials were encapsulated in the General's leave-taking. He accepted the applause, pumped Senator Wiley's hand effusively, then, as he turned to go, reached across a six-foot gap to clasp McCarthy's outstretched hand. It was, as one reporter put it, a "strange handshake." [36]

The occupants of the "Look Ahead Neighbor" Special sighed with relief after the train left Wisconsin. "We've been through the valley of the shadow," one of the candidate's aides declared. Having made the reconciliations necessary to bind the frayed party together, Eisenhower would once again court the discontented independents. For the rest of the campaign, Ike's crusade would wend its way solely through sunny uplands. "The general's compromises," pledged another anonymous advisor, "are all behind him." "From now on you'll hear more of the old Ike." [37]

In Duluth, first stop over the state line, the General took care to explain that "when we go after corruption or Communism we do it in the American way." In Salt Lake City, he criticized anticommunist zeal "that takes no account of our civil liberties." "We cannot pretend to defend freedom with weapons suited only to the arsenal of tyrants." To a Newark audience he praised General Marshall and stressed his own independence—he had, he said, made no "deals" with anyone.[38] On the day before a nationally televised speech by McCarthy, Ike recorded his opposition to the use of "irresponsible smears." In Chicago, he promised again to expunge "communist contamination" from government, but he differentiated himself from "those who believe that any means are justified by the end of rooting out communism." A day later, he made the same guarantee, while ruling out "witch hunts or character assassination." [39] Although Eisenhower blamed the Democrats for permitting communist infestation and attacked Stevenson for dismissing that issue as an uproar over officials of the Bureau of Wildlife and Fisheries, there was an element of temperateness to his attack. He did his red-baiting with single-gang hooks.

Other Republicans used less measured phrasing in their indictments. Very early it appeared that the GOP would portray the position of the Democratic candidate as lying far to the left, blending with socialism and merging, unintentionally perhaps, with communism. The association of several Stevenson advisors with the Americans for Democratic Action provided grist for Republican mills. National Chairman Summerfield declared that the choice of Wilson Wyatt as campaign manager "clearly demonstrates that the ultra-left-wingers . . . will have complete charge of [Stevenson's] campaign." Speechwriters Arthur M. Schlesinger, Jr., and Archibald

MacLeish received comparable pummeling. Noting the Republican concern with his dangerous liaisons, Stevenson expected momentarily, he said, to be declared "the 'captive' of a girl named Ada." [40]

The Republicans also castigated the Illinois Governor for having executed a character deposition for Alger Hiss. Governor McKeldin of Maryland declared the subject a "legitimate . . . point of attack." Senator Jenner predicted: "If Adlai gets into the White House, Alger gets out of the jail house." Both, after all, were "a couple of Ivy League boys who made good in the State Department under Secretary Dean Acheson." Not to be outdone, McCarthy suggested that if Stevenson rather than Nixon had served on HUAC, Hiss might be Secretary of State or a presidential candidate. [41]

Richard M. Nixon received primary jurisdiction over the communist issue. At first, the Californian was content to link Stevenson with "the Truman gang"; he deferred comment on the Hiss deposition until he had had a chance to digest the full transcript of the trial. In the meantime, he challenged the Governor to state "wherein he disagrees with the Truman-A.D.A.-Wyatt program." He found Stevenson unfit to be President because he had "ridiculed and poohpoohed the Communist threat from within." Responding to Stevenson's comment that many of the alleged reds of whom the Republicans orated were "phantoms," Nixon inquired whether that label was applicable to Hiss, Lee Pressman, Nathan Witt, John Abt, and Julian Wadleigh. Yet all this was prologue: Nixon confided that his "real slugging" would begin on September 15. [42]

Soon after that date, Nixon found himself on the defensive; on September 20, the first "Nixon Fund" stories appeared, carrying the implication that the $18,000 fund subscribed to by friendly California businessmen for political expenditures had obligated the Senator to certain "interests." Waiving the question of the fund's propriety, Nixon defended himself in the rhetoric of anticommunism. As he ended a whistle stop in Marysville, a bystander cried, "Tell us about the $16,000." Ordering the train to hold up, Nixon exclaimed that the "crooks and Communists have another guess coming if they think they can stop this attack." He had been warned that if he persisted in exposing these villains, "they would continue to smear me." Later, Nixon was greeted with a sign cautioning, "S-h-h-h. Anyone who mentions $16,000 is a Communist." McCarthy came to his colleague's support: "The left wing crowd hates Nixon because of his conviction of Alger Hiss." He noted that James Wechsler, editor of the New York *Post,* which broke the story, had admitted having once belonged to the Young Coummunist League.[43]

In his ultimate rejoinder, the famous "Checkers" speech, Nixon sketched a Horatio Alger background, pursued the cocker-spaniel and cloth-coat vote and, with proper intimations of martyrdom, confessed his awareness that this would not be "the last of the smears." Some of the same columnists and commentators, he recalled, "were violently opposing me at the time I was after Alger Hiss." Undeterred, he read the Democratic record—600 million souls lost to communism, 117,000 casualties in Korea, and Stevenson's minimizing of the internal communist threat. "I say that a man who says that isn't qualified to be president of the United States." [44]

His position on the ticket reaffirmed, Nixon went on to advocate the party's cause with vigor. He soft-peddled the "corruption" issue and placed more emphasis on the topic of communism. He would rather have a general in the White House, a "khaki-clad President than one clothed in State Department pinks," he declared. As for foreign policy, he classified Stevenson as "Adlai the appeaser," who "carries a Ph. D. from Dean Acheson's cowardly college of Communist containment." "Somebody had to testify for Alger Hiss," Nixon conceded, "but you don't have to elect him President of the United States." In Wisconsin, he endorsed his "good friend, Joe McCarthy," and in Minnesota he charged that if Truman and the State Department "had their way, the traitor-spy Alger Hiss would be free today and voting for the Truman candidate." Nixon's rhetoric had a more strident tone than did the more balanced cadences of Eisenhower.[45]

Perhaps because of the welter of other voices, McCarthy played a less prominent role on the national level than might have been expected. He inflated his rhetoric accordingly. He bragged that he had researchers combing Stevenson's past to uncover not just "association," but "collaboration" with Hiss. If, after they heard what McCarthy planned to reveal, "the American people want Gov. Stevenson, they can have him." "If you'll give me a slippery elm club and put me aboard Adlai Stevenson's campaign train," he stated in his most notable oratorical excess, "I could use it on some of his advisors and I might be able to make a good American out of him." [46]

Only once, however, when he gave a speech over network television, did the Wisconsin Senator break in on the coverage given to the national campaign. His assiduously ballyhooed performance of October 27 was sponsored by a group of midwestern businessmen headed by Robert E. Wood, the Sears Roebuck magnate and former principal in the America First organization. For his "very carefully documented history" of the Democratic nominee's past seventeen years, McCarthy shuffled together a gaggle of falsehoods, half-truths, and harmless truisms. He blamed Stevenson for the American policy during World War II which sought to force the Italians to accept Communists in a coalition government. (The policy had been precisely the opposite.) He "exposed" Stevenson's membership in the Institute of Pacific Relations; the well-known character reference for Hiss; the Governor's alleged (but disproved) sponsorship of Hiss at a Northwestern University forum; the Daily Worker's support of his candidacy (again, not true). In a calculated "slip" of the tongue, one which he had made on at least four prior occasions, he referred to "Alger—I mean Adlai." [47] The address, which droned on forty minutes past the allotted half-hour of network coverage, disappointed its sponsors; one irately labeled it "a waste of time as well as money." Newsday declared it "the biggest television bust since Dagmar" and, in a similar vein, Alben Barkley commented: "The lightning flashed, the thunder roared—and killed a chigger." [48]

Democratic strategists who believed that McCarthy was a liability to the GOP could find confirmation of their views in the tepid reaction to the Senator's Chicago speech. Implicit in some Democratic rhetoric and, presumably, planning, was the assumption that linking McCarthy with the Republican national ticket would benefit the Democrats. Stories trickled out of Stevenson headquarters to the effect that Eisenhower's association with McCarthy and other members of the Class of '46 would turn fair-minded independents away from the Republican candidate. Confidence that raising the charge of McCarthyism would gain votes for Stevenson was alloyed, however, with a degree of trepidation; no one took the Wisconsinite's talents for granted. Still, even the less sanguine Democrats perceived that since the Republicans were attacking on the communist issue, it was essential to reinforce that part of the line.[49] To be sure, the Democrats did not give their main emphasis to this issue. As November approached, they stressed economic and social-welfare issues and concentrated on reintegrating the old party coalition built up under FDR. "Don't Let Them Take It Away" became a Democratic theme song. In St. Paul, Governor Stevenson avowed that he did not want to "run against Herbert Hoover," but then proceeded more or less to do so.[50]

Yet even with their recourse to bread-and-butter questions, the Democrats, particularly Stevenson, devoted considerable attention to McCarthy and his activities. In his message to the American Legion, the Governor warned against those "who use 'patriotism' as a club for attacking other Americans." He belittled the "men who hunt Communists in the Bureau of Wild Life and Fisheries while hesitating to aid the gallant men and women who are resisting the real thing in the front lines of Europe and Asia," thus sounding the recurrent Democratic theme that GOP isolationism obstructed the fight against communism. His opponent, Stevenson noted with distress, "included on his team people who have called General Marshall . . . a traitor to his country." Stevenson rejected "the proposition that party regularity is more important than political ethics." In horror he surveyed the "murderers row" of potential committee chairman in a Republican Senate: McCarthy, Capehart, Cain, and others of the Old Guard. In McCarthy's home state, the Governor made a plea to the Wisconsin tradition of progressive tolerance and warned of those who "in the name of anticommunism would assail the community of freedom itself . . . by pillorying the innocent." Acknowledging Ike's endorsement of McCarthy and criticism of his own campaign humor, the Democrat declared: "My opponent has been worrying about my funnybone. I'm worrying about his backbone." The General, he chided, was "a Taft Republican in Ohio, a Dirksen Republican in Illinois, a Jenner Republican in Indiana, a McCarthy Republican in Wisconsin." [51]

The Illinois Governor's campaign utterances contained another, more defensive theme. Accepting the salience of the loyalty-security issue, Stevenson and his supporters argued that their party had taken effective action, whereas the Republicans, mere naysayers, talked the game of anticommunism but rarely played it. "We have tightened up our espionage and security legislation," the nominee proclaimed. "We have instituted a Federal Loyalty system—and we did so . . . three long years before the Senator from Wisconsin made his shrill discovery of the Communist menace." It was the Democratic Congressman John F. Kennedy, he proudly noted, "and not Senator Nixon who got the first contempt citation of a Communist [Harold Christoffel, a Milwaukee labor leader] for perjury." Deriding vigilante-style anticommunism, Stevenson declared the fight against disloyalty to be "a job for professionals" like the FBI and "an infinitely tougher and harder battle" than most Republicans comprehended. Contrasting Truman's resolute stand against communism in Korea with the carping of critics, Stevenson wondered whether the GOP might be charging Truman and Stalin with having been "boyhood friends in outer Mongolia" if the President had not intervened.[52]

Stevenson also combined the communist issue with the Democrats' campaign staple—memories of the dismal thirties. The Republican bungling which fastened the Depression upon the country afforded communism "it's first real chance in America," he reasoned. "Once the laissez-faire Kismet boys start swinging away at the economic defenses we have enacted . . . anything could happen." Pursuing the line that the GOP and the Bolsheviks were each other's best allies, he argued that the "mentality of the Republican party in foreign trade has been well assessed by Stalin." Republican cries that present prosperity was based on war echoed "the Kremlin story." The "economic reactionaries" and "isolationists" were "allies of communism . . . even if they don't know it." [53]

Additionally, Stevenson answered Republican use of the communist issue, particularly their criticism of his character deposition for Hiss, with *tu quoque* arguments. The National Volunteers for Stevenson produced "tangible evidence" that Eisenhower had had "faith" in Hiss—otherwise he would not have consented in 1948 to serve as a trustee of the Carnegie Endowment for International Peace, of which Hiss was president. Similarly, the General had not objected to the trustees' refusal to accept Hiss's resignation when he first came under fire. If anything, Ike was "more vulnerable" than Adlai on the issue. In his fullest reply to the charge of fraternizing with Hiss, Stevenson suggested that if the Republicans "were to apply the same methods" to Eisenhower and John Foster Dulles as to himself, "they would find that both these men were of the same opinion" about Alger Hiss "and more so." Dulles, as chairman of the Carnegie trustees, had initially found "no reason to doubt Mr. Hiss' complete loyalty." The Governor did not mean to imply that either man was "soft toward Communists," but to demonstrate how "the mistrust, the innuendoes, the accusations" of the Republicans imperiled the "integrity of our institutions." [54]

John Sparkman, the vice-presidential candidate, employed an approach to the issues of communism and McCarthyism similar to Stevenson's. The Alabama Senator countered Republican charges of weakness toward Russia by quoting Ike's 1945 statement that "nothing guides Russian policy so much as a desire for friendship with the United States." He asserted that "there are more Communists and Communist infiltrators" from Eisenhower's own Columbia University "than from any other school in the United States." [55] McCarthyism, he said, was a grave moral flaw in the "so-called great crusade," and he criticized Eisenhower for hobnobbing with Jenner and McCarthy, the vilifiers of General Marshall. He was certain that Americans would not "stomach a crusade" joined by such men.[56]

President Truman enjoyed a still more vigorous workout with these rhetorical exercises; there was a sharper edge to his criticism of Eisenhower than to the language of other Democrats. The President leaned heavily into the charge that Ike had deserted his old friend Marshall by endorsing Jenner and McCarthy.* Truman had no patience for a man who would surrender to such "moral pygmies." Eisenhower, he claimed, had thereby "compromised every principle of personal loyalty." [57] He found Eisenhower's anticommunism insufficiently obdurate—as allegedly shown in the 1945 statement that the Soviets sought peace and friendship. Since the General's advice had "carried great weight" at the time, it "did a great deal of harm"

---

* Truman's acerbity was part of his style, but it may have been accentuated by his reported sense of betrayal at the hands of a man he had once respected and trusted. Eisenhower's treatment of General Marshall particularly vexed Truman, in whose lexicon of virtues personal loyalty ranked high. *New York Times,* Oct. 12, 1952; Washington *Post,* Oct. 11, 12, 1952; Charles S. Murphy Oral History Interview (Truman Library), p. 49. Cf. Edward T. Folliard Oral History Interview (Truman Library), p. 53.

(the nature of which Truman did not elaborate). The cocky Missourian stated that after the Potsdam Conference he had instructed Ike to work out the details of American access to Berlin; Eisenhower delegated the chore and the result, said Truman, was a flimsy oral agreement rather than a firm written one. Furthermore, the President alleged, Eisenhower as Chief of Staff had recommended withdrawal of U.S. troops from Korea in 1947—a decision which the Republican candidate was now attacking.[58]

Truman extolled the effective anticommunism of his administration. His party, he noted, had cured the Depression, whereas the GOP had fought all reform measures as "communistic." The Democrats had expedited the effective work of the FBI in capturing spies, had jailed key Communist leaders, had obtained hundreds of convictions for perjury and contempt,* and had instituted the federal loyalty program.[59] In recent months, he bragged, "we have been indicting and convicting the Communist conspirators and putting them where they belong—in jail." The Democrats, he exulted, had "stopped the advance of communism all over the globe." The Republicans, by contrast, in condoning McCarthy's activities were guilty of exploiting the "Big Lie"—a tool used by Hitler and Stalin.[60] In the event of a GOP victory, Truman predicted "A wave of smear and fear"—not to mention a "third world war" and a possible return to depression. "You cannot trust your human rights," he warned, "to a party that is running on the coattails of Joe McCarthy." [61]

While the Democratic willingness to grapple with McCarthy and the issues he personified bespoke a degree of confidence, a note of fear also insinuated itself into the debate, for the Democrats remained aware of the Senator's reputation as a political heavy. In Maryland, Truman conjured up memories of the 1950 "back street" campaign. "I don't know what sort of composite pictures or other frauds they

* During the autumn the Justice Department was in active pursuit of Communists. Its internal security section added new staff; among them was Roy Cohn, who had helped prosecute the Rosenbergs and would shortly join McCarthy's stable. Eighteen second-echelon Communist leaders were indicted under the Smith Act in September; the Earl Browders were arraigned for perjury in connection with passport applications; and the Attorney General moved with more than deliberate speed for the deportation of eight prominent Party members. There is no evidence that these vigorous steps were more than coincidental to the campaign; in any case, their impact upon the election was imperceptible. *New York Times,* Sept. 5, Oct. 1, 23, 1952.

are going to try to put off on you this year. But I am sure they will try something of the sort." The President remarked later that McCarthy, in his October 27 telecast, had tried "to see if he could do to Governor Stevenson what was done to Senator Tydings." When a New York advertising executive's plan for a radio-television "blitz" for Ike in the last days of the campaign was publicized, such Stevensonians as Senator Fulbright and George W. Ball feared that it portended a parallel to the Maryland campaign, down even to the composite photo. (Ball saw a similarity between the 1950 composite and a proposal to splice taped questions from local citizens together with canned answers by Eisenhower.) In anticipation of McCarthy's television extravaganza, Stevenson declared that Eisenhower must accept responsibility for the perpetration of "calumny" and, in a phrase applied to the Maryland election, "the big doubt." He warned New England crowds to expect "perhaps the most magnificent of all smears of all time." [62]

A prominent figure of speech in the Democrats' national campaign, McCarthy also served as the chief target of Democrats in Wisconsin. His opponent Fairchild asserted that the Senator had "done nothing about communism but shout about it." The election, Fairchild warned, would "go far far toward determining whether we give the green light to a home grown gestapo . . . or whether we stop this ugly threat to American freedom." Fairchild stressed that McCarthy exploited the communist issue to distract attention from a sorry voting record, to which the Democrats gave considerable attention. However, Fairchild's campaign was circumscribed by the fact that McCarthy had developed a patent on anticommunism. "No one is more opposed to communism than I am," Fairchild asserted; but no one was more directly identified with anticommunism than McCarthy. Democratic strategists recognized the latter fact, but they could do little about it. [63]

The confident Senator waged a considerable portion of his campaign through proxies—including Robert Vogeler, the businessman who had been imprisoned by the Czechs on spurious charges of spying, Arthur Bliss Lane, a former Ambassador to Poland, and Harvey Matusow, a confessed ex-Communist. [64] McCarthy spent much of his time campaigning for others. His stunning primary victory had convinced party leaders of his usefulness, and within the week he had been invited to take his case into other states. His efforts were bent primarily toward the election of senatorial candidates; although he had a kind word for Nixon, who, he said, "knows a Communist when he sees one," he offered little more than bland endorsements for the party's presidential candidate.[65]

McCarthy's travels took him into thirteen different states. In Arizona, he criticized Senator McFarland for opposing his attempts to uncover Communists. In a later appearance, he shared the platform with McFarland's foe, Barry Goldwater.[66] In Nevada, he came to the aid of Senator George ("Molly") Malone, who was locked in a close race with Thomas Mechling, an upstart Democrat who had triumphed over the McCarran machine in the primary. At a public forum in Las Vegas, McCarthy inadvertently labeled the local editor Hank Greenspun an "ex-Communist" (he meant "ex-convict"); he beat a hasty retreat after Greenspun seized the microphone for a half-hour's refutation and counterattack. He campaigned in Wyoming for Frank Barrett against Senator Joseph C. O'Mahoney and in Montana for Senator Zales Ecton against his challenger, Congressman Mike Mansfield. He did not accuse Mansfield of being a Communist agent, but since the Democrat had once received the praise of the *Daily Worker*, he must be "either stupid or a dupe." In Washington, McCarthy lauded Senator Harry Cain as "perhaps more hated by Communists, Communistic and fellow-traveler elements than any man alive." [67]

From surface indications, McCarthy's western swing seemed less than a rousing success. His Las Vegas meeting was assessed as falling somewhere between a "fiasco" and a "debacle." His speech at a Riverton, Wyoming, picnic, while well received, was followed by an outbreak of food poisoning. In Washington, his efforts received treatment unbecoming the knight-errant of anticommunism. One talk had to be delivered by telephone after fog grounded his plane; when he tried to make a serious address at the Washington Press Club gridiron dinner, he was heckled by the celebrants, who insisted on humorous fare. "I didn't come 2,300 miles to be a funnyman," he fumed. He left early to keep another engagement only to find that a Seattle television station refused to carry his speech because he declined to excise certain possibly slanderous allegations.[68]

McCarthy also spoke in several midwestern senatorial campaigns.

On October 31, he offered a rehash of his Chicago speech to assist James Kem of Missouri in his uphill battle against Stuart Symington. Earlier, in Michigan, he spoke for Congressman Charles Potter, who was seeking to displace Senator Blair Moody, and for his friend Alvin Bentley, a candidate for Congress. In Indiana, he lauded Senator Jenner, who was "guilty" only of being "a great American," for having become the target of the "Eastern bleeding hearts." Jenner, Nixon, and himself, McCarthy claimed, were opposed by the "Communists, pinks and fellow travelers." In West Virginia, on behalf of former Senator Chapman Revercomb, he criticized the Truman administration for cutting a recent wage increase won by coal miners. Leon Keyserling, whom he had previously accused of procommunist leanings, was, the Wisconsinite asserted, "instrumental" in the settlement.[69] Although McCarthy did not go to North Dakota, his recorded voice termed "entirely untrue" the charges that his friend Senator William Langer was "a communist, socialist, fellow traveler" or "a front man for various subversive organizations." If Langer had voted against the McCarran Act, "as he had a right to do," so had "such outstanding men" as Lehman, Green, Murray, and "perhaps the most outstanding foe of communism in the Senate," Dennis Chavez.[70]

McCarthy journeyed twice to Connecticut, where his archenemy William Benton faced a challenge from William Purtell (also a Senator, having been appointed to the seat of the late Brien McMahon). McCarthy spoke at Bridgeport and Danbury in September, making no direct references to Benton but promising that his fight with the Reds would get "rougher and rougher." He had been invited to appear by a local group of Republicans, not by the state party leaders; the latter, unenthusiastic about the proffered aid, grudgingly turned out to welcome him. Purtell had stated that he had no time for the McCarthy-Benton "feud" and would "beat Mr. Benton without any help from anybody." But he conceded, as he introduced McCarthy at Bridgeport, "Communism is a paramount issue." Prescott Bush, running for the other Senate seat, prefaced McCarthy's talk with a partial disclaimer that there were "many, like myself, who approve heartily of his goals but hold reservations at times concerning his methods." For his principles, the crowd booed Bush. Later in the campaign, at Waterbury, McCarthy declared that "little Bill Benton" was "worth a hundred million dollars to the Kremlin on the floor of the United States Senate." [71]

McCarthy had no monopoly on the communist issue, however; others exploited it energetically both in races in which he intervened and in those he ignored. The Missouri campaign of Senator Kem offered some of the most full-blown red-baiting. Kem also accused his foe, Stuart Symington, of having been a war profiteer; of being a cosmopolite, "the idol of New York cafe society"; of having gone to Yale (Kem did not mention his own studies at Harvard Law School); of having commenced his campaign after a sinister meeting with a British banker (not a Rothschild, alas) in Bermuda. He claimed that Symington was a "personal friend, a crony and intimate of William Sentner," a labor leader recently arrested as a member of the Communist Party. "Does Symington deny," taunted Kem, "that on innumerable occasions he took Sentner to luncheon and dinner at a downtown club in St. Louis, that he and Sentner played golf together and visited in each other's homes?" (As a business executive Symington had had to deal with Sentner's union. They had broken bread together, but never par.)[72]

In a fashion typical of Democratic attacks on members of the Class of '46, if more vigorously, Symington labeled his rival "the most reactionary isolationist" in that reactionary, isolationist group; Kem's opposition to the Marshall Plan, aid to Greece, and NATO showed him sharply at odds with Ike's bipartisan views. The incumbent's votes, Symington argued, were "strikingly similar" to those of Vito Marcantonio, which in turn were the "key to the wishes of the Politburo." (Symington did not "mean to imply" that Kem was a Communist, only that isolationism was "strikingly similar to the Communist party line.") He also accused Kem of "following the tactics" of that "arch-priest of character assassination in the North."[73]

In Washington, Joe Stalin's candidacy was less obvious. Senator Cain did not claim that Representative Henry Jackson was "a Communist" or belonged to "Communist front organizations"; but his opponent had gone along with congressional left-wingers in the surrender of China to the Communists in 1944–1945 and had "approved each step the Administration took on the road to Korea." Jackson, in turn, derided Cain's red-baiting as "the last plaintive cries of a politician going down for the last time." Cain might be "A swashbuckling enemy of Communism when he talks to a luncheon club, but when he gets down to hard votes in the Senate he isn't much of a fighter." In the gubernatorial contest between Arthur Langlie, seeking reelection, and Congressman Hugh Mitchell, there were exchanges over the challenger's ADA affiliation. Langlie warned against candidates who "play footsie with Communists and their dupes." [74]

Montana provided parallels to Washington, including the emphasis on China. Senator Ecton attacked the Democrats' Asian policies and linked his rival Mike Mansfield, who had participated in a wartime mission to China, to them. He termed Mansfield a "captive candidate of the Truman-Acheson gang" who was "duped by people in the State Department." Mansfield's tough talk against Andrei Vishinsky while a member of the American delegation to the UN was a "political deathbed repentance"; it could not erase his efforts to force Chiang Kai-shek into a coalition with the Communists nor his naivete in assuming the latter to be "peace-loving agrarian reformers." Mansfield contrasted his debates with Vishinsky and his introduction of a bill outlawing the Communist Party to Ecton's "failure to take definite action against Communism." [75]

In Arizona, Barry Goldwater raised the issues of spending, socialism, corruption, and Korea against Ernest McFarland, who, as Senate Majority Leader, was closely identified with the Truman administration's vulnerabilities. Goldwater pronounced it "time we drive Communists and Communist sympathizers" from government and "time we quit bending on our knees to Russia." "I haven't heard my New Deal opponent . . . mention one thing about running Communists out of the halls of Washington," he avowed. Pressing for a reversal of the current "appeasement" policy in Korea, he advocated the use of Nationalist Chinese troops ("they may not be the best troops in the world, but they are not American boys either"). McFarland's flaccid campaign failed to match that of the aggressive Goldwater. On November 1, he was rebutting statements his adversary had made in March. His standard rejoinder was to ask the Republicans "which socialistic measure" they intended to alter. [76]

In Indiana, Senator Jenner faced the popular Democratic Governor Henry Schricker, to whom the early polls gave the lead. Consequently, notwithstanding the fact that the staunchly isolationist Jen-

ner disagreed with the foreign-policy views held by Eisenhower, he
clutched for the candidate's coattails. "It was an inspiration to discover that Gen. Eisenhower and I see eye to eye" on the major issues, he declared. Jenner also associated himself with McCarthy;
they both, he claimed, had been "marked for liquidation by an administration which . . . consorts openly with Reds and Pinks." Jenner campaigned stridently against the Korean War, fought, he lamented, under the "spider-web flag" of the UN. If the Democrats
won, "the bodies of thousands more American boys will be tossed on
Truman's funeral pyre in Asia." In response to Schricker's charge
that his isolationism threatened relations with America's allies, Jenner cried: "We have no allies worthy of the name"—only "destitute
relatives with their hands in our pockets." He stressed that his opponent had vouched for Stevenson (having nominated him at the Democratic convention), while Stevenson in turn had vouched for Hiss,
"his Harvard Law School crony." If Schricker and Stevenson were
elected, "the Red network will continue to work secretly and safely
for the destruction of the United States." [77]

In Ohio, similar charges were bandied, but in somewhat more temperate language. Senator John Bricker labeled the Korean War "un-
constitutional"; he demanded a halt to "trading the blood of American boys for synthetic propaganda to elect Harry Truman or his
satellites." He charged that the Truman administration ignored the
threat of Communist infiltration and argued that "hundreds of persons who were dangerous . . . are now out of federal service because of Joe McCarthy." Michael V. DiSalle, one-time mayor of
Toledo and former director of the Office of Price Stabilization, criticized Bricker's isolationist votes, which had "weakened Europe's
capacity to resist Communist encroachment." He chided his rival for
"clubbiness" with the McCarthy-Jenner-Kem-Malone axis endorsed
by McCormick of the Chicago *Tribune*. [78]

In Michigan, Republican Congressman Charles Potter challenged
Senator Blair Moody. Aided by hearings which HUAC, of which he
was a member, had held in Detroit, Potter traded heavily on his identification with red-hunting. Following local custom, Potter classified
his opponent as a "captive of the little band of overlords who rule the
CIO" and a minion of the CIO-PAC, the ADA, and "Moscow-
trained" Walter Reuther. The voters could choose "between a man

who believes in fighting Communism and destroying it, and a man who would destroy the committee [HUAC] which is fighting Communism." Moody countered by pointing out Potter's frequent absences from his committee's sessions. He labeled Potter a lackey of the auto magnates and the NAM and a member of the "isolationist claque which rules the Michigan Republican congressional delegation." [79]

In Maryland, McCarthy's activities two years earlier sufficed to plant his impress lightly upon the campaign. The Republican senatorial candidate, J. Glenn Beall, decried the nation's headlong rush "down the path of precepts dictated by the teachings of Karl Marx." "We have got to slug it out, toe to toe," he warned, "with the parlor pinks and so-called liberals, who call themselves Democrats." He asserted that "we haven't scratched the surface yet" in the search for Reds in government and challenged his listeners to find "one charge that McCarthy ever made that he's been wrong on." Maryland's Democrats as well as a number of visiting party leaders frequently referred scathingly to the Butler campaign, counting on a presumed popular "revulsion" against the tactics used in 1950.[80]

As in Maryland, the GOP candidate for Senator in West Virginia banked heavily on the communist issue; it was, perhaps, Chapman Revercomb's chief weapon in his fight with Senator Harley M. Kilgore. He charged that his foe had "aided and appeased Communist causes" and "consistently taken a sympathetic and protective attitude" toward Reds in office and had a record of "continuous sympathy to the Communist thinkers." Kilgore stressed Revercomb's "reactionary isolationist" record during his term in the Senate (1943–1949), which showed that "he was not, as you might think from his speeches now, a leader in the fight to stop Communist aggression." [81]

Possibly the strangest epicycle of the campaign unfolded in Massachusetts, where neither Senator Henry Cabot Lodge, Jr., nor Congressman John F. Kennedy found much in the other's record against communism to criticize and where McCarthy's name was mentioned only in hushed tones. Though McCarthy was conspicuous by his absence, the anxieties he raised agitated the deeper currents of Bay State politics. Lodge's prominence as an Eisenhower backer had embittered conservative Taftites, who reportedly might either cut him or aid his Democratic foe. Two influential pro-Taft newspapers did, in fact, support Kennedy. Massachusetts was also presumed to contain many Democrats—Boston Irish—who approved of McCarthy. When Lodge allegedly had once asked the Democratic Governor, Paul Dever, about home-state reaction to his colleague, Dever had replied: "Your people don't like him, but unfortunately mine do." [82]

Kennedy did nothing to alienate such voters; to the chagrin of liberals, he failed to speak out on McCarthyism. It was no surprise that McCarthy did not electioneer for Lodge, for the two, notwithstanding the latter's endorsement of the Wisconsinite, had no rapport. More remarkably, several conservatives had a kind word for young Kennedy. Westbrook Pegler alleged that the Congressman "would be glad to embrace McCarthy on a platform in South Boston and the only consideration that prevents that is Joe's party loyalty, not any hypocrisy on Jack's part." Another journalist reported Kennedy's "great appeal to the same pro-American elements . . . that Lodge represented before he turned his coat." [83]

If undeserving of these encomiums, Kennedy did move cautiously. Late in the campaign, some of his liberal-academic advisors pressed him to speak in opposition to McCarthyism; Senator Benton complied with a request for material on McCarthy, but it was never used. On one occasion, the candidate's father Joseph P. Kennedy vociferously and effectively opposed an advertisement critical of McCarthy (whom he counted as a friend). The future president confined himself to writing to the American Civil Liberties Union of his concern over excesses perpetrated in congressional investigations and suggesting that committees hire counsel whose job would be to cross-examine the accusers on behalf of the accused. He conceded that some legislators had made irresponsible charges, but he concluded that "the ultimate remedy for all abuses of power lies in resort to . . . free debate and to the ballot box." [84]

In Connecticut, McCarthy's number-one target, Bill Benton, tried to make an asset of his opposition to the Senator. When McCarthy accused him of being worth money to the Kremlin, he tallied his support of the Voice of America, the Marshall Plan, Point Four, and defense spending against McCarthy's nonsupport of these programs and asked which of the two was the Kremlin's best investment. After McCarthy's second speech in Connecticut, Benton accused him of "following chapter and verse the instructions of the Communist party handbook on how to destroy a democracy." He hit the "cowardly compromise" Connecticut's Republicans had made with McCarthy and compared his own and his party's effective anticommunism (collective security, defense, and an end to "bread lines") with the GOP's "hot air method" of fighting the battle.[85]

Throughout much of the campaign, however, the interest of Connecticut was focused on the presidential race. State Republicans pinned their hopes on Eisenhower's ability to generate support for the entire ticket. William Purtell dealt with national issues, notably Korea, which the election of Ike would resolve, and with local problems. ("The clock industry has little for which it can thank the Truman Administration.") Until Benton began linking him to the conservative views expressed by the Connecticut Manufacturers' Association (of which he had once been president), Purtell paid little heed to his opponent. Purtell castigated his foe for this resort to "smear by implications" and "accusations of guilt by association, something which he has piously protested against." [86] Aside from this acrimony, Purtell restricted himself to attacks on the Truman regime, while Benton ran primarily against McCarthy, Taft, Hoover, and to some degree Eisenhower. Benton wrestled strenuously with the communist issue (one advertisement credited him with "four right hooks to Joe Stalin's jaw"), but Purtell left the question to others. Connecticut provided a haven of relative gentility in a campaign which several observers considered worthy of comparison to 1928 in its bitterness.[87]

Interested onlookers eagerly awaited the November 4 returns to gauge the extent of McCarthy's appeal across the nation. The results were not impressive. In his own race, McCarthy's 870,000 votes provided 54 percent of the two-party total and an easy, but far from overwhelming, victory over Fairchild. McCarthy was low man on the ticket. He lagged behind Eisenhower, who captured 980,000 votes and 61 percent of the total in the presidential column. One reporter termed the outcome a "rebuke" to the Senator. The other GOP state candidates outdistanced both Ike and McCarthy; Fred Zimmerman, the perennial secretary of state who had registered outspoken opposition to McCarthy, amassed 66 percent of the votes in his contest. Compared to his 1946 showing, McCarthy maintained or increased his grip (measured by percentage of the vote) on only sixteen of the state's seventy-one counties. He ran poorly in the more urbanized counties and in union strongholds, and while he picked up significant support in strongly Catholic areas, the results did not appear to confirm the legendary appeal he was supposed to exert upon such voters. Czechs and Poles, for whom communism was a particularly trenchant issue, seem to have supported him, but his strength came primarily from the state's rural regions. The McCarthy vote derived largely from traditional, rural, conservative, organizational Republicans.[88]

The Wisconsin Senator's efforts on behalf of the Republicans in other states produced mixed results. James Kem of Missouri, Harry Cain of Washington, and Zales Ecton of Montana were defeated despite McCarthy's intervention. His assistance to ex-Senator Revercomb proved unavailing, as did his help to General Patrick J. Hurley of New Mexico. On the other hand, Arthur Watkins of Utah, Jenner of Indiana, and Malone of Nevada, all endorsed by McCarthy, were victorious. Several challengers backed by McCarthy—Barry Goldwater in Arizona, Frank Barrett in Wyoming, Charles Potter in Michigan, and William Purtell and Prescott Bush in Connecticut—also achieved election.

These results produced rejoicing among McCarthyites and chagrin among the Senator's adversaries, even though the causal link between McCarthy's intervention and the outcome was rarely clear. McCarthy's support probably did not hurt Jenner, who identified his cause with that of his colleague. McCarthy's appearance on behalf of Barrett, who was running against Senator O'Mahoney in Wyoming, made a "favorable impression," Senator Hunt noted ruefully. The Connecticut election provoked the greatest number of raised eyebrows and afforded McCarthy his greatest pleasure: "How do you like what happened to my friend Benton?" he inquired of an interviewer.[89]

However, Eisenhower's landslide victory proved far more influential in the Senate races than did McCarthy's activities. Nowhere was this more apparent than in Connecticut. Benton attributed his defeat to Ike's drawing power. He conceded that McCarthy might have swung some Irish votes to Purtell, a fact whose chief significance resided in its impact upon Democratic Party leaders, most of whom were Irish. Benton may have lost some Catholic support, but statis-

tical analysis failed to find a correlation between Catholicism and opposition to Benton. In any case, the McCarthy issue may have swung
two or three thousand votes, but that number was insignificant in
view of Benton's 88,000-vote margin of defeat.[90]

McCarthy's incursions produced no visible statistical damage to
the electoral standing of his Connecticut adversary. Benton's 1952
performance was roughly comparable to his 1950 showing: in both
years his percentage of the vote lagged behind that of the rest of the
Democratic ticket by a minute fraction; he managed to stay close to
the party "norm." Although he trailed the popular Congressman Abe
Ribicoff, who was contesting the state's other Senate seat, Benton
ran about 6,000 votes (1.7 percent) ahead of Adlai Stevenson. In
comparison to the lure of Eisenhower, all other influences, including
McCarthy, were minor; "in one easy phrase," Benton "got caught in
the Eisenhower landslide." [91]

The General's coattails exerted a similar pull in other Senate contests.[92] They apparently assured William Jenner's reelection.[93] Barry
Goldwater benefited from Ike's appeal (as well as from that of the
popular Governor Howard Pyle and from a two-year campaign in
which he traveled the equivalent of twice the circumference of the
world).[94] In Nevada, Senator Malone's narrow victory was facilitated
by Eisenhower's strong showing (and insured by the rift in the Democratic Party caused by the Mechling candidacy).[95] Eisenhower led the
ticket in Utah and aided the cause of Senator Watkins.[96] His popularity was "clearly the deciding factor" in O'Mahoney's loss to Governor Barrett in Wyoming.[97] Eisenhower's coattail influence may have
been more influential in the Western states than in the other sec-
tions.[98]

Far from assisting the recipients of his favor, McCarthy, according
to one analysis, actually impaired their prospects. By comparing the
1952 performances of McCarthy's political legatees to past GOP
strength in the states (and even counties) where the Wisconsin Senator campaigned, the political statistician Louis H. Bean found that
McCarthy-backed candidates ran an average of 5 percent behind the
Republican norm. Seemingly, a Democrat who faced an adversary
assisted by McCarthy could count on a five-percent advantage in the
two-party vote. Every Democrat opposed by McCarthy without exception ran ahead of Stevenson (and also improved upon Democratic

senate-race performances of past presidential years). In the Northern states which were not graced by McCarthy's presence, senatorial contestants ran about evenly with Stevenson.[99]

The Republican conservatives, including McCarthy's allies, generally fared poorly in 1952, while Republicans who took middle-of-the-road positions closer to Eisenhower's were more prolific vote-getters. Senate moderates like Ralph Flanders, Irving Ives, H. Alexander Smith, Edward Thye, and John Sherman Cooper usually ran better than conservatives such as Bricker, Jenner, Revercomb, Cain, Kem, Ecton, and Malone. The former group amassed an average vote of 54.3 percent, while the latter received an average vote of only 51.6 percent. Although only one right-wing Republican out of the thirteen running equaled Eisenhower's share of the two-party vote, of nine moderates, five bettered his mark.[100]

Polling statistics also indicate that the "pure" communist issue, emphasizing domestic infiltration, exercised less influence than McCarthy's allies or enemies anticipated. It generated more noise than substance. The authors of *The American Voter* found that the topic of domestic communism had little salience in 1952. While Korea and corruption, the first two elements of the K_1C_2 formula, were frequently mentioned in interviews, the issue of communism or subversion received even fewer mentions than did such esoteric subjects as Point Four or Adlai Stevenson's divorce. Louis Harris reached a similar conclusion: few people singled out domestic communism as a crucial problem unless they were "confronted" with it in the interview. A study of voting in the western states concluded that the issue of domestic communism was not "primary," was seldom volunteered by interviewees, and tended to be subsumed under broader concerns, such as the Korean War.[101]

McCarthy's strength lay in the fact that "his" issue could not be separated from the cluster of topics raised by the GOP in 1952; but his weakness stemmed from the fact that the communist problem was not dominant in the voters' consciousness. McCarthy was unquestionably popular among certain groups, particularly conservative, isolationist Germans, Irish, Poles, and, in Wisconsin at least, Czechs. He had some claim to the allegiance of Catholic voters, but it was by no means overwhelming.[102] The one true test of his vote-getting prowess, his own campaign in Wisconsin, produced modest results.

Thanks to his talent for publicity and its reflection in the media, Mc-Carthy possessed an appeal which struck deeply in spots, but not as widely as suspected.

Nonetheless, many politicians and observers exaggerated McCarthy's effectiveness at the grass-roots. Both the Senator's partisans and his critics overestimated his political impact. Westbrook Pegler, incensed at Eisenhower's standoffishness, warned that Joe was "one of the most popular Republicans in the country, with his own bandwagon capable of cruising far beyond the borders of his own Wisconsin." "Only the people are for him," the Indianapolis *Star* editorialized. "The political scalps dangling from his belt," claimed *Newsweek,* were "irrefutable evidence" of McCarthy's influence. Benton had "thought he could succeed where Tydings failed" and was returned to "private life" for his pains. William S. White cited respectfully the view of the Wisconsin Senator's friends that in two elections he had "influenced the success at the polls of no less than eight present Senators." Later, describing McCarthy as "The Man with the Power," White declared that the "political landscape" was "increasingly littered with the wreckage of anti-McCarthy careers." [103]

Whether from fear or from confidence in the righteousness of their own position on the communist issue and McCarthyism, the Democrats also exaggerated the salience of these concerns. If, as some Democrats assumed—and as statistics eventually confirmed—McCarthy was a GOP liability, it made sense to emphasize his role and sins. However, there is no evidence that it was the Democratic offensive against McCarthyism which made inroads upon Republican strength. Though such rhetoric showed the flag for liberalism, it may, equally, have granted McCarthy an importance beyond his due.* With that hindsight which has yet to lose an election, one might conjecture that the Democrats would have been wiser to play down the

* This would argue that McCarthy himself—not anti-McCarthy speeches—may have been worth votes to the Democrats. While McCarthy was an *apparent* liability to candidates he assisted, the correlations on which that assumption is based do not preclude the possibility that some other factor explains the results. Moreover, there was a curious nonmeshing between McCarthy's campaign and those of senatorial candidates whom he opposed. It was not so much these Democrats as the party's national leaders who spoke out against the Wisconsinite.

McCarthy-communism argument and hit harder the one issue which, according to various polls, the voters considered a positive party attribute—Democratic identification with prosperity and Republican association with the Depression.[104] Despite Stevenson's initial reluctance to run against Hoover, the Democrats eventually pitched their campaign in that direction and might have profited by further emphasis on the issue, although there is no reason to suspect that they were in danger of winning the election no matter what their tactics.

Given the silence of large sectors of the Democratic Party before the election and their return to passivity after the ballots were counted, how is the vocal anti-McCarthyism of the campaign to be explained, and why did it so quickly ebb? In the first place, a presidential campaign differs from the diurnal round of Senate activities. The Senate may not often have asserted itself against McCarthy, but the White House had roused itself, and Harry Truman had exchanged numerous salvos with McCarthy in the year prior to the election. During the campaign, Truman continued to supply a large portion of the Democrats' anti-McCarthy commentary; much of the rest issued from Stevenson, to a lesser extent his running mate, and his close supporters. With a few exceptions, the Senators who spoke out against McCarthy had, like Lehman, Kefauver, Benton, and Monroney, already acquired the habit.* The strong liberal-academic coloration of Stevenson's speechwriters and advisors helped shape the resolute anti-McCarthyism of his campaign. Also, despite the Governor's pains to remain free of the shadow of the Truman administration, the President's active barnstorming and the general thrust of Stevenson's campaign cemented a sort of "executive-branch" continuity with the administration on many issues, including McCarthyism. After the election, the Democrats tended to slip back toward inactivity under the influence of the congressional leaders with whom power now rested. They reasoned that McCarthy had, after all, been vindicated by his constituents and that he had become a "Republican problem."

* Other Senators who assailed McCarthy during the campaign were Robert Kerr, who was thus an exception to this generalization, and Hubert Humphrey, whose occasional previous demurrers regarding the Wisconsin Senator put him in a borderline category. Among administration officials who voiced criticism of McCarthy were Oscar Ewing, Charles Brannan, James McGranery, and Maurice Tobin.

During the months to come, despite the equivocal mandate with which McCarthy's campaign efforts had been crowned, his colleagues and members of the press continued to exaggerate his capacity to sway the American voter. Once again, the perception of power was taken for power itself and served to deter opposition. "There is no doubt that Senator McCarthy's power lies with his hold on public opinion," Senator Humphrey observed. "The fate of ex-Senators Tydings and Benton would indicate that opposing Senator McCarthy within the Senate—as a political matter—is not likely to succeed." [105]

Some of McCarthy's foes, perceiving that inflated estimates of his influence hampered their cause, strove to educate opinion leaders and Senators in the less impressive reality of the Wisconsinite's appeal. William Benton emphasized the need for refuting the "myth of invincibility" surrounding McCarthy. Soon the National Committee for an Effective Congress (NCEC), an organization becoming increasingly engaged in the fight against McCarthy, saw the utility of a "carefully detailed analysis" which would prove that McCarthy did not "defeat seven Senators" or "elect ten Senators." [106] The NCEC, Benton, and other interested parties commissioned such a study from Louis Bean, a former statistician with the Agriculture Department and noted political prognosticator. Ready in April 1954, the Bean pamphlet was distributed to Senators and White House insiders. It confirmed that McCarthy's electoral prowess had been overrated. A number of political leaders were impressed; it was "conceivable" that the pamphlet had some influence upon the Republican National Committee's decision not to use McCarthy in the 1954 campaign. [107] By that time, however, the information was secondary to events on Capitol Hill. Throughout most of McCarthy's reign as a national figure, his reputation as an electoral mover and shaker remained intact, with a consequent retardative effect upon Senate opposition.

CHAPTER 9

". . . A Republican Problem"

AT THE ONSET of the Eisenhower administration, the Democrats did not hasten to initiate conflict with the Senator from Wisconsin. Partisan considerations had much to do with their reticence, but they could also, if desirous, seek justification for their position in the expressed hopes of the administration's well-wishers. Eisenhower's supporters had argued that their candidate was the one man who could put a halter on Senator McCarthy. Walter Lippmann and other political commentators had reasoned that an Eisenhower victory would do more than anything else to quash McCarthyism. More partisan Republican sources concurred in that assumption. "[W]hen the regular branches of government function as they should," the Hartford *Courant* editorialized, "Senator McCarthy will emerge as a much less noteworthy figure than he was under the Truman Administration," to whose mishandling of the communist issue he owed his "speedy rise to national prominence." One columnist predicted that Eisenhower would "soon chop McCarthy down to size." [1]

Such hopeful predictions, however, did not allow for the remarkable passivity which Eisenhower maintained in his relations with McCarthy. Despite the tribulations McCarthy heaped on him, the new President persisted in the belief that the best solution to the problem was to "pursue a steady, positive policy in foreign relations, in legal procedures in cleaning out the insecure and disloyal, and in all other areas where McCarthy seems to take such a specific and personal interest." He felt he could not afford to "'name names." [2]

The administration had weighty reasons for avoiding a confrontation. Controlling the Senate by only a forty-eight to forty-seven margin, the Republicans knew that each seat was crucial to the preservation of their majority. The administration assumed it would have to squeeze out every last vote for its programs, a circumstance which augured tolerant treatment of McCarthy and other nettlesome legislators. Several of Eisenhower's advisors, including C. D. Jackson, Emmet John Hughes, and Robert Cutler, urged that the McCarthy issue be met vigorously. At the same time, other staff members, particularly those whose work demanded close contact with Congress, advocated a more noninterventionist policy toward McCarthy. White House aides General Wilton B. Persons and Bernard Shanley and Republican National Chairman Leonard W. Hall advocated a conciliatory line, lest the President's legislative program suffer. Hall warned Eisenhower to beware of those journalists who "tried to crucify every Congressman or Senator who has stuck his head above water in the fight against Communists in government." [3] Others, notably Vice-President Nixon, occupied an intermediate position, seeking to mute conflict between McCarthy and the White House, sometimes trying to restrain the Senator, at other times interceding on his behalf. [4]

Eisenhower's conception of his duties as President served to deter White House opposition to the Wisconsin Senator. Ike considered McCarthy primarily the Senate's responsibility and reasoned that presidential dictation to Congress regarding its own affairs would only stir resentment without achieving a solution. To a Congressman who bespoke support for a code of committee procedures to blunt McCarthyite investigative excesses, a White House aide replied: "The President feels strongly that the Executive should not intrude into matters that are within the exclusive province of the Legislative Branch. . . . You have probably noted how careful he has been not to comment on any Congressional investigation or the manner in which it might be conducted." Eisenhower also desired to return the Presidency to a dignity from which, by implication, it had lapsed in recent years. In furtherance of that goal, he refused to be drawn into personal conflict with McCarthy; as he reiterated in his press conferences, he would not "talk personalities." [5]

Strategically, too, Eisenhower believed a pugnacious policy to be ill-founded. "It is a sorry mess," he conceded, but "nothing would probably please [McCarthy] more than to get the publicity that would be generated by public repudiation by the President." When C. D. Jackson, the staunchest anti-McCarthyite on his staff, proposed a sharp reply to one of the Senator's attacks, Ike exclaimed: "I will not get into the gutter with *that* guy." [6] Throughout the final two years of McCarthy's ascendancy, Eisenhower generally hewed to that position, with the result that momentum remained with the Senator.

Although McCarthy's keener adversaries surmised that the administration's pattern of evasion and temporizing permitted the Senator to run further amok, certain Eisenhower supporters commended the General's forbearance; they theorized that when McCarthy had been given "enough rope," he would eventually hang himself.[7] The argument has plausibility. "How long, O how long?"—the Ciceronian question that might have been put at the opening of the Eisenhower administration—was answered in less than two years, which is not a long time, as demagogues go. Conceivably, a personal attack upon the Senator would only have strengthened him. On the other hand, Eisenhower's personal prestige was so immense that, in all probability, it could have overborne McCarthy. If, as the "enough rope" theory seemed to imply, a confrontation was inevitable, the sooner, one could argue, the better.

McCarthy promptly seized the initiative from the hesitant Executive branch and capitalized on the willingness of a number of Eisenhower's lieutenants, notably John Foster Dulles, to appease him. Dulles demanded "positive loyalty" of State Department employees, then shuffled uncertainly between assurances that the Foreign Service consisted primarily of unimpeachably patriotic, able men and hints that heads might roll. R. W. Scott McLeod, a McCarthy ally, was appointed chief security officer of the State Department.[8] John Doerfer, a home-state ally of McCarthy's, was appointed to the Federal Communications Commission. Barely had he taken office before he asked the White House to rule on whether or not the FCC should honor McCarthy's request for confidential records. Such goings-on could only provoke acutely arched eyebrows among those who knew the Senator's methods.[9]

After the Republican victory in November 1952, McCarthy had given some indications that, with his own party in power, he might restrain himself. "The situation's a lot different now," he had said, "with a good man president, and a Republican house and senate." As chairman-presumptive of the Committee on Government Operations and its Permanent Investigations Subcommittee, McCarthy encouraged inferences that he would shift his sights from communism to influence-peddling and corruption; not surprisingly he volunteered such intentions while colleagues were considering his committee's appropriation. But simultaneously he was jockeying to insure himself a leading role in the coming hunt for communists.[10]

The search for subversion stimulated a zeal comparable to that which sent the Sooners plunging into the Indian Territory—a fact attested to by the requests of some 185 of the 221 Republican Congressmen for assignment to the House Un-American Activities Committee. The incoming chairman of HUAC, Harold Velde, and William Jenner, who took over the Senate Internal Security Committee, both hastened to stake out claims. Under the ministrations of party leaders, Velde, Jenner, and McCarthy negotiated warily and mapped out a tentative division of labor; Jenner's group would be given primary jurisdiction over the communist problem, while McCarthy contented himself with secondary rights to the field. McCarthy's acquiescence allayed the misgivings of his colleagues sufficiently to ease through the Senate his committee's appropriation of $200,000, twice the amount voted to the panel in 1952. The only negative voice was that of Senator Allen Ellender, an inveterate economizer who predicted that the investigations would duplicate each other. Earlier, chuckling over the Wisconsin Senator's rear-corridor committee assignment, Robert Taft had confided: "We've got McCarthy where he can't do any harm." [11] A less accurate boast would be hard to imagine, for McCarthy was soon romping joyously across plots thought to be reserved for other committees.

Briefly, McCarthy's subcommittee delved into the administrative warrens which were its normal domain. Such mundane labors as a probe of welfare "chiselers," of improper influence in connection with a pipeline project, and of "bad buying" in the strategic materials stockpiling program did not engage the Senator's interest, however, and he shifted back to familiar pursuits. In February, as a sort of warm-up, his panel heard testimony that the State Department's personnel files were in grave disarray and that employees had virtually unimpeded access to their own dossiers.[12]

McCarthy moved on to the Voice of America. Long criticized by conservatives, the Voice and the entire State Department information program were in need of reorganization, proposals for which were under study. But McCarthy declined to give the new team or Dr. Robert Johnson, recently appointed to head the State Department's International Information Agency, a chance even to get settled. His subcommittee heard testimony from unhappy Voice employees. One woman recounted a job interview at which the personnel officer allegedly asked her to consider taking up a form of housekeeping or "collective living" short of marriage. Some functionaries implied that decisions to cut programming in certain languages or to alter the content of some scripts reflected ambivalent attitudes toward communism; others testified that the supposed mislocation of two Voice transmitters suggested that someone did not want to mount an effective broadcast program.[13]

McCarthy's subcommittee next placed the State Department's overseas libraries under scrutiny. On the pretext that their "pro-Communist" books were stocked in the libraries, McCarthy summoned witnesses ranging from the anticommunist editor James Wechsler, a trenchant critic, not coincidentally, of the Senator, to such left-wing perennials as Howard Fast and Dashiell Hammett, to Earl Browder. The International Information Agency (IIA), timid and vacillating, played into McCarthy's hands; on February 19 it circulated a memo proscribing the use of books by "Communists, fellow-travelers, et cetera." The next five months were consumed in interpreting and altering this and subsequent directives. From Germany James B. Conant, in amusement mingled with chagrin, called for clarification of "et cetera." IIA workers hastily removed numerous books from the libraries, including some by Foster Rhea Dulles, the Secretary's cousin, and even Whittaker Chambers's anticommunist testament, *Witness*. A few books were actually burned.[14] Meanwhile, Roy Cohn, the subcommittee's chief counsel, and G. David Schine, its unpaid chief consultant, embarked on a tour of IIA facilities in Europe which foreign observers found at once diverting and alarming. After six hours in London, the two envoys generously allowed that the American Ambassador there was doing a pretty good job; a brief stop in Bonn unearthed "millions of dollars worth of waste and mismanagement." All told, said Schine, it was an "extremely interesting" trip.[15]

In his relations with the Executive, McCarthy behaved almost as if Harry Truman still occupied his beloved White House sun porch. He stopped short of a public rupture with the administration over the appointment of James B. Conant as High Commissioner to Germany, but only because it "would not accomplish his defeat and would furnish . . . ammunition" to European Communists.[16] The sputtering fuse ignited, however, when Eisenhower nominated Charles Bohlen to be Ambassador to the Soviet Union. Bohlen, a career diplomat, had sinned by having been present at Yalta; he compounded the evil by refusing to repudiate that pact. Although the Secretary of State vouched for Bohlen's loyalty, McCarthy, with McCarran and Bridges, persisted in questioning it. McCarran and McCarthy asserted that McLeod, on the basis of Bohlen's FBI file, had not been able to recommend the appointment. When McCarthy asked that Dulles testify under oath, Taft termed the proposal "ridiculous." Finally, Taft and John Sparkman were delegated to inspect Bohlen's dossier; after they reported that it in no way impeached Bohlen's loyalty, the nomination was approved, seventy-four to thirteen. The administration had won, but the right wing had shown its capacity for obstruction. Taft, after gamely backing Eisenhower in the fight, informed the White House that there could be "no more Bohlens!" [17]

On March 28, 1953, just after the Bohlen skirmish, McCarthy announced his "Greek ship deal," by which he claimed to have persuaded several Greek shipping magnates to halt all trade with Communist China. Harold Stassen, Director of Mutual Security, promptly castigated McCarthy: the deal, he said, "undermines enforcement instead of helping it" by trampling in an area where the Executive branch was proceeding circumspectly. Secretary Dulles abruptly exposed Stassen's flank by conceding with some reservations that McCarthy's activities were "in the national interests," and Eisenhower undercut his subordinate by asserting that Stassen had not so much accused McCarthy of "undermining" foreign policy as of "infringement." Besides, said the President, McCarthy was not "negotiating" anything. "He can discuss, suggest, advise"—just so long, apparently, as he did not violate the imprecise semantic boundaries which surrounded "negotiate." Stassen initialed the articles of capitulation by agreeing that he had indeed meant "infringe" rather than "undermine." [18]

These persisting trials finally goaded the President to express public irritation. On June 14, in the midst of the overseas libraries controversy, Eisenhower offered some extremporaneous advice to the graduating class of Dartmouth College. "Don't join the book burners. . . . Don't be afraid to go into your library and read every book. . . . How will we defeat communism" he asked, "unless we know what it is . . . ?" The Dartmouth remarks greatly heartened McCarthy's foes. At last Eisenhower seemed to have committed his prestige to the battle. Quickly, however, the impact of the speech was dissipated. Asked if he had referred to McCarthy, the President executed a fast barrel roll away from any dogfight: "I think we will get along faster . . . if we remember that I do not talk personalities." Queried about the conflicting directives sent out to the overseas libraries, Ike responded: "I don't mean to say that I have dropped this; I just mean to say I don't know any more about that possibly than you do." A fusillade of tangled syntax produced the impression that the President saw no reason why the nation, by stocking blatantly communist books, should support "something that advocates its own destruction," and that the State Department, rudderless as it was, should proceed as it saw fit. [19]

During the early months of Republican rule, Democrats had generally emulated the administration's hands-off policy toward McCarthy. He was, the Democrats commonly asserted, a "Republican problem" over which they had little control. Democratic National Committee Chairman Stephen A. Mitchell stressed the need to "keep hammering away at the necessity for Republican action on the McCarthy matter." Thus Mitchell and, through him, Sam Rayburn warned Adlai Stevenson against a rumored speech on McCarthyism. It would divert McCarthy's attacks from Republicans to Stevenson and would rescue the Senator from "the decline that has already started." Moreover, McCarthy remained "the Republicans' responsibility and we have been doing all right in making them bear the burden he is, and thus eventually force them to discipline him." [20] Lyndon B. Johnson, the Senate Minority Leader, also promoted this strategy. Johnson's elevation to his new post was primarily the work of conservative Southerners, with whom he was in close touch. ("I think Lyndon is entitled to a promotion," wrote Richard Russell, dean of the Southern Democrats.) His views on McCarthy corresponded closely at the tactical level with those of the Southerners. Although inwardly, according to one biographer, Johnson was angry at McCarthy, he refused to let his or any other Democrat's distaste inadvertently play—as he assumed it would—into McCarthy's hands. He reiterated that he would not involve the Democrats in a "high school debate on the subject 'Resolved that Communism is good for the United States,' with my party taking the affirmative." On several occasions, he headed off Democratic colleagues who were eager to challenge McCarthy.[21]

To be sure, not all Democrats followed such counsels of reticence. The irrepressible Herbert Lehman spoke up: he defended Bohlen and lashed out at the menacing growth of "McCarthyism and Jenneritis." [22] Senator Hennings seized upon the President's "bookburning" remarks to belabor Secretary Dulles for his department's waffling on the standards of suitability for books used in overseas libraries. While gratified that Missouri's own Mark Twain had not been purged, Hennings awaited with wonderment "the next episode in this literary comedy." Quoting Senator Tobey's declaration that McCarthy and his allies in the Bohlen ruckus were "unworthy to tie the shoelaces of either Acheson or Bohlen," Robert S. Kerr expressed delight that Republicans finally "were telling the truth about each other." [23]

Most Democrats, however, preferred to consider McCarthy his own party's responsibility. "Whenever the Republicans decide that they have enough of him, they will act," wrote Senator Hoey. "He can be checked when the other Republicans make up th[e]ir minds to do it, but not until then." Democrats also cautioned that any intervention by them in the conflict germinating between McCarthy and the administration might only cause his Republican colleagues to rally around the Senator. If a leading Democrat were to defy Ike, Dulles or McCarthy, J. William Fulbright explained, "it would become a partisan matter and that, instead of weakening Mr. McCarthy, . . . would more likely draw the Republicans together in their support. Until public opinion has been more definitely crystallized regarding Mr. McCarthy, a Democrat who would seek to challenge him would be doing a futile thing." First, "some leading Republican" must "take the curse of partisanship off the matter." [24]

Many Democratic critics of McCarthy were prepared to hold their fire until prominent Republicans—particularly the President—chose to take on the Wisconsin Senator. Certain that McCarthy was "riding for a fall," Wyoming's Senator Hunt argued that "the break will need to be on the highest level between the President and McCarthy." "I am hopeful," Senator Fulbright confided, "that President Eisenhower will seek to curb some of the abuses which we feel exist in the McCarthy type hearings." If Eisenhower ever saw fit to make a statement, Fulbright ventured, "I think the opportunity for the Democrats to join in support of him would be presented." In a similar vein, Senator Humphrey declared that "the most effective opposition should come from the Administration itself." [25]

Given this strategic prerequisite, the controlling fact of Eisenhower's reluctance to do battle with McCarthy kept the Democrats equally inactive. They could only wait, cheering at each Republican counterblow, however glancing, against McCarthy, in the hope that it portended a stiffening resistance on the part of the administration. For example, by the summer of 1953 Lester Hunt was writing optimistically that, as the split between McCarthy and the White House widened, "it may be that the President has gained enough courage to take him on." In December, Hubert Humphrey was sanguine that administration "leadership" in the fight against McCarthy "has now come to the fore." The Democrats could sense difficulties in the situation as they described it. In the same letter in which he expressed hope that the President might confront McCarthy, Senator Hunt passed on a recent definition of the "Eisenhower waltz": "one step forward, two steps backward and one sidestep!" Senator Humphrey confessed at one point that he expected no anti-McCarthy "action by the Administration—at least until 1955." Thus, Democratic Senators waited on a President who in turn steadfastly left it to the Senate to commence hostilities against McCarthy. As William S. White noted, if the administration were not to move against McCarthy, "no one will." [26]

In the meantime, many Democrats sheltered behind battlements constructed of tested clichés: the voice of the people, the majority party's responsibility for its own miscreants, and traditional Senate protocol. "The Senate," Clinton Anderson explained, "has been very slow to say to the people of a state that knowing all the facts about candidates they do not still have the right to pick out the person they want." "Certainly [McCarthy's] record is open to great criticism," Clyde Hoey conceded, "but the people of Wisconsin elected him after all of this was published." [27] As for McCarthy's excesses as Chairman of the Permanent Investigations Subcommittee, the Democrats, Senator Anderson argued, were powerless to challenge his status because "a) we stick by the princip[le of] seniority in the Senate and b) if the Democratic members voted against a Republican nomination when the Republicans have a majority, they would lose." Southerners were especially leery of establishing such departures. It would be a "very revolutionary measure," said Senator Hoey, for the Senate to "take charge of a Committee and tell the Committee how to run or conduct its hearings." Senators would reject such a move "because they would not want to establish a precedent of having the Congress tell them how to run their Committee hearings." "You cannot change the whole Senate merely because one Senator is running wild on a Committee." [28]

Weighted down by such tactical burdens, the Democrats moved cautiously where McCarthy was concerned. They took no action to prevent the Republicans from pigeonholing the Hennings report. Excepting Senator Ellender, they did not cavil at doubling McCarthy's committee appropriation. When it became clear that McCarthy would head the Permanent Investigations Subcommittee, Senator Hoey, the outgoing chairman, resigned from it. He had kept McCarthy, as a minority member, under control, but with that situation altered, Hoey "did not wish to be responsible for what might develop." [29] The only Democratic countermeasure at this stage was Lyndon Johnson's subtle stroke of assigning to the Government Operations Committee Stuart M. Symington, Henry Jackson, and John F. Kennedy, newcomers who would not have to face an election for six years. These selections signaled to the Washington *Post* the Democrats' intention "to throw the party's weight effectively against McCarthyism." [30]

In fact, the appointments did not impede McCarthy. The Republicans gave him free rein over the committee, granting him exclusive control of the investigative agenda and the hiring of staff. The Democrats were scarcely less permissive. The ranking minority member, John McClellan, was a crusty conservative often in harmony with McCarthy's political leanings (although subsequently he would lead Democratic opposition to McCarthy himself). The Democrats offered little resistance to McCarthy and attended subcommittee hearings sporadically. McCarthy and his chief aide Cohn had something to do with this situation, for they gave scant notice of meetings or of their plans in general and operated as if the subcommittee were their wholly owned subsidiary.*.

Thus, the Democrats' various tactical parameters became self-fulfilling prophecies. The Republicans *had* to trigger any significant opposition to McCarthy, because the Democrats would not. And of course McCarthy would ultimately, as predicted, bring retaliation upon himself, since the Republicans would only move against him after severe provocation. It was a comforting, closed system of thought which afforded everyone a convenient rationale for inaction.[31] The politics of the past decade had thrust the Republicans into a tolerance of McCarthyism and had rendered the Democrats impotent against it. The initiative lay entirely with the Senator from Wisconsin.

While McCarthy's opponents within the Senate bided their time, those outside labored under great frustrations. William Benton continued to devote his vast energies to anti-McCarthy activities after 1952, but he was aware of their diminished impact. His assistant John Howe felt "like a boxer who is sparring against an opponent who is fifty yards away—with his back turned." [32] Officials of the Americans for Democratic Action, a frequent adversary of McCarthy, had by 1953 grown sensitive about the amount of attention their organization expended on the Senator. The ADA Executive Committee admonished itself that "activities re McCarthy should not dominate the ADA's interest and activities," yet, inevitably, they did. The ADA did not relish the situation, but, it was argued, "this is not of

* The other Democrats on the subcommittee were Jackson and Symington. Kennedy did not go on despite overtures which McCarthy reportedly made. McCarthy had dated Kennedy's sister Eunice and offered his brother Robert a job with the subcommittee. Kennedy, uncharacteristically, had recently criticized McCarthy for proposing to investigate communism in the colleges. Washington *Post*, Jan. 13, 18, 1953; *New York Times*, Jan. 24, 1954.

our doing but of his." [33] The American Committee for Cultural Freedom—and intellectuals generally—spent endless hours debating methods and priorities in the fight against McCarthyism and, in some instances, whether it or communism constituted the primary threat. [34] Hubert Humphrey put his finger on "McCarthy's real threat to American democracy . . . the fact that he has immobilized the liberal movement. Liberals just don't talk about anything else any more." It had approached the point of "a national neurosis." [35]

Along with other groups which moved in the orbit of liberalism, the National Committee for an Effective Congress (NCEC) perceived that its chief activities—initially the subsidizing of the Senate campaigns of more or less liberal Democrats and Republicans—were overshadowed by the presence of McCarthyism. By 1953, as its directors realized that the attainment of an "effective" Congress required the destruction of McCarthy's influence, they began to direct their efforts to that end. The NCEC high command, including Maurice Rosenblatt and George Agree in particular, developed perhaps the most thoroughgoing assessment of the McCarthy problem offered by any of the opposition. In a manner strikingly similar to the analytical approach of contributors to *The New American Right*,* the NCEC principals saw that McCarthy and his allies were "aiming at the conservative foundations of the country," specifically "the moral underpinning (particularly Protestant) of our secular traditions," the "Atlantic Union and its various backers," "international financial and trade interests, identified as 'Wall St.,' " the internationalist wing of the GOP, and the universities. Yet the putative victims were ignorant of the Senator's true targets (as were many of McCarthy's supporters). The NCEC set itself the task of exposing to "the conservative elements the real nature and direction of the McCarthy attack" and "putting McCarthy in juxtaposition to the groups he is really at-

---

* Daniel Bell, ed. (New York, 1955). Some of the contributors' views had appeared in articles in 1954. On the parallel with the NCEC's strategy, see Harry Scoble, *Ideology and Electoral Action: A Comparative Study of the National Committee for an Effective Congress* (San Fancisco, 1967). Scoble, and Griffith in *Politics of Fear*, pp. 224–29 and passim, provide valuable coverage of the NCEC. NCEC participants found their theoretical models in William Bolitho's essay on Catiline in *Twelve Against the Gods* (New York, 1929) and Hannah Arendt's *The Origins of Totalitarianism* (New York, 1951). Personal interview with Maurice Rosenblatt (June 27, 1967); cf. Griffith, pp. 225–26.

tacking." The NCEC, then, operated primarily to mobilize elite groups—ultimately, of course, the Senate.[36]

Early in 1953, the NCEC sponsored several meetings to deliberate methods of opposing the Wisconsin Senator. The participants included, as well as the NCEC regulars, Robert R. Nathan of the ADA (and NCEC); Gerhard P. Van Arkel, Senator Benton's attorney in his legal battles with McCarthy; Warren Woods, counsel for Drew Pearson in his suit against McCarthy, Herman Edelsberg of the Anti-Defamation League; and Kenneth Birkhead of the Democratic Senatorial Campaign Committee. Occasionally other anti-McCarthyites, including ex-Senator Tydings, various labor lobbyists, and Senate staff members were brought into the consultations. Out of these preliminaries evolved the so-called Clearing House, a research-oriented agency which collected and filed information and channeled it to those of McCarthy's opponents who asked for it. The Clearing House, loosely structured, consisted initially of a single employee, Lucille Lang [Olshine], who took charge of the anti-McCarthy archives, comprising primarily the files of Warren Woods, Benton, Van Arkel, and the material amassed by Jack Anderson and Ronald W. May for their muckraking biography of the Senator. In the summer of 1953, the files were moved from a downtown Washington location into the office of the Senate Democratic Campaign Committee, where Senator Earle Clements, in some agitation, tolerated their presence.[37]

Increasingly, the Clearing House-NCEC activists saw their function as that of a tough-minded lobbying group. "It is the kind of thing one would set up if one were interested in lifting an excise tax, helping Israel get a loan, or winning a government subsidy," wrote Maurice Rosenblatt. They sought to win "new strength and new allies in Congress, adding to rather than working over the same old people." The Clearing House eschewed "debate, argument, denunciation or contradiction." Rather, it stood ready to help in a "strictly technical" fashion when Senators asked for aid. Such efforts cost money, and the Clearing House, suffering under straitened finances, maintained only a skeletal program throughout 1953.[38] It essayed "preclusive operating" in certain areas: a study of the general problem of internal security legislation was launched to enable the liberals to shape a better loyalty program and "take the ball away from the wolfpack Senators."[39] But few opportunities for direct attacks on

McCarthyism materialized so that members of the Clearing House, like other anti-McCarthyites, waited upon events.

On June 18, 1953, McCarthy announced the appointment of J. B. Matthews as executive director of the Investigations Subcommittee and presented opponents in several quarters with an occasion ripe for intervention. Dr. Matthews, a one-time Methodist minister active in many leftist causes during the 1930s, had made the transit to the far right; at the end of the thirties, he had been employed by the House Un-American Activities Committee and later served as the Hearst newspapers' resident expert on communism. The hiring of Matthews would probably have brought no complications but for his article in the current *American Mercury*. "The largest single group supporting the Communist apparatus in the United States today," it began, "is composed of Protestant clergymen." [40]

The NCEC moved to exploit McCarthy's *faux pas*. Armed with a report on Matthews prepared by Lucille Lang, Clearing House agents "went to work on the Democrats" soon after the appointment was announced. John McClellan, reportedly "enraged" by the *American Mercury* piece, assumed leadership of the subcommittee minority. The three Democrats conferred on July 2 and went to McCarthy to ask for Matthews's dismissal. McCarthy refused, whereupon the Democrats issued a statement condemning the "shocking and unwarranted attack" on the clergy and demanding a subcommittee meeting to "consider appropriate action." The Clearing House, operating through influential Michigan clerics, also exerted "pressure" upon Senator Charles Potter, a Republican subcommittee member. On July 3, Potter publicly criticized Matthews. In an executive session on July 7, the three Democrats and Potter sought Matthews's removal, but McCarthy insisted that the Reorganization Act of 1946 gave him complete control over the hiring of "nonprofessional" staff, in which category he placed Matthews. McClellan rejected this interpretation, and the Democrats stood fast. [41]

In the meantime, the White House had entered the fray; presidential assistants who advocated a hard line against McCarthy saw a chance to strike a blow. Emmet John Hughes and Deputy Attorney General William Rogers undertook to solicit a protest to the President from the National Conference of Christians and Jews (NCCJ) against Matthews. Leaders of the Conference were given their cue, and

Hughes drafted a presidential reply to the anticipated telegram. The message from three prominent religious leaders got enmeshed in the White House's bureaucratic thicket before it was finally located. It became increasingly evident that McCarthy was going to fire Matthews; lest his declaration precede and thus preempt the White House, the anti-McCarthyites scrambled furiously to beat McCarthy to the headlines. Encountering the Wisconsin Senator on his way to announce the ouster, Rogers and Nixon stalled him in the Vice-President's office with probing inquiries about his coming activities until the press at last received the text of Ike's response to the three clergymen: "Generalized and irresponsible attacks that sweepingly condemn the whole of any group of citizens are alien to America." When such attacks "create doubt in the loyalty" of all clergymen, "the damage to our nation is multiplied." [42]

McCarthy's antagonists had scored a triumph, admittedly within very narrow confines. The President had criticized him obliquely and abstractly, and four men on his subcommittee had thwarted his plans. Members of the Clearing House saw in the episode a lesson that McCarthy had been defeated thanks to "a tough, knowing, internal procedural battle over firing or retention of an employee of a subcommittee of a minor Senate committee, joined around issues involving Senate operation." Proof that "the bully" could be beaten heartened McCarthy's colleagues. [43]

The Matthews affair generated further repercussions. After the Permanent Investigations Subcommittee voted four to three to jettison Matthews, Potter rejoined the Republicans to support a face-saving resolution affirming the Chairman's full powers to hire and fire staff. The three Democrats promptly resigned from the subcommittee, protesting "the impossible position of having responsibility without any voice, right or authority." The withdrawal of Symington, Jackson, and McClellan marked the first real, concerted counterblow by Democrats against McCarthy's activities under Republican hegemony. [44]

Eisenhower's telegram to the NCCJ leaders marked the latest in a series of publicized displays of presidential disapproval of McCarthy. There had been the Dartmouth speech. Late June brought another occasion for a general statement of Ike's commitment to traditional liberties; after careful negotiations with the White House (chiefly Emmet Hughes), the American Library Association elicited a message of greeting to its convention from the President. The letter warned against the "zealots" who, "with more wrath than wisdom . . . would try to defend freedom by denying freedom's friends the opportunity of studying Communism in its entirety." Freedom, Ike lectured, "cannot be censored into existence." Speculation regarding the likelihood of a head-on battle between the White House and Mc-Carthy grew, but Eisenhower, in keeping with his views of the presidential function, returned to public silence regarding the Wisconsin Senator.[45]

In the Senate, too, McCarthy received criticism more taxing than he had encountered in recent months. In fact, he even succeeded in provoking the anger of the Southerners, who had hitherto been fairly tolerant of his antics. McClellan's leadership in the Matthews fight was significant enough, but in addition Harry Byrd of Virginia, the beau ideal of Dixie conservatism, issued a statement calling on Matthews to document his charges "or stand convicted as a cheap demagog." After checking with the Director of the FBI, Byrd subsequently accounted it a "remarkable thing" that Hoover had not found a single churchman who could be prosecuted as a Communist agent.[46]

The Southerners had other grievances against McCarthy. At an appropriations hearing in June, McCarthy jumped on High Commissioner James B. Conant concerning overseas library policies and members of his staff in Germany and reached a verdict that Conant was "not doing a good job." Senator Maybank quickly interjected, "I think you're doing a good job." Incredulously, McCarthy asked if he had heard correctly; assured that he had, he could only reply, "I guess I can't trust another Senator, can I?" [47]

In late July, McCarthy antagonized J. William Fulbright, among others, at a hearing on the scholar-exchange program which Fulbright had authored. The episode began with Senator A. Willis Robertson protesting the presence of klieg lights and television cameras in the hearing room, for which Ferguson, the acting chairman, denied blame; it developed that McCarthy was responsible for the unexpected apparatus as well as the transfer of the proceedings to larger quarters. In the course of the hearing, McCarthy seized Ferguson's gavel and banged loudly to demand that Fulbright answer a question. "Who is running this committee?" Senator Ellender inquired angrily.

Later, excusing himself briefly to attend to business on the floor, Mc-
Carthy announced, "I don't want the witness to disappear while I am
gone." Ferguson retorted that there was "no justification" for such
an inference. When McCarthy resumed his harassment of Fulbright,
John McClellan came to the aid of his fellow Arkansan. McCarthy
broke off with a crack that, while he customarily referred to the
Fulbright as the "half-bright" program, he intended no reflection
upon the Senator.[48]

In July, McCarthy also incurred the wrath of Senator Monroney.
The Oklahoman was eager to join the opposition; he seized upon Mc-
Carthy's attempt, as a covering maneuver for his retreat in the
Matthews incident, to subpoena employees of the top-secret Central
Intelligence Agency. McCarthy had demanded the appearance before
his committee of William Bundy, chiefly notorious as Dean Ache-
son's son-in-law, as a one-time contributor to a defense kitty for
Alger Hiss, and presently as the recipient of a promotion for which
McCarthy thought him unfitted. The CIA declined to produce Bundy,
McCarthy bristled, and CIA Director Allen Dulles hastened to a conference with McCarthy arranged by the Vice-President. As the controversy simmered, Monroney pounced. The proposed CIA probe, he
declared on July 13, "puts the Senate up to a choice of giving the
distinguished Senator from Wisconsin carte blanche authority to fully
explore . . . the innermost secrets" of the agency, exposing data
"that even the Kremlin's best spy apparatus could not get." Criticizing McCarthy's recent activities, Monroney also ridiculed the "Key-
stone cop" chase by Cohn and Schine through Europe. He quoted
illustratively from the "pan" mail he received from McCarthy's
more frenzied advocates. ("You are a murderer and a traitor. Read
this, fall dead.") Eventually, Monroney offered Senate Resolution
146, which empowered the Senate to discharge any committee of further investigation in an area deemed to be outside its prescribed
domain. Although the motion expired in committee, Monroney remained hopeful, believing that McCarthy was "off balance." [49]

While McCarthy took these rhetorical lumps, the Democrats on his
subcommittee stayed out on strike, a situation which other Republicans, not relishing sole responsibility for their colleague, viewed
unhappily. McCarthy first tried to twit the Democrats into returning.
"If they don't want to take part in uncovering the graft and corrup-

tion of the old Truman-Acheson Administration," they were "entitled to refuse." But he soon adopted a more conciliatory tone, expressing hope that "housekeeping" details would not keep them away. Then he returned to threats, charging that the Democrats had withdrawn because they found their work on the subcommittee discomfiting in view of the discoveries he had made.[50]

The Democrats stood fast. Symington dismissed McCarthy's insinuations of embarrassment by noting that, since McCarthy's past and future probes dealt with the Eisenhower regime, their substance would, if anything, lure the minority members back. McClellan, feisty and pugnacious, rejected reconcilation: "so far as I'm concerned it's a closed issue." When Alton Lennon, newly appointed to the Senate (upon Willis Smith's death) and to the Government Operations Committee, saw no reason why he should not accept assignment to the subcommittee, his senior colleagues swiftly enlightened him. "I didn't know very much about it yesterday," he confessed, adding that he would not "be in any hurry" to join the subcommittee. There were, in addition, rumors that the Democrats, not satisfied with Matthews's scalp alone, would seek the ouster of another staffer, reportedly Roy Cohn.[51]

However, the Democrats did not capture control of the subcommittee, nor were there indications of much effort to that end. Their absence, moreover, in no way curbed the peregrinations of McCarthy, who, after Congress adjourned in August, embarked on a series of one-man investigations. The Democrats were optimistic that McCarthy had been wounded by recent events. "It appears," Lester Hunt wrote, "that McCarthy is about at the end of his string." "It is now obvious," Hubert Humphrey reported, "that McCarthy is in trouble. The conservative forces in the Congress are beginning to speak up." Between June and August, the Gallup poll showed a decline of those with favorable opinions regarding McCarthy from 35 to 34 percent, while unfavorable responses rose from 30 to 42 percent.[52] However, poll results were mercurial (in six months McCarthy's support would reach a new high). The tumult of July brought only a subtle diminution of McCarthy's standing. Though it might be argued that these summer storms were instrumental in McCarthy's undoing, the Democrats did almost nothing to accelerate the process. Some of the Southerners had shifted from passivity to irritability, the Republicans had grown more disturbed, but no one, aside from Monroney and Lehman, was willing to seize the initiative against McCarthy.

During the remainder of 1953, McCarthy was left to his own numerous devices. In August, the subcommittee heard testimony that Edward Rothschild, an employee of the Government Printing Offices, was a Communist; Rothschild and the witnesses whose appearance his lawyer had requested unhelpfully took the Fifth Amendment.[53] McCarthy also toyed briefly with an investigation of alleged communist infiltration among civilian employees of the Army.[54] Then he rushed, "more or less through the back door," as he put it, into a two-day investigation of security at the UN, questioning an American employee of the Polish delegation who two ex-Communists asserted had been a Party functionary.[55]

McCarthy quickly returned to the spore of communist infiltration of the nation's defenses. He labored to show that "Psychological and Cultural Traits of Soviet Siberia," a study for and by G-2, was an effort to "indoctrinate" Army Intelligence officers with communist propaganda. Louis Budenz and two escapees from the Soviet Union obligingly attested to the document's reddish tinge. When General Richard Partridge defended the study as "an honest attempt," McCarthy, aghast at the General's ignorance of the fact that the book quoted Stalin without attribution, declared the witness "completely and hopelessly incompetent." (McCarthy had begun to show flashes of the abusiveness which would soon lock him in mortal combat with the Army.)[56] In October, the Senator began hearings on purported communist infiltration and espionage at the Army Signal Corps Center at Fort Monmouth. He interrogated witnesses from the radar labs in executive session, then emerged with lurid accounts for waiting newsmen. On October 12, he claimed to have found traces of "extremely dangerous espionage" striking at "our entire defense against atomic attack." The next hearing yielded the alleged information that "top secret" documents from Fort Monmouth showed up in East Germany; at another briefing McCarthy surmised that the spy ring set up by Julius Rosenberg "may still be in operation." The next day's headline blared: "Radar Witness Breaks Down; Will Tell All About Spy Ring." The espionage, it turned out, was a product solely of McCarthy's inventiveness and the newpapers' gullibility. While thirty-three scientists were suspended during the inquiry, the majority were exonerated and reinstated and no spy was unmasked.[57]

As these events unfolded, McCarthy's relations with the Army, already uneasy because of the Monmouth probe, were further complicated when G. David Schine, the subcommittee's unpaid consultant, received his draft notice. Despite efforts by McCarthy and, more vigorously, by Roy Cohn to secure a special assignment or direct commission for Schine, in early November he was inducted as a private. At the same time that the Senator and his aides were seeking unusual privileges for Schine, the Army was trying to convince McCarthy to ease off on the Monmouth investigation. As the outlines of the coming conflict dimly emerged, the Army had to look to its own defenses, since administration leaders remained tolerantly noninterventionist toward McCarthy.[58]

Notwithstanding its desire for disengagement, the White House soon found itself embroiled with the Senator. The difficulty arose when Attorney General Herbert Brownell decided to tack around to McCarthy's windward and claim red-baiting for the administration. On November 6, he delivered a speech asserting that President Truman, despite FBI reports charging Harry Dexter White with being a Soviet agent, had nominated him to be Director of the International Monetary Fund in 1946.[59]

The spark ignited dry tinder. Truman angrily denied the accusation; his inaccurate rendering of the events of seven years earlier only fanned the flames, however. Chairman Velde of HUAC subpoenaed him along with former officials of his administration—an act which Eisenhower disavowed. Truman ignored the subpoena and, in his televised rebuttal to the charges, castigated the Eisenhower administration for resorting to "McCarthyism"; the Wisconsin Senator demanded equal time. In his response, McCarthy made the requisite indictment of the Democrats, but he also criticized Republicans. The Eisenhower regime marked a substantial improvement, he conceded, but it, too, had sins for which to answer: it still employed John Paton Davies (as Counselor to the Embassy in Lima), American fliers remained in captivity in China, and the "blood trade" between America's allies and Red China continued. Eisenhower had recently expressed the hope that the communist issue would be "a matter of history and of memory" by the time of the 1954 elections; Mc-

Carthy, however, assured his listeners that it was and would be a burning question.[60] Brownell's initiative in the White case, far from taking the topic of communism out of McCarthy's court, had lobbed it invitingly to his forehand.

McCarthy's not-too-veiled attack on the administration made members of the President's staff "hopping mad," prompting some to counsel a snappy response. C. D. Jackson, who admitted to feeling that McCarthy posed "the biggest menace to the world short of Malenkov," urged Ike to reply sharply at his next press conference. Jackson suggested that the President contrast the administration's "patient, quiet, thorough, and decent investigation and corrective action" against communist infiltration with McCarthy's "darting hither and yon before the television cameras spreading fear." [61] Other staffers implored the President to seize "one of the most dramatic moments" in his career to stand "on the side of the angels" against McCarthy. Eisenhower emphatically refused to descend to McCarthy's level—this was the occasion of his "gutter" remark—and issued a less pointed response to the Senator than these advisors advocated. McCarthy rewarded Ike's mildness by summoning those who supported his own position to "write or wire the President" of their feelings.[62]

Nevertheless, the administration persisted in the assumption that McCarthy could be appeased, domesticated. C. D. Jackson compared the current conciliatory view "that the Senator is really a good fellow at heart" to the discredited notion that Mao Tse-tung "was just an agrarian reformer." The softer policy prevailed. Army Secretary Robert Stevens, eager to nudge the McCarthy committee out of its Fort Monmouth investigation, tried to placate McCarthy in a fashion which, in view of the Army's subsequent charges that McCarthy and Cohn had exerted undue pressure on behalf of Schine, appeared abject, if not compromising.[63]

Stevens was only reflecting administration attitudes, however. Eisenhower himself had a conference with McCarthy in December, after which Leonard Hall congratulated the President for averting the "open fight" which the "Left Wing newspaper and magazine writers" sought to "foment." I. Jack Martin, a White House assistant, tried to cajole McCarthy into toning down his investigative activities, and late in December, Nixon and Deputy Attorney General

William Rogers tried to impress upon him the need for a more responsible attitude. McCarthy shortly indicated to the press that he might shift his attention to questionable tax settlements reached by the Truman administration, but when news stories suggested that Nixon had shunted him in that direction, the Wisconsinite angrily denied such reports.[64]

As if in tandem with the White House, the Democratic high command—particularly Lyndon Johnson—continued to advocate a hands-off doctrine regarding McCarthy. "I have nothing to say," said Johnson, "except that he is a Republican problem." Pat McCarran and John Sparkman echoed the Minority Leader. A number of Democrats believed their best strategy lay in allowing McCarthy to go on contesting for dominance in the GOP, thus widening the divisions in that party.[65]

Despite the unassertiveness of the Democratic leadership, McCarthy felt the buffets of growing opposition. In 1953 he had managed to affront numerous colleagues in both parties. Some resented his poaching on the territories of other committees. Even Pat McCarran complained that McCarthy's subcommittee had "stepped over into a field where it was not intended to function at all," adding that the Internal Security Subcommittee could "do all the work necessary on the Senate side" in probing subversion. "How many Communists have been punished because of his investigations?" Senator Ellender asked skeptically. Other Democrats proposed to restrain McCarthy's investigative wanderlust. Even Guy Gillette promised to seek curbs upon investigations of communism which intruded upon the domain of his own Foreign Relations Committee. Some Senators, including McClellan and Russell, suggested the creation of a combined House-Senate committee and Un-American activities.[66] The peppery Ellender announced that he would demand an accounting of its previous accomplishments to justify any committee's requests for new funds. He sensed that a year of McCarthy's "trampling on the toes of others" had created a favorable "climate" for his fund-cutting efforts. Carl Hayden also urged a fight against "waste and extravagance" on the part of committees.[67]

The Republicans had become sensitive to these crosscurrents. Majority Leader William F. Knowland expressed a lukewarm willingness to consider a joint committee on subversive activities, and others of his party perceived the need for limiting the investigative excesses of committees. "One cannot be a member of the Congress," wrote Senator Hendrickson, "without realizing the ever-growing need for a well-defined set of rules to govern . . . investigations." On February 26, the Republican Policy Committee voted unanimously to study the question; meetings were held in March, and seven "minimum rules and procedures" were framed for the "earnest consideration" of the various chairman. This démarche evinced a presumption that McCarthy had become a burden to the GOP. "Its meaning," said Senator Flanders, "can be reduced to these few words. 'Joe McCarthy is beginning to worry us.' " [68]

McCarthy trimmed sail before the shifting breeze. He humored reports that he would pursue such innocuous subjects as corruption and inefficiency; he announced a probe of "false claims, bribery" and "waste" in federal programs in Alaska. He strove to coax the Democrats back on to his subcommittee. On January 25, he agreed to surrender his plenary power over committee staff; he also gave the Democrats a minority counsel and other assistance and yielded to their demand for a rule which would permit them to veto—subject to a vote by the full committee—any public hearing which they considered unwarranted. The Democrats thereupon ended their boycott. [69]

McCarthy gave way lest he jeopardize his committee appropriation. Senator Hayden had moved quietly to apply constraints. He let it be known that he would insist on full enforcement of Senate rules: a committee's request for funds must lie over one day to "give the Senate an opportunity to consider the necessity for proposed investigations"; and the majority of a committee's members must approve the hiring of an employee before funds could be appropriated to pay him. Hayden would cut off McCarthy's funds until the Democrats on the committee approved his appropriations request. McCarthy, according to Senator Hoey, "completely surrendered" to Democratic demands. (The Democrats, in turn, went back on the subcommittee, Hayden wrote, "because they thought it would be a mistake to give the Chairman an opportunity to pose as a martyr" by denying him funds.) With the Democrats' return to the Permanent Investigations Subcommittee, Senator Ellender's movement to question the spending and jurisdiction of that body collapsed; only Fulbright voted against its appropriation. [70]

After the minority members of the subcommittee had won their point, the Democrats did not press the fight against McCarthy. Their leadership chose, for example, to ignore an opportunity to administer another rebuff to the Wisconsin Senator on the issue of the confirmation of Robert E. Lee as a Federal Communications Commissioner. After Lee, a friend and political ally of McCarthy's, had received the appointment the previous autumn, the NCEC prepared a memorandum detailing Lee's previous activities and links to McCarthy for Mike Monroney and other interested Senators. Lee's sole experience with broadcasting consisted of service as emcee of "Facts Forum," an ultraconservative television program subsidized by H. L. Hunt. Monroney put up a fight in the Interstate and Foreign Commerce Committee and on the Senate floor, and twenty-five Senators voted against the nomination, but, lacking the support of party leaders and Lyndon Johnson in particular, the insurrection failed.[71]

Notwithstanding these examples of timidity, the Democrats were altering, slowly but perceptibly, their posture of restraint toward the Wisconsin Senator and the controversies in which he was embroiled. Though they still embraced the "Republican problem" strategy, events were nudging them out of their passivity. Ironically, the Democrats' growing testiness was piqued by the efforts of prominent members of the Eisenhower administration to preempt the internal security issue and to shunt McCarthy aside.

During the autumn, administration spokesmen had begun to vaunt the achievements of the security program which Eisenhower had instituted the previous May. On October 23, 1953, the White House had announced that 1,456 employees had been removed from federal service under Executive Order 10450. Other Republicans took up the theme. Herbert Brownell yoked it to his exposé of the Harry Dexter White case, and White House Counsel Bernard Shanley trumpeted on the same day that the Republicans had ousted "1,456 subversives." Governor Dewey cited the figure in speculating on Democratic fears that Americans would "discover what a nice feeling it is to have a Government which is not infested with spies and traitors," In his January State of the Union message, Eisenhower raised the ante: now, over 2,200 had been "separated" as security risks. The new statistic received further oratorical embellishment.[72]

In the furor and fustian, the distinction between loyalty and security risks continued to blur, and the Republicans did not hasten to clarify it. Political and journalistic inquiries soon revealed a number of interesting facts about the administration's claims. It developed that some of the 2,200 (or 1,456) had resigned with no knowledge of the derogatory information, if any, in their files; many had merely resigned to take positions in other government agencies; some had been Republican-appointed. Very few of the dismissals stemmed from charges of disloyalty. The 2,200 figure covered tipplers, blabbermouths, a woman the birth of whose child antedated nine full months of marriage, few subversives, and considerable hokum.[73] In addition, as a ploy to silence the Senator from Wisconsin, the entire medicine-show failed egregiously. McCarthy only heightened the din. He embroidered the statistics with the claim that 90 percent of the 1,456 employees and "practically all" of the 2,200 were let go because of "Communist connections and activities or perversion." He angered the administration by managing to find room to criticize it despite its boasted accomplishments. He enraged the Democrats with his nine-stop Lincoln Day tour, sponsored by the Republican National Committee, on which he castigated the party of Roosevelt and Truman for "twenty years of treason." [74]

The Democrats rebelled. On January 25, Senator Olin Johnston, the ranking Democrat on the Post Office and Civil Service Committee, decried the administration's "practice of deceit and demagoguery" and introduced a resolution requiring the Chairman of the Civil Service Commission to present a "breakdown" of the 2,200 removals. Senator Thomas Burke labeled the Eisenhower regime's figures "a shoddy shell game." On February 8, after consulting other party members, Sam Rayburn and Stuart Symington launched a simultaneous counterattack. Rayburn denounced the "mean," "untrue," and "dastardly" attacks on his party, and warned that "the backs of some of us are getting pretty sore." Symington criticized the Republicans' " 'rat-alley' partisan approach" and, like Rayburn, held the President accountable for the rhetorical excesses and warned of their effect upon Democratic cooperation. Lyndon Johnson later added that "irresponsible statements by high Administration officials" were "not conducive to the kind of bipartisanship I should think the 'Great Crusade' would require." President Eisenhower finally disavowed any notion that the opposition party was tainted with communism, but the net effect of the agitation over security risks had been to vex and sensitize the Democrats.[75] If McCarthy had received any wounds, they were inflicted not by any direct hits from the administration, but by unintended caroms. Similarly, the Democrats directed their wrath not so much at the Wisconsin Senator as at the Administration, which appeared to have taken up his methods.

Unaffected by the Democrats' diffuse response to developments, McCarthy was steering a course toward ruin. The shoal on which he foundered was the United States Army. In January, McCarthy attempted to stir up the Fort Monmouth probe, demanding the appearance of the loyalty-security appeals board members who had decided the cases of the radar scientists. The Army seemed unwilling to yield, and, after a meeting with the Republicans on his subcommittee, McCarthy backed down.[76] But in the meantime, he discovered Irving Peress, a dentist who, despite having invoked the Fifth Amendment on his application for a commission under the Doctors Draft Act, had been inducted into the Army, excused from an overseas assignment, and promoted to Major. On January 30, McCarthy questioned Peress; three days later, the Army imprudently granted the Major, at his own request, a hasty but honorable discharge, in spite of McCarthy's demand that the dentist be court-martialed. On February 18, McCarthy grilled Peress's C.O., General Ralph W. Zwicker, who, under orders, declined to reveal the identity of those responsible for the bizarre turns in the Peress case. After tendentious and hypothetical questioning, McCarthy described the General, who had been decorated for his part in the Battle of the Bulge, as "not fit to wear that uniform." "You should be removed from any command," he told the witness.[77]

The harassment of Zwicker goaded the Army reluctantly into action. Secretary Robert T. Stevens objected to the "unwarranted abuse" of the General, declared that under existing conditions no other officers were to honor McCarthy's demands for testimony, and made ready to appear before McCarthy's subcommittee to defend his officers. On February 24, however, on the urging of Senator Mundt, Stevens attended the famed "chicken luncheon" with the Republican members of the subcommittee. He went up to the Hill, he said, to insist upon the rights and dignities of his men; he assumed he had received appropriate guarantees from the Republican Senators, but signed a "memorandum of understanding," composed jointly by all present, which made no mention of these safeguards. The document, indicating that the Secretary was now willing to hand over privileged information regarding the Peress case and to let Zwicker go before the committee, seemed to signal an ignominious retreat.[78]

Consternation prevailed in all quarters. "I wish to express my congratulations to you for taking the position you did. It is," wrote Senator Hunt to the beleaguered Army Secretary, "to be regretted you were forced to change your position." "Private Schine," one Pentagon brass hat commented, "is the only man left in the Army with any morale." Under White House tutelage, Stevens issued a statement on February 25 which attempted to recoup some of the lost ground. "I shall never accede to the abuse of army personnel," he declared, professing to have received "assurances" from subcommittee members that there would be no recurrence. McCarthy promptly branded the latter claim "completely false." Karl Mundt, rounding into form as a conciliator of the irreconcilable, said that Stevens was correct in stating that he had received "assurances" from individuals (but not the subcommittee), although these, as he wrote a constituent, had not been "formalized." "We all [presumably excluding McCarthy] told Bob we did not consider the memo of understanding a capitulation" and consented to the issuance of his February 25 "post script statement" despite a prior agreement to forego further public comment. The trouble arose, Mundt contended, from slanted reporting after "we succeeded in depriving blood-thirsty reporters of the Roman holiday they had envisioned" if Stevens had testified before the subcommittee as originally planned. (The cancellation of this hearing was the only item in the memorandum of understanding which could even remotely be interpreted as a concession to Stevens; but since Stevens thus backed away from an intended defense of his subordinates, the engagement did end in a surrender.) [79]

Words and clarifications could not drown our the clank of massing armor. The Army became the spearhead—however blunt—of a tentative counterattack against the Wisconsin Senator. McCarthy's demand for the names of the members of the Army loyalty screening board had prompted a meeting on January 21 of Sherman Adams, Herbert Brownell, Henry Cabot Lodge, presidential aide Gerald Morgan, and John G. Adams, the Army's Counselor. Sherman

Adams had then suggested that the Army draft an account of the improper exertions by McCarthy and Cohn on Private Schine's behalf. The former chief consultant had undergone an unusual basic training. He was excused from training exercises to make or accept some 250 phone calls—on committee business for which his knowledge was assertedly essential. He received numerous weekend passes as part of the Army's effort to make him available for subcommittee work. When his fellow trainees were at the firing range, Schine was discovered in the cab of a truck, "studying logistics," he explained. The private was also reported to have hired other soldiers to clean his rifle. By February, several Democrats, including John McClellan, were pressing the Army to release the details of Schine's military career. In March, ostensibly in response to Senator Potter's request for information, the Army published its "Chronology" of the attempts by McCarthy, Cohn, and Francis P. Carr, another subcommittee staff member, to exert undue influence. McCarthy and Cohn countercharged that the Army had tried to head off the Monmouth inquiry with various blandishments and by holding Schine as a "hostage." [80]

As tensions, publicity, and recriminations mounted, the subcommittee voted on March 16 to investigate the accusations issuing from both sides. McCarthy yielded his chairmanship temporarily to Karl Mundt, and Henry Dworshak of Idaho took the vacant seat on the subcommittee. Several members of the panel favored bucking the investigation up to the parent committee or surrendering it to the Armed Services Committee, and Mundt preferred to yield it to a blue-ribbon committee outside of Congress. In a preliminary meeting, Everett Dirksen voiced prophetic doubts that an investigation would achieve much. It would consume several weeks and shed little light, all to produce a result attainable immediately: the dismissal of Roy Cohn and polite advice to the Army to do likewise with John G. Adams. However, the Democrats, taking the position they would occupy throughout the hearings, refused to countenance less than a full airing of the dispute. "It is our linen," McClellan intoned, "and we have got to wash it." The special subcommittee commenced public hearings on April 22.[81]

Grand army battles appear chaotic and chance-ridden in their immediacy, but take on logical patterns in retrospect; in contrast, the Army-McCarthy hearings seemed to possess a sort of order as they unfolded which, with the passage of time, was obfuscated. For thirty-six days the hearings unraveled and overlapped until the involuted tangle they produced denied easy synopsis or explanation. Conducted with the trappings of legalism affected by Chairman Mundt, by Ray Jenkins, the special subcommittee's chief counsel, and by counsel for the principals, the hearings were at once something less and something more than a trial. No legal verdict resulted; the pursuit of several charges stopped short of definitive truth; and the proceedings often jumped their quasi-judicial tracks before the last words were uttered on June 17. It took two and a half months more for Jenkins to summarize the hearings, for his condensation to be condensed in turn, and for the members to probe the full extent of their disagreement. The Republicans issued a majority report harder on the Army than on McCarthy and Cohn; the Democrats offered a report more critical of McCarthy and his staff than of the Army; Potter issued individual views which struck evenhandedly at both sides, and Dirksen published separate conclusions. By August 31, the swift flow of events had bypassed the questions which the reports tried to resolve.[82]

Not so much a set of findings of fact as a melange of visual images and dramatic vignettes emerged from the hearings, which television carried to millions of viewers. James St. Clair, who helped present the Army's case (and, twenty years later, President Richard M. Nixon's), reported his child's lament: "When is Daddy going to get off [television] so we can see Howdy Doody again?" There was McCarthy, no Howdy Doody, glowering, menacing, breaking in with incessant points of order; Robert Stevens in his grand indecisiveness; and Joseph N. Welch, the Army's special counsel, parrying McCarthy's mace with the foil of his wry rejoinder. There was the "cropped photo" incident and, most memorably, Welch's powerful reply to McCarthy's blurted charge that a young member of his firm, Frederick G. Fisher, had once belonged to the National Lawyers Guild, named "oh, years and years ago, as the legal bulwark of the Communist Party." As McCarthy continued, Welch asked: "Have you no sense of decency, sir, at long last?" Still McCarthy plunged on, and Welch cut him off. Forbidden applause reverberated through the room in what was the climactic episode of the hearings.[83]

The style of the hearings left a more enduring impression than did the content. One public opinion sampler theorized that viewers had generally not grasped the constitutional or civil-libertarian significance of the proceedings; instead, they saw the contest as soap opera, as a morality pageant exemplifying the value of "The Lone Hero" (McCarthy) to some and the sin of "tattling on one's peers to others." As Eric Sevareid argued: "The real cleavage in the nation is not political or philosophical, but emotional." [84]

The Democrats were only marginally involved in the public preliminaries to the Army-McCarthy hearings. Party Chairman Stephen Mitchell had noted in mid-March that the McCarthy situation not only "hurt the Republicans," but, more importantly, it "hurt the country." Adlai Stevenson, in his much heralded speech of March 6, deprecated the GOP as "a political party divided against itself, half McCarthy and half Eisenhower." The barb sank deeply; in his next press conference, Ike labeled the charge "nonsense," but he took care to list his administration's own anticommunist bona fides and to commend a recent speech by Ralph Flanders which had criticized McCarthy. Then replying to Stevenson's speech for the GOP, Richard Nixon warned that some who had previously "done effective work exposing Communists . . . have, by reckless talk and questionable method, made themselves the issue rather than the cause they believe in so deeply." [85] Clearly, McCarthy had emerged as a serious "Republican problem."

Other developments underscored McCarthy's growing vulnerability. The Republicans had grown less sure of his value as a party totem. National Chairman Leonard Hall had maneuvered artfully to have Nixon, not McCarthy, answer Stevenson's critique. The President had expressed doubt as to whether McCarthy would be speaking for the party in the coming campaign. Even Karl Mundt told a constituent that "all of us are of the same view that [McCarthy] overstepped his bounds in the last investigation" and were working to "reconcile the duties" of the Senator with the "success of this administration." [86] In another quarter, Edward R. Murrow had tackled McCarthyism on his television show, "See It Now." McCarthy also received adverse publicity when he dropped his libel suit against William Benton.[87]

Despite the sniping at McCarthy, Senate Democrats, not wishing to promote GOP unity in the face of an external threat, trod lightly as the intraparty battle went on. McClellan and Jackson issued a statement following the "chicken luncheon" that, having been excluded from the festivities, they would "accept no responsibility" for what was "primarily a Republican quarrel." They had, however, expressed an interest in the Army's first intimation of impropriety in regard to Private Schine and had been counseling Stevens since the Zwicker blow-up. Stevens had consulted with McClellan and, particularly, with Symington about his difficulties; Symington also called on Clark Clifford, then practicing law in Washington, to render advice, as the transcripts of the phone calls monitored by the Army revealed when they were subsequently read at the hearings. While Clifford's was a minor role, Symington had stoutly encouraged Stevens to stand up to McCarthy, though warning that "this boy gets awfully rough." [88]

Amid the growing animosity between the Army and McCarthy, the Democrats were discreetly supportive of Secretary Stevens. Although the three Democrats on the Permanent Investigations Subcommittee had not instigated the dispute (nor initiated the contacts with Stevens), once the controversy became public, they exerted their influence upon the subcommittee's deliberations to insure that the issues were thoroughly and publicly aired. They forestalled efforts to palm the squabble off on another committee or to defuse it, and, with considerable Republican assistance, they successfully insisted that McCarthy, as one of the principals, step down from the subcommittee so as not to serve as judge or prosecutor of his own cause. When McCarthy tried to disengage himself from what he called "the dispute between Mr. Cohn and Mr. [John G.] Adams" and entered the disclaimer that "this isn't my case," Senator McClellan quickly rejoined that it was. Once the subcommittee started to pursue the mutual recriminations of the Army and McCarthy, the Democrats kept it pointed toward that objective alone, resisting McCarthy's attempts to deflect its course. [89]

Even before the Army-McCarthy hearings began, the three Democrats showed a stiffened resolve to keep the subcommittee and its chairman in check. On February 23, they began attending hearings for the first time since the previous July and quickly embroiled themselves in a fight over McCarthy's treatment of Annie Lee Moss, a Pentagon clerical worker. McCarthy had sneeringly explained that her testimony had been deferred since too many perjury cases were already pending. He claimed—erroneously—that the employee had access to decoded messages and belonged to the Communist Party. (She had received Communist mailings, but hers seemed to be another case of mistaken identity—there were three Annie Lee Mosses in the Washington telephone directory.) Mrs. Moss convinced the Democrats of her innocence; McClellan feared she had been unjustly dealt with and Symington offered to find her a job if she lost her present one. Eager to move against McCarthy's lieutenant Cohn, the three Democrats expressed indignation at his questioning of the bewildered witness. Henry Jackson took occasion to belittle McCarthy's accomplishments, denying that he had found any "new Communists." [90]

During the Army-McCarthy hearings, the Democrats often played secondary roles as McCarthy battled with the Army's representatives and stepped on the toes of his Republican colleagues. Partisan configurations often blurred, although McCarthy attempted from time to time to focus the debate on the sins of the Democrats. He charged that the minority members—particularly Symington—had instigated the controversy. He hinted bluntly to fellow Republicans that surely they wanted neither to emulate Democratic methods nor aid Democratic prospects. The Pentagon troublemakers, he argued, were Truman "hangovers." To the unknowing in the television audience he explained that the Clifford referred to in the monitored phone calls was "the chief political adviser of President Truman at the time they were most vigorously fighting my attempts to expose Communists in the last administration." [91]

Although they occupied a peripheral position in the action, the Democrats, led by McClellan, entered the discussion frequently enough. In lawyerly fashion, McClellan upheld due process and orderliness. In one of his first spoiling maneuvers, McCarthy accused a witness, General Miles Reber, of having ulterior motives in the controversy because his brother had allegedly been asked to resign from the Foreign Service on security grounds. McClellan angrily objected that McCarthy was "giving testimony." In another exchange the Arkansas Senator took issue with McCarthy's unproven assertion that one of the Fort Monmouth scientists he had investigated was a Communist. Once, when McCarthy volunteered that Clark Clifford was not in McClellan's wing of the Democratic Party, McClellan retorted that "maybe the President of the United States is not of your wing of the party, either." McClellan also marshaled the Democrats in opposition to the several Republican efforts to end, recess, or take the hearings behind closed doors. [92]

With low-keyed effectiveness, Senator Henry Jackson, too, came to grips with McCarthy. He probed hard at the "purloined letter" McCarthy produced—a report from J. Edgar Hoover to Army Intelligence which had been passed off as a true copy, but turned out to have been altered. The Democrats attack on the authenticity of the memorandum occasioned one of McCarthy's recurrent remarks that the minority had returned to the subcommittee only to "obstruct any attempt to dig Communists out of Government." That charge, said Jackson, was "an old stock-in-trade, and you can expect that all through the hearing." McCarthy, he noted, had made similar statements in the 1952 campaign against Symington and himself, "and the people repudiated him." Jackson also needled McCarthy with an interrogation regarding the much-puffed "Schine plan" for psychwar against communism; Jackson referred mirthfully to a scheme for using pin-up pictures in the war for men's minds, for creating a "deminform" to counter the Cominform and, he extrapolated, for working with Elks' lodges in Pakistan. (It was this ribbing which allegedly prompted Roy Cohn to remark to the Democratic aide, Robert F. Kennedy, that they were going to "get" Jackson and which led to a brief flurry between the two young assistants.)[93]

Stuart Symington offered the most protracted opposition to the Wisconsin Senator on the part of the Democrats. Sometimes it was mere niggling: once when McCarthy claimed a point of order, the Senator from Missouri responded that it was a point "out of order." "Oh, be quiet," snapped McCarthy, to which Symington rejoined, "I haven't the slightest intention of being quiet." On another day, Symington rebuffed one of McCarthy's habitual first-name references: "Let's keep this on a formal basis." Other objections were more substantial. Symington was disturbed by McCarthy's stubborn insistence that federal employees had a higher duty to give him secret information than to obey the law. If McCarthy was right, said Symington, "we haven't got a good government, we haven't got a bad government, we just don't have any government at all." [94]

McCarthy and Symington generated the most acrimonious exchanges of the hearings. One developed as McCarthy was badgering Symington to testify about his involvement in the maneuvers which led to the inquiry. Alluding to the Gillette subcommittee, Symington interjected that nobody "knows more about how to avoid testifying than the junior Senator from Wisconsin." McCarthy snarled back at "Sanctimonious Stu," whereupon Symington advised: "You better go to a psychiatrist." Like Jackson, Symington deemed it important to declare his fearlessness: "I want you to know from the bottom of my heart that I am not afraid of anything about you or anything you got to say, at any time, any place, anywhere." He capped the exchange with a peroration that he found nothing fundamentally "wrong" with America, "and that is the great and basic difference between the junior Senator from Wisconsin and the junior Senator from Missouri." It might look at times like the Boy Scouts against what McCarthy liked to label "Indian Charlie" tactics, but Symington did land some telling, if transient, blows.[95]

The hearings, however clouded their message, had a sharply negative impact on McCarthy's popularity. According to the Gallup poll, McCarthy had reached a peak of acclaim in January, when 50 percent of the respondents had had a favorable opinion of him; in June, only 34 percent of those polled reacted positively toward the Senator. (29 percent had opposed him in January; the figure rose to 49 percent in May and fell off to 45 percent in June.) Even before the hearings had begun, McCarthy's popularity had declined (by 4 percent), and some Republican leaders had pressed for a harder line against him. Leonard Hall commented admonishingly that McCarthy had "done more harm than good." [96] Congressman George H. Bender, seeking the late Bob Taft's Senate seat, informed the President that the hearings had prompted "growing impatience with the Republican Party" and the equating of " 'McCarthyism' " with "witch-hunting." From the chairman of the Republican National Finance Committee came the news that his associates found the hearings "a disgraceful affair." Their harmful effect prompted Congressman John Vorys to urge his old friend Karl Mundt to curtail them. Mundt was fully aware "that these hearings are doing neither the country nor the Republican Party any good." [97]

The GOP moved swiftly away from the tottering edifice of Mc-

Carthy's prestige. In May, the Republican National Committee let it be known that McCarthy would not be invited to take a leading role in the campaign. Several candidates sought to put distance between themselves and the Senator. Hugh Butler asserted that he had had nothing to do with booking McCarthy as a speaker at the Nebraska Republican convention, that the invitation had been tendered "before this present controversy," and that McCarthy would only be an "evening speaker," not the keynoter. (The Army hearings prevented McCarthy from filling the engagement.) Congressman Thomas E. Martin, running for the Senate in Iowa, explained that he had no involvement in plans to bring McCarthy into his state, adding that he would not "undertake to bar anyone" the speakers bureau saw fit to schedule. Governor Kohler commented that McCarthy was losing friends in Wisconsin and, during the hearings, a recall movement against the Senator was being waged.[98]

In other ways, McCarthy's Republican colleagues demonstrated a sensitivity to the damage he had done. Spurred by the Army-McCarthy hearings, Prescott Bush called for procedural standards for investigating committees; he felt "a sense of shame" that previous laxity had brought the Senate to its present pass. H. Alexander Smith and Wallace F. Bennett also gave consideration to committee reform proposals as a means of closing the rifts the hearings had opened. During the summer, William Jenner's Subcommittee on Rules heard testimony on proposed standards of committee procedure.[99]

If less secure than before, McCarthy's power had not yet fully evaporated, and so the Democrats, while willing to take further steps against him, moved cautiously. The minority members of the Permanent Subcommittee on Investigations kept McCarthy pinned down by sniping at his lieutenants. They pressed for a "housecleaning" of the subcommittee staff before any new inquiry was begun. Cohn, presumably, would go with the first flourish of the mop; since Charles Potter also thought the youthful aide expendable, it appeared that McCarthy would be outvoted. The Democrats' call for a showdown was thwarted first by McCarthy's absence, then by his refusal to accept the proxy of Senator McClellan, who was campaigning in Arkansas. McClellan angrily objected to this "arbitrary" act, but before the issue came to a head, Cohn resigned.[100]

McCarthy's embarrassments multiplied. In June the Democrats

disclosed that two other staff employees had failed to obtain security clearances from the Defense Department. After first denying the charges, McCarthy transferred one assistant, Don Surine, to his Senate staff payroll; the other, Thomas La Venia, was retained by the subcommittee in a "non-security" post. McCarthy suffered another reversal when, on typically short notice, he scheduled a hearing in Boston; Majority Leader Knowland himself blocked this venture. Later in the month, McCarthy was again rebuffed when the Government Operations Committee refused to approve his nomination of ex-Senator Owen Brewster as general counsel; the appointment fell through because the Democrats did not support it and several Republicans declined to press it over their opposition.[101]

Gradually, the Democrats, in conjunction with Republicans who sought to stem the Wisconsin Senator's ravages upon his party, brought the Permanent Subcommittee on Investigations under a tighter rein. McCarthy's power over the employment of staff, over the docketing of hearings—in short his very ability to generate the publicity which inflated his political balloon—had been steadily crimped. He was still a popular speaker on the banquet (if not the campaign) circuit. Indeed, it seemed that as his colleagues narrowed the amount of play afforded him by Senate institutions, he compensated by going to his wider constituency. His speaking schedule at some stages in the Army controversy was almost frenetic and remained heavy afterward. However, his mass appeal, always more apparent than real, had shown slippage. His colleagues, while still wary of his grip on public sentiment, had become less fearful. They had begun to see the separability of the communist issue from the McCarthy issue; while continuing to insure themselves against the former, they were less disturbed by risks posed by the latter. The storms of spring and summer had sharply buffeted McCarthy. "It is not pretty," a fellow Senator observed, "to see a man when circumstances are gathering about him." [102]

The Democrats had played a growing part in keeping hostile forces ringed tightly about the Wisconsin Senator, closing off alleys of escape, allowing "circumstances" to proliferate. Yet all the while, they still perceived McCarthy as a Republican problem. This formulation served as a rhetorical convenience and tactical ploy, but it was more than that. Not many Democrats chafed to launch personal challenges or act as champions for the nebulous forces seeking Mc-Carthy's downfall. The next move, after McCarthy's powers as sub-committee chairman had been circumscribed, was not clear. To what further measures, if any, the Democrats might have resorted independently cannot be known, for more drastic steps took the initiative largely out of their hands.

CHAPTER 10
". . . Contrary To Senatorial Traditions"

IT TOOK Ralph E. Flanders, initially acting alone, to channel the various pulses and energies surging against McCarthy into an effective force of opposition. The seventy-three-year-old junior Senator from Vermont was a remarkable character. Born of a family so poor that he was "bound out" to a farmer in his youth, Flanders had worked his way up as a machinist, draftsman, and machine-tool designer, married the boss's daughter, and finally became president of the Jones and Lamson Machine Tool Company. He was a member in good standing of the American Establishment, serving as president of the Federal Reserve Bank of Boston and belonging to the Committee for Economic Development. In 1946 he went to the Senate. He supported Eisenhower Republicanism and advocated a "wise liberalism" for the GOP, though these were positions with which his pronounced independent streak sometimes coincided and at other times clashed. He pushed harder for disarmament than most of his peers. In 1953 he challenged the government's explanation for the presence of an American plane attacked in Soviet airspace. Yet he shared with such fellow Republicans as H. Alexander Smith and John Foster Dulles a penchant for investing the nation's foreign policy with heavy doses of morality. This cast of mind led him to believe that the Korean armistice of 1953 required too costly a moral compromise. A deeply contemplative and spiritual man, he closed one of his addresses on the McCarthy problem with an eighth-century hymn by St. Andrew of Crete.[1]

For some time Flanders had brooded over McCarthy's baleful influence. He was a friend of William Benton, and Mrs. Flanders had taxed him for not joining in Benton's earlier battle with McCarthy. Though he agreed with the basic tenet of the Republican Right that "the New Deal was possessed of ideas which closely paralleled the Communists" and was disturbed by communist success in infiltrating the American government, he was skeptical about his Wisconsin colleague. "I have at no time been convinced as to the soundness" of McCarthy's charges, he told his constituents in 1950. He surmised that 90 percent of McCarthy's allegations were "baseless," but the remaining 10 percent troubled him. Until the spring of 1954, he continued to believe that the best answer to McCarthy's extravagances lay in implementing alternatives to the wrong-headed, damaging policies of the Democrats.[2]

On March 9, 1954, in his first frontal attack, Flanders ridiculed McCarthy's anticommunism: "He dons his war paint. He goes into his war dance. He emits his war-whoops. He goes forth to battle and proudly returns with the scalp of a pink army dentist." Flanders toyed with the possibility that McCarthy was a "hidden satellite of the Democratic Party." On June 1, he addressed himself to the "colossal innocence" of the Wisconsin Senator, whom he likened to "Dennis the Menace." More seriously, he suggested that McCarthy's schismatic activities betrayed parallels to the rise of Hitler. "Established and responsible government is besmirched. Religion is set against religion, race against race. Churches and parties are split asunder. All is division and confusion." Flanders made a more peremptory challenge on June 11. Having informed his adversary of his intentions—before the television cameras at the Army hearings— Flanders submitted to the Senate a resolution to "separate" McCarthy from his committee and subcommittee chairmanships if he did not within a reasonable time purge himself of his contempt of the Senate by answering the six questions posed to him by the Privileges and Elections Subcommittee in 1952.[3]

To the extent that they took it seriously, fellow Republicans did not welcome Flanders's motion. McCarthy dismissed it as a product not of "viciousness" but of "senility." Majority Leader Knowland labeled it a "mistake," "contrary to the established procedure," and obstructive to the administration's legislative program. Twice at dinner parties Flanders was "dealt with to be reasonable"—once by Knowland and once by Treasury Secretary George Humphrey. The resolution was allowed to lie on the table until June 15, when, with Flanders's approval, it was sent to the Rules Committee. However, the Senator from Vermont insisted that he would not permit the measure to get lost in the rush to adjourn; he would, if necessary, propose its discharge in mid-July—after giving McCarthy ample time to purge himself of contempt. Though Flanders maintained that the resolution was "very much alive," the prospects did not seem encouraging. The Republican Policy Committee declared its unanimous opposition to any tampering with existing committee arrangements, and the Majority Leader announced that he himself would move to table Flanders's motion. He did promise that he would put up no "artificial obstructions"—Flanders would get a vote, but no more.[4]

Most ominously, many Democrats greeted Flanders's resolution with a palpable lack of enthusiasm. To be sure, a few supporters declared themselves. Herbert Lehman introduced a similar resolution on June 17, but it was consigned to the same grave as Flanders's. Senators Sparkman, Monroney, Fulbright, Hill, and Hennings were reported to have offered aid; Hubert Humphrey planned to give his "full backing" but feared that the Flanders and Lehman resolutions had been effectively "pigeon-holed." Earle Clements, the Minority Whip, indicated that he would waive his "technical objections" if Flanders could show "real support," but beyond this, Democratic aid was scanty. Maurice Rosenblatt of the NCEC estimated that twenty-five Democrats (and twelve Republicans) could be "counted for the resolution." Others would follow suit if a division were taken, but therein lay the problem: to pressure the Senate's leaders into permitting a vote.[5]

Reluctant Democrats had several motives for caution. They fell in behind the old argument which one of them stated anonymously: "Joe's their problem, let them battle it out." Where such a formulation had once represented a defensive rationale, as McCarthy's contentiousness increasingly roiled his own party, the stock phrase now masked considerable pleasure. At the same time, however, some Democrats viewed a roll call on McCarthy with trepidation. As the fall elections approached, no candidate relished having to declare his stand regarding the Wisconsin Senator: he stood to lose votes no matter how he voted.[6]

The nature of the punishment Flanders wished to mete out also troubled his colleagues—particularly the Southerners. Committee chairmanships were based on the seniority principle, than which there was nothing dearer to these senior Senators. The Democrats professed to be thinking "deeper" than the McCarthy issue. If the minority party disrupted the present majority party's arrangements, what, they asked, would prevent recurrences of this when roles were reversed? "If we get back in power we don't want a simple motion like Senator Flanders' to throw us out of joint," said one Democrat. Such arguments, it was predicted, might incline as many as 50 percent of the Democrats to vote against Flanders's motion. The Senate's "club" feeling also operated against Flanders's prospects, although he argued that since McCarthy was "himself unprecedented," there need be no worry about establishing a bad precedent.[7]

The inhospitality of the Democratic Party leaders posed a further obstacle. "The greatest stumbling block," wrote Maurice Rosenblatt, "is the alliance between the Republican and Democratic leadership . . . which is trying [to] mousetrap the Flanders motion." "Clements and Lyndon Johnson are working their party into a spot where the Democrats will be responsible for a vote of confidence in McCarthy." The Democrats, though ready to "back any sound move emanating from a Republican," were "milling around without leadership or purpose." Overcoming the resistance of Democratic sachems loomed as one of the chief objectives of those seeking the success of the Flanders resolution.[8]

To answer the objections of the traditionalists, Senator Flanders announced on July 16 that in two weeks he would offer a new motion calling for McCarthy's censure. He would resolve that McCarthy's conduct "is unbecoming a member of the United States Senate, is contrary to Senatorial traditions, and tends to bring the Senate into disrepute, and such conduct is hereby condemned." The new motion had the advantage that there was precedent, albeit sparse, for censure, and such a move would not disturb the normal dispositions of power so important to the Southerners. It asked merely a moral judgment.[9]

The Democrats looked with greater favor upon the censure resolution than upon Flanders's original motion. Senator Fulbright announced his support—and his continuing aid would play an indispensable role in the success of the enterprise. About sixteen Democrats were thought to be "sure" supporters of censure; with twelve more "very probable" plus perhaps fourteen Republicans, a total of forty-two votes for the Flanders motion was possible but far from guaranteed. A number of Democrats, including some leaders, were willing to back a Republican initiative but had first to be convinced that Flanders had "real support." [10] Lyndon Johnson continued to be "the root of all difficulties on the Democratic side," according to the NCEC, which fired off an open letter telling him and other party captains to stand behind Flanders. The Minority Leader's immobility tied down other Democratic votes: John F. Kennedy waited upon the decision of Johnson or McClellan to determine his course—and Leverett Saltonstall in turn was keying on Kennedy. The quiescence of the party high command stood athwart the efforts of Flanders's allies to demonstrate visible increases in support for censure.[11]

Despite the hostility of his own party's leadership and the unreliability of the Democrats, Flanders could count on significant help. After he introduced his first resolution, the NCEC had come to his aid. It supplied research, lobbying, and staff assistance which were essential. NCEC partisans labored to produce both the substance and the impression of growing momentum. They labored to stimulate displays of public opinion in favor of the Flanders resolution, but more importantly, to mobilize significant elites to put the heat on wavering Senators. The NCEC retained William Frye for public relations work; hired Lawrence Henderson, whose experience on the Hill included previous stints in the offices of Benton and Flanders, to aid the Vermonter; obtained the services of Raimond Bowles to maintain contact with the Republicans; and tapped such sources of funds for these expensive operations as Benton, Paul Hoffman, and Marshall Field.[12]

An important accretion of strength for the cause came when Senator John McClellan gave it his blessing. Fulbright brought him to a meeting with Flanders on July 18; McClellan told Flanders he was "vitally interested" in the censure motion, but would like its consideration delayed until July 30, after his difficult primary race. Flanders agreed to the postponement and thus was able to commit McClellan and, it was assumed, other Southerners (and even some Northerners) to the enterprise. Other leaders were implored to lend support. Senator Humphrey lectured Lyndon Johnson "in no uncertain words" that it was the "duty and the responsibility of the Democratic Party to line up behind . . . Senator Flanders' motion." [13]

The Democratic leadership, however, refused to make the Flanders resolution a party issue. The Democratic Policy Committee declared it "a matter of conscience upon which each individual Senator should vote his convictions without regard to party affiliations." Lacking direction from the top, a number of Democrats waffled. Chavez was reported "completely evasive"; J. Allen Frear of Delaware was "trying to duck"; George Smathers was "unresolved"; and John F. Kennedy was described as "non-committal." Senator Jackson, "wearing [a] judicial mantle," reasoned that his role in the Army-McCarthy proceeding precluded taking a stand on Flanders's motion. "His legalisms [were] beginning to weaken Symington." Thus, the prospects for punishing McCarthy remained fluid. [14]

On July 30, Flanders introduced Senate Resolution 301, calling for censure. He grounded it chiefly upon McCarthy's contempt for the Gillette subcommittee and its members, upon the European follies of Cohn and Schine, and upon the Senator's "habitual contempt for people" as glaringly demonstrated in the hazing of General Zwicker. Formidable opposition immediately surfaced. Everett Dirksen charged that the Communist Party, along with such groups as the CIO, ADA, and NCEC, had "climbed into bed" with Flanders. Beyond such outright resistance lay further shoals. H. Alexander Smith, a McCarthy critic but an inveterate conciliator, had long sought to bring the Wisconsinite back to the administration "team." In lieu of censure, he proposed that a select committee study the "divisiveness" in the Senate and nation over both communism and the methods employed against it. The panel was to report back by February 1955, a date promising obvious relief to those who wished to duck hard choices in an election year. On July 31, Prescott Bush introduced a resolution calling for a uniform code of committee behavior as yet another solution to the McCarthy problem. [15]

Guy Cordon of Oregon broached the most serious objection to Flanders's motion when he noted that it neither specified of what McCarthy was guilty nor gave the Senator a forum before which to defend himself. Cordon urged that the resolution be referred to a committee. This argument had a powerful impact on the Southern Democrats. Price Daniel of Texas enjoined that it was "doubly important" to employ "proper rules of procedure" since McCarthy himself had been accused of neglecting such niceties. Walter George considered it "unthinkable" not to send the motion to committee; McClellan and Spessard Holland supported him.[16]

Flanders and his allies distrusted the clamor for specifications, fearing endless debate and a plethora of addenda; however, to oblige his critics, Flanders introduced thirty-three charges (which the NCEC had drafted). Earlier, Fulbright had submitted six specifications as amendments to Senate Resolution 301, and Morse added seven more later; the result was forty-six overlapping charges. The anti-McCarthy activists similarly questioned the wisdom of referring the motion to committee: as Monroney pointed out, McCarthy had made a shambles of five other committees. Nevertheless, Knowland moved that the Flanders proposal and all amendments and substitutes be referred to a six-man select committee chosen by the Vice-President. The Majority Leader, after conferring with Ives and Lyndon Johnson, accepted an amendment by Ives requiring the panel to report back before the session adjourned; Knowland's motion passed, 75 to 12, the nay votes being cast by those who wanted an immediate showdown.* Herbert Lehman, one of the twelve, felt the pro-Flanders forces had "temporarily been defeated." Fulbright, also disheartened, remarked that "Joe can buffalo any committee on earth." However, other censure supporters saw the creation of the select committee as a victory.[17]

After a series of conferences, the majority and minority leaders agreed upon the make-up of the select committee. On August 5, it was announced that Senator Arthur V. Watkins of Utah would head the panel and would serve along with Francis Case (South Dakota) and Frank Carlson (Kansas), Republicans, and John Stennis (Mississippi), Sam Ervin (North Carolina), and Ed Johnson (Colorado),

* Voting against referral were Republicans Flanders, Cooper, and Duff, and Democrats Chavez, Douglas, Fulbright, Hennings, Hill, Humphrey, Lehman, Magnuson, and Monroney.

Democrats. None of the Republicans was particularly high in party counsels. Carlson had been an early Eisenhower backer; Case was noted as a cautious moderate (somewhat more conservative than Carlson). Watkins, also a conservative, was calm and deliberate, but capable of anger when provoked, as he would be shortly. Ervin and Stennis had enjoyed distinguished judicial careers prior to elevation to the Senate, and Ed Johnson, who was giving up his Senate seat to run for Governor of Colorado, was a potent party leader, a "senior adviser" to Lyndon Johnson. Except for the Coloradan, none of the six wielded great power, but each was highly "respected," conservative, and representative of the values cherished by Senate insiders. None could be classified a liberal. It was also noted that the McCarthy issue did not cut too deeply in their home states. (Although the McCarthy issue, by Ed Johnson's own estimate, cost him 50,000 votes, he won his gubernatorial contest easily.) [18]

In an intangible way, the ground had already shifted out from under McCarthy. Possibly the first sign had been the sheer fact that Knowland sent the Flanders motion to a committee. Referral might not please those who sought an immediate showdown, but it showed, Hubert Humphrey wrote, that "seventy-five of Senator McCarthy's colleagues, including nearly all the Republicans in the Senate, believed the charges against him are serious enough . . . to set up a special committee to investigate them." The solid, impeccable appointments to the select committee also reassured censure backers. While McCarthy, encouraged perhaps by the panel's conservatism, conceded that it was a "good bunch of people," Flanders, too, was "very well satisfied." Under Watkins, the Vermonter predicted, "they will hold the reins, and to have someone else hold the reins will be a new experience for the junior Senator from Wisconsin." [19]

As if to prove Flanders correct, Watkins announced that the proceedings would not be televised: There would be no crowd to play to. Characteristically, the Mormon elder from Utah also forbade smoking during the hearings. When McCarthy tried to intervene in the deliberations over ground rules, he was rebuffed. He demanded that his accusers be hailed before the tribunal for cross-examination, but the committee announced that such testimony would probably not be solicited: most evidence received would be documentary, and only witnesses with personal knowledge would be called. Watkins also ruled that either McCarthy or his attorney might question a witness, but not both. The panel, Watkins explained, would treat procedural and evidential questions; it did not assay the flaming issues which characterized previous debate over McCarthy. The Senators adopted the suggestion of Frank Carlson at their first meeting: "Let it be clearly understood that he [McCarthy] was not running the committee." Similarly, Ervin proposed that the group "sustain all rulings of the Chairman on evidence and if any disagreement, to consider that in private meetings; also that hearings be conducted as if it were a court." [20]

Before the hearings began, the Watkins committee set aside the more dubious specifications offered by Flanders, Morse, and Fulbright and boiled the remainder down into five categories which seemed the likeliest grounds for censure. These involved charges relating to "contempt of the Senate or a Senatorial committee"; "encouragement" of federal employees to violate the law and their oaths of office; receipt or use of confidential material from executive files; "abuse of colleagues"; and the Zwicker incident.[21]

The first public hearing on August 31 set the pattern to follow. McCarthy's attorney Edward Bennett Williams led off with an argument that the contempt power, on which censure would presumably be based, died at the end of each Congress—hence McCarthy could not be punished for actions in the previous Congress. Watkins terminated the plea, instructing Williams to submit a brief on the precedents, and blandly informed him that the committee's "preliminary determinations" had refuted his line of reasoning. Later, Williams and McCarthy questioned Ed Johnson's impartiality in view of his statement in March to the effect that all of McCarthy's colleagues loathed him. Watkins cut McCarthy off. As McCarthy persisted, Watkins declared him out of order and shouted him down. "We are not going to be interrupted by these diversions and sidelines." The Chairman's gavel banged down, the hearing was recessed, and McCarthy, agog, could only term the proceeding "the most unheard of thing I ever heard of." [22]

Throughout the rest of the hearings—there were only nine public sessions—McCarthy was kept on a short leash. The committee counsel E. Wallace Chadwick and his assistant laboriously recited the documentation of the Flanders-Fulbright-Morse charges. The result, for a McCarthy hearing, was most unusual. As one journalistic wag phrased it, the committee might not censure McCarthy, "but it may well bore him to death." As black-and-white proof of what Mc-Carthy had done and said over the years was read into the record, each session, according to James Reston, was "a form of censure of its own." McCarthy and Williams made their defense, and the committee withdrew to consider the evidence and write a report. They did so with a unity which obliterated party lines. (During the hearings, it was noted, they sat at random around the table rather than according to party.) [23]

On September 27, the Watkins Committee issued a unanimous report urging McCarthy's censure on two counts: for his "contemptuous, contumacious, and denunciatory" conduct toward the Privileges and Elections Subcommittee and its members (notably Hendrickson); and for his "reprehensible" treatment of General Zwicker. McCarthy was found guilty of irresponsibility and impropriety in other actions, but not to a degree meriting censure. As for inviting employees to break the law and possessing classified documents, these raised thorny constitutional questions, and the committee gave McCarthy the benefit of the doubt. The report condemned McCarthy for violating the ethical values of the Senate as an institution, for breaches of the "club's" decorum. (William S. White astutely described the Watkins panel as something like a private club's house committee.) The Watkins report said nothing about "McCarthyism," engaged almost none of the liberal criticisms of McCarthy, and rehabilitated no victims; it merely declared his ruffianly behavior in a gathering of gentlemen to be distasteful. [24]

From the day the select committee was created, it—and the whole McCarthy issue—operated within fundamentally conservative and institutional parameters. Flanders himself appreciated this fact. In a letter to the Watkins Committee, he noted that McCarthy, as subcommittee chairman, "did not function in the traditional or accepted manner," but employed "radically new methods of an entirely alien nature," and posed a "threat to the very traditions and foundations of our orderly democratic procedures." In his own more biblical fashion, Watkins commented on what he called McCarthy's " 'unrighteous use of authority.' " In a sense, the emerging alignments bore out the strategic perception of NCEC operatives that McCarthy must be placed in juxtaposition to his conservative targets. However, the NCEC itself and the early proponents of censure moved out of center stage. Flanders would play no leading role in the coming floor fight—that task would devolve upon members of the Select Committee.[25]

Before their reckoning with McCarthy, his colleagues required fortification against the anxieties upon which the Wisconsin Senator had thrived, and so once more they confronted the "communist issue" in its legislative dimension. On August 11, the Senate debated S. 3706, John Marshall Butler's proposal to add a new category, "Communist-infiltrated" organizations, to those which fell under the Internal Security Act of 1950; such organizations—presumably labor unions—would lose their bargaining and representational rights before the National Labor Relations Board. Liberals were perturbed by what Senator Lehman termed a "blunderbuss bill" and "deadly anti-union weapon." Morse and Humphrey urged caution, while citing their own demonstrated concern with the problem. Liberal foes of the Butler bill rallied behind Senator Magnuson's proposal to refer the whole issue to a presidential Commission on Security. Their numerical weakness was revealed, however, when Magnuson's amendment was defeated, 57 to 31. (The losing side comprised 28 liberal and moderate Democrats plus Ives, Cooper, and Morse; 12 conservative Democrats voted on the other side.) [26]

Having failed to turn the left flank, Democratic liberals next tried to maneuver to the right. Hubert Humphrey called up his amendment, which, as a substitute for the Butler bill, declared the Communist Party to be no true political party, but rather "an instrumentality of a conspiracy to overthrow the Government of the United States." Consequently, anyone who "knowingly and willfully" became a member of it would, upon conviction, be subject to a fine and imprisonment. Cheered on by such liberal cosponsors as Morse, Lehman, and Kennedy, Humphrey declared it time "to quit 'horsing around.' " "I am tired of reading headlines about being 'soft' toward communism," he complained. "I am tired of having people play the Communist issue as though it were a great overture which has lasted for years. . . . I want Senators to stand up and to answer whether they are for the Communist Party, or are against it." It was left to Senators Ferguson and Cooper to question the amendment's constitutionality and effect on civil liberties. Senator Price Daniel muddled the parliamentary situation by folding Butler's bill, with some alterations, back into the Humphrey amendment. Eighty-five Senators gulped down this concoction; only Lehman voted nay, and even he assented to the Humphrey amendment and the Butler bill itself, both of which were passed unanimously.[27]

In the House of Representatives, the Butler-Humphrey measure encountered second thoughts. Some argued that the measure would nullify Title I of the Internal Security Act, which specifically denied that membership in the Communist Party was a crime. (Otherwise the earlier bill would undermine the Fifth Amendment: Communists who sought to register as the law required could be whipsawed with prosecutions under the Smith Act.) Aided by Justice Department officials, members of the lower house rewrote S. 3706 so that Communist Party membership would no longer constitute a crime *per se;* the Party was simply denied legal political standing and its members were made subject to the penalties prescribed in the McCarran Act.[28]

In the Senate, Humphrey strove to reinsert his amendment in the House version of the Butler bill, while Estes Kefauver stood virtually alone in resisting the headlong rush to enact an anticommunist statute. Humphrey complained that though the House had defined communism as "a man-eating bear . . . it went forth with a powderpuff and touched the bear on the nose." He found it strange that after "all the speeches we have heard on communism," when the chance to act arose, "we start backing away from it." Morse relished the irony of the administration's unenthusiastic response to the measure: apparently the White House thought Humphrey "a little too harsh on the Communists." McCarran and Ferguson warned that Humphrey's amendment would gut the Internal Security Act, but, after Senators Lennon and—surprisingly—Kefauver withdrew their nay votes, the proviso was reinstated by a 41 to 39 margin. Then the entire bill passed 81 to 1, with only Kefauver dissenting. At Martin Dies's urging, the House instructed its conferees to accept the Humphrey amendment. When the conference report came before the Senate, Kefauver again expressed concern that the bill might penalize those with unorthodox beliefs. "Let them join the party of Mars or the party of Jupiter, if they want to be different," Humphrey responded. The Senate finally approved the measure 79 to zero, and the House followed suit by a 265 to 2 vote.[29]

The legislative history of the Communist Control Act attested to one lawmaker's dictum that this was "not a normal time." There was no agreement on what, precisely, the measure would do—whether it really did "outlaw" the Communist Party or not. Martin Dies received credit for having originated portions of the liberals' bill, though Humphrey insisted that he "took only a few provisions from the Dies bill." With deep conviction Humphrey maintained that the Communist Party was a conspiracy, ought to be treated as such, and must not be allowed to masquerade as a political party. Far from stirring up hysteria, he argued, his amendment would end "star-chamber proceedings" and "remove the Communist issue from the political arena to the courts." (Other legislators allayed their doubts about the measure by arguing that the courts could be trusted to decide the question.) [30]

Despite Humphrey's vigorous appeals to principle, the Communist Control Act also carried a heavy burden of partisan calculation. The *Wall Street Journal* scored the coup as "political skulduggery." Humphrey's legislative aide stated that the question of the political wisdom of the maneuver was resolved "when we considered the long range desirability of the Liberals beginning to assume the initiative on the question of anti-subversive legislation." As a dividend, the enterprise reportedly abetted Senator James Murray's quest for reelection, and some of Humphrey's backers believed that it helped shield him from red-baiting. The Communist Control Act solaced Democrats angered by months of Republican manipulation of the security-risk "numbers game." "We called them and raised them," gloated one leading Democrat, "and they fell in line, like stampeding cattle." [31]

Such elation aside, the Democrats continued to worry about the electoral potency of the communist issue. Indeed, as soon as the Republicans had begun to trumpet the number of security risks fired by the Eisenhower administration, the Democrats had assumed that their rivals would rely heavily on red-baiting during the 1954 campaign. In January 1954, Stephen A. Mitchell had warned that recent Republican oratory prefigured an effort "to link the Democratic Party with the words 'socialist,' 'communism,' 'marxist,' and 'left-winger.'" In June, Mitchell predicted that the Republicans would "use the President to smile and McCarthy to smear" in the campaign.[32]

The latter prophecy failed, however, to account for McCarthy's fall from grace. State GOP leaders had already begun backing away from the schismatic Senator. McCarthy, while claiming to have received "hundreds" of invitations to speak, announced that he would decline all but three previously accepted requests in order to get on with his investigations. Only one speech was billed as a political outing, and a spokesman even tried to minimize the local Republican organization's responsibility for the affair. A hospital sojourn later forced McCarthy to cancel even these engagements. Consequently, he intervened in the campaign only from a distance. He declared his support for all Republican candidates except Clifford Case of New Jersey, who had expressed forthright opposition to him.* In late October, McCarthy sent a telegram to Guy Gillette challenging him to "give a yes or no answer" on whether he would vote for censure. He also wired Paul Douglas that the latter's claim of an "open mind" on the censure issue was "a revolting exhibition of hypocrisy" and a "cowardly" evasion. GOP National Chairman Leonard Hall encapsulated McCarthy's personal influence on the campaign, however, in his comment that Americans were "sick and tired" of the subject.[33]

Nevertheless, McCarthy's "enforced silence" did not prevent Republicans from merchandising the wares in his line. GOP rhetoric featured the topic of security-risk firings prominently. Opportunely, the Civil Service Commission announced on October 11 that there had been 6,926 security dismissals in the year ending June 30, heartening Republicans who had banked on the continued salience of the communist issue. (Earlier, when a reporter asked Everett Dirksen if the new figures could be expected about two weeks before the election, the Illinois Senator had grinned broadly.) Vice-President Nixon, the administration's chief campaigner, boasted that the Eisenhower administration had "put the Reds on the run," that it had "kicked the Communists out of Government not by the hundreds, but by the

---

* Case's liberalism and anti-McCarthyism embroiled him with New Jersey's more conservative Republicans, who tried briefly to dump him from the party ticket. In October, a news story of unknown inspiration linked his sister with several Communist fronts. This smear probably worked to Case's advantage. In November, he won election to the Senate. *New York Times,* July 8, Aug. 11–12, Sept. 21–22, 26, 28, Oct. 14–19, 1954.

thousands." He warned that the Communist Party "had determined to conduct its program within the Democratic party." Oratory such as this prompted Adlai Stevenson to accuse Nixon of "McCarthyism in a white collar." [34]

Nixon also upbraided the Democrats for their "leftwing" proclivities. When the Republicans came in, he revealed, "we found in the files a blueprint for socializing America" through a "well-oiled scheme" calling for socialized medicine, housing, agriculture, water and power, and atomic energy. He attacked five western-state senatorial candidates (Glen Taylor, Joseph T. O'Mahoney, Sam Yorty, John Carroll, and Richard E. Neuberger) as "members of the Left Wing of their party" and warned that Democratic election gains "must inevitably come from their Americans for Democratic Action Wing." He noted areas of congruence between the programs of the ADA and those of the Communist Party.[35]

State-level campaigns reflected a similar thematic range. In Colorado, the question was asked (again): "How Red is John Carroll?" Foes of Joseph O'Mahoney, who sought the Wyoming Senate seat of the late Lester Hunt, labeled him "foreign agent 783" (he was so registered as the representative of Cuban sugar interests) and stressed that he had served as an attorney for Owen Lattimore. In Montana, luridly illustrated pamphlets flooded the state with their message about "Senator Murray and the Red Network over Congress." In Idaho, where Glen Taylor essayed a comeback, his enemies, not surprisingly, resorted to flamboyant red-baiting. However, the more flagrant political smears in several contests originated outside of official Republican Party circles, and the campaign generally hit slightly less strident notes than these. More commonly Republicans attacked their opponents for socialist or left-wing tendencies. In Illinois, for instance, the Republican candidate Joseph T. Meek did toll off Senator Douglas's leftist affiliations, but more characteristically he scored the incumbent as "Mr. Capital 'S' of Socialism," the "friend of the tax collector" and the "sponsor of the fishy-eyed bureaucrat." [36]

The elections produced a nominal victory for the Democrats, who narrowly recaptured both houses of Congress, and seemed to confirm the decline in potency of the communist issue and its corollaries. Democratic incumbents who had been attacked as leftists had a high rate of survival. Senators Murray, Douglas, Anderson, Kefauver, and Humphrey won; only Gillette of Iowa and Thomas Burke of Ohio were retired. While the Democratic challengers Sam Yorty in California and Glen Taylor in Idaho were beaten, O'Mahoney and the venerable Alben Barkley were returned to the Senate, and W. Kerr Scott in North Carolina and Richard Neuberger in Oregon made good their election bids.* Congressmen Kit Clardy, Fred Busbey, and Charles Kersten, three noted red-hunters, failed of reelection.

Across the country, the issues were diffuse, but various polling data indicated that McCarthy, had he campaigned actively, would have operated as a net liability to most fellow Republicans. A late-summer poll taken for the CIO found that voters in nine of eleven states would react negatively in heavy proportions (and by a slim margin even in Massachusetts) to a candidate endorsed by McCarthy; only in New Jersey would McCarthy's approval redound (slightly) to a candidate's advantage. An office-seeker who appplauded McCarthy would find that stand helpful only in Massachusetts, and one who advocated McCarthy's removal from his committee chairmanship would suffer only in the Bay State. The fact that 50 percent of the respondents in Iowa would hold it against a candidate who thought McCarthy had done "a fine job," while 16 percent would hold it in his favor, seemed to indicate that the McCarthy issue did not explain Gillette's defeat. (The polling figures did explain why both Senate candidates in Massachusetts were happy to discuss other topics.) Communists-in-government was not a very salient issue to the 1954 electorate. In one public opinion study, only 3 percent of those sampled volunteered praise for Republican efforts at "getting Communists out of government." To a query about the "worst thing" done by the GOP, the most frequent answer (13 percent) was "mishandled McCarthy." These data compelled two political scientists to conclude that McCarthy's influence at this stage had been "grossly misjudged in many quarters." As issues, McCarthy and censure were "almost

* It was suggested (without proof) that Burke's pro-censure position aided his foe. McCarthyism was not an issue between Barkley and John Sherman Cooper. Scott took several pokes at McCarthyism with no ill effect. *New York Times,* Nov. 4, 1954; Barkley to Mrs. Jim Vaden, June 26, 1954, Campaign, Senate, 1954, Barkley MSS; speeches, May 21, 26, 1954, Box 9.18, Scott MSS, North Carolina State Dept. of Archives and History.

as passé," according to William S. White, "as the Boxer Rebellion or William McKinley." [37]

However, a number of McCarthy's colleagues, unready to make so optimistic a reading of public opinion prior to the 1954 elections, exerted strong pressure to defer consideration of the report of the Watkins panel until after the campaign. Leverett Saltonstall, for example, facing a close reelection contest in Massachusetts, reportedly had no enthusiasm for a record vote prior to the election. The Democrats termed the question of scheduling the debate "a Republican matter," and Lyndon Johnson professed that his side was prepared to take up the report immediately, but several Democrats, including Ed Johnson who was running for Governor in Colorado, welcomed the delay. Senator Fulbright reported that both Lyndon Johnson and William Knowland favored postponement even before the decision was thrust upon them, and so the confrontation was deferred. [38]

When Congress reconvened November 8, Watkins introduced his committee's report and, the next day, its recommendations in the form of amendments to Flanders's resolution. McCarthy issued a statement claiming that the Communist Party had made the Watkins Committee "its unwitting handmaiden." This and subsequent attacks on the Select Committee helped alienate the last neutrals and negate the efforts of those who sought compromise. Wallace Bennett, who had previously not taken sides, announced that he would offer an addition to the censure motion dealing with McCarthy's denigratory remarks about the Watkins Committee. John Stennis defended his chairman; he could not "approve such slush and slime as a proper standard of senatorial conduct." He accused McCarthy, in his relations with the Gillette Committee, of having perpetrated "an insult to the constituted authority of the Senate, which was carrying out a constitutional mission." Three days later Senator Ervin exclaimed that if McCarthy had made his "fantastic and foul accusations" without believing them, he was morally incompetent to serve as a Senator; if he did believe them, he "ought to be expelled from the Senate for mental incapacity." On November 16, Watkins tossed aside his prepared remarks and, speaking extemporaneously, brought tears to the eyes of his colleagues. Declaring McCarthy's aspersions an affront to the Senate itself, he challenged: "What are you going to do about it?" [39]

During the debates, the Democrats pursued a strategy of silence in order to prevent the battle from forming along partisan lines and to insure that the matter was settled before the Eighty-third Congress expired. On November 8, Dennis Chavez impulsively intervened in a preliminary discussion; Lyndon Johnson strode over and whispered to him, and the New Mexican promptly took his seat. Johnson worked to dissuade those Democrats who were tempted to speak to the broader issues of "McCarthyism." "The burden is being carried by the very conservative members of the Watkins Committee," Senator Lehman's assistant wrote, "and those of us who have been holding the banner up for years are staying in the background." "Lyndon Johnson and others," he said, "are literally demanding that we refrain from rocking the boat." The Democrats agreed that the "best strategy is to remain silent and let the Republicans fight it out." [40]

In the heat of debate, several Democrats appeared to forget the Johnson program. Despite pressures from the leadership, Herbert Lehman made two speeches which went beyond the narrow indictment of the Watkins report; Senator Fulbright spoke on the "great sickness" abroad in the land evidenced by the public response to the censure question. Understandably, Ervin and Ed Johnson spoke in support of the Select Committee's recommendations. Alton Lennon, Price Daniel, and Russell Long also advocated censure; their pleas were couched in the old-school rhetoric of the Watkins report. On December 1, Lyndon Johnson abandoned silence and added his support to the motion. McCarthy's slanders upon the members of the Select Committee, said the Texan, "do not belong in the pages of the Congressional Record," but "would be much more fittingly inscribed on the wall of a men's room." The "real issue" was whether the Senate, "the greatest deliberative body in the history of the world, will permit abuse of a duly appointed committee" pursuing its duty.[41]

The Johnson tactic of keeping quiet and holding the lines was well fitted to offset the McCarthyite counterstrategy credited to Styles Bridges. Under this scheme, the twelve to fifteen McCarthy stalwarts would woo eight or twelve fellow Republicans who were amenable to compromise, then go to the rest of the GOP and point out that if the party split, "only the Democrats can win." With some additional support from this group, McCarthy's allies would be in a position to go to Johnson and say: "You don't want this to become a party issue,

do you? Let us find a compromise." Whether or not so elaborate a
plan was concocted, Bridges, Dirksen, Mundt, Barry Goldwater,
H. Alexander Smith, and Vice-President Nixon were all working on
proposals to avert censure. Most of these called for an apology by
McCarthy and a Senate approval of civility. However, the time for
such balm had passed. On December 1, Mundt's resolution substitut-
ing a disavowal of McCarthy's "intemperate statements" for censure
was defeated, 74 to 15; it lacked the support of either McCarthy's
"warmest friends or his hottest enemies," as Mundt put it.[42]

The pro-censure forces faced another threat in the defection of
Senator Francis Case from the solid ranks of the Watkins Committee.
Case demurred at censuring McCarthy for his abuse of General
Zwicker. He explained that new evidence revealed that the Army had
received, but dismissed, McCarthy's urgent request to hold Major
Peress for court-martial before the dentist left the Army. Thus the
treatment of Zwicker was somewhat mitigated by this great "provocation." (However, Senators Mundt and Humphrey suspected that it
was constituent pressure which influenced Case, and even before
learning of the new evidence, Case had invited McCarthy to apologize for his offenses and thus escape censure.) A number of Democrats also had doubts about the Zwicker censure count: McCarthy was
not the first to bullyrag a witness. Seeking "to maintain a full and
united front," the Democratic leaders decided to eliminate the
Zwicker clause and replace it with Bennett's amendment dealing with
McCarthy's contumacy toward the Watkins panel. The leadership
thought this gambit preferable to a leakage of Democratic votes
"with the possibility that Senator McCarthy might even win that particular censure count vote." [43]

Those who sought censure sat through the long defenses of Mc-
Carthy by his friends and through his hospitalization with a swollen
elbow; they resisted compromises and distractions, defeating palliat-
ing substitutes; and finally, on December 2, 1954, they approved the
resolution condemning his behavior toward the Privileges and Elections Subcommittee and his abuse of its members and those of the
Watkins Committee. The final vote was 67 to 22. Lyndon Johnson
had succeeded in massing every one of the 44 Democrats present
behind the motion; the Republicans split evenly, 22 on each side of
the issue.[44]

By censure, McCarthy lost not a single privilege of office. Senator Watkins described the action as "a formal slap on the wrist." Shortly after the final vote, Senator Bridges inquired of the Chair whether the resolution actually did "censure" McCarthy. The Vice-President confessed that the term was found only in the title, from which he removed it; the operative verb in the resolution was "condemned." Fulbright brought in a dictionary, which proved that neither word was complimentary to McCarthy. Welker, one of those who chortled when the oversight was discovered, had himself stated earlier that while one could not censure a man to death, one could condemn him to death.[45]

Censure, condemnation—whatever—had been voted on very narrow grounds. The Senate abjured "McCarthyism" only insofar as it impinged upon institutional proprieties. The proceedings, wrote Norman Thomas, were "in no way handsome," for McCarthy's "outrages against individual rights and freedom" had been ignored. "We have condemned the individual," Herbert Lehman fretted, "but we have not yet repudiated the 'ism.' " In the debates, McCarthy's colleagues acknowledged his previous achievements in varying degrees but had declared the issue to lie elsewhere; or they denied that he had a monopoly on anticommunism; or they belittled the number of notches on his gun. They never questioned the virtues of muscular anticommunism. Price Daniel, Harry Byrd, and Ed Johnson introduced an amendment to Senate Resolution 301 stating that censure should not be interpreted as an attack on the power of congressional committees to investigate communism. Having been sidetracked during the censure debate, Daniel successfully pressed for a similar resolution in 1955; Senator McClellan took the occasion to avow his determination to get to the bottom of the Peress case, and, under his chairmanship, the Permanent Subcommittee on Investigations pursued some of the quarry McCarthy had flushed in the previous Congress. Neither the deeper premises of McCarthyism nor the legitimacy of cold-war rhetoric had been questioned.[46]

Still, slight breezes of change were blowing. In 1955, the Democrats, while seldom attacking central postulates of the cold-war consensus, began to probe at some of its more exposed corollaries. Two years of Republican boasts about security-risk firings had soured them on the numerical approach to that problem. In the Democratic-controlled Eighty-fourth Congress, the Eisenhower security program was scrutinized by three different groups. Under Senator Humphrey, the Subcommittee on Reorganization of the Government Operations committee examined the structure of federal and private regulations with a view to recommending creation of a Commission on Government Security. (In August, Congress passed the Humphrey-Stennis resolution, which called for such a body; it was appointed in November.) [47] Olin Johnston led a subcommittee of the Post Office and Civil Service Committee in a parallel probe. Under Senator Hennings, the Subcommittee on Constitutional Rights (of the Judiciary Committee) considered the subject from a civil-libertarian perspective. The findings of these committees undercut past Republican claims. The Johnston Subcommittee ascertained, for instance, that the number of dismissals under Eisenhower's security order as of mid-1955 totaled only 343.[48]

Other episodes brought the security program under further critical scrutiny. In November 1954, John Paton Davies, Jr., long a target of the McCarthyites, was finally removed from the State Department; a chorus of condemnation greeted the decision. A few weeks later, Wolf Ladejinsky, a noted expert on land reform and devout anticommunist attached to the U.S. Embassy in Tokyo, was denied a transfer to the Agriculture Department on grounds that he was a security risk. The flimsiness of the allegations against Ladejinsky further discredited the security program and, in part, inspired Senator Humphrey's call for a Commission on Government Security. The case also provided ammunition for the attacks on the program which were mounted by Harry Cain, the former Senator and McCarthy ally then serving on the Subversive Activities Control Board. The loyalty-security apparatus fell into further disesteem when Harvey Matusow, an active, professional ex-Communist witness, confessed that he had perjured himself in several proceedings. The Supreme Court also made inroads on the loyalty mania, handing down decisions which greatly incensed McCarthy and other conservatives.* Even the sym-

* McCarthy singled out the *Slochower, Nelson* and *Cole* cases. Ironically, his arguments against *Pennsylvania v. Nelson* dovetailed with the states' rights rationale used by Southern foes of civil-rights decisions. Had the McCarthy miasma lasted longer (or civil-rights cases come sooner), a more seasoned McCarthyite-Dixiecrat alliance might have emerged. However, McCarthy never opposed racial equality *per se*—and

bols of the anticommunist crusade were blurring. In the week before McCarthy was censured, Alger Hiss was released from prison. (In the same penitentiary, another symbol disappeared when William Remington was beaten to death by a fellow-inmate.) [49]

In foreign policy, too, changes were coming. The Eisenhower administration had begun to act as if "coexistence" was not a dirty word. This development greatly perturbed the right wing of the GOP. During the censure debates, Knowland and Jenner salted the *Record* with addresses castigating this more accommodating approach to the Soviet Union. In 1955, as Ike prepared to leave for the Big Four summit conference, McCarthy fought a rear-guard battle against the "spirit of Geneva" in the name of militant anticommunism; his bellicose resolution was trounced 77 to 4, a lopsided repudiation which demonstrated the Wisconsin Senator's altered status.[50]

If these *démarches* represented only gingerly probing at the periphery of the conservative, anticommunist, cold-war presuppositions of America in the 1950s, McCarthy's own reaction revealed his appreciation that they posed a deeper threat to the politics of McCarthyism. In speeches delivered in late 1955 he attributed the recent brazen antics of the Communist Party to the "spirit of Geneva," which he equated with "illusion, folly and appeasement." He also warned of ongoing efforts to "reduce awareness of the Communist menace" and "destroy our security program," singling out the exertions of the Fund for the Republic and of the subcommittee headed by Tom Hennings, "Missouri's special contribution to the left-wing bleeding hearts club." The "Democrat Party," he insisted, must repudiate "activities which give aid and comfort to our country's enemies." [51]

However, censure had precipitated McCarthy's downward slide. After 1954, his floor speeches elicited conscious inattention. The press ignored his handouts; the politicians, his challenges. His effort to resuscitate the issue of subversion for the 1956 election failed. His angry letters to the President about American captives in China or the weakening of the security program received noncommittal replies; the Senator was no longer welcome at the White House. The denouement

at one time his opponents fretted over a rumor that he would preempt that liberal cause. *Cong. Record,* 102 (April 11, 1956): 6603–64, (June 14, 1956): 10319–21; Maurice Rosenblatt to Gifford Phillips, Aug. 31, 1953, File 4, Drawer 1, NCEC MSS.

of the McCarthy issue had helped crystallize a right-wing faction in the GOP, but also isolated it. Thus, when McCarthy, on December 7, 1954, felt compelled to "apologize" for supporting Eisenhower in 1952, he drew criticism even from several Republicans who had fought against his censure.[52]

As his shrewder critics had noted, McCarthy was the symbol and exemplar of McCarthyism, but not its single cause, and liberal opponents of the "ism" often did themselves a disservice in allowing themselves to be transfixed by the man. Hubert Humphrey had held that one danger of McCarthyism lay in "the addiction of liberals in politics to concentrate their entire attention upon him." McCarthy's censure brought only partial mitigation of the perils of McCarthyism. The cold war was far from over, as the spirit of Geneva proved evanescent. Reforms of the federal security apparatus—for example, those announced by Attorney General Brownell in March 1955—were meager. The Commission on Government Security, slow in starting, offered pallid recommendations for reform. It was the courts which cautiously took the lead in battening down American liberties against the cold-war gale.[53]

Nevertheless, the personal discredit which McCarthy suffered in national politics, while of limited scope, did produce thoroughgoing results. As an electioneering tactic, red-baiting did not entirely disappear, but in the future it would be carried on with far less gusto, frequency, or effect. As one ADA official argued in response to a criticism of the narrowness of the attack upon McCarthy, "the same forces in American political life that finally do away with McCarthy are the anti-bodies that will bring the infection under control. . . . He is a political ailment and must be cured politically." Later, Senator Hennings would write that, while censure did not directly confront McCarthyism, "we are gradually coming out of the wilderness and . . . the majority of people are beginning to realize that intolerance and conformity are in no sense acceptable elements in a democratic political economy." W. Kerr Scott, the freshman Senator from North Carolina, could report nine months after censure that McCarthy "no longer had any serious following here in Washington or in the country at large." [54] The change had been subtle and partial, but profound.

Epilogue

OBSERVERS HAVE FOUND it hard to explain the abruptness of McCarthy's political decline. On its face, censure did not look like a terribly stern punishment. Karl Mundt could believe that McCarthy emerged from it "pretty much unweakened and undamaged" (until his attack on the President alienated many supporters). As with his rise, so McCarthy's fall depended upon the confluence of a number of circumstances—a slackening of cold-war tensions, a subtle downward shift in his popularity, a related decline in fear on the part of his colleagues. The Eisenhower Administration had resolved to end further appeasement, but the Army's resistance fell short of the heroic and the White House's defense, anchored in the redoubt of "executive privilege," seems less than inspirational in the aftermath of Watergate. The damage to McCarthy did not appear irreversible at first; millions continued to revere him. Yet he was finished as a major actor on the national scene.[1]

McCarthy's last years are almost as sketchily documented as his early days. Onlookers sensed that he labored under a feeling of having been betrayed—by financial advisers who sold out and left him to suffer sizable losses, according to Richard Rovere; by erstwhile political allies who deserted him, according to Roy Cohn. His political performance—and his mood—grew unpredictable. He did not forgive Arthur Watkins, but he held no enduring grudge against Flanders and even sought reconciliation with Drew Pearson toward the end. There were numerous physical ailments, including a liver whose failure was hastened by drink. On May 2, 1957, Joe McCarthy died.[2]

It was cruel, but appropriate, that McCarthy, thriving as he had on semantic violence, should leave his name as a label for that activity. By 1968, usage was such that Spiro Agnew, rebuked for his rather tame red-baiting of Hubert Humphrey, confessed that if he had known his remark "would in some way cast me as the Joe McCarthy of 1968, I would have turned five somersaults to avoid saying it." The comment marks the essence of McCarthy's political success and the frustrations of his opponents: he had inseparably identified himself with the issue of communism. Yet his contemporaries exaggerated his personal grip on the American political pulse, for he was as much the product of events as their shaper. Though McCarthy was a formidable figure, it was the broader contingencies of partisan politics and the exigencies of world developments which ignited the flame of prominence in 1950 and, shifting in 1954, snuffed it.

Notes

CHAPTER 1   THE RED PERENNIAL

1. Mosinee *Times,* April 12, 19, 26, May 3, 1950; Milwaukee *Journal,* April 30–May 2, 1950; Minneapolis *Tribune,* May 1, 1950.

2. *New York Times,* March 4, 1949; Rovere, *Senator Joe McCarthy,* pp. 8–9; Milwaukee *Journal,* Oct. 29, 1952.

3. John M. Fenton, *In Your Opinion . . .* , p. 85; *Public Opinion Quarterly,* 11 (Winter 1947–48): 665; Gallup poll, Washington *Post,* Feb. 2, 1951. However, 45 percent of the 1951 respondents (the largest category) were uncertain what the cold war was. Still, a poll taken just before Truman requested aid for Greece and Turkey found that 52 percent believed the Soviets wanted to dominate the world; one year earlier, 39 percent had held that opinion. Washington *Post,* March 21, 1947.

4. Goldman, *The Crucial Decade —and After,* ch. 5; U.S. State Department, *United States Relations with China, With Special Reference to the Period 1944–1949* (Washington, 1949), pp. iv, vii, xv, and passim.

5. Tsou, *America's Failure in China,* pp. 195–235, 446, 453, 465, 493, and passim; Westerfield, *Foreign Policy and Party Politics,* pp. 262–68; Washington *Post,* March 20, 1947; *New York Times,* Aug. 6, 21–22, 1949; *Cong. Record,* 96 (Jan. 11, 1950): 298, (Jan. 13, 1950): 389.

6. Young, *Congressional Politics in the Second World War,* p. 156; Graebner, *The New Isolationism,* pp. 55, 58–59, 74–76; Westerfield, *Foreign Policy and Party Politics,* pp. 241–45; Adler, *The Isolationist Impulse,* pp. 317, 412, 447; *New York Times,* Nov. 28, 1945.

7. Minneapolis *Tribune,* Feb. 12, 1950; Westerfield, *Foreign Policy and Party Politics,* pp. 245–50; Graebner, *The New Isolationism,* pp. 14–16; Vandenberg, ed.,

Private Papers of Senator Vandenberg, pp. 351, 519–20, 523, 531; *Cong. Record*, 96 (Jan. 5, 1950): 79, 90.

8. *Public Papers of the Presidents, Harry S. Truman, 1949* (Washington, D.C., 1964), p. 485 (cited hereafter as *Truman Papers*); U.S. House of Representatives, *Directing the Secretary of Commerce to Transmit to the House of Representatives a Certain Letter With Respect to Dr. Edward U. Condon*, 80th Cong., 2nd Sess., 1948, H. Rept. 1753, p. 17.

9. On *Amerasia*, see Latham, *The Communist Controversy in Washington*, pp. 203–16; Griffith, *The Politics of Fear*, pp. 35–38; U.S. Senate, Subcommittee of the Committee on Foreign Relations, *A Resolution to Investigate Whether There Are Employees in the State Department Disloyal to the United States: Hearings Pursuant to S. Res. 231*, 81st Cong., 2d Sess., 1950; U.S. House of Representatives, *Report of Subcommittee IV of the Committee on the Judiciary in pursuance of H. Res. 430*, 79th Cong., 2d Sess., 1946; U.S. Senate, Internal Security Subcommittee, Committee on the Judiciary, *The Amerasia Papers: A Clue to the Catastrophe of China*, 2 vol., 91st Cong., 1st Sess., 1970; Service, *The Amerasia Papers*.

10. *Cong. Record*, 95 (Oct. 19, 1949): A6626; Washington *Post*, Dec. 14, 1951; George Sokolsky in Wheeling *Intelligencer*, March 16, 1950; *New York Times*, April 23, 1950.

11. Wolfskill, *Revolt of the Conservatives*, pp. 108, 152. Red-baiting antedated the 1930s. The Republican National Committee, for instance, had referred to those who probed the Harding scandals as "senatorial Bolshevists." Robert James Maddox, "Keeping Cool with Coolidge," *Journal of American History*, 52 (March 1967), 778*n*.

12. Schlesinger, *Age of Roosevelt: Coming of the New Deal*, pp. 457–60. The Hiss case, said the Chicago *Tribune* (Feb. 2, 1950), "proved that Dr. Wirt . . . knew what he was talking about." Cf. Wheeling *Intelligencer*, April 10, 1950 (Sokolsky). Significantly, Wirt was thrust into the spotlight by foes of a bill to regulate the stock exchanges.

13. Schlesinger, *Age of Roosevelt: Politics of Upheaval*, pp. 518, 619–24, and passim; McCoy, *Landon of Kansas*, pp. 265, 272, 307–8, 321, 324; Moos, ed., *H. L. Mencken on Politics*, p. 327.

14. *New York Times*, Sept. 21, Oct. 26, 31, 1944; cf. Gaddis, *The United States and the Origins of the Cold War, 1941–1947*, pp. 58–60.

15. *New York Times*, Sept. 26–27, Oct. 6–8, Nov. 2, 5, 1944.

16. *Ibid.*, Feb. 8, June 2, July 27, Sept. 27, 1946; Washington *Post*, Nov. 2–3, 6, 1946; Hamby, *Beyond the New Deal*, p. 157.

17. Shelton, "Nine G.O.P. Senate Freshman," pp. 10–12; Cater, "Senator Cain," p. 15; Washington *Post*, Jan. 20, 1952; *Public Opinion Quarterly*, 10 (Fall 1946): 423; Milwaukee *Journal*, Oct. 17, 23, Nov. 6, 1946.

18. August Ogden, *Dies Committee,* pp. 48, 74, and passim; Dies, *Trojan Horse in America,* p. 285. On the Dies Committee versus labor, see Auerbach, *Labor and Liberty,* pp. 164–66, 169–71.

19. Ogden, *Dies Committee;* Hadley Cantril, ed., *Public Opinion, 1935–1946,* p. 164; Goodman, *The Committee,* pp. 48–50, 161, 167–244.

20. Goodman, *The Committee,* pp. 252–67; Cooke, *A Generation on Trial,* passim; Carr, *House Committee on Un-American Activities,* pp. 88–131.

21. Cooke, *Generation on Trial,* pp. 9–11; Carr, *House Committee on Un-American Activities,* p. 99; Goldman, *Crucial Decade,* pp. 104–6, 111; Fiedler, *An End to Innocence,* pp. 20–22.

22. *Cong. Record,* 96 (Jan. 23, 1950): 755, (Jan. 25, 1950): 891, 902–3; "President's Press Conference of Aug. 5, 1948," *Truman Papers, 1948,* p. 433; Milwaukee *Sentinel,* Jan. 22, 1950. On Yalta, see Theoharis, *The Yalta Myths.*

23. Goodman, *The Committee,* pp. 244–47, 249–53, 267–68; Carr, *House Committee on Un-American Activities,* pp. 88–92, 153–65.

24. Acheson, "Crisis in Asia—An Examination of United States Policy," *Department of State Bulletin,* 22 (Jan. 23, 1950): 111–18; Tsou, *America's Failure in China,* pp. 536–37; Westerfield, *Foreign Policy and Party Politics,* pp. 366–67; Milwaukee *Sentinel,* Jan. 6, 1950.

25. *New York Times,* Jan. 26, Feb. 1, March 1, 5, 1950; Chicago *Tribune,* Feb. 2, 1950; Acheson, *Present at the Creation,* p. 101.

26. Chicago *Tribune,* Feb. 5, 1950; *New York Times,* March 1, 1950.

27. *Truman Papers, 1950,* p. 138; *Time,* 56 (Aug. 7, 1950): 17, (Oct. 2, 1950): 12–14, (Oct. 16, 1950): 112. On the debate over whether to build the hydrogen bomb, see Gilpin, *American Scientists and Nuclear Weapons Policy,* pp. 73–111; Lilienthal, *The Journals of David E. Lilienthal,* vol. 2: *The Atomic Energy Years, 1945–1950,* pp. 580–84, 587–91, 613–14.

28. *New York Times,* Feb. 4–5, 11, March 2, 8, 11, 13, June 9, 1950.

29. Abels, *Out of the Jaws of Victory;* Latham, *Communist Controversy,* pp. 393–99.

30. *New York Times,* Sept. 22, 26, 28, Oct. 2, 5, 1948.

31. Latham, *Communist Controversy,* p. 396; Ross, *The Loneliest Campaign,* pp. 49–53; Schuyler, *Black and Conservative,* pp. 311–12; Berelson, Lazarsfeld, and McPhee, *Voting,* pp. 236.

32. *Truman Papers, 1948,* p. 860. For other illustrations of this theme, see also pp. 559, 610–11, 802, 845, 926–29.

33. "Address in Oklahoma City," Sept. 28, 1948, *ibid.,* pp. 609–14; "Address at Mechanics Hall in Boston," Oct. 27, 1948, *ibid.,* pp. 882–86.

34. Clark address, Kiamesha Lake, Sept. 18, 1948; Clark speech, Des Moines, Sept. 6, 1948; Democratic National Committee, "Files of the Facts: V. Loyalty and Subversive Activities," n.d. [1948], all in White House Assignment File, Spingarn Papers, Truman Library.

35. Elsey note, "Random thoughts 26 August [1948]"; memoranda, Elsey to Clark Clifford, Aug. 16 and 27, 1948; memorandum, Clifford to the President, Aug. 4, 1948, all in Elsey Papers, Internal Security—Congressional Loyalty Investigations, Truman Library; Stephen J. Spingarn Oral History Interview, pp. 40–43, Truman Library.

36. Berman, "Civil Rights and Civil Liberties," p. 203; Schmidt, *Henry Wallace,* p. 247; Lubell, *Future of American Politics,* pp. 200–1, 204; Westerfield, *Foreign Policy and Party Politics,* pp. 323–24; Yarnell, *Democrats and Progressives,* pp. 109–10.

37. Schmidt, *Henry Wallace,* pp. 159, 252–53, 261; Bernstein, "America in War and Peace;" pp. 309–10; Theoharis, "The Rhetoric of Politics," p. 221; Yarnell, *Democrats and Progressives,* ch. 7 and passim; Clifford, "Memorandum for the President," n.d. [Nov., 1947], Clifford Papers, Truman Library; Birkhead Oral History Interview, p. 2, Truman Library.

38. Berelson et al., *Voting,* p. 10; Campbell, Converse, Miller, and Stokes, *American Voter,* pp. 531–32. For the thesis that Truman exerted a "conservative" appeal in 1948, see Lubell, *Future of American Politics,* pp. 158–60, 164–65.

39. Theoharis, "The Rhetoric of Politics," p. 221; Yarnell, *Democrats and Progressives,* pp. 85, 107. To say that liberals "legitimized" red-baiting in 1948 also seems to ignore thirty years in the development of this political art.

40. Latham, *Communist Controversy,* pp. 394–95, 398; Westerfield, *Foreign Policy and Party Politics,* pp. 325–26; David B. Truman, *The Congressional Party,* pp. 16–17; Chicago *Tribune,* Feb. 11, 1950. Irwin Ross has speculated that "a Dewey victory would have spared the country the vast trauma of the McCarthy era." Ross, *Loneliest Campaign,* p. 267.

41. Westerfield, *Foreign Policy and Party Politics,* pp. 119, 371–72; Vandenberg, ed., *Private Papers,* p. 546.

42. Dulles was charged with anti-Semitism for a remark (made upstate) which, he argued, was merely anticommunist: "If you could see the kinds of people in New York City making up this bloc that is voting for my opponent . . . with your own eyes, I know that you would be out, every last man and woman of you, on election day." *New York Times,* Sept. 20, 23–24, Oct. 4, 6, 11, 15, 21, 26, 31, Nov. 1, 5, 1949.

43. *Cong. Record,* 96 (Jan. 11, 1950): 298; Milwaukee *Sentinel,* Jan. 22, 1950; *New York Times,* Feb. 7, 1950.

44. Pollard, "The White House News Conference as a Channel of Communication," p. 665; Theoharis, "Rhetoric of Politics," pp. 222–24, 226; Wester-

field, *Foreign Policy and Party Politics*, pp. 326–30; Vandenberg, ed., *Private Papers*, pp. 468–71; President's News Conference of Dec. 9, 1948, *Truman Papers, 1948*, p. 959; Acheson, *Present at the Creation*, pp. 309–10.

45. Bontecou, *Federal Loyalty-Security Program*, pp. 10–30; Chase, "Controlling Subversive Activities," pp. 61–82, 107–17; Latham, *Communist Controversy*, pp. 362–64; "Report of the President's Temporary Commission on Employee Loyalty," Feb. 20, 1947, OF 252-I, Truman Papers.

46. Bontecou, *Federal Loyalty-Security Program*, pp. 21–22; Harper, *Politics of Loyalty*, pp. 22–24; Latham, *Communist Controversy*, pp. 365–66; Phillips, *Truman Presidency*, pp. 360–61; Theoharis, "Threat to Civil Liberties," pp. 268–69; Theoharis, "Document: Attorney General Clark, Internal Security, and the Truman Administration," pp. 16–23; Theoharis, "Escalation of the Loyalty Program," pp. 242–43, 246–47; memorandum, John C. Collet to Dr. John Steelman, Sept. 18, 1946, OF 252-I, Truman Papers; Subcommittee of the House Post Office and Civil Service Committee, Report (with Minority Views), July 20, 1946, OF 252, *ibid.*

47. Stephen J. Spingarn, Memorandum for the File, Jan. 15, 1947; Minutes of President's Temporary Commission on Employee Loyalty, Jan. 13, 1947; memoranda, Spingarn to Edward H. Foley, Jr., Jan. 19 and 29, 1947; Spingarn, "Notes on Commission Meeting of Feb. 14, 1947," all in Treasury Department File—President's Temporary Commission on Employee Loyalty, vol. II, folder 1, Spingarn Papers.

48. 12 *Federal Register* 1935; Harper, *Politics of Loyalty*, pp. 26–44; Theoharis, "Escalation of the Loyalty Program," pp. 247–50; "The Report of the President's Temporary Commission on Employees Loyalty," OF 252-I, Truman Papers.

49. Washington *Post*, Dec. 1, 1950, quoted in Ekirch, Jr., *The Decline of American Liberalism*, p. 356; Harper, *Politics of Loyalty*, pp. 47–48.

50. Freeland, *The Truman Doctrine and the Origins of McCarthyism*, pp. 115, 127–28, 142.

51. Washington *Post*, March 13, April 11, 1947; *New York Times*, June 18, 1950; undated MS [ca. April 1950], "The Cold Civil War," Box 11, Rovere MSS, State Historical Society of Wisconsin.

52. It was reported that the Loyalty Commission held a "secret meeting" the day *Friedman* was handed down. Washington *Post*, March 18–19, 23–24, 1947; *Friedman v. Schwellenbach*, 330 U.S. 838 (1947). For the initial assumption that the loyalty report would be released on February 21, see Spingarn, "Memorandum for the Temporary Commission File," Feb. 20, 1947, Treasury Department File— President's Temporary Commission on Employee Loyalty, vol. II, folder 1, Spingarn Papers.

53. *Cong. Record*, 93 (June 12, 1947): 8943, 8979–81; Spingarn, "Notes on Commission Meeting of Feb. 14, 1947," Treasury Department File—President's Temporary Commission on Employee Loyalty, vol. II, folder 1, Spingarn Papers; Tanner,

"The Passage of the Internal Security Act of 1950," pp. 150–51; Theoharis, "Escalation of the Loyalty Program," p. 248.

54. Washington *Post*, March 23, 1947; Tanner, "Passage of the Internal Security Act of 1950," pp. 147, 150–51.

55. Washington *Post*, March 12, 1947; Theoharis, "Rhetoric of Politics," p. 214n; McGrath speech before the Advertising Club of New York, April 19, 1950, McGrath Papers, Truman Library. The speech is quoted in Theoharis, "Rhetoric of Politics," p. 215; Theoharis, *Seeds of Repression*, p. 136; Bernstein, "America in War and Peace," p. 310; LaFeber, *America, Russia, and the Cold War*, p. 106.

56. Bernstein, "America in War and Peace," pp. 309–10; Theoharis "Rhetoric of Politics," pp. 201–19 (esp. pp. 202, 213).

57. For examples of "balance," see *Truman Papers, 1947*, pp. 490–91; *Truman Papers, 1948*, pp. 181, 612–13; *Truman Papers, 1950*, pp. 270–71.

58. *Public Opinion Quarterly*, 9 (Spring 1945): 102–3, 10 (Fall 1946): 436, 10 (Winter 1946–47): 640, 11 (Winter 1947–48): 653.

59. McLellan and Reuss, "Foreign and Military Policies," p. 23; Freeland, *Truman Doctrine*, passim; *New York Times*, Sept. 27, 1946; Milwaukee *Journal*, Oct. 2, 1946; Hamby, *Beyond the New Deal*, p. 135; Washington *Post*, Nov. 5, 1946; Jennings Randolph to Truman, July 25, 1946, OF 252, Truman Papers; Smith and Sarasohn, "Hate Propaganda in Detroit," pp. 44–45.

60. For the notion that each party has a congressional and a presidential faction— parties within the parties—see Burns, *Deadlock of Democracy*.

61. Ripley, *Power in the Senate*, p. 15; cf. Schattschneider, *Party Government*, ch. 6.

62. Kogan, "Illinois: A Sorry State," pp. 362–63; New York *Post*, July 6, 1951; Harper, *Politics of Loyalty*, pp. 246–49; Evans and Novak, *Lyndon B. Johnson*, pp. 51–53; cf. White, *Citadel*, p. 106.

CHAPTER 2   "A LIST OF 205 . . ."

1. Rovere, *Senator Joe McCarthy*, pp. 77–78; cf. Roy Cohn, *McCarthy*, p. 14. On McCarthy's early life, see Anderson and May, *McCarthy*, pp. 6–10 and passim; Rovere, pp. 75ff. I am also highly indebted to Griffith, *The Politics of Fear*, ch. 1.

2. Anderson and May, *McCarthy*, pp. 11–36; *Christian Science Monitor*, April 7, 1950 (Max K. Gilstrap); also see the series by Oliver Pilat and William V. Shannon, "Smear Incorporated," New York *Post*, Sept. 4–23, 1951.

3. Anderson and May, *McCarthy*, pp. 37–71; Steinke, "The Rise of McCarthyism," pp. 38–41 and passim. The prime example of McCarthy's questionable jurisprudence was the Quaker Dairy case, in which he destroyed parts of the court record: *State ex. rel. Department of Agriculture v. McCarthy*, 232 Wis. 258.

4. Anderson and May, *McCarthy*, pp. 78–84; Steinke, "Rise of McCarthyism," ch. 2; Milwaukee *Journal*, March 16–19, May 4–6, 1946; *Wisconsin State Journal*, March 18, 1946; Madison *Capital-Times*, Jan. 8, Feb. 24, March 24, May 7, 1946.

5. *Wisconsin Blue Book 1948* (Madison, 1948), pp. 604, 675; Milwaukee *Journal*, June 16, 24, July 7, 15, 18, 26, Aug. 1, 8–9, 1946. On the primary, see Roger T. Johnson, *Robert M. La Follette, Jr.*; Meyer, "The Politics of Loyalty"; Fried, "Young Bob La Follette"; Michael James O'Brien, "Senator Joseph R. McCarthy," ch. 1.

6. On Communist oppostition to La Follette: Morris Rubin, *The Progressive*, 10 (Aug. 26, 1946): 1; Marquis Childs, *Wisconsin State Journal*, Aug. 19, 1946; William T. Evjue, "Young Bob," p. 200; Anderson and May, *McCarthy*, pp. 103–5. For critical treatments of this theory, see note 5 *supra*, and Steinke and Weinstein, "McCarthy and the Liberals," pp. 43–50.

7. Milwaukee *Journal*, Oct. 2, 17, 23, Nov. 6, 10, 1946; Steinke, "Rise of McCarthyism," pp. 56–59.

8. Rovere, *Senator Joe McCarthy*, pp. 104–11; Anderson and May, *McCarthy*, pp. 122–57; U.S. Senate, Hearings before a Subcommittee of the Committee on Banking and Currency, *Study of Reconstruction Finance Corporation. Lustron Corp— Transportation Contract*, 81st Cong., 2nd Sess., 1950; Rep. John Vorys to author, Sept. 19, 1966; Davies, *Housing Reform During the Truman Administration*, pp. 68–72, 93–94.

9. Griffith, *Politics of Fear*, pp. 20–26; Anderson and May, *McCarthy*, pp. 158–64; U.S. Senate, Committee on Armed Services, *Malmedy Massacre Investigation*, 81st Cong., 1st Sess., 1949. For major debates, see *Cong. Record*, 95 (Jan. 27, 1949): 598–99, (July 26, 1949): 10160–74, (Oct. 14, 1949): 14511–34.

10. *Cong. Record*, 96 (Jan. 12, 1950): 342–43, (Jan. 18, 1950): 512–41, (Jan. 23, 1950): 744–54, (Jan. 24, 1950): 802–9; see also Milwaukee *Sentinel*, Nov. 19, 1949; Anderson and May, *McCarthy*, pp. 165–71.

11. *Cong. Record*, 96 (Jan. 12, 1950): 343, (Jan. 18, 1950): 536–37, 540.

12. Understandably, McCarthy turned increasingly to nonlegislative activities. See Griffith, *Politics of Fear*, pp. 13, 17–20; New York *Post*, Sept. 4, 1951 (Pilat and Shannon); cf. Minneapolis *Tribune*, April 2, 1950.

13. Rovere, *Senator Joe McCarthy*, pp. 121–22; Miles McMillin Memoir, Cornell University Oral History Program, pp. 18–24; *State v. McCarthy*, 255 Wis. 234; O'Brien, "McCarthy and Wisconsin," ch. 2.

14. Anderson and May, *McCarthy*, pp. 172–73; cf. Washington *Post*, March 14, 1950 (Drew Pearson).

15. Cohn, *McCarthy*, pp. 8–10; New York *World-Telegram*, July 13, 1954 (Frederick Woltman).

16. O'Brien, "McCarthy and Wisconsin," ch. 3; Madison *Capital-Times*, Nov. 9–11, 1949; Milwaukee *Journal*, Nov. 9–12, 1949.

17. Milwaukee *Journal*, Oct. 17, 23, 25, 1946; "Radio Address by Judge Joseph R. McCarthy," Oct. 1, 1946, Box 49, Edward Thye MSS, Minnesota Historical Society; Anderson and May, *McCarthy*, p. 145; *Cong. Record*, 81st Cong., 1st Sess., 95 (Sept. 15, 1949): 12877–79, (Oct. 14, 1949): 14507–08.

18. *Cong. Record*, 95 (Oct. 19, 1949): A6625–27, A6631–32.

19. O'Brien, "McCarthy and Wisconsin," pp. 95–96; Madison *Capital-Times*, Dec. 12, 1949; *Cong. Record*, 96 (Jan. 5, 1950): 86.

20. Milwaukee *Sentinel*, Jan. 22, 1950; *Cong. Record*, 96 (Jan. 25, 1950): 895, (Feb. 8, 1950): 1635.

21. McCarthy did deal with some of these economic issues in a question-and-answer period after his speech. Wheeling *New-Register*, Feb. 8, 10, 1950; Wheeling *Intelligencer*, Jan. 31, 1950. On McCarthy and crime, see Milwaukee *Journal*, Jan. 23, 1950; Milwaukee *Sentinel*, Feb. 15, 1950. On pensions, see Paul Douglas to McCarthy, Feb. 21, 1950, General Outgoing Correspondence, Douglas MSS., Chicago Historical Society; Elmer Thomas to McCarthy, Feb. 6, 1950, Box 455, Thomas MSS, University of Oklahoma.

22. Valuable on the sources of the Wheeling speech is Griffith, *Politics of Fear*, pp. 48–49; also Rovere, *Senator Joe McCarthy*, pp. 124–25.

23. Draft reprinted in U.S. Senate, Subcommittee of the Committee on Foreign Relations, *A Resolution to Investigate Whether There Are Employees in the State Department Disloyal to the United States. Hearings Pursuant to S. Res. 231*, 81st Cong., 2d Sess., 1950, pp. 1759–67. Cited hereafter as *Tydings Committee Hearings*. For McCarthy's own version, from which the rough draft differs in several details, see *Cong. Record*, 96 (Feb. 20, 1950): 1954–57.

24. Affidavits of Whitaker and Myers, April 25, 1950, in *Tydings Committee Hearings*, pp. 1756–57. Copies of these can also be found in Box 74, Harley M. Kilgore MSS, Franklin D. Roosevelt Library, Hyde Park.

25. Wheeling *Intelligencer*, Feb. 10, 1950; Wheeling *News-Register*, Feb. 10, 1950. The latter account follows Desmond's quotation of McCarthy verbatim and was probably derived from Desmond's article.

26. Chicago *Tribune*, Feb. 10, 1950; cf. Toledo *Blade*, Feb. 10, 1950; St. Louis *Post-Dispatch*, Feb. 10, 1950. Reports drawn from the AP referred to the 205 as Communist Party members but not spies.

27. See note 23 *supra*. The most thorough review of evidence regarding the Wheeling speech is U.S. Senate, Committee on Rules and Administration, Subcommittee on Privileges and Elections, "Report of Preliminary Investigation of Senator William Benton's Charges Against Senator Joseph R. McCarthy Relating to Senate Resolution 187," (Jan. 1952), Case One, passim. This report of the subcommittee staff, never published, is cited hereafter as "Report of Preliminary Investigation." The copy I have consulted (of the nine made) is in Box 17, Robert C. Hendrickson MSS, Syracuse University.

28. "Report of Preliminary Investigation," Case One, pp. 2, 5–7, 13, 22a–23, 30–31a; Wheeling *Intelligencer*, Feb. 11, 1950. It has been suggested that Gieske got *his* figures from accounts of McCarthy's post-Wheeling speeches, in which the number 57 was used.

29. "Report of Preliminary Investigation," Case One, pp. 4–5, 28–28a, 33. Later testimony from Wheeling became hopelessly snarled. Whitaker and Myers altered parts of their testimony (though maintaining a belief that McCarthy had spoken of 205 Communists). See U.S. District Court for District of Columbia, *McCarthy v. Benton*, Civil Action No. 1335–52, Depositions of Millard Tydings and Edward P. Morgan, Sept. 3, 1952, pp. 85–109, 152–57, stenographic copy in Tydings MSS.

30. "Report of Preliminary Investigation," Case One, pp. 3–4, 15–16, 24–27; cf. "Joint statement of James K. Whitaker and Paul A. Myers," July 15, 1952, attached to memorandum, Senator William Benton to Gerhard Van Arkel, July 30, 1952, Box 5, Benton MSS, State Historical Society of Wisconsin.

31. "Report of Preliminary Investigation," Case One, pp. 2–2a, 4, 9–13, 26–27; *Cong. Record*, 96 (Feb. 20, 1950): 1953, 1957–58; *U.S. News & World Report*, 31 (Sept. 7, 1951): 37, 39.

32. Byrnes to Sabath, July 26, 1946, in *Cong. Record*, 92 (Aug. 1, 1946): A4892; *ibid.*, 96 (Feb. 20, 1950): 1953.

33. Denver *Post*, Feb. 11, 1950; [Salt Lake City] *Deseret News*, Feb. 11, 1950; Salt Lake *Tribune*, Feb. 11, 1950; U.S. Senate, *State Department Employee Loyalty Investigation. Report of the Committee on Foreign Relations Pursuant to S. Res. 231*, 81st Cong., 2d Sess, 1950, p. 2. (Hereafter cited as *Tydings Committee Report*.)

34. Telegram, McCarthy to Truman, Feb. 11, 1950, OF 3371, Papers of Harry S. Truman, Truman Library; Washington *Post*, Feb. 12, 1950.

35. Reno *Evening Gazette*, Feb. 13, 1950; Washington *Post*, Feb. 12, 1950; [Reno] *Nevada State Journal*, Feb. 12, 1950 (Edward Conners). Conners wrote that McCarthy "had first typed a total of 205 employees of the State Department who could be considered disloyal to the United States and pro-Communists" but changed it to " '57 card-carrying members'. . . ."

36. *Nevada State Journal*, Feb. 15, 1950; Los Angeles *Times*, Feb. 15, 1950; [Huron] *The Huronite and the Daily Plainsman*, Feb. 16, 22, 1950; Milwaukee *Journal*, Feb. 15, 1950; Milwaukee *Sentinel*, Feb. 17, 1950.

37. Washington *Post*, Feb. 12, 1950; Los Angeles *Times*, Feb. 11–12, 1950.

38. *New York Times*, Feb. 12, 1950; Washington *Post*, Feb. 12, 1950; cf. Milwaukee *Journal*, Feb. 12, 1950; Denver *Post*, Feb. 11, 1950; Rovere, *Senator Joe McCarthy*, p. 126.

39. *New York Times*, Feb. 5, 7, 1950; Notes for Lincoln Day talk, Feb. 14, 1950, South Bend, Indiana, 67A1541, Box 30, Karl E. Mundt MSS, Mundt Library, Dakota State College.

40. Minneapolis *Tribune,* Feb. 22, 1950; *New York Times,* Feb. 5, 1950. A White House aide correctly anticipated that the President would be asked about McCarthy's charges at his February 16 press conference. Memorandum, Stephen J. Spingarn to Charles S. Murphy, Feb. 15, 1950, Internal Security File, Spingarn Papers, Truman Library.

41. Washington *Post,* Feb. 12, 1950; *New York Times,* Feb. 14, 1950; *Truman Papers, 1950,* p. 163; Los Angeles *Times,* Feb. 19, 1950.

42. Hoey, though expressing willingness to examine the charges, was not sure that his committee had jurisdiction; Lucas noted the difficulty posed by the fact that McCarthy was a member of the Hoey panel. Salt Lake *Tribune,* Feb. 11, 1950; Los Angeles *Times,* Feb. 15, 19, 1950; Milwaukee *Journal,* Feb. 20, 1950; Reno *Evening Gazette,* Feb. 21, 1950; Denver *Post,* Feb. 20, 1950; Milwaukee *Sentinel,* Feb. 17, 1950.

43. Washington *Post,* Feb. 14, 1950; Milwaukee *Journal,* Feb. 14, 17, 1950; Salt Lake *Tribune,* Feb. 19, 1950. Cf. Anderson and May, *McCarthy,* p. 180; Rovere, *Senator Joe McCarthy,* p. 130.

44. *Cong. Record,* 96 (Feb. 20, 1950): 1952–58.

45. *Tydings Committee Report,* pp. 6–9; U.S. House of Representatives, *State, Justice, Commerce and the Judiciary Appropriation Bill, Fiscal Year 1949. Report* [*To accompany H. R. 5607*], 80th Cong., 2d Sess., 1949, pp. 3–4; U.S. House of Representatives, *Report No. 1595,* 80th Cong., 2d Sess, 1948, p. 3. For references to the 108 list, see *Cong. Record,* 94 (March 3, 1948): 2062–86, (March 4, 1948): 2157–60, (March 25, 1948): A1912–21, (April 21–May 3, 1948): A2438–39, A2456, A2512, A2547, A2569, A2584–85, A2696, (Aug. 2, 1948): 9643–44.

46. Alfred Friendly, "The Noble Crusade of Senator McCarthy," p. 37; "Preliminary Report on Robert E. Lee," Dec. 17, 1953 (mimeographed), File 9, Drawer 1, NCEC MSS; telephone interview with former Congressman Walter H. Judd, Aug. 22, 1973.

47. *Cong. Record,* 96 (Feb. 20, 1950): 1958–59, 1962–64, 1967–68, 1972–73; Washington *Post,* Feb. 21, 1950. Lucas noted that McCarthy had named the first names himself when he attacked Service, Shapley, Duran, and Mrs. Keeney.

48. The original "108 list" is reprinted in *Tydings Committee Hearings,* pp. 1771–1809. See also Friendly, "The Noble Crusade of Senator McCarthy," pp. 35–37; Griffith, *Politics of Fear,* pp. 54–57.

49. *Cong. Record,* 96 (Feb. 20, 1950): 1980–81 and passim; I am indebted to Griffith, *Politics of Fear,* p. 55, for calling to my attention the role of Senator Ferguson.

50. *Cong. Record,* 96 (Feb. 20, 1950): 1955, 1958, 1970–72, 1981. Wherry and Ferguson were partial to their own Appropriations Committee, with crusty Senator Kenneth McKellar as chairman. The Democrats, including the Secretary of State preferred the Foreign Relations Committee. Minutes, Majority Policy Committee, Feb. 21, 1950, Box 326, Scott W. Lucas MSS, Illinois State Historical Library.

51. Minutes, Majority Policy Committee, Feb. 21, 1950; *Cong. Record,* 96 (Feb. 21, 1950): 2062–68; *New York Times,* Feb. 22, 1950.

52. *Cong. Record,* 96 (Feb. 22, 1950): 2141–50. Lucas also accepted an amendment by Senator Wayne Morse which guaranteed a suspect an open hearing before any formal finding was made against him. *Ibid.,* 2129–41.

53. Interview with Adrian S. Fisher (Aug. 27, 1968); Jack K. McFall Memoir, Cornell Oral History Program, p. 24.

54. Washington *Post,* March 5, 1950; "Was the McCarthy Investigation the Wrong 'Sure-Thing' Flier in the Political Stock Market?" unsigned MS, March 20, 1950, Tydings MSS. This memo, probably written by a participant in the State Department machinations against McCarthy, noted the Wisconsinite's "stale stuff" and poor research.

55. Jack K. McFall oral history interview, Truman Library, pp. 16–18.

56. *Christian Science Monitor,* March 10, 1950; Kilgore to Mrs. John Mayne, Feb. 22, 1950, Box 29, Kilgore MSS, Franklin D. Roosevelt Library.

57. Milwaukee *Journal,* Feb. 27, 1950; Sen. Lester Hunt to Mrs. Floyd C. Reno, March 20, 1950, Box 2, Hunt MSS, University of Wyoming.

58. Interview with Adrian S. Fisher; unsigned memorandum [Max Lowenthal], May 5, 1950, "The McCarthy Business," Internal Security File, Spingarn Papers; *Christian Science Monitor,* April 24, 1950. Soon, however, the White House was receiving a good deal of mail regarding the charges of communist infiltration from writers especially disturbed by Truman's unwillingness to release the loyalty files to Congress. Note, Spingarn to Charles Ross, March 4, 1950, and attached memorandum, n.d., by Spingarn, "Suggested reply . . . ," OF 419–K, Truman Papers, Truman Library.

59. *Cong. Record,* 96 (July 20, 1950): 10716; Salt Lake *Tribune,* Feb. 11, 1950; also see *Tydings Committee Report,* pp. 7, 176–79.

60. Providence *Evening Bulletin,* Feb. 23, 1950; Washington *Post,* Feb. 23, 1950; penciled note on clipping of latter story, Internal Security—McCarthy Charges, George M. Elsey Papers, Truman Library.

61. Tydings to Fritz Moses, Sept. 7, 1952, Tydings MSS; see also Friendly, "The Noble Crusade of Senator McCarthy," p. 38.

62. Rovere, *Senator Joe McCarthy,* p. 65; Wheeling *Intelligencer,* April 28, 1950.

CHAPTER 3   THE TYDINGS INVESTIGATION

1. *New York Times,* Feb. 24, 1950; Wherry to Thomas J. Sheehan, Jr., April 13, 1950, Wherry MSS, University of Nebraska; Milwaukee *Journal,* Feb. 27, 1950; *Christian Science Monitor,* March 10, 1950. McCarthy reportedly told associates he anticipated "another Hiss case." New York *Post,* March 8, 1950.

2. *New York Times,* Feb. 22, 25, 1950; Jack K. McFall Memoir, Cornell Oral History Program, pp. 24–25, 51–52; New York *Post,* March 8, 1950; *Christian Science Monitor,* March 18, 1950.

3. Interview with Adrian S. Fisher (Aug. 27, 1968); G. W. Foster, Jr., Memoir, Cornell Oral History Program, p. 23. The Fisher group (as well as the Tydings Subcommittee) dispatched investigators to Wheeling to determine what McCarthy had said on February 9. Photostat, William E. Rine to William O. Player, Jr., March 27, 1950, Box 1106, Theodore Francis Green MSS, Library of Congress; Wheeling *Intelligencer,* March 24–25, 1950.

4. Transcript of Tydings's weekly radio broadcast (interview with Macon Reed), April 23, 1950, File 2, Drawer 1, Tydings MSS; Minneapolis *Tribune,* March 12, 1950; *New York Times,* Nov. 9, 1950; *Christian Science Monitor,* March 10, 1950.

5. H. Alexander Smith Diary entries of Feb. 25–26, 1950 (pp. 71–72), Smith MSS, Princeton University.

6. Fisher interview; *Christian Science Monitor,* April 24, 1950. For criticism of Truman's overconfidence, see Theoharis, "The Rhetoric of Politics," pp. 230, 232. For White House countermeasures, see Stephen J. Spingarn Oral History Interview, Truman Library, pp. 125–26.

7. *Tydings Committee Hearings,* pp. 1–32.

8. *Ibid.,* p. 17; H. Alexander Smith Diary, March 12–14, 1950 (pp. 91, 93–94), Smith MSS; Washington *Post,* March 15, 1950. On the question of who was responsible for public hearings, cf. unsigned memo, n.d. [April 1950], "Public Disclosure of Names," Tydings MSS; *Cong. Record,* 81st Cong., 2d Sess., 96 (March 30, 1950): 4373; Latham, *Communist Controversy,* pp. 271–72.

9. Washington *Post,* March 9, 1950; New York *Post,* March 10, 1950; Latham, *Communist Controversy,* p. 271. Panuch had been Deputy Assistant Secretary of State for Administration until January 1947.

10. *Tydings Committee Hearings,* pp. 18–32; *Christian Science Monitor,* March 10, 1950; Washington *Post,* March 9, 1950.

11. *Tydings Committee Hearings,* pp. 33–72.

12. *New York Times,* March 9, 13, 1950.

13. *Ibid.,* March 10, 14, 1950; *Tydings Committee Hearings,* p. 109; Washington *Post,* March 13, 1950; Washington *Times-Herald,* March 14, 1950; Milwaukee *Sentinel,* March 22, 1950; Green to Tydings, March 11, 1950, Box 1108, Green MSS.

14. *Tydings Committee Hearings,* pp. 28, 73–174.

15. *Ibid.,* p. 207; *Tydings Committee Report,* p. 47. A useful genealogy of these much-hackneyed charges is in Griffith, *Politics of Fear,* pp. 68–72. I have found Griffith's account of the Tydings investigation to be of great value.

16. *Tydings Committee Hearings,* pp. 175–275, 293–313, 341–71.

17. *Ibid.*, pp. 9–11, 34; Adrian Fisher interview.

18. *Cong. Record*, 96 (Feb. 22, 1950): 2148; cf. Clinton P. Anderson's remarks, *ibid.* (March 4, 1950): 2795–98; Transcript of President's News Conference of Feb. 23, 1950, *Truman Papers, 1950* (Washington, D.C., 1965), p. 180. Truman's reference was to *Cherokee Nation v. Georgia* (1831).

19. Unsigned memorandum [George M. Elsey], "Murphy Says," March 1, 1950; clipping, New York *Herald-Tribune*, March 2, 1950 (Robert J. Donovan), both in Elsey Papers, Internal Security—McCarthy Charges; Transcript of News Conference of March 2, 1950, *Truman Papers, 1950*, p. 183. The clipping is annotated: "This leaked from Pres's Big 4 meeting 27th" [*sic*].

20. *New York Times*, March 3, 1950; Atlanta *Journal*, March 23, 25, 1950. An alternative was to have the Senators consult the files at the White House. Elsey memorandum, "Murphy Says," March 1, 1950.

21. *Tydings Committee Hearings*, pp. 249, 252; New York *Post*, March 16, 1950; Washington *Post*, March 16, 1950. Much of Tydings's optimism seems to have been stimulated by the State Department, which would not be making the final decision.

22. Adrian Fisher interview; *New York Times*, March 21, 1950; Washington *Post*, March 22, 1950; memorandum, J. Howard McGrath to the President, March 17, 1950, OF 419-K, Truman Papers.

23. *Tydings Committee Hearings*, pp. 315–39, 1767–70; Truman to Tydings, March 28, 1950, and Truman to Seth W. Richardson, March 28, 1950, *Truman Papers, 1950*, pp. 229–32; Washington *Post*, March 29, 1950.

24. *New York Times*, March 19, 28–29, 31, 1950; *Christian Science Monitor*, April 1, 1950.

25. *New York Times*, March 11, 22, 26, 28, 1950; Washington *Post*, March 13, 1950.

26. *New York Times*, March 5, 19, 21, 26, 1950; *Christian Science Monitor*, March 15, 1950; Chicago *Tribune*, Feb. 19, 1950.

27. *New York Times*, March 29, April 2, 7, 9, 1950; Truman to Styles Bridges, March 26, 1950, OF 419-K, Truman Papers, reprinted in Harper, *The Politics of Loyalty*, pp. 265–66.

28. *Christian Science Monitor*, April 10, 1950; Hugh Butler press release, April 6, 1950, Box 299, Butler MSS, Nebraska Historical Society; *New York Times*, April 1, 1950. Some Republicans were unhappy about the parley with Bridges. Westerfield, *Foreign Policy and Party Politics*, p. 378.

29. John Foster Dulles also took exception to the attacks on Acheson. *New York Times*, March 24, 29, April 9, 1950; *Christian Science Monitor*, March 29, 1950.

30. *New York Times*, March 26–27, 1950; Vandenberg, ed., *Private Papers of Senator Vandenberg*, p. 561; Vandenberg to Jack Bell, April 5, 1950, Vandenberg MSS, William L. Clements Library.

31. *New York Times,* March 19, 31, April 9, 1950.

32. There are several versions of the statement—which Taft himself denied having made. For this version, see White, *The Taft Story,* p. 85; also *Christian Science Monitor,* March 24, 1950. Cf. Milwaukee *Journal,* March 25, 1950. The *New York Times* (March 23, 1950) does not quote Taft directly.

33. Unsigned memo, n.d., "Taft" (probably material assembled by journalists Jack Anderson and Ronald W. May for their biography of McCarthy), File 4, Drawer 3, NCEC MSS; *New York Times,* March 23, 1950 (but cf. March 31, April 9, 1950).

34. Wheeling *Intelligencer,* March 20, 1950; Atlanta *Journal,* March 5, 1950; *Christian Science Monitor,* June 8, 1950. Also see Rovere, *Senator Joe McCarthy,* p. 135. The best analysis of Taft's position is Patterson, *Mr. Republican,* pp. 444–49.

35. Smith Diary, March 12–14, 22–28, 1950 (pp. 91, 93–94, 106–9, 111, 113), Smith MSS; *Cong. Record,* 96 (March 27, 1950): 4098–4107. Smith's remarks did register with some Democratic tacticians. Unsigned MS [Max Lowenthal], "The Senate Debate That Is A Landmark In the History of the Nation . . . ," n.d. [ca. April 4, 1950], Loyalty, Communism and Civil Rights, Spingarn Papers.

36. *Truman Papers, 1950,* pp. 234–36, 252, 258; *New York Times,* April 1, 1950; cf. Theoharis, "The Rhetoric of Politics," pp. 232—33.

37. Senator Warren Magnuson and W. Averell Harriman also scored McCarthy. *Cong. Record,* 96 (March 22, 1950): 3763, (March 27, 1950): 4102, 4121–23; *New York Times,* April 14, 16–17, 20, 1950; New York *Post,* March 27, 1950; *Capital Comment,* vol. 4, no. 10 (March 18, 1950), Box 431, Clinton P. Anderson MSS, Library of Congress.

38. *New York Times,* March 19, 26, April 23–24, 1950; Fisher interview; *Department of State Bulletin,* 22 (May 8, 1950): 711–16; Elsey memorandum, April 26, 1950, "Mr. Acheson's Speech to the Society of Newspaper Editors," Internal Security—McCarthy Charges, Elsey Papers.

39. State Department Press Release No. 491, in *Tydings Committee Hearings,* p. 1818; Fisher interview.

40. *Tydings Committee Hearings,* pp. 92, 277–87; *New York Times,* March 24, 27–28, 1950.

41. Oddly—for so important a speech—McCarthy first asked to insert the text in the *Record;* Clinton Anderson objected. *Cong. Record,* 96 (March 30, 1950): 4372–4408 (quotations on pp. 4374–75, 4385); *Christian Science Monitor,* March 31, 1950.

42. *New York Times,* March 25, 29, 1950; Minneapolis *Tribune,* March 31, 1950; *Tydings Committee Hearings,* p. 484. The file summary was in consonance with the agreement Truman had made with his legislative leaders on February 27. Elsey memorandum, "Murphy Says," March 1, 1950, Internal Security—McCarthy Charges, Elsey Papers.

43. *Tydings Committee Hearings,* p. 484; *New York Times,* April 8, 10–11, 1950; *Cong. Record,* 96 (April 3, 1950): 4572.

44. *New York Times,* April 23, 1950; *Tydings Committee Hearings,* pp. 490–92, 495, 526. Critical of Budenz's reliability as a witness is Packer, *Ex-Communist Witnesses,* ch. 4.

45. Budenz had also been consulted by others interested in McCarthy's charges: J. B. Matthews, Robert Morris, and Charles Kersten. *Tydings Committee Hearings,* pp. 526–27, 536–37, 583–84, 608, 610, 622.

46. *Ibid.,* pp. 660–67; *New York Times,* April 26–27, 1950.

47. *Tydings Committee Hearings,* pp. 632–60, 699–707, 709–35, 737–95.

48. *Cong. Record,* 96 (May 3, 1950): 6259; *New York Times,* April 23, 30, 1950.

49. Memorandum, Tydings to Truman, April 12, 1950, OF 419-K, Truman Papers. Tydings noted that a similarly forthright handling of the Pearl Harbor investigation had averted "a political catastrophe."

50. *Public Opinion Quarterly,* 14 (Fall 1950): 596; Minneapolis *Tribune,* April 30, 1950; cf. *New York Times,* April 30, 1950.

51. *New York Times,* April 2, 9, 16, 30, 1950; minutes, Majority Policy Committee, March 14, 21, 28, April 4, 11, May 2, 1950, Box 326, Lucas MSS.

52. *Cong. Record,* 96 (April 25, 1950): 5697–5712. See also *New York Times,* April 10, 17, 19, 25, 1950.

53. *New York Times,* March 23, April 25, 1950.

54. *Truman Papers, 1950,* pp. 270–71; *New York Times,* May 5, 7, 1950; Minneapolis *Tribune,* May 5, 1950; "Release by Sen. Tydings," May 4, 1950, File 2, Drawer 5, Tydings MSS; unsigned MS [Tydings], "McCarthy and Communism" [July 1952], Tydings MSS; unsigned memorandum, May 10, 1950, "The Possible Republican Complaints Against the Safeguards on Their Access to the Loyalty Files," Elsey Papers, Internal Security—McCarthy Charges.

55. *New York Times,* May 7–8, 11, 1950; Washington *Evening Star,* June 4, 1950 (C. Holland), clipping in Box 1108, Green MSS.

56. *New York Times,* May 11–12, 1950.

57. Griffith, *Politics of Fear,* p. 93; *New York Times,* May 12, June 15, 24, 1950; Lodge, "Individual Views," Part 2 of *Tydings Committee Report,* pp. 19–20. "You don't seem very excited" about the files, Tydings was told. "No comment," he replied. Radio interview (with Charles Parmer), WBAL (Baltimore), May 14, 1950, File 2, Drawer 1, Tydings MSS.

58. *New York Times,* April 19, 30, May 21–22, June 15, 1950; *Cong. Record,* 96 (April 25, 1950): 5704; Spingarn memorandum, "Hoey Sex Pervert Investigation," July 24, 1950; Spingarn, "Memorandum for the Hoey Subcommittee Sex Pervert Investigation File," June 29, 1950, both in Chronological File, Spingarn Papers.

59. *New York Times*, April 18, 23, 1950.

60. Frank Bielaski, who led the OSS raid on the *Amerasia* office, testified—after McCarthy had told the press—that he had found one document referring to "a new bomb" or " 'A' bomb." Strangely, he had not reported this to an earlier congressional inquiry. *Tydings Committee Hearings*, pp. 931–32, 954–56; Griffith, *Politics of Fear*, pp. 96–97.

61. Tydings claimed that 99 percent of the stolen documents were "casual and routine." *New York Times*, May 7, 23–24, June 4, 14, 20, 1950; Smith diary, May 17, 1950 (p. 167), Smith MSS; *Cong. Record*, 96 (June 13, 1950): 8486–87.

62. *New York Times*, June 16–17, 22, 1950; McCarran quoted in *Cong. Record*, 96 (June 13, 1950): 8487; transcript of phone call, Hickenlooper to John G. Brunini, June 16, 1950, Hickenlooper MSS; "Presentment of Conclusions of Grand Jury Investigation into Espionage," submitted to Judge John W. Clancy, June 15, 1950, *ibid*. A July Gallup poll found that only 25 percent of its respondents had ever heard of the case. *Public Opinion Quarterly*, 14 (Winter 1950–51): 801.

63. *Cong. Record*, 96 (May 3, 1950): 6246–62. For Karsten's attack, see *ibid.*, 96 (May 1, 1950): 6108–13.

64. Peurifoy supplied some of the data Rep. Karsten used in his speech; it may also have been significant that two senior Democrats, John McCormack and John Rooney, assisted Karsten in debate. Radio broadcast, week of May 7, 1950, Box 151, Flanders MSS, Syracuse University; *Newsweek*, 35 (May 15, 1950): 25; Minneapolis *Tribune*, May 5, 1950.

65. *Cong. Record*, 96 (May 9, 1950): 6696 (May 12, 1950): 6969–75; memorandum, Benton to John Howe, Feb. 21, 1955, Box 4, Benton MSS, State Historical Society of Wisconsin; *New York Times*, May 14, 1950. Chavez also raised questions about Budenz's previous moral carriage. See *Tydings Committee Hearings*, pp. 1691ff.

66. *New York Times*, May 9, 15–16, 21, 26–29, 1950; Minneapolis *Tribune*, May 10, 1950. Earlier, one White House advisor had recommended further attacks. "Memorandum for Mr. Dawson," unsigned, May 8, 1950, OF 419-K, Truman Papers.

67. *Cong. Record*, 96 (March 27, 1950): 4099 (May 8, 1950): 6594.

68. *New York Times*, March 23, 1950; *Cong. Record*, 96 (April 3, 1950): 4571–72.

69. *New York Times*, April 4, 1950; Tydings to Edward P. Morgan, April 11, 1950, and attachments: "Confidential—Memorandum" (*re* grounds for censure) and "Memorandum on Precedents For Censuring A Member of the U.S. Senate," all File 2, Drawer 5, Tydings MSS. Tom Connally thought the investigation would be "pretty well" ended during the same week (with the exoneration of Lattimore). *Christian Science Monitor*, April 10, 1950.

70. *New York Times*, April 4, 1950; *Christian Science Monitor*, April 1, 4, 1950; Baltimore *Sun*, April 6, 1950, clipping in Box 1105, Green MSS; Kem to Larry E. Spivak, May 11, 1950, Box 1, Kem MSS, University of Missouri.

71. *New York Times,* April 24, May 28, 1950; Memorandum, Charles S. Murphy and Stephen J. Spingarn to the President, May 24, 1950, OF 252-K, Truman Papers; Spingarn, memorandum, May 22, 1950, National Defense and Individual Rights, Vol I, Spingarn Papers; memorandum, Spingarn to Dawson, May 20, 1950, Chronological File, *ibid.;* copy of draft letter, McMahon to Truman, May 19, 1950, Box 1110, Green MSS. In a memo of May 22, Green surmised that the letter was never sent.

72. Memorandum, Murphy and Spingarn to the President, May 24, 1950; Spingarn memorandum, May 22, 1950. The Washington *Post* (May 22, 1950) came out for a commission with still more ambitious goals than Murphy and Spingarn projected.

73. Tydings to Joseph R. Byrnes, May 25, 1950, File 1, Drawer 2, Tydings MSS; Tydings to Theodore F. Green, June 14, 1950, Box 1105, Green MSS; *New York Times,* June 6, 1950. For conjecture on the imminence of a commission, see *ibid.,* May 28, 1950; Milwaukee *Journal,* June 5, 1950; Washington *Post,* June 6, 1950; Washington *Evening Star,* June 5, 1950 (Fleeson), clipping in Box 1108, Green MSS.

74. Minneapolis *Tribune,* May 23, 1950; *New York Times,* June 16, 1950.

75. *Cong. Record,* 96 (June 1, 1950): 7894–95; *Christian Science Monitor,* June 2, 1950; Elbert D. Thomas to Richard E. Cottam, June 2, 1950, Box 275, Thomas MSS, Franklin D. Roosevelt Library. The other signers of the "Declaration" were Charles Tobey, George Aiken, Wayne Morse, Irving Ives, Edward Thye, and Robert Hendrickson.

76. *New York Times,* June 4, 19, 22, 1950.

77. *Ibid.,* June 4, 11, 1950; President's News Conference of June 1, 1950, *Truman Papers, 1950,* p. 451.

78. Spingarn, "Memorandum for the Files," June 23, 1950, National Defense and Individual Rights, Vol. I, Spingarn Papers. Seth W. Richardson also opposed the idea. Richardson to Donald S. Dawson, June 26, 1950, OF 419-K, Truman Papers.

79. Spingarn, "Memorandum of Pros and Cons on the proposal to establish a Commission on Internal Security and Individual Rights," June 26, 1950, National Defense and Individual Rights, Vol. I, Spingarn Papers; Spingarn, "Memorandum for the Files," June 23, 1950, *ibid.;* memorandum, Spingarn to Stephen Mitchell, Oct. 30, 1952, Internal Security—McCarthy, *ibid.*

80. Charles S. Murphy, George M. Elsey, and Stephen J. Spingarn, Memorandum to the President, July 11, 1950; Spingarn, Memorandum for the Record, July 21, 1950, both National Defense and Individual Rights, Vol. I, Spingarn Papers; Washington *Post,* July 9, 1950 (Drew Pearson).

81. *New York Times,* June 28, 1950; *Christian Science Monitor,* July 3, 1950. Cf. *New York Times,* June 29, July 2, 1950; Wheeling *Intelligencer,* July 13, 1950.

82. *Tydings Committee Hearings,* pp. 2511–25; Washington *Evening Star,* July 18, 1950, clipping in Box 1108, Green MSS; *New York Times,* July 8, 1950.

83. *New York Times,* July 18, 1950; *Tydings Committee Report,* pp. 151, 154, 159–63, 167, and passim.

84. *New York Times,* July 19, 1950; Baltimore *Evening Sun,* July 18, 1950.

85. *New York Times,* July 18–19, 1950; *Cong. Record,* 96 (July 19, 1950): 10568-70.

86. *Cong. Record,* 96 (July 20, 1950): 10686–89, 10691–10707; *Christian Science Monitor,* July 21, 1950.

87. *Cong. Record,* 96 (July 21, 1950): 10773–92 (July 24, 1950): 10805–21 (July 25, 1950): 10912–50. Democrats subsequently cited Lodge's statement to discredit McCarthy's charges. E.g., Lester Hunt to D. W. Ogilbee, Aug. 25, 1950, Box 2, Hunt MSS; Clyde Hoey to J. F. Mullen, July 27, 1950, Box 22, Hoey MSS, Duke University; Clinton P. Anderson, "Article prepared by CPA for Democratic Digest" [Aug. 1950], Box 430, Anderson MSS.

88. Tydings to Fritz Moses, Sept. 11, 1952, Tydings MSS; Providence *Evening Bulletin,* Feb. 23, 1950; Washington *Post,* Feb. 23, 1950.

89. Unsigned MS (apparently by a member of the "floating crap game"), March 20, 1950, "Was the McCarthy Investigation the Wrong 'Sure-Thing' Flier in the Political Stock Market?" Tydings MSS; Lilienthal to William W. Waymack, March 24, 1950, Waymack MSS, State Historical Society of Iowa; New York *Post,* March 8, 1950, *Christian Science Monitor,* March 10, 1950; cf. Griffith, *Politics of Fear,* p. 66.

90. Minneapolis *Tribune,* March 19, 1950; "Was the McCarthy Investigation the Wrong 'Sure-Thing' Flier . . . ?" Tydings MSS. For other slighting assessments of McCarthy, see unsigned MS, n.d., "Preliminary Analysis and Appraisal of Senator McCarthy's Job to Date in Support of His Charges," *ibid.;* unsigned memorandum, n.d., "The Senate Inquiry Into State Department Personnel," Box 1107. Green MSS; unsigned MS, March 13, 1950, "The McCarthy Saga: Four Chapters of the Story of the Spearpoint of the Brewster-Ferguson-McCarthy Adventure," *ibid.*

91. Edward Thye to Tom Connally, July 19, 1950, Box 213, Connally MSS, Library of Congress; McFall Oral History Interview, Truman Library, pp. 17–18. For editorials favoring a commission, see *New York Times,* June 17, 1950; Washington *Post,* May 22, 1950; Milwaukee *Journal,* July 18, 1950; *Christian Science Monitor,* June 19, 1950; Detroit *Free Press,* July 22, 1950; Baltimore *Evening Sun,* July 18, 1950.

92. *Cong. Record,* 96 (June 6, 1950): 8119.

93. Flanders Radio Broadcast, week of May 7, 1950, Box 151, Flanders MSS, Syracuse University; Radio Broadcast, week of July 23, 1950, *ibid.;* Flanders to Paul Hoffman, Oct. 15, 1951, Box 105, *ibid.; Cong. Record,* 96 (July 21, 1950): 10798.

94. *New York Times,* June 4, 1950; *Cong. Record,* 96 (June 6, 1950): 8120, (July 21, 1950): 10773; "Congressional Investigations," speech on WHAM (Rochester), June 19, 1950, Box 108, Ives MSS, Cornell University; Milwaukee *Journal,* June 7, 1950; Smith Diary, May 28, July 19, 1950 (pp. 184–85, 259), Smith MSS.

95. Tydings to William Benton, Sept. 6, 1951, Tydings MSS; *Christian Science Monitor*, July 19, 1950. For provocative speculation about alternative scenarios for the McCarthy investigations, see Griffith, *Politics of Fear*, pp. 106–14.

96. Denver *Post*, Nov. 14, 1950; McCarthy to Truman, July 12, 1950, OF 20, Truman Papers; unsigned MS [Tydings], "America's Shame," n.d., p. 42, Tydings MSS.

CHAPTER 4   ON THE TRACK OF THE "COMMIECRAT" PARTY

1. *Time*, 55 (May 15, 1950): 25; Malafronte, "Claude Pepper," pp. 11–12, 39, and passim; Key, *Southern Politics in the State and Nation*, pp. 82ff.

2. Quoted in Stoesen, "The Senatorial Career of Claude D. Pepper," pp. 332, 329.

3. *Time*, 55 (April 3, 1950): 23; *New York Times*, April 7, 1950; Miami *Herald*, Jan. 13, 1950, quoted in Malafronte, "Claude Pepper," p. 33; Ralph McGill, "Can He Purge Senator Pepper?" p. 33; *Newsweek*, 35 (April 10, 1950): 23.

4. Smathers denied the latter story. Price, *The Negro in Southern Politics*, pp. 56, 60–61; *Time*, 55 (April 3, 1950): 23; *ibid.*, 55 (April 17, 1950): 28.

5. *New Republic*, 122 (May 15, 1950): 5; Malafronte, "Claude Pepper," p. 107; *New York Times*, April 9, 1950; *Time*, 55 (April 17, 1950): 27; *Newsweek*, 35 (April 10, 1950): 23.

6. Price, *The Negro in Southern Politics*, pp. 63, 86; Malafronte, "Claude Pepper," p. 115 and (quoting Pepper) p. 52.

7. Pepper to Herbert H. Davidson, Aug. 28, 1950, Box 86, Pepper MSS, Federal Records Storage, Alexandria, Va.

8. Price, *Negro in Southern Politics*, p. 63; Price, "The Negro and Florida Politics, 1944–1954," pp. 216–17; Doherty, "Liberal and Conservative Voting Patterns in Florida," pp. 413–14.

9. *U.S. News & World Report*, 28 (April 28, 1950): 17; *Newsweek*, 35 (April 10, 1950): 24; *New Republic*, 122 (May 15, 1950): 5; Pepper to W. G. Ward, June 8, 1950, Box 85, Pepper MSS.

10. Malafronte, "Claude Pepper," pp. 25–26, 86–87, 108; Stoesen, "Senatorial Career of Claude D. Pepper," pp. 338–39; interview with Congressman Claude Pepper, June 19, 1967; Kelley, *Professional Public Relations and Political Power*, ch. 3.

11. *Time*, 55 (May 15, 1950): 25; Raleigh *News and Observer*, May 5, 1950 (Marquis Childs); Charlotte *Observer*, May 6, 1950 (Thomas L. Stokes).

12. Raleigh *News and Observer*, May 2, 3, 7, 21, 24, 1950; Charlotte *Observer*, May 7, June 14, 1950; Jonathan Daniels to Isador Lubin, May 5, 1950, Box 49, Daniels MSS, University of North Carolina; Jefferson D. Johnson, Jr. (Graham's campaign manager) to William J. Smith, April 14, 1950, Johnson MSS, Duke University.

13. Raleigh *News and Observer*, May 4, 5, 20, 21, 1950. On Graham's role on the Civil Rights Committee, see the correspondence of his fellow members in Johnson MSS and Personal Files, 1949, 1950, Graham MSS, University of North Carolina.

14. Raleigh *News and Observer*, May 21, 1950.

15. *Ibid.*, May 24, 25, 1950. Copies of this and other handbills are in Political Campaign Literature, 1841–1964, Box 3, Misc. Collections, North Carolina State Department of Archives and History, Raleigh.

16. Raleigh *News and Observer*, May 11, 13, 16, 17–19, 21–23, 25, 26, 1950; quotations from *ibid.*, May 13, 18, 1950.

17. *Ibid.*, May 21, 24, June 20, 1950.

18. *Ibid.*, May 20, 21, 1950; Greensboro *Daily News*, May 28, 1950.

19. Raleigh *News and Observer*, June 3, 1950; Greensboro *Daily News*, June 26, 1950; Jonathan Daniels to Will Alexander, June 27, 1950, Box 50, Daniels MSS.

20. Raleigh *News and Observer*, June 14, 17, 20, 1950; Greensboro *Daily News*, June 21, 1950; Charlotte *Observer*, June 7, 1950; "Southern White People Must Organize in Self Defense," unsigned handbill, Johnson MSS; "White People Wake Up," unsigned handbill, Political Campaign Literature, Box 3, North Carolina State Department of Archives and History. Cf. Lubell, *Future of American Politics*, p. 109.

21. J. W. Jeffries to Gov. W. Kerr Scott, June 8, 1950, Johnson MSS; Lubell, *Future of American Politics*, pp. 110–11.

22. Daniels to Maurice Rosenblatt, June 27, 1950, Box 50, Daniels MSS; to Roger N. Baldwin, July 1, 1950, *ibid.*; Jefferson D. Johnson, Jr., to D. Hiden Ramsey, July 3, 1950, Johnson MSS. See also Greensboro *Daily News*, June 25, 26, 1950; Charlotte *Observer*, June 23, 26, 1950; Raleigh *News and Observer*, June 25, 1950; *New York Times*, June 26, 1950.

23. Lubell, *Future of American Politics*, p. 111. On the role of economic conservatism in the Florida and North Carolina votes, see *ibid.*, pp. 112–14, 119–20. For the political geography of North Carolina, see Key, *Southern Politics*, ch. 10.

24. McMillan, "Who Beat Frank Graham?" pp. 3–6.

25. *New York Times*, June 4, 1950; Los Angeles *Times*, May 11, 16, 20, 23, 24, 1950; Mazo and Hess, *Nixon*, pp. 67–68.

26. Peterson, *Prophet Without Honor*, pp. 159–71; Pratt, "Senator Glen Taylor," pp. 160–61; Boyd A. Martin, "The 1950 Elections in Idaho," pp. 76–79; *New York Times*, July 16, Aug. 6, 1950.

27. Mundt to E. Y. Berry, n.d. [August 1950], Political Letters August, 1950, Mundt MSS, Dakota State College; *Cong. Record*, 96 (June 28, 1950): 9322; *New York Times*, Aug. 17, 20, 1950. See also Caridi, *The Korean War and American Politics*.

28. *New York Times,* July 3, 7, Aug. 13, 1950.

29. *Ibid.,* Aug. 12, 14, 20, 1950.

30. On the PCISIR, see Stephen J. Spingarn, "Memorandum of Pros and Cons on the proposal to establish a Commission on Internal Security and Individual Rights," June 26, 1950, National Defense—Internal Security and Individual Rights, Vol. I, Spingarn Papers.

31. *New York Times,* Sept. 13, 1950.

32. *Ibid.,* July 19, Aug. 4, 7, 24, Sept. 23, 1950.

33. *Ibid.,* Aug. 28, Sept. 12, 14, 17, 1950.

34. *Ibid.,* Aug. 1, 2, 4, 6, 14, 26, 1950; Carl Hayden to Mrs. Ellen Thompson, Aug. 8, 1950, Folder 2, Box 42, Hayden MSS, Arizona State University.

35. *New York Times,* July 30, Aug. 10, 1950; Stephen J. Spingarn, memorandum, July 21, 1950, "Proposal for Presidential leadership . . . ," National Defense—S. 2311, Spingarn Papers; *Cong. Record,* 96 (Sept. 5, 1950): 14186.

36. Theoharis, "The Rhetoric of Politics," pp. 227–28; Theoharis, *Seeds of Repression,* ch. 6; Stephen J. Spingarn and Charles S. Murphy, memorandum to the President, "Suggestion for Improving Executive Branch Formulation in the field of Internal Security Legislation," May 16, 1950, OF 2750, Truman Papers.

37. Spingarn memorandum, "Proposal for Presidential leadership . . . ," July 21, 1950; Spingarn, memorandum to the President, July 14, 1950, "Background and analysis of H.R. 4703," Chronological File, Spingarn Papers.

38. *Truman Papers, 1950,* pp. 571–76; Spingarn, memorandum for the file, Aug. 11, 1950, Chronological File, Spingarn Papers; *New York Times,* Aug. 14, 1950; transcript of radio recording, Aug. 9, 1950, File 2, Drawer 2, Wherry MSS, University of Nebraska.

39. *New York Times,* Aug. 10, 11, 18, 1950. The most thorough study on the subject is Tanner, "Passage of the Internal Security Act of 1950." Also see Tanner and Griffith, "Legislative Politics and 'McCarthyism,' " pp. 172–89; Cater, "A Senate Afternoon," pp. 27–30; Cotter and Smith, "An American Paradox," pp. 20 33; Griffith, "The Political Context of McCarthyism," pp. 26–31.

40. *New York Times,* Sept. 3, 7, 8, 11–13, 1950; *Cong. Record,* 96 (Sept. 11, 1950): 14548; Paul Douglas to Howard E. Shuman, Jan. 17, 1951, Douglas MSS, Chicago Historical Society; Lucas radio script, Sept. 15, 1950, Box 73, Lucas MSS.

41. *Truman Papers, 1950,* pp. 645–53.

42. Theoharis, "The Rhetoric of Politics," pp. 228–29; Bernstein, "America in War and Peace," p. 320 (note 106); Patrick Murphy Malin to Truman, Sept. 20, 1951, vol. 16, file 20 (1951), American Civil Liberties Union MSS, Princeton University. For Truman's declared opposition to repressive legislation, see Stephen J. Spingarn, "Memorandum for the File on Internal Security and Individual Rights," July 22, 1950, Chronological File, Spingarn Papers.

43. *New York Times,* Sept. 25, 1950. For the political pressures on Lucas, see Everett Dirksen to Karl Mundt, July 29, 1950; Mundt to Dirksen, Sept. 16, 1950, both in "Political Letters Out-of-State, June–Aug., 1950," Mundt MSS; Lucas to Edward Clamage, July 3, 1950, Box 25, Lucas MSS.

44. Washington *Post,* Oct. 23, 1950; Hyman, *The Lives of William Benton,* pp. 433–35; *Cong. Record,* 96 (Sept. 22, 1950): 15520, (Sept. 23, 1950): 15674; Paul Douglas to Howard E. Shuman, Jan 17, 1951, Douglas MSS; Herbert H. Lehman to Harry S. Truman, Jan. 7, 1959, Special File, Lehman MSS, Columbia University; Cotter and Smith, "An American Paradox," pp. 32–33.

45. Andrew Biemiller to William L. Langer, Sept. 28, 1950, Box 95-2, Langer MSS, University of North Dakota; Milwaukee *Journal,* Oct. 25, 29, 1950; San Francisco *Chronicle,* Nov. 1, 1950; Los Angeles *Times,* Oct. 5, 11, 1950; press release, Oct. 4, 1950, Box 174, Helen Gahagan Douglas MSS, University of Oklahoma; Lucas speech, American Legion Convention, Chicago, Sept. 9, 1950, Box 56, Lucas MSS.

46. Herbert H. Lehman Address Over WCBS, Oct. 2, 1950, Campaign Files, Drawer 4, Lehman MSS. Also see memorandum, J. Carter to T. V. Brunkard, Sept. 25, 1950, Drawer 5, *ibid.; New York Times,* Oct. 22, 26, 30, 1950.

47. Radio recording, Republican National Committee, Sept. 23, 1950, File 2, Drawer 2, Wherry MSS.

48. Detroit *Free Press,* Sept. 13, 1950; *New York Times,* Sept. 13, 14, 16, 1950; *Nation,* 171 (Sept. 23, 1950): 261.

49. Kenneth W. Hechler to John Gunther, Oct. 18, 20, 1950, Series 5, Box 5, ADA MSS; copy, Michel Cieplinski to William M. Boyle, Jr., Nov. 29, 1950, Box 584, Theodore F. Green MSS; Radio Address by J. Howard McGrath, Nov. 1, 1950, Campaign Files, Drawer 4, Lehman MSS; Anderson article in *The Democratic Digest* (Aug. 1950), pp. 13–14.

50. Philadelphia *Inquirer,* Oct. 25, 1950; Seattle *Post-Intelligencer,* Nov. 3, 1950. On the use of the "isolationist" theme, see *New York Times,* Sept. 17, 22, Oct. 15, 27, Nov. 4, 1950.

51. Los Angeles *Times,* Feb. 16, 1950; Truman to Clinton P. Anderson, Aug. 5, 1950, Box 430, Anderson MSS; *Truman Papers, 1950,* pp. 697–703.

52. Philadelphia *Inquirer,* Oct. 26, 1950; *New York Times,* Nov. 5, 1950; *Public Opinion Quarterly,* 15 (Summer 1951): 386–87. On the electoral impact of Korea, see *New York Times,* Oct. 29, 1950; Detroit *Free Press,* Oct. 5, Nov. 5, 1950; Cleveland *Plain Dealer,* Oct. 22, 1950; Chicago *Tribune,* Nov. 7, 8, 1950; San Francisco *Chronicle,* Nov. 6, 1950.

53. Los Angeles *Times,* Oct. 1, 3, 5–7, 29, Nov. 2, 1950; San Francisco *Chronicle,* Nov. 5, 1950; Mazo and Hess, *Nixon,* pp. 71–72.

54. Douglas speech to International Oil Workers of America, Aug. 18, 1950, Box 206, Douglas MSS; *New York Times,* Oct. 15, Nov. 1, 1950; San Francisco

Chronicle, Nov. 3, 5, 1950; Washington *Post,* Oct. 22, 1950, March 3, 1951; Los Angeles *Times,* Oct. 17, 24, 1950; *U.S. News & World Report,* 29 (Nov. 17, 1950): 30; Mazo and Hess, *Nixon,* pp. 72–74.

55. *New York Times,* Oct. 22, 1950; *New Republic,* 123 (Nov. 20, 1950): 8; Brazil, "The 1950 Elections in California," p. 67; McCarthy quoted in William Costello, *The Facts About Nixon,* p. 70; Milwaukee *Journal,* Nov. 8, 1950.

56. Jonas, "The 1950 Elections in Utah," pp. 83, 88–90; Jonas, "The Art of Political Dynamiting," pp. 374–78; Denver *Post,* Oct. 18, 1950; *Deseret News* [Salt Lake City], Oct. 3, 4, 10, 12, 19, 1950. Minions of Gerald L. K. Smith were also active against Thomas. Epstein and Forster, *The Trouble-Makers* p. 248.

57. Elbert D. Thomas to Theodore Cannon, Feb. 24, 1950, Box 291, Thomas MSS, Franklin D. Roosevelt Library; Jonas, "The 1950 Elections in Utah," pp. 86–88; Jonas, "Setting the Stage for the Political Dynamiter," pp. 70–71; *New Republic,* 123 (Nov. 20, 1950): 10; *Deseret News* [Salt Lake City], Oct. 14, 15, 24, 1950.

58. Boyd A. Martin, "The 1950 Elections in Idaho," pp. 76–79; Neuberger, "Stand-off in the Northwest," p. 334; Seattle *Post Intelligencer,* Nov. 8, 1950.

59. Seattle *Post Intelligencer,* Oct. 26, 27, 1950; *New York Times,* Oct. 23, 1950; Bone, "The 1950 Elections in Washington," p. 94.

60. Curtis Martin, "The 1950 Elections in Colorado," pp. 73–74; Denver *Post,* Oct. 3, 17, Nov. 2, 5, 1950; Epstein and Forster, *The Trouble-Makers,* p. 248. The Denver *Post* and Millikin's speech files reveal only occasional and vague references to Hiss and communist infiltration. E.g., speech of Oct. 2, 1950, Book III; speech of Nov. 3, 1950, Book IV, Millikin MSS, University of Colorado.

61. Des Moines *Register,* June 4, Oct. 11, 12, Nov. 9, 1950; *New York Times,* Nov. 1, 1950.

62. *New York Times,* Oct. 31, 1950; *Daily Oklahoman* [Oklahoma City], Oct. 14, 19–21, 25, 27, 1950.

63. Philadelphia *Inquirer,* Sept. 26, 29, Oct. 7, 11, 29, Nov. 1, 1950; *New York Times,* Oct. 31, Nov. 4, 1950; Robert Bendiner, "Anything Goes in Pennsylvania," p. 386.

64. Cleveland *Plain Dealer,* Sept. 15, Oct. 5, 13, 22, 30, 1950.

65. *Ibid.,* Oct. 19, 21, 1950; *New York Times,* Oct. 29, 1950; Lubell, *Future of American Politics,* pp. 183–89. On the CIO-PAC's difficulties in mobilizing support for Ferguson, see Calkins, *The CIO and the Democratic Party,* pp. 34–36.

66. Detroit *Free Press,* Sept. 3, Oct. 17, 20, 27, 31, Nov. 4, 6, 9, 15, 1950.

67. *New York Times,* March 31, May 19, June 11, Sept. 17, 1950; Milwaukee Journal, Oct. 1, 29, 31, 1950.

68. Milwaukee *Journal,* March 19, April 1, 2, Oct. 1, 5, 9, 11–13, 19, 1950.

69. *Ibid.,* Oct. 5, 12, 1950.

70. *Ibid.*, Oct. 17, 27, 29, 1950.

71. *Ibid.*, Nov. 8, 1950.

72. *Ibid.*, Nov. 10, 1950; Leon D. Epstein, *Politics in Wisconsin*, p. 4. Cf. Washington *Post*, Nov. 28, 1950 (Pearson); *Nation*, 171 (Nov. 25, 1950): 472.

73. Washington *Post*, Nov. 4, 1950; *U.S. News & World Report*, 29 (Nov. 17, 1950): 33; Chicago *Tribune*, Oct. 28, 30, Nov. 1, 1950.

74. Milwaukee *Journal*, Oct. 22, 1950; Chicago *Tribune*, Oct. 22, 1950.

75. Text of Nov. 6 [1950] Radio Broadcast by Lucas, Box 73, Lucas MSS; *New York Times*, Aug. 18, Oct. 25, 27, 1950; Milwaukee *Journal*, Oct. 18, 1950; Chicago *Tribune*, Oct. 21, 25, 29, 31, Nov. 4, 7, 1950.

76. *New York Times*, Oct. 25, Nov. 10, Dec. 10, 1950; Washington *Post*, Nov. 3, 4, 1950; Chicago *Tribune*, Oct. 16, 18, 26, 30, 31, Nov. 8, 1950; Kogan, "Illinois," p. 363.

77. Indianapolis *Star*, Oct. 1, 3, 4, 8, 13, 18, Nov. 1–3, 1950; Detroit *Free Press*, Nov. 10, 1950.

78. *New York Times*, Oct. 31, 1950; Milwaukee *Journal*, Oct. 24, 1950; Kemper, *Decade of Fear*, pp. 28–32; Kirschten, "Donnell Luck and Missouri Scandal," pp. 332–33.

79. Washington *Post*, Oct. 28, 1950; Milwaukee *Journal*, Oct. 31, Nov. 6 1950; Hyman, *Lives of William Benton*, pp. 440–41.

80. Bean, *Influences in the 1954 Mid-Term Elections*, pp. 23–24; *New York Times*, Oct. 31, 1950; Bowles, *Promises to Keep*, p. 240.

81. *New York Times*, Jan. 7, 1951; Atlanta *Journal*, July 7, 1950; Washington *Post*, Nov. 10, 28, 1950. Cf. *Christian Science Monitor*, Aug. 9, 1951; *Newsweek*, 36 (Nov. 13, 1950): 27.

82. William A. Glaser in McPhee and Glaser, eds., *Public Opinion and Congressional Elections*, p. 275; Washington *Post*, Oct. 8, 1950; *New York Times*, Oct. 29, 1950.

83. *Cong. Record*, 82d Cong., 1st Sess., 97 (Feb. 28, 1951): 1657, 1659; *New York Times*, Nov. 9, 1950; Washington *Post*, Aug. 10, 1951.

84. Felknor, *Dirty Politics*, p. 10; *New York Times*, Oct. 31, Nov. 9, 1950; Kenneth W. Hechler, memorandum, "The 1950 Elections," Nov. 15, 1950, 1950 Elections File, George Elsey Papers, Truman Library. I am indebted to Prof. Alonzo Hamby, Ohio University, for calling this memo to my attention.

85. Kelley, *Professional Public Relations and Political Power*, passim.

86. Flynn, *The Road Ahead*; Schriftgeisser, *The Lobbyists*, ch. 13; Raleigh *News and Observer*, June 12, 17, 1950; Madison *Capital-Times*, March 1, 1951, clipping in File 4, Drawer 2, NCEC MSS; LaPalombara, "Pressure, Propaganda, and Political Action in the Elections of 1950," pp. 303–25.

87. Glaser in *Public Opinion and Congressional Elections*, p. 206. Liberals tended to run better than conservatives in the GOP in 1950. Washington *Post*, Dec. 17, 1950.

88. Hechler memorandum, Nov. 15, 1950, previously cited; cf. Tyler, "The Mid-Term Paradox," pp. 14–15; "The Elections," *Nation*, 171 (Nov. 18, 1950): 451.

89. Memorandum, Violet Gunther to ——, n.d. [1950], Series 5, Box 34, ADA MSS; Karl Mundt to Everett Dirksen, Sept. 13, 1950, Political Letters Out-of-State, Sept.–Oct., 1950, Mundt MSS.

90. Polsby, "Towards an Explanation of McCarthyism," pp. 268–71.

CHAPTER 5   FOOTLOOSE IN MARYLAND

1. *Biographical Directory of the American Congress* (Washington, D.C., 1961), p. 1736; *Time*, 55 (April 3, 1950): 20.

2. Baltimore *Sun*, March 14, 1950, clipping in Tydings MSS; New York *Post*, March 21, 1950; Washington *Times-Herald*, March 23, 1950, clipping in Box 1111, Green MSS. For Tydings's denial of such stories and of reports that he was in line for a prestigious ambassadorship, see Hagerstown *Morning Herald*, Sept. 1, 1950; cf. Atlanta *Journal*, July 16, 1950.

3. Jon M. Jonkel, campaign manager for Tydings's Republican opponent, noted this tactical error. U.S. Senate, *Maryland Senatorial Election of 1950. Hearings before the Subcommittee on Privileges and Elections of the Committee on Rules and Administration, Pursuant to S. Res. 250*, 82d Cong., 1st Sess., 1951, p. 286. (Cited hereafter as *Maryland Election Hearings*.)

4. John H. Fenton, *Politics in the Border States*, pp. 172, 178, 182–86, 196, 201; Cumberland *Evening Times*, Sept. 13, 1950.

5. Baltimore *News Post*, Feb. 27, 1950; Annapolis *Evening Capital*, Feb. 1, 1950; *ibid.* (undated), all clippings in Tydings MSS; *Maryland Election Hearings*, p. 306.

6. Fenton, *Border States*, pp. 184–85; Baltimore *Evening Sun*, July 7, Sept. 11, 1950.

7. Office memo from "vk," March 10, 1950, File 2, Drawer 5, Tydings MSS; William Curran to Tydings, May 4, 1950, Tydings MSS.

8. David A. Halley to Tydings, April 4, 1950, Tydings MSS; Robert L. Otto, "The Maryland Senatorial Election of 1950: Butler vs. Tydings" (M.A. Thesis, University of Maryland, 1962), pp. 10–11.

9. Various memoranda, July 1950, File 2, Drawer 5, Tydings MSS.

10. The Maryland Action Guild also called for the ouster of Acheson, Jessup, Service, and Vincent from the State Department. Baltimore *Evening Sun*, July 7, 14, 1950.

11. Baltimore *Sun*, July 9, 1950.

12. Baltimore *Evening Sun,* Aug. 17, 19, 31, 1950.

13. *Ibid.,* Aug. 14, 31, Sept. 1, 1950; Cumberland *Evening Times,* Sept. 8, 1950.

14. Baltimore *Evening Sun,* July 13, Sept. 1, 11, 1950; Cumberland *Evening Times,* Sept. 11, 13, 1950; *Maryland Election Hearings,* pp. 288–89. Markey had initially planned to run for Governor, but when Theodore R. McKeldin announced for that office, he shifted to the Senate race.

15. *Maryland Election Hearings,* pp. 183–90, 198, 236; U.S. Senate, Committee on Rules and Administration, *Maryland Senatorial Election of 1950,* 82d Cong., 1st Sess., 1951, p. 5. (Cited hereafter as *Maryland Election Report.*)

16. *Maryland Election Report,* pp. 31–32; Baltimore *Evening Sun,* Sept. 28, 1950.

17. Baltimore *Sun,* Aug. 9, 1950; Baltimore *Evening Sun,* Aug. 21, 1950, clippings in Tydings MSS. The latter step was taken "by arrangement." Kelley, *Professional Public Relations and Political Power,* p. 116.

18. Memorandum by "vk," July 20, 1950, File 2, Drawer 5, Tydings MSS.

19. The questionnaires are in File 1, Drawer 2, *ibid.* Their reliability is, of course, debatable. The more optimistic responses may have constituted whistling in the dark or the results of a natural reluctance to tell one's Senator that he might be defeated.

20. Kirwin, *The Inevitable Success,* pp. 508–9.

21. *Ibid.;* Baltimore *Evening Sun,* Aug. 15, 1950; Otto, "The Maryland Senatorial Election of 1950," p. 33.

22. "A Serious Message to the People of Maryland," address of Aug. 31, 1950, File 2, Drawer 4, Tydings MSS.

23. Questionnaires in *ibid.* Some respondents were encouraged by the reaction to Tydings's televised speech.

24. *Maryland Manual, 1953–54* (Baltimore, 1953), pp. 273–74; Baltimore *Evening Sun,* Oct. 16, 1950; *New York Times,* Oct. 20, 1950.

25. Baltimore *Evening Sun,* Sept. 19, 1950; *Maryland Election Hearings,* pp. 273, 291–92; cf. Hagerstown *Morning Herald,* Sept. 26, 1950.

26. Baltimore *Evening Sun,* Sept. 25, 30, Oct. 2, 3, 27, 1950; Washington *Post,* Oct. 1, 3, 1950; Hagerstown *Morning Herald,* Oct. 3, 1950; *Maryland Election Hearings,* p. 300; Kelley, *Professional Public Relations and Political Power,* p. 120.

27. Baltimore *Evening Sun,* Sept. 12, 15, 1950; letter from John J. O'Connor, Jr., in *ibid.,* Sept. 19, 1950; memorandum, Willard H. Becker to Tydings, Sept. 16, 1950, File 1, Drawer 1, Tydings MSS; Washington *Evening Star,* Oct. 4, 1950, cited in Otto, "Maryland Senatorial Election of 1950," p. 38; Milwaukee *Journal,* Oct. 15, 1950; "If We Were Tydings, Here's What We'd Say to McCarthy," reprint from Madison *Capital-Times,* Sept. 12, 1950, Tydings MSS.

28. For Evjue's interest in the Maryland contest, see Evjue to Tydings, Sept. 5, 6, 8, 1950, File 2, Drawer 5, Tydings MSS.

29. Virgil P. Lary, Jr., to Lt. Michael Garon (Maryland Veterans Committee), Sept. 18, 1950, *ibid.;* Garon to Lary, Sept. 16, 1950; Tydings to Evjue, Sept. 27, 1950, File 1, Drawer 3, *ibid.; New York Times,* June 5, 1950. Lary was one of the survivors of Malmedy.

30. "ADA Voters Guide" (Baltimore), undated [1950], File 1, Drawer 1, Tydings MSS.

31. Rollins J. Atkinson to Tydings, Sept. 13, 1950, File 2, Drawer 1, *ibid.;* N. Bancroft Williams, "An Examination of the Factors Leading to the Defeat of Millard E. Tydings in the Maryland Senatorial Election of 1950," p. 35; *Maryland Election Hearings,* p. 252.

32. Baltimore *Evening Sun,* Sept. 28, 1950; *New York Times,* Sept. 24, 1950; "Address by Senator Joseph R. McCarthy before the Republican Club of the District of Columbia," Oct. 30, 1950, Tydings MSS; Washington *Post,* Oct. 31, 1950. Another speech McCarthy was slated to make was canceled due to a schedule mix-up. *Ibid.,* Oct. 14, 1950.

33. *Maryland Election Hearings,* pp. 272–73, 276–80; Washington *Post,* Oct. 10, 1950.

34. Baltimore *Sun,* Nov. 1, 1950; Baltimore *Evening Sun,* Nov. 6, 1950; Washington *Post,* Oct. 22, 1950; Hagerstown *Morning Herald,* Oct. 17, 26, 1950.

35. Tydings speech of Oct. 30, 1950, File 2, Drawer 5, Tydings MSS; Hagerstown *Morning Herald,* Oct. 24, 1950; Baltimore *Evening Sun,* Oct. 24, 1950; Washington *Post,* Oct. 29, 1950; *Maryland Election Hearings,* pp. 286–87.

36. *Maryland Election Hearings,* pp. 275–76, 293–94, 298, 734, 755; *Maryland Election Report,* pp. 5–8

37. *Maryland Election Report,* pp. 5, 16, 19, 23, 31–34; *Maryland Election Hearings,* pp. 233, 257, 265, 327, and passim.

38. As Robert Griffith has noted (*Politics of Fear,* pp. 62–63), these individuals were members of an unofficial "McCarthy Lobby."

39. *Maryland Election Report,* pp. 20, 23–25, 27–28, 31, 35–36; *Maryland Election Hearings,* pp. 253, 257, 327, 370, 386—94, 425–31, 442, and passim. On behalf of the *Times-Herald* it was claimed that the standard price for printing the tabloid was charged.

40. For Tydings's complaints about the tabloid, see *Maryland Election Hearings,* pp. 8–14, 1061–63; for McCarthy's defense of it, *Maryland Election Report,* pp. 44–66.

41. Baltimore *Evening Sun,* Oct. 11, 1950. The constituent in question did not catch the speaker's identity at first, but either way—Harding or Tydings—he thought the candidate was "a bunch of baloney."

42. Baltimore *Evening Sun,* Oct. 16, 1950. There was some ambivalence on this point, however: while Tydings speakers were instructed to wage an "affirmative" campaign, it was considered unlikely that the subject of the State Department inves-

tigation could be wholly avoided. "Memorandum for Speakers for Senator Tydings," n.d. [late Sept.–Oct., 1950], File 1, Drawer 1, Tydings MSS. Tydings headquarters distributed a pamphlet, "The Real Facts about the Tydings Subcommittee Investigation of the State Department," to answer such charges.

43. *New York Times,* Oct. 15, 1950; Washington *Post,* Oct. 11, 29, 1950; Baltimore *Evening Sun,* Oct. 16, Nov. 4, 1950.

44. Washington *Post,* Oct. 13, 17, 1950.

45. Washington *Post,* Oct. 20, 1950; cf. Otto, "The Maryland Senatorial Election of 1950," pp. 64–65.

46. Transcripts of Lewis broadcasts, March 24, Oct. 13, 16, 17, 1950, File 2, Drawer 5, Tydings MSS; "Speech of Senator Tydings Over Mutual Network—Oct. 20, 1950," *ibid.;* telegram, Tydings to Lewis, Oct. 20, 1950, *ibid.;* Washington *Post,* Oct. 19, 20, 1950; Milwaukee *Journal,* Oct. 20, 1950.

47. Transcripts of Lewis broadcasts, Oct. 23, 24, 1950, File 2, Drawer 5, Tydings MSS; Kelley, *Professional Public Relations and Political Power,* p. 131.

48. Baltimore *Evening Sun,* Oct. 18, Nov. 3, 6, 1950; Baltimore *Sun,* Nov. 1, 1950; Kirwin, *The Inevitable Success,* pp. 509–10; "Statement by Senator Millard E. Tydings," Nov. 3, 1950, File 1, Drawer 2, Tydings MSS.

49. Baltimore *Evening Sun,* Nov. 6, 7, 1950; Hagerstown *Morning Herald,* Nov. 7, 1950; Tydings statement of Nov. 5, 1950, File 2, Drawer 5, Tydings MSS.

50. Wentworth, *Election Statistics in Maryland,* pp. 37, 39; Baltimore *Evening Sun,* Nov. 8, 1950; *New York Times,* Nov. 8, 1950.

51. *New York Times,* Nov. 12, 1950 (James P. Connolly), Jan. 7, 1951 (White); Baltimore *Evening Sun,* Nov. 13, 1950.

52. Washington *Post,* Nov. 9, 1950; Baltimore *Evening Sun,* Nov. 8, 1950.

53. Washington *Post,* Nov. 9, 1950.

54. Kelley, *Professional Public Relations and Political Power,* pp. 140–41; Baltimore *Evening Sun,* Nov. 8, 1950; cf. Lubell, *Future of American Politics,* p. 153.

55. Baltimore *Afro-American,* Aug. 26, Sept. 9, 16, 30, Nov. 4, 18, 1950. Lane was unpopular among blacks both for his racial views and for the sales tax. On Robeson, cf. Pittsburgh *Courier,* Aug. 19, 1950.

56. Kirwin, *The Inevitable Success,* pp. 510–11; *The Catholic Review,* Nov. 17, 1950 (Rev. John Sinnott Martin). The editorial contested the view that Tydings was "almost solidly opposed" by Catholics. *Time,* 56 (Nov. 13, 1950): 13.

57. Vote percentage declines are computed from Wentworth, *Election Statistics in Maryland,* pp. 27, 39. Figures on Catholic population are from National Council of Churches, *Churches and Church Membership in the United States,* Series A, No. 1.

58. Bean, *Influences in the 1954 Mid-Term Elections,* pp. 28–30.

59. Using Spearman's coefficient of rank correlation, rho = 0.29, which is not statistically significant.

60. Bean, *Influences*, pp. 30–32. An attempt was made to assess the effect of Lane's candidacy upon Tydings's, correlating the rank order declines from their vote totals of 1946 and 1944 respectively. Spearman's coefficient yielded a rho = 0.25, which was not statistically significant.

61. Baltimore *Evening Sun*, Nov. 8, 1950; Tydings to William Boyle, Nov. 16, 1950, File 1, Drawer 1, Tydings MSS; *U.S. News & World Report*, 29 (Nov. 17, 1950): 33.

62. Tydings to Polk Bramble, Dec. 12, 1950; to W. J. Mann, Jr., Dec. 12, 1950, Tydings MSS.

63. Baltimore *Evening Sun*, Nov. 29, 1950; Washington *Post*, Dec. 17, 22, 1950; Tydings to Gillette, Dec. 15, 1950, in Tydings press release of Dec. 17, 1950, File 2, Drawer 5, Tydings MSS; *New York Times*, Dec. 22, 1950.

64. Washington *Post*, Dec. 29, 1950, Jan. 9, 1951; Anderson to Irving Dilliard, Jan. 10, 1951, Box 264, Anderson MSS, Library of Congress. The tabloid had come to symbolize most graphically the skulduggery in Maryland. Memorandum, Edward A. McDermott to Senators Gillette, Monroney, Hennings, Hendrickson, and Margaret Chase Smith, "Status of Pending Investigations," Jan. 19, 1951, File 9, Drawer 3, NCEC MSS.

65. *New York Times*, Jan. 7, 1951; Washington *Post*, Jan. 3, 4, 1951; *Cong. Record*, 97 (Jan. 3, 1951): 3.

66. Baltimore *Sun*, Nov. 28, Dec. 6, 29, 1950; Washington *Post*, Jan. 3, 18, 21, 1951; *Cong. Record*, 97 (Daily Digest, Feb. 19, 1951): D49, (Feb. 28, 1951): 1670–71.

67. Hendrickson to Albert E. Burling, July 13, 1951, Box 13, Hendrickson MSS, Syracuse University; *New York Times*, Jan. 27, 1951; Margaret Chase Smith, *Declaration of Conscience*, pp. 21–24; Griffith, *Politics of Fear*, p. 154. Democrats emphasized the desirability of an even partisan balance on the four-man subcommittee. *Cong. Record*, 97 (Feb. 28, 1951): 1664, 1671.

68. *Maryland Election Hearings*, pp. 312–13, 1021, 1144–60, 1180; Washington *Post*, Feb. 17, March 31, 1951; *New York Times*, March 25, 1951.

69. *Maryland Election Hearings*, pp. 75–81, 1008, 1010, 1026–36, 1049, 1083–85. While critics charged that Fried, a garage owner, did not seem qualified for the post, he had held investigative jobs in the past—with a law firm and with the WPA.

70. *Ibid.*, pp. 86–88, 91–92, 126–31, 921, 1093; Washington *Post*, March 29, 31, April 5, 1951.

71. *Cong. Record*, 97 (Feb. 28, 1951): 1655–64, 1670–73 (March 6, 1951): 2001–10; Washington *Post*, April 4–6, 1951. Formal hearings did end soon after Wherry's appeal, however.

72. Hugh Butler to John Riddell, March 9, 1951, Box 356, Hugh Butler MSS, Nebraska Historical Society; *New York Times,* March 6, 25, 1951; but cf. Washington *Post,* March 11, 1951.

73. *Maryland Election Hearings,* pp. 1–6.

74. *Ibid.,* p. 1091; Washington *Post,* April 6, 1951.

75. *Maryland Election Hearings,* pp. 7–28.

76. *Ibid.,* pp. 32–179, 957–1005. At the time of the election, Nilles worked for Senator Edward Martin.

77. *Ibid.,* pp. 636–729, 1128–43 (Surine), 593–635 (Moore), 842–89 (Nilles).

78. *Ibid.,* pp. 104–05, 108–13, 116, 125–30, 1003. On the other hand, there were inaccuracies and evasiveness in the testimony of those who had disputed Fedder's account.

79. Washington *Post,* March 16, 1951; *Maryland Election Hearings,* pp. 233, 280, 303.

80. *Maryland Election Hearings,* pp. 196–97, 199–212, 225, 524, 532, 1018, 1191, 1209–10; Washington *Post,* Feb. 28, 1951.

81. Jonkel had also acted illegally by functioning as Butler's political agent without so registering and by so serving while a nonresident of Maryland. Washington *Post,* June 4, 5, 1951.

82. *Maryland Elections Hearings,* pp. 285, 305.

83. *Ibid.,* 260–63, 273, 275, 277, 785, 790; *Maryland Election Report,* pp. 5–8.

84. *Maryland Election Report,* pp. 23, 72–73; Washington *Post,* March 13, April 1, 7, 1951.

85. *Maryland Election Report,* pp. 41–43.

86. Washington *Post,* April 25, June 19, July 5, 1951.

87. *Ibid.,* April 29, 1951; *New York Times,* May 9, June 23, 1951; Kemper, *Decade of Fear,* p. 38. Republican leaders, however, may have been less concerned with such motives than with appeasing McCarthy and keeping him off the Policy Committee, on which he sought a place. Washington *Post,* June 28, 1951.

88. Washington *Post,* July 5, 6, 1951; Margaret Chase Smith, *Declaration of Conscience,* pp. 27–28; *New York Times,* Aug. 3, 1951. Opinions vary on who deserved credit for driving the project through to completion. For accounts favorable to Hennings, see Washington *Post,* July 15, 19, 1951. For an account more favorable to Monroney, see *ibid.,* Aug. 10, 1951.

89. *Maryland Election Report,* pp. 2–3, 8–9.

90. *Ibid.,* pp. 3–9 and passim. The Justice Department found no evidence that federal law had been violated. Copy, Attorney General Herbert Brownell, Jr., to William E. Jenner, Oct. 15, 1953, Box 30, Hennings MSS, University of Missouri.

91. Kemper, *Decade of Fear*, pp. 39–40; Griffith, *Politics of Fear*, p. 219; Hendrickson to Albert E. Burling, July 13, 1951, Box 13, Hendrickson MSS. For earlier doubts that Butler would be disciplined, see Washington *Post*, April 16, 1951; *New York Times*, March 25, 1951.

92. Washington *Post*, Aug. 4, 1951. For Senator Butler's reaction, see Baltimore *Sun*, Sept. 12, 1951.

93. Washington *Post*, Aug. 9, 1951; McCarthy to Wherry, Aug. 8, 1951, File 5, Drawer 1, Wherry MSS.

94. Washington *Post*, Aug. 9, 1951; *Cong. Record*, 97 (Aug. 9, 1951): 9703–18. McCarthy had been waving the list for some time, although he was not always certain whether the number was twenty-nine or twenty-six. Washington *Post*, July 16, 18, 24, 1951.

95. *Cong. Record*, 97 (Aug. 20, 1951): 10304–08.

96. *Ibid.*, 97 (Aug. 20, 1951), 10319–36.

97. *Ibid.*, 10337.

CHAPTER 6   THE MARINE AND THE ARTILLERYMAN

1. Truman to Alben Barkley, June 21, 1950, Barkley MSS, University of Kentucky. For analyses of Truman's attitudes toward McCarthyism, see Theoharis, *Seeds of Repression*, pp. 149–50, 183; and especially Hamby, *Beyond the New Deal*, pp. 396–97, 421.

2. George M. Elsey to Erwin D. Canham, Sept. 2, 1950, OF 2750-B, Truman Papers; Truman to Alben Barkley, Sam Rayburn, Scott Lucas, and John McCormack, Aug. 28, 1950, Barkley MSS; Charles Van Devander to John Gunther, March 17, 1951, Series 5, Box 39, ADA MSS; Jonathan Daniels, Memorandum, Sept. 28, 1950, Box 52, Daniels MSS.

3. The study was prepared by White House staffer Kenneth Hechler, working from an earlier, less wieldy study commissioned by Robert Landry, Truman's Air Force Aide. Memorandum, George M. Elsey to Stephen J. Spingarn, Aug. 24, 1950, Internal Security File, Spingarn Papers; unsigned memorandum [Spingarn], June 25, 1950, "Books on Civil Rights," Chronological File, *ibid.*

4. "Special Message to Congress on the Internal Security of the United States," Aug. 8, 1950, *Truman Papers, 1950*, p. 572.

5. *New York Times*, Dec. 13, 21, 1950; Cecil V. Crabb, Jr., *Bipartisan Foreign Policy*, pp. 88–94.

6. *New York Times*, Nov. 9, 15, Dec. 3, 5, 7, 8, 1950; Washington *Post*, Nov. 30, 1950.

7. *New York Times*, Dec. 1, 6, 1950; Washington *Post*, Nov. 27, Dec. 9, 1950; Clyde Hoey to James Furlong, May 7, 1951, Box 26, Hoey MSS; Hunt to A. E. Deru, Dec. 21, 1950, Box 2, Hunt MSS.

8. E.g., Milwaukee *Journal*, Nov. 6, 1950; *New York Times*, Nov. 9, 12, 1950; Washington *Post*, Nov. 27, 1950; Denver *Post*, Nov. 15, 1950.

9. Washington *Post*, Nov. 8, Dec. 14, 22, 1950; *New York Times*, Nov. 18, 19, 1950.

10. *New York Times*, Nov. 12, Dec. 7, 8, 10, 16, 1950.

11. *Ibid.*, Dec. 20, 1950; Clyde Hoey to R. W. Troutman, Dec. 21, 1950, Box 25, Hoey MSS; President's News Conference of Dec. 19, 1950, *Truman Papers, 1950*, p. 751.

12. G. W. Foster, Jr., Oral History Interview (Cornell University), pp. 26, 34, 36; personal interview with Adrian S. Fisher (Aug. 27, 1968).

13. Congressmen Richard Bolling, Chet Holifield, Emmanuel Celler, and John Huber also defended Acheson. Washington *Post*, Dec. 17, 31, 1950; *New York Times*, Dec. 8, 19, 1950.

14. Clinton P. Anderson to R. A. Caldwell, Feb. 8, 1951, Box 433, Anderson MSS; *New York Times*, May 17, June 1, 1951; Washington *Post*, June 2, 1951.

15. Washington *Post*, Sept. 16, Oct. 5, 11, 1951; *New York Times*, Sept. 11, Dec. 13, 1951.

16. Acheson, *Present at the Creation*, pp. 360, 730; *New York Times*, July 5, 1951; Washington *Post*, Nov. 17, 1950, Nov. 4, 1951.

17. Coral Bell, *Negotiation from Strength*, pp. 76–77; Harper, *The Politics of Loyalty*, p. 252; Hamby, *Beyond the New Deal*, pp. 436–40.

18. *New York Times*, Nov. 28, 1950; Chicago *Tribune*, Nov. 10, 13, 1950.

19. Detroit *Free Press*, Nov. 10, 1950; *New York Times*, Nov. 10, 20, 21, Dec. 12, 1950, Jan. 2, 1951; Washington *Post*, Nov. 11, 1950.

20. Washington *Post*, Dec. 1, 1950, March 11, 1951; *New York Times*, Jan. 25, Feb. 10, 11, 17, 1951. On the McCarran subcommittee, see Latham, *The Communist Controversy in Washington*, pp. 296–316.

21. Washington *Post*, Aug. 11, 1951; *New York Times*, Aug. 19, Nov. 4, 1951; Latham, *Communist Controversy*, pp. 269n, 297, 305, 314; *U.S. v. Lattimore*, 112 Fed. Supp. 507; 127 Fed. Supp. 405.

22. Personal interview with Adrian S. Fisher; Harper, *Politics of Loyalty*, pp. 217–19; Griffith, *Politics of Fear*, pp. 140–41; Willis Smith to Fred J. Kerr, March 25, 1952, Box 12, Smith MSS. Griffith notes that McCarthy benefited from "fallout" generated by the communist issue.

23. Tydings to Truman, July 24, 1950, OF 252-K, Truman Papers.

24. Presidential aide Stephen J. Spingarn also continued to press for a PCISIR. Herbert H. Lehman, James Murray, and Estes Kefauver to Truman, Sept. 20, 1950; Harley Kilgore to Truman, Sept. 14, 1950; Helen Gahagan Douglas to Truman, Sept. 20, 1950, all OF 2750-C, Truman Papers; Memorandum, Spingarn to Donald

Dawson, Sept. 30, 1950, Internal Security Legislation, Spingarn Papers; Spingarn, first revised draft of message on internal security, July 23, 1950, Murphy Files, Internal Security, Truman Papers.

25. Tydings to William M. Boyle, Jr., Nov. 16, 1950, File 1, Drawer 1, Tydings MSS. Cf. Arthur Krock in *New York Times,* Jan. 25, 1951.

26. Francis Biddle to Truman, Dec. 5, 1950, Records of the President's Commission on Internal Security and Individual Rights, HSTL (hereafter referred to as R. G. 220); Washington *Post,* Nov. 11, 1950.

27. *Christian Science Monitor,* Nov. 16, 1950; memorandum, Charles S. Murphy to Truman, draft of Nov. 15, 1950, *re* "Proposed President's CISIR," Murphy Files, Internal Security, Truman Papers; memorandum, David E. Bell to Murphy, Nov. 13, 1950, Internal Security—Nimitz Commission, Elsey Papers; memorandum, Elsey to Murphy, Nov. 22, 1950, *ibid.* For postelection speculation regarding the PCISIR, see Washington *Post,* Nov. 19, 1950; Denver *Post,* Nov. 15, 1950.

28. Truman to Hoover, Nov. 25, 1950; Hoover to Truman, Nov. 26, 1950, both in OF 2750-A, Truman Papers. The best account of the PCISIR, on which I have relied heavily, is Harper, *Politics of Loyalty,* ch. 8.

29. Truman to Nimitz, Jan. 4, 1951, OF 2750-A, Truman Papers; Nimitz to Truman, Jan. 9, 1951, *ibid.; New York Times,* Jan. 24, 1951; *Truman Papers, 1951,* pp. 119–21; Washington *Post,* Jan. 25, 1951. Owen Roberts apparently also rejected the proffered chairmanship. Phone memo, "M.N." to Elsey, Dec. 8, 1950, Internal Security—Nimitz Commission, Elsey Papers.

30. *New York Times,* Jan. 26, 1951; Washington *Post,* Jan. 26, 1951. For Father Walsh's opposition to McCarthyism, see *ibid.,* Nov. 29, 1951.

31. Harper, *Politics of Loyalty,* pp. 177–79. Harper calls the membership of the PCISIR on the whole "second string." Learned Hand turned down an appointment as general counsel. Copy, Learned Hand to Nimitz, March 11, 1951, R.G. 220.

32. Harper, *Politics of Loyalty,* pp. 181–84; Leffingwell to Nimitz, March 20, 1951, R.G. 220; but cf. *New York Times,* April 22, 1951. For another critical view of the PCISIR, see Theoharis, *Seeds of Repression,* pp. 168–69.

33. Truman to Nimitz, Jan. 4, 1951, OF 2750-A, Truman Papers; unsigned memorandum, Feb. 12, 1951, "Commission on Internal Security and Individual Rights," Internal Security—Nimitz Commission, Elsey Papers; marginal note by Elsey on memorandum, David E. Bell to Charles S. Murphy, Nov. 14, 1950, *ibid.*

34. Telegram, Jacob Blaustein to Truman, Jan. 24, 1951; Patrick Murphy Malin to Truman, Jan. 24, 1951; Hugh C. Wolfe to Truman, Feb. 9, 1951, all OF 2750-A, Truman Papers; Paul Hoffman to Chester W. Nimitz, March 14, 1951, R.G. 220; Chester C. Davis to John A. Danaher, March 12, 1951, Box 26, Fund for the Republic MSS, Princeton University.

35. Nimitz to John Danaher, March 10, 1951; Danaher to Nimitz, March 8, 1951; Nimitz to Paul Hoffman, March 16, 1951, all R.G. 220; memorandum, Chester C.

Davis to Paul Hoffman, Robert M. Hutchins, et al., March 9, 1951, Box 26, Fund for the Republic MSS.

36. Eric Sevareid News Analysis, Jan. 25, 1951, Box 12, Sevareid MSS, Library of Congress; Washington *Post,* Jan. 25, 26, 1951; *Cong. Record,* 97 (Jan. 25, 1951): 680–84; Washington *Times-Herald,* Feb. 18, 1951, clipping in R.G. 220; Danaher to Nimitz, March 19, 1951, *ibid.*

37. McCarran to Truman, May 26, 1951, OF 2750-A, Truman Papers; Danaher to Nimitz, March 19, April 9, 1951, R.G. 220. The law also thwarted the hiring of a prestigious lawyer as general counsel.

38. McCarran to Nimitz, Feb. 21, 1951; Danaher to Nimitz, March 2, 1951; Nimitz to Danaher, March 2, 8, 1951; Nimitz to Truman, May 8, 1951, all R.G. 220.

39. *New York Times,* May 1, 1951; Nimitz to Truman, May 8, 1951; Truman to McCarran, May 12, 1951; McCarran to Truman, May 26, 1951, all OF 2750-A, Truman Papers; George Elsey, memorandum for the record, May 2, 1951, Internal Security—Nimitz Commission, Elsey Papers.

40. *New York Times,* May 23, 1951; Washington *Post,* June 5, 19, 1951. Congressman Gerald R. Ford, after consulting with Senator Ferguson, blocked the rider under a unanimous consent rule.

41. Unsigned, undated [ca. Sept. 1951] notes [Elsey], Internal Security—Nimitz Commission, Elsey Papers; memorandum, Elsey to the President, Oct. 5, 1951, *ibid.;* Harold E. Benson to Rev. Karl Morgan Block, Sept. 28, 1951, R.G. 220; Charles S. Murphy to Prof. E. M. Morgan, Oct. 11, 1951, OF 2750-A, Truman Papers; Mary Alice Baldinger to Alan Reitman, July 27, 1951, vol. 16 (1951), ACLU MSS; memorandum, David Freeman and Bernard L. Gladieux, "The Current Status of Projects and Agencies Dealing with National Security and Individual Freedom in the United States," Sept. 26, 1951, Box 26, Fund for the Republic MSS; *New York Times,* Oct. 3, 28, 1951.

42. Nimitz memorandum, "Discuss with Mr. Murphy," May 11, 1951, OF 2750-A, Truman Papers. Following a suggestion by Truman, the American Bar Association undertook a study of federal programs. Washington *Post,* Sept. 22, 1951, March 2, 1952.

43. Patrick Murphy Malin to Morris L. Ernst, Nov. 1, 1951; Alan Reitman to Mary Alice Baldinger, July 24, 1951; Baldinger to Reitman, Aug. 1, 1951, all in vol. 16 (1951), ACLU MSS.

44. Truman to James S. Lay, Jr., July 14, 1951, *Truman Papers, 1951,* p. 394; Washington *Post,* Sept. 16, 1951; Truman to Robert Ramspeck, Aug. 8, 1952, *Truman Papers, 1952,* pp. 513–14; "Report to National Security Council from Interdepartmental Committee on Internal Security . . . ," April 29, 1952, Martin Friedman Files, Civil Service Commission—Loyalty Review Board, Truman Papers.

45. *Truman Papers, 1951,* pp. 605–06; Washington *Post,* Nov. 2, 1951; *New York Times,* Oct. 28, 29, 1951.

46. Anna Lord Strauss wanted further information before giving her approval for the change. Copy, Hiram Bingham to Nimitz, Feb. 16, 1951, R.G. 220; Nimitz to Truman, April 4, 1951, *ibid.;* Washington *Post,* Feb. 14, April 27, 1951; *New York Times,* Jan. 23, April 15, 29, 1951; *Truman Papers, 1951,* p. 156; Harper, *Politics of Loyalty,* pp. 181–82; Theoharis, "The Escalation of the Loyalty Program," pp. 258–59.

47. Danaher to Russell C. Leffingwell, April 7, 1951, R.G. 220; *New York Times,* April 6, 15, 1951.

48. Theoharis, "The Escalation of the Loyalty Program," pp. 257–59; Bontecou, *The Federal Loyalty-Security Program,* pp. 55, 70; *Peters v. Hobby,* 349 U.S. 331 (1955).

49. Washington *Post,* May 1, 1953.

50. Some Republicans also resented Richardson's service as general counsel in the congressional investigation of Pearl Harbor, which they considered yet another Democratic "whitewash." *New York Times,* Nov. 20, 1950, Jan. 2, Feb. 11, April 15, May 28, June 3, 7, 1951; Washington *Post,* Oct. 23, 1951, March 18, 1953; McCarran to Truman, May 26, 1951, OF 2750-A, Truman Papers.

51. Francis Biddle to Truman, May 22, 1951, and attached "Memorandum for the President Concerning some aspects of the Loyalty Program," OF 2750-A, Truman Papers; memorandum, Truman to Charles Murphy, May 24, 1951, *ibid.;* Truman to James S. Lay, Jr., July 14, 1951, *Truman Papers, 1951,* p. 394; Washington *Post,* Feb. 8, 1953.

52. Washington *Post,* April 11, 1951, Nov. 21, 22, 1952; *New York Times,* June 19, 1951; mimeographed newsletter, Esther C. Brunauer to "My Friends and Former Colleagues," Dec. 8, 1952, Box 30, Fund for the Republic MSS.

53. *New York Times,* July 13, 1951, Oct. 11, 12, 1952; Washington *Post,* Dec. 21, 1951, Feb. 26, Oct. 12, Nov. 15, 1952. Davies was dismissed by John Foster Dulles in 1954 for "lack of judgment, discretion and reliability." Reinvestigated, he was given a security clearance in 1969. *New York Times,* Nov. 6, 1954, Jan. 15, 1969.

54. *New York Times,* July 13, 1951, Feb. 12, March 9, 10, 1952; Washington *Post,* March 6, 1952; Clubb, *The Witness and I.*

55. Washington *Post,* March 3, 1951; *New York Times,* July 14, Aug. 24, Dec. 18, 1951, Jan. 31, Feb. 20, Dec. 16, 1952, Jan. 4, Feb. 1, March 5, 1953.

56. Washington *Post,* March 4, Oct. 26, Dec. 14, 22, 1951, Nov. 2, 1952; *Service v. Dulles,* 354 U.S. 363 (1957).

57. Washington *Post,* Feb. 5, 11, Oct. 11, 1952; *New York Times,* April 22, Oct. 2, 1952, Jan. 10, 1953; telegram, McCarthy to Truman, Feb. 3, 1952, OF 3327, Truman Papers.

58. Boorstin, *The Image,* pp. 21–23. For valuable treatments of the role of the press in the McCarthy era, see Cater, *The Fourth Branch of Government,* pp. 68–74,

106–7; Rovere, *Senator Joe McCarthy*, pp. 162–67; Davis, *But We Were Born Free*, pp. 160–64, 176–77; Griffith, *Politics of Fear*, pp. 139–42; Washington *Post*, Nov. 30, 1970; Edwin Lahey Reminiscences, Columbia Oral History Project, pp. 134–35.

59. Personal interview with Maurice Rosenblatt (June 27, 1967); cf. Boorstin, *The Image*, pp. 22–23; Clyde Hoey to E. P. Yarborough, March 11, 1954, Box 35, Hoey MSS; Humphrey to Dr. Frederick J. Kottke, March 8, 1954, Box 109, Humphrey MSS, Minnesota Historical Society; Lester Hunt to Wandell Elliott, March 12, 1954, Hunt MSS.

60. "Suggested Agenda for Discussion," attached to "A Message to Our Guests," unsigned mimeographed program, March 31, 1953, Box 12, Richard H. Rovere MSS, State Historical Society of Wisconsin. The meeting, under the aegis of the ADA, brought together various individuals, particularly from the mass media, who were concerned about McCarthy. Susanna Davis to Robert Nathan, April 2, 1953; Audrey Stone, "Draft of Minutes of meeting held March 31, 1953," both in Series 7, Box 81, ADA MSS.

61. Washington *Post*, Feb. 8, 1952.

62. Washington *Post*, Sept. 10, 1951; *New York Times*, Aug. 27, 1952. Cf. Zechariah Chafee, Jr., in Washington *Post*, Nov. 15, 1952.

63. Philip L. Graham to Elmer Davis, Aug. 13, 1952, Box 3, Elmer Davis MSS, Library of Congress; *New York Times*, Jan. 14, 1954.

64. Memorandum, Elsey to Charles S. Murphy, Aug. 24, 1951, Internal Security—McCarthy Charges, Elsey Papers.

65. *Truman Papers, 1951*, p. 433.

66. *Ibid.*, pp. 462–64; Washington *Post*, Sept. 3, 1951; *Truman Papers, 1951*, p. 523; *New York Times*, Sept. 20, 1951.

67. *New York Times*, Aug. 30, 1951. In a less publicized speech to the Knights of Columbus, Tobin called on "all Catholics" to repudiate "a campaign of terror against free thought in the United States." Washington *Post*, Nov. 21, 1951.

68. *New York Times*, Sept. 13, 15, 16, 1951.

69. *Ibid.*, Oct. 19, Nov. 12, 1951; Washington *Post*, Oct. 26, 1951. For an earlier attack by Acheson, see Washington *Post*, Aug. 20, 1951.

70. Truman, too, raised the specter of the "big lie." *New York Times*, Aug. 12, Dec. 14, 1951; *Truman Papers, 1951*, p. 636. Two eventual presidential aspirants, Governor Adlai Stevenson and Senator Estes Kefauver, also spoke out against McCarthy. *New York Times*, Nov. 20, 1951; Washington *Post*, June 24, 1951.

71. *New York Times*, Oct. 25, 1951; Washington *Post*, Dec. 20, 1951. During this period McCarthy also encountered resistance of unwonted vigor from Democratic colleagues (see ch. 7).

72. Madison *Capital-Times*, Sept. 29, 1951, clipping in File 4, Drawer 2, NCEC Files; *New York Times*, Sept. 2, 9, 15, Oct. 7, 1951.

73. *New York Times*, Sept. 30, Oct. 7, 1951; Douglass Cater, "Is McCarthy Slipping?" *Reporter*, 5 (Sept. 18, 1951): 25–26. Cater hedged his answer to this question.

74. Washington *Post*, Sept. 2, Nov. 21, 1951; *New York Times*, Sept. 9, 16, 30, 1951; Baltimore *Sun*, Sept. 9, 1951, clipping in Tydings MSS; Des Moines *Register*, Aug. 13, 1951; New York *Post*, Aug. 21, 1951.

75. Washington *Post*, April 13, 1951; *Cong. Record*, 97 (April 24, 1951): 4259–70, (June 14, 1951): 6556–6603.

76. *New York Times*, July 1, Sept. 9, 30, 1951; Kenneth W. Hechler to Sen. Robert S. Kerr, July 3, 1951, Kerr MSS, University of Oklahoma; Washington *Post*, Aug. 18, 1951.

77. Washington *Post*, Nov. 21, 1951.

78. *Ibid.*, July 31, 1951; McCarthy to Truman, Aug. 3, 1951, President's Personal File (PPF) 200, Truman Papers; *New York Times*, Aug. 16, 17, 23, 30, 31, 1951.

79. Baltimore *Evening Sun*, Sept. 27, 1951; *New York Times*, Sept. 9, Oct. 23, 1951.

80. *New York Times*, Oct. 19, 24, 1951; Washington *Post*, Sept. 27, 1951. For observations that McCarthy had lost support within the GOP, see Washington *Post*, Nov. 21, 1951; *New York Times*, Oct. 7, 1951; Madison *Capital-Times*, Sept. 29, 1951, clipping in File 4, Drawer 3, NCEC MSS; New York *Post*, July 2, 1951; *Christian Science Monitor*, Sept. 27, 1951.

81. Washington *Post*, Dec. 30, 1951. From his previous low (24 percent in June), Truman's stock had risen (to 32 percent in October). Cf. *ibid.*, July 11, Sept. 9, Oct. 17, 1951, Feb. 8, 1952.

82. *Ibid.*, April 22, 29, June 28, Aug. 22, 1951; *New York Times*, Jan. 31, May 9, June 23, 1951, Jan. 11, 1952; Griffith, *Politics of Fear*, p. 117.

83. Harry S. Truman, *Memoirs by Harry S. Truman*, Vol. II: *Years of Trial and Hope*, p. 313. Cf. Washington *Post*, Dec. 23, 1953.

84. T. Harry Williams, *Huey Long*, pp. 636–38, 689, 692, 794–98, 816, 819–28. Williams notes, however, that the patronage squeeze against Long achieved indifferent results, partly because Long did not depend heavily upon federal largesse. For other points of comparison; see Rovere, *Senator Joe McCarthy*, pp. 19–20; Luthin, *American Demagogues*, chs. 10–12; Washington *Post*, Dec. 28, 1950, Oct. 2, 1951; New York *Post*, Sept. 23, 1951.

85. Washington *Post*, Aug. 13, Oct. 2, 5, 1951, Feb. 28, March 4, 1952.

86. Unsigned memorandum for the president, n.d. [late July–early Aug., 1951], "Subject: McCarthyism," General File (1951), Barkley MSS.

CHAPTER 7   THE CORPORAL'S GUARD

1. Frank J. Kendrick, "McCarthy and the Senate," pp. 117–18.

2. New York *Post*, Sept. 19, 1951 (Pilat and Shannon); *New Republic*, 125 (Oct. 1, 1951), 6.

3. U.S. Senate, Subcommittee of the Committee on Foreign Relations, *Nomination of Philip C. Jessup to be United States Representative to the Sixth General Assembly of the United Nations*, 82d Cong., 1st Sess., 1951, p. 10 (cited hereafter as *Jessup Hearings*); *Cong. Record*, 97 (Aug. 9, 1951): 9703 04; *ibid.*, 97 (Feb. 12, 1951): 1224.

4. Hoey to Rev. E. L. Kirk, Nov. 18, 1950, Box 5, Hoey MSS; to Lewis R. Lawson, July 28, 1950, Box 22, *ibid.;* Smith to Richard D. Korn, Aug. 17, 1951, Box 12, Smith MSS, Duke University. On Lattimore and the IPR, see Smith to Hornell Hart, June 6, 1952, Box 6, *ibid.;* to E. M. Hoffman, March 3, 1952, Box 9, *ibid.*

5. White, *Citadel*, New York *Post*, Aug. 8, 1951; cf. Matthews, *U.S. Senators and Their World*, pp. 97–99.

6. White, *Citadel*, pp. 122, 126; Hunt to Wandell Elliott, March 12, 1954, Hunt MSS; Atlanta *Journal*, Aug. 7, 1951; cf. Kendrick, "The Senate and Senator Joseph R. McCarthy," pp. 65–66.

7. Hoey to Junius D. Grimes, April 5, 1950, Box 19, Hoey MSS.

8. Memorandum, William Benton to John Howe, Feb. 26, 1953, Box 4, Benton MSS.

9. Rovere, *Senator Joe McCarthy*, p. 35; New York *Post*, Sept. 23, 1951 (Pilat and Shannon); *Christian Science Monitor*, Aug. 9, 1951; *New Republic*, 125 (Oct. 29, 1951): 5; *Madison Capital-Times*, Aug. 27, 1951, Feb. 20, 1952, clippings in File 4, Drawer 2, NCEC MSS and Tydings MSS respectively. For perhaps the strongest emphasis on the "fear" theme, see Griffith, *Politics of Fear*, pp. 122, 151, and passim.

10. *New Republic*, 125 (Aug. 27, 1951): 3; Seattle *Times*, Oct. 1, 1952; Douglas to author, April 23, 1971; Sherrill and Ernst, *The Drugstore Liberal*, pp. 82–83; Humphrey to K. L. Shisler, Sept. 16, 1954, Box 104, Humphrey MSS, Minnesota Historical Society.

11. *Cong. Record*, 96 (Sept. 12, 1950): 14577; *New York Times*, Oct. 8, 1951.

12. Epstein and Forster, *The Trouble-Makers*, pp. 27, 30, 33, 53–56; U.S. Senate, Committee on Armed Services, *Nomination of Anna M. Rosenberg to Be Assistant Secretary of Defense*, 81st Cong., 2d Sess., 1950, pp. 26–27, 38–39, 42–43, 54–55 (cited hereafter as *Rosenberg Hearings*). For useful accounts of the Rosenberg episode, see Epstein and Forster, pp. 25–61; Griffith, *Politics of Fear*, pp. 136–39; and the articles by Alfred W. Friendly in the Washington *Post*, Jan. 15–19, 1951.

13. Epstein and Forster, *Trouble-Makers*, pp. 29, 41, 45; *Rosenberg Hearings*, pp. 10–11, 26–27, 38–39, 42–43, 85, 96, 115–22, 127, 204, 271–72, 285, 326; unsigned "Confidential Report," Feb. 25, 1951; unsigned "Confidential Report," Feb.

17, 1951; unsigned memorandum, "Report No. 30: Grand Jury Action on Perjury in Anna Rosenberg Case," March 20, 1951, all in File 4, Drawer 3, NCEC MSS. The reports came from a Drew Pearson agent.

14. Epstein and Forster, *Trouble-Makers*, pp. 35, 52, 54–55; *Rosenberg Hearings*, pp. 85, 372–73; Griffith, *Politics of Fear*, p. 139; New York *Post*, Sept. 21, 1951.

15. Washington *Post*, Oct. 25, 1951; *New York Times*, Sept. 18, Oct. 19, 1951; Chicago *Tribune*, Sept. 19, 1951, clipping in File 4, Drawer 3, NCEC MSS; Tom Connally to Larry Odom, Feb. 8, 1952, Box 57, Connally MSS; "Speech by Senator [Connally] (American Foreign Policy) 1951," Box 571, *ibid.*

16. *Jessup Hearings*, pp. 2, 6, 9, 12, 68–69, and passim; *New York Times*, Sept. 28, 1951; Johnson and Gwertzman, *Fulbright the Dissenter*, p. 132. Also valuable is Griffith, *Politics of Fear*, pp. 146–51.

17. Madison *Capital-Times*, Sept. 29, 1951, clipping in File 4, Drawer 2, NCEC MSS; *New York Times*, Sept. 30, Oct. 7, 1951.

18. Stassen himself had opposed recognition of Red China—"not at least for a question of a couple of years." *Jessup Hearings*, pp. 601–3, 610, 620, 687, 696–99, 710–22, 744, 774–76, 782, 789, 797, 820–21; *New York Times*, Oct. 10, 12, 1951; Washington *Post*, Oct. 3, 12, 1951.

19. *Jessup Hearings*, pp. 178, 401–2, 620–21, 710; Washington *Post*, Oct. 2, 1951; Hoey to C. W. Tillett, Oct. 13, 1951, Box 26, Hoey MSS.

20. *New York Times*, Oct. 19, 1951. Cf. Gillette's earlier remark that he would not consider it a disqualification even if Jessup *had* been among those who urged cutting off aid to Chiang. Washington *Post*, Oct. 8, 1951.

21. *New York Times*, Oct. 19, 1951; H. Alexander Smith to John Crider, Nov. 9, 1951; to Albert Linton, Oct. 31, 1951, both in Box 104, Smith MSS.

22. Washington *Post*, Oct. 17, 24, 1951; *New York Times*, Oct. 20, 1951; Tom Connally to Olin G. Bell, Jan. 29, 1952, Box 49, Connally MSS; *New Republic*, 125 (Nov. 5, 1951): 17.

23. Truman subsequently gave Jessup an interim appointment. *New York Times*, Oct. 19, 23, 28, 1951; Washington *Post*, Oct. 17, 19, 1951.

24. Smith Diary, Aug. 10, 1951 (p. 275), Smith MSS; *Cong. Record*, 97 (June 14, 1951): 6556–6603; on the background of the Marshall speech, see Rovere, *Senator Joe McCarthy*, pp. 170–78.

25. Hendrickson to James Kerney, Jr., July 10, 1951, Box 13, Hendrickson MSS; McCarthy to Dulles, June 25, 1951, Correspondence, 1951, Dulles MSS, Princeton University; Flanders to Paul Hoffman, Oct. 15, 1951, Box 105, Flanders MSS, Syracuse University; Washington *Post*, June 31, 1951; *New York Times*, Oct. 23, 1951.

26. Senator Estes Kefauver, an exceptional case, was quick to criticize McCarthy for the speech. Washington *Post*, June 16, 19, 24, 1951. The issue became more

salient, of course, after Eisenhower—Marshall's protégé—became the Republican presidential nominee.

27. *Cong. Record,* 97 (Aug. 9, 1951): 9703–12; *New York Times,* Sept. 9, 1951.

28. *Cong. Record,* 97 (Feb. 1, 1951): 865–68, (Feb. 12, 1951): 1223; Benton to Herbert H. Lehman, Feb. 17, 1951, Special File—William Benton, Lehman MSS.

29. *Cong. Record,* 97 (Feb. 12, 1951): 1218–24.

30. *Ibid.,* 97 (Aug. 24, 1951): 10604; memorandum, M. A. Baldinger to Alan Reitman, July 6, 1950, vol. 20 (1950), ACLU MSS; Washington *Post,* Jan. 20, 1951.

31. *Cong. Record,* 97 (Aug. 24, 1951): 10602–05. Kefauver became interested in the problem of committee fairness during his celebrated crime hearings. Kefauver to Herbert Monte Levy, April 14, 1951, Legislative File, Box 14, Kefauver MSS, University of Tennessee.

32. *New York Times,* Dec. 22, 1950; *Cong. Record,* 97 (Aug. 24, 1951): 10603–04. Hunt also suggested, but dismissed as unlikely, an amendment removing congressional immunity from the Constitution.

33. Washington *Post,* Oct. 18, 1951; *Cong. Record,* 97 (Aug. 10, 1951): 9774–75, (Aug. 24, 1951): 10603.

34. Madison *Capital-Times,* Aug. 27, 1951, clipping in File 4, Drawer 3, NCEC MSS.

35. Hyman, *Lives of William Benton,* pp. 406, 453, 591, and passim. I have relied heavily on Hyman's book. On Benton's offensive against McCarthy, Griffith, *Politics of Fear,* ch. 5, is useful; my analysis and his are frequently parallel.

36. Benton to Alben Barkley, Nov. 16, 1950, Box 22, Barkley MSS; *New York Times,* Nov. 28, 1950.

37. Telegram, Benton to Tydings, Nov. 8, 1950, Tydings MSS; Benton to Kilgore, Feb. 17, 1951, Box 75, Kilgore MSS, Franklin D. Roosevelt Library. Benton and Kilgore had discussed the McCarthy problem soon after the election.

38. Benton to Mrs. Kathleen Wilkins, Jan. 9, 1961, Box 4, Benton MSS; John Howe to Herbert Agar, May 22, 1957; *ibid.;* Hyman, *Lives of William Benton,* pp. 452–55; *Cong. Record,* 97 (Aug. 6, 1951): 9494–9501.

39. Washington *Post,* Aug. 9, 1951; Hartford *Courant,* Aug. 7, 1951; Atlanta *Journal,* Aug. 7, 1951.

40. *Cong. Record,* 97 (Aug. 20, 1951): 10306; Washington *Post,* Aug. 9, 1951; *New York Times,* Aug. 9, 1951. Some Democrats also questioned the "timing" of the resolution. Hartford *Courant,* Aug. 9, 1951.

41. *New York Times,* Aug. 9, 1951. Cf. *Christian Science Monitor,* Aug. 8, 1951, quoting Gillette as saying it would be "considerable time" before the subcommittee acted.

42. On precedents, see *New York Times,* Aug. 12, Sept. 30, 1951; Hyman, *Benton,* p. 455; cf. Doris Fleeson in Atlanta *Journal,* Aug. 14, 1951. On elections, see

Washington *Post*, Aug. 13, 1951; Hartford *Courant*, Aug. 12, 1951; *New York Times*, Feb. 10, 1952.

43. Smith to Hornell Hart, June 6, 1952, Box 6, Smith MSS. Nor were well-wishers sanguine—though urging support for the move, one ADA functionary observed: "We are fully aware that Benton won't get very far." Evelyn Dubrow to Joseph L. Rauh, Aug. 14, 1951, Series 5, Box 39, ADA MSS.

44. Transcript of interview, "Reporters Roundup," Aug. 30, 1951, Fulbright MSS.

45. Atlanta *Journal*, Aug. 14, 1951 (but cf. *ibid.*, Aug. 7, 1951); Baltimore *Sun*, Sept. 9, 1951 (Frank R. Kent), clipping in Tydings MSS.

46. Smith Diary, Aug. 7, 1951 (p. 272), Smith MSS; Flanders to Paul Hoffman, Oct. 15, 1951, Box 105, Flanders MSS,; Benton to Flanders, Oct. 27, 1958, *ibid.*

47. *Christian Science Monitor*, Aug. 9, 1951; Benton to Clinton P. Anderson, Sept. 1, 1951, Box 103, Anderson MSS; memorandum, Howe to Benton, n.d. [ca. Aug. 1951], Box 4, Benton MSS; Hennings to Tom F. Baker, Aug. 31, 1951, Box 73, Hennings MSS. For indications of Benton's willingness to amend his resolution and of the consideration being given to censure instead of expulsion, see *New York Times*, Sept. 26, 30, 1951; *New Republic*, 125 (Sept. 17, 1951): 8; New York *Post*, Sept. 20, 1951; Hartford *Courant*, Sept. 29, 1951.

48. Benton to Clinton Anderson, Aug. 20, 1951, Box 73, Anderson MSS; copy, Charles Van Devander to Benton, Aug. 16, 1951, *ibid.*

49. Benton sought to rig a response, but the reply was tardy and ineffective. Benton to McGrath, Aug. 25, 1951, with suggested draft of same date, Box 5, Benton MSS; Benton to McGrath, Aug. 31, 1951, *ibid.;* Washington *Post*, Sept. 2, 1951; *New York Times*, Dec. 19, 1951; Assistant Attorney General James M. McInerney to Benton, Nov. 15, 1951, J. Howard McGrath Papers, Truman Library.

50. Memorandum, Benton to Howe, June 9, 1954, Box 5, Benton MSS. Benton did confer with Lister Hill and Carl Hayden on August 6 and 7; later, he received help from Kenneth M. Birkhead of the Democratic National Committee. Hartford *Courant*, Aug. 8, 1951; Hyman, *Lives of William Benton*, pp. 455, 462.

51. Gillette said he expected to hold hearings "unless something unforeseen develops," then denied having given any assurances. Hartford *Courant*, Aug. 28, Sept. 20, 23, 1951; New York *Post*, Sept. 10, 1951.

52. McCarthy claimed to have been misquoted; the story was based on an exclusive interview. Atlanta *Journal*, Sept. 20, 1951; *Christian Science Monitor*, Sept. 22, 1951.

53. *New York Times*, Sept. 19, 1951; McCarthy to Hennings, Sept. 18, 1951, in *Cong. Record*, 97 (Sept. 22, 1951): 11857; Hennings speech in *ibid.*, 11855–58. A valuable account of the controversy is in Kemper, *Decade of Fear*, pp. 43–50.

54. Though hardly the "conservative" White and Richard Strout declared him to be, Hennings was representative of the Senate's conservative traditions and folkways. Atlanta *Journal*, Sept. 21, 25, 1951; *New York Times*, Sept. 23, 1951 (White);

Christian Science Monitor, Sept. 22, 1951 (Strout); Kemper, *Decade of Fear,* pp. 46–48.

55. Kemper, *Decade of Fear,* pp. 48–50; *New York Times,* Sept. 25, 27, 1951; Washington *Post,* Sept. 18, 27, 1951; *Christian Science Monitor,* Sept. 22, 1951.

56. U.S. Senate, Committee on Rules and Administration, Subcommittee on Privileges and Elections, *Investigation of Joseph R. McCarthy,* 82d Cong., 1st Sess., 1952, pp. 1–53 (cited hereafter as *Benton Investigation*). In drafting his brief, Benton had the aid of John Howe, Kenneth M. Birkhead and, on two "cases," Adrian Fisher of the State Department. Hyman, *Lives of William Benton,* p. 462; interview with Adrian Fisher (Aug. 27, 1968).

57. Benton to Ben Sonnenberg, Oct. 13, 1959, Box 4, Benton MSS; Washington *Post,* Oct. 10, 1951.

58. The delay was partly occasioned by the subcommittee's investigation of the 1950 Ohio senatorial campaign and by the need to find additional staff. Washington *Post,* Oct. 27, Nov. 2, 1951; *New York Times,* Nov. 30, 1951; Hennings to Carl Hayden, copy, Oct. 15, 1951, File 9, Drawer 2, NCEC MSS.

59. *New York Times,* Oct. 10, 1951; Washington *Post,* Oct. 10, 16–18, 1951; memorandum, Howe to Benton, n.d. [ca. March 1952], Box 4, Benton MSS; memorandum, Benton to Howe, Oct. 8, 1954, *ibid.*

60. Hartford *Courant,* Aug. 7, 1951.

61. McCarthy to Gillette, Oct. 4, 1951, in U.S. Senate, Committee on Rules and Administration, Subcommittee on Privileges and Elections, *Investigation of Senators Joseph R. McCarthy and William Benton,* 82d Cong., 2d Sess., 1952, pp. 61–62 (cited hereafter as *Benton Report*); Washington *Post,* Oct. 11, 1951.

62. *New York Times,* Nov. 30, 1951; McCarthy to Gillette, Dec. 6, 7, 19, 1951, all in *Benton Report,* pp. 62–65.

63. Buckley was later hired by the Republican National Committee. Washington *Post,* Dec. 18, 28, 1951, June 19, 1952; Buckley press release, Dec. 27, 1951, in *Benton Report,* pp. 106–7; Confidential Memorandum, John P. Moore to Senator Gillette, Jan. 11, 1952, Box 18, Hendrickson MSS.

64. U.S. Senate, Committee on Rules and Administration, Subcommittee on Privileges and Elections, "Report of Preliminary Investigation of Senator William Benton's Charges Against Senator Joseph R. McCarthy Relating to Senate Resolution 187," Jan. 1952, Box 18, Hendrickson MSS (cited hereafter as "Preliminary Report"); *New York Times,* Jan. 19, 1952.

65. Washington *Post,* Jan. 16, 19, 1952; *New York Times,* Jan. 17, 1952; cf. Margaret Chase Smith, *Declaration of Conscience,* pp. 31–34.

66. The maneuver was widely held to be a product of considered Republican strategy. Washington *Post,* Jan. 19, 23, 1952; *New York Times,* Jan. 20, 1952; Margaret Chase Smith, *Declaration of Conscience,* pp. 34–35.

67. Washington *Post*, Jan. 23, 1952; *New York Times*, Jan. 24, 1952; Smith to Hayden, Jan. 22, 1952, in *Cong. Record*, 98 (March 18, 1952): 2246.

68. Benton recalled that the Subcommittee on Rules was the body "to which things were referred for . . . burial." Memorandum, Benton to Howe, Jan. 6, 1955, Box 4, Benton MSS; memorandum, Benton to Howe, Dec. 20, 1954, *ibid.; Benton Investigation*, p. 69.

69. The caricature was a bit unfair in view of the "preliminary report." Moreover, the subcommittee, apparently at the request of Chief Counsel Moore, had asked the Bureau of Internal Revenue for access to McCarthy's tax returns. Hartford *Courant*, Feb. 1, 1952; memorandum, Ralph Mann to Benton, Jan. 3, 1952, Box 4, Benton MSS; Washington *Post*, Jan. 25, Feb. 6, 1952.

70. Benton to Mr. and Mrs. Clayton Knowles, Feb. 18, 1952, Box 2, Benton MSS; Benton to Ernest McFarland, April 14, 1952, Box 4, *ibid.*

71. Washington *Post*, Dec. 8, 1951, Feb. 7, 22, 1952; memorandum, Howe to Benton, n.d. [ca. March 1952], Box 4, Benton MSS; *New York Times*, March 6, 8, 1952; *Cong. Record*, 98 (April 8, 1952): 3701. The Senate's Democratic leadership was not enthusiastic about the maneuver, apparently out of "sensitivity about Senator McCarthy and his position and rights as a Senator." Benton to Ernest McFarland, March 28, 1952, Box 4, Benton MSS.

72. *Cong. Record*, 98 (April 10, 1952): 3933–34.

73. *Ibid.*, 3935–54; memorandum, Howe to Benton, n.d. [ca. March 1952], Box 4, Benton MSS; cf. *New York Times*, May 18, 1952.

74. *New York Times*, May 8, 1952; Benton to Ben Sonnenberg, Oct. 13, 1959, Box 4, Benton MSS; Hyman, *Benton*, p. 464; Gillette to Hayden, Sept. 10, 1952, in *Benton Report*, p. 95.

75. Providence *Evening Bulletin*, Feb. 20, April 15, 19, 21, 1952. On April 10, McCarthy had criticized the subcommittee for these leaks.

76. Memorandum, Benton to Howe, April 27, 1955, Box 4, Benton MSS; *Benton Investigation*, pp. 76–92, 106–316.

77. McCarthy to Gillette, Monroney, and Hennings, May 11, 1952, in *Benton Investigation*, p. 72. The man in question was no "star witness" and not criminally insane; he had been institutionalized after suffering a stroke. *Ibid.*, p. 73.

78. *Ibid.*, pp. 225–28, 248–51; *New York Times*, May 16, 1952.

79. *Benton Investigation*, pp. 102–5; Washington *Post*, June 13, 1952.

80. *New York Times*, May 22, 1952; Washington *Post*, May 29, 1952.

81. *New York Times*, Jan. 27, April 22, 1952; Providence *Evening Bulletin*, Feb. 20, 1952; Washington *Evening Star*, May 18, 1952, clipping in Tydings MSS; *New Republic*, 125 (Sept. 17, 1951): 8; Benton to Alfred A. Knopf, Oct. 16, 1951, Box 2, Benton MSS.

82. *New York Times,* March 19, 27, 28, 1952; memorandum, Benton to Howe, March 31, 1952, Box 5, Benton MSS; Washington *Evening Star,* May 18, 1952, clipping in Tydings MSS; personal interview with Gerhard P. Van Arkel (Aug. 26, 1968). Cf. Griffith, *Politics of Fear,* p. 174.

83. *New York Times,* April 24, May 6, 27, June 5, 6, Aug. 20, 1952; Washington *Post,* May 9, 1952; Gerhard P. Van Arkel to Benton, Aug. 11, 1952, Box 4, Benton MSS.

84. Interview with Van Arkel; George R. Donahue, Orton H. Hicks, and Sidney H. Scheuer to "Dear Friend," July 19, 1954, File 7, Drawer 3, NCEC MSS; memorandum, Howe to Benton, June 10, 1954, Box 4, Benton MSS; Hyman, *Lives of William Benton,* pp. 484–85.

85. Memorandum, Howe to Benton, April 14, 1952, Box 4, Benton MSS; *New York Times,* July 4, 5, 1952; Washington Post, July 4, 1952; Hartford *Courant,* Sept. 15, 1951.

86. Washington *Post,* July 5, 1952; memorandum, Howe to Benton, Aug. 22, 1952, Box 4, Benton MSS.

87. Van Arkel to Benton, Aug. 11, 1952; telegram, Benton to Van Arkel, n.d. [ca. Aug. 11, 1952]; memorandum, Howe to Benton, Aug. 12, 1952; Benton to A. M. Gilbert, Aug. 14, 1952, all Box 4, Benton MSS.

88. Telegram, Poorbaugh to Gillette, Sept. 8, 1952, *Benton Report,* p. 93; copy, telegram, Welker to Gillette, Sept. 8, 1952, Box 4, Benton MSS. Poorbaugh was in contact with the office of Fulton Lewis, Jr., just before he resigned. *Benton Report,* p. 14.

89. There were reports that the impatient Hayden had planned to demand that Gillette either get moving or resign. Des Moines *Register,* Sept. 26, 1952; Washington *Post,* Sept. 6, 8, 1952; Gillette to Hayden, Sept. 10, 1952, in *Benton Report,* p. 95.

90. *New York Times,* Sept. 27, 1952; Des Moines *Register,* Sept. 27, 1952; memorandum, Howe to Benton, Aug. 22, 1952, Box 4, Benton MSS.

91. Borrowed from the RFC, Cotter was familiar with the Lustron episode. Washington *Post,* Nov. 27, 1952; night letter, Hayden to Darrell St. Claire, Oct. 14, 1952; telegram, Hayden to Hennings, Sept. 23, 1952; Hayden to Sen. Earle C. Clements, Sept. 23, 1952, all Folder 6, Box 60, Hayden MSS; Benton to Monroney, Nov. 11, 1952, Box 5; memorandum, Howe to Benton, n.d. [March 1952], Box 4; Hendrickson to Benton, Nov. 14, 1952, Box 4, all Benton MSS.

92. Copy, Ben H. Brown, Jr., to Hayden, containing text of Monroney message from Rome, Nov. 20, 1952, Folder 4, Box 120, Hayden MSS; Hayden to St. Claire, Nov. 20, 1952, *ibid.;* Washington *Post,* Nov. 20, 1952; Hyman, *Benton,* p. 415.

93. Washington *Post,* Nov. 11, 19, 1952; memorandum, Paul Eaton to Robert Koch, Sept. 27, 1954, Folder 28, Box 128, Hayden MSS; Mary K. Garner to Hayden, Sept. 13, 1954, *ibid.;* cf. *Benton Report,* pp. 9–10.

94. *New York Times*, Nov. 19, 23, 1952; Washington *Post*, Nov. 11, 1952; Paul J. Cotter to McCarthy, Nov. 7, 21, 1952; Ray Kiermas to Cotter, Nov. 10, 1952; Hennings to McCarthy, Nov. 21, 1952; McCarthy to Hennings, Nov. 28, Dec. 1, 1952, all in *Benton Report*, pp. 96–99, 101–4.

95. *New York Times*, Dec. 25, 1952; Hyman, *Benton*, pp. 482–83; Abell, ed., *Drew Pearson Diaries*, pp. 239–41; Washington *Post*, Jan. 3, 1953; memorandum, Benton to Howe, Sept. 17, 1954, Box 5, Benton MSS. Cf. memorandum, Benton to Howe, June 11, 1959, Box 4, *ibid.;* Kemper, *Decade of Fear*, pp. 23, 214.

96. Telegram, Hendrickson to Charles Johnston, Jan. 6, 1953, Box 36, Hendrickson MSS.

97. Clinton P. Anderson to Mrs. James Calvin Hobart, Jan. 12, 1953, Box 283, Anderson MSS; Abell, ed., *Drew Pearson Diaries*, p. 246. Technically, though all three Senators approved the report, none "signed" it. Hendrickson to Benton, Sept. 20, 1954, Box 5, Benton MSS.

98. Memorandum, Benton to Howe, June 11, 1959, Box 4; memorandum, Benton to Howe, Sept. 17, 1954, Box 5, Benton MSS; cf. draft, Benton to Arthur Hays Sulzberger, Dec. 8, 1954, Box 4, *ibid*.

99. Nearly eight of the fifty pages of text dealt with Benton's "badly handled" donation from Cosgriff. *Benton Report*, pp. 10–11, 13, 20–23, 26–32, 41, 45–52, and passim. Cf. Griffith, *Politics of Fear*, pp. 182, 187.

100. Washington *Post*, Jan. 3, 1953; memorandum, Howe to Benton, Oct. 12, 1954, Box 5, Benton MSS; Clinton P. Anderson to Mrs. James Calvin Hobart, Box 283, Anderson MSS; draft of unanimous consent resolution, n.d., Folder 5, Box 120, Hayden MSS; cf. Abell, ed., *Drew Pearson Diaries*, pp. 245–47.

101. Washington *Post*, Jan. 4, 1953; *New York Times*, Jan. 3, 4, 1953.

102. Kemper, *Decade of Fear*, p. 60; memorandum, Howe to Benton, Oct. 12, 1954, Box 5, Benton MSS; Washington *Post*, Jan. 4, 6, 1953.

103. Washington *Post*, Jan. 3, 6, 1953; Hennings to Ralph Torreyson, Feb. 7, 1953, Box 84, Hennings MSS. It would have been a "vote of Republican support which they might not give to him at some later time." Clinton P. Anderson to Mrs. James Calvin Hobart, Jan. 12, 1953, Box 283, Anderson MSS.

104. *New York Times*, Jan. 3, 1953; Humphrey to John Forbes, Jan. 21, 1953, Box 97, Humphrey MSS; Washington *Post*, Jan. 4, 6, 1953.

105. Washington *Post*, Jan. 7, 8, 22, 1953; *Christian Science Monitor*, Jan. 7, 1953; Hennings to Robert E. McWilliams, Jan. 28, 1953, Box 82, Hennings MSS. Some of the subcommittee files also were sent to the Justice Department.

106. Kemper, *Decade of Fear*, p. 62; Kenneth M. Birkhead to Benton, n.d. [ca. March 1953], Box 4, Benton MSS; Benton to Birkhead, March 9, 1953, *ibid.;* Lester Hunt to L. G. Flannery, Feb. 24, 1953, Hunt MSS. The Americans for Demo-

cratic Action undertook a photo-offset reproduction of the rare document. John J. Gunther to Ralph Flanders, June 14, 1954, Series 5, Box 39, ADA MSS.

107. Telegram, Benton to Truman, Jan. 16, 1953, OF 3371, Truman Papers; *New York Times,* Jan. 19, 1953; copy, Brownell to Jenner, Oct. 15, 1953, Box 30, Hennings MSS.

108. Hendrickson to Daniel J. P. Hendrickson, Dec. 3, 1952, Box 21, Hendrickson MSS.

109. Memorandum, Violet Gunther to James Loeb, Jr., Dec. 14, 1950, "Senate Situation on McCarthyism, et al.," Series 5, Box 34, ADA MSS.

110. Washington *Post,* Sept. 5, 1952; Washington (Sunday) *Star,* May 18, 1952, clipping in Tydings MSS; Hartford *Courant,* April 20, 23, 1952.

111. U.S. Senate, Select Committee to Study Censure Charges, *Hearings on S. Res. 301,* 83d Cong., 2d Sess., 1954, p. 68; cf. Washington *Post,* Jan. 3, 1953. For the impact of the H-H-H Report on censure, see Griffith, *Politics of Fear,* p. 187; Kemper, *Decade of Fear,* pp. 63ff.

112. Flanders to Benton, Nov. 3, 1958, Box 102, Flanders MSS. The Vermont Senator believed, however, that "any endeavor of a Democrat to censure McCarthy was doomed to failure. It could only be done by a Republican." Flanders to author, Sept. 19, 1968.

113. Maurice Rosenblatt to Gifford Phillips, Aug. 31, 1953, File 4, Drawer 1, NCEC MSS.

114. Memorandum, Howe to Benton, June 2, 1953, Box 4, Benton MSS; Benton to Ralph Flanders, Oct. 27, 1958, Box 102, Flanders MSS.

CHAPTER 8   "ALGER . . . I MEAN ADLAI"

1. Wheeling *Intelligencer,* Feb. 11, 1952.

2. *New York Times,* Sept. 9, 1951; Milwaukee *Journal,* Aug. 27, 1951; Madison *Capital-Times,* Dec. 15, 1951, clipping in Tydings MSS; McCarthy to Douglas MacArthur, Oct. 18, 1951, VIP File, MacArthur MSS, MacArthur Memorial Library, Norfolk, Va. For speculation regarding McCarthy's role in 1952, see *New York Times,* Nov. 21, 1951, Feb. 3, April 27, 1952.

3. *New York Times,* Oct. 5, 1951, Feb. 17, March 25, 29, 1952; David, Moos, and Goldman, eds., *Presidential Nominating Politics in 1952,* vol. 4: *The Middle West,* pp. 135–38. Phil La Follette had served on MacArthur's staff in the Pacific, and his brother had made laudatory references to the General prior to the 1944 election. On the 1948 MacArthur boom, see Schonberger, "The General and the Presidency," pp. 201–19.

4. *New York Times,* Feb. 20, March 15, April 8, 1952.

5. Milwaukee *Journal*, Aug. 22, 1951; *Life*, 31 (Oct. 1, 1951): 32; *Collier's*, 128 (Aug. 18, 1951): 74; Washington *Post*, Feb. 14, March 9, Oct. 23, 1951, Jan. 28, 1952. Also see Patterson, *Mr. Republican*, pp. 503, 530.

6. *New York Times*, Oct. 23, 1951, Jan. 22, March 23, 1952. For conservative anger at Taft's ambivalence, see George Creel to Sen. Karl E. Mundt, March 7, 1952, Box 4, Creel MSS, Library of Congress.

7. *New York Times*, Feb. 23, 1952; Washington *Post*, June 23, 1952 (Walter Lippmann), July 11, 1952 (Alsops).

8. *New York Times*, July 3, 1952; cf. *ibid.*, Oct. 14, 1951.

9. *Ibid.*, June 8, Oct. 20, 1950, Jan. 8, May 9, 1952.

10. *Ibid.*, June 6, 1952; Washington *Post*, June 6, 8, 23, 1952; Elmer Davis radio script, Aug. 7, 1952, Box 23, Davis MSS, Library of Congress; cf. *New Republic*, 126 (June 16, 1952): 5–6.

11. Washington *Post*, July 6, 1952; *New York Times*, July 10, 1952.

12. Schoeppel to Butler, July 16, 1952; Butler to Schoeppel, July 21, 1952, both Box 353, Hugh Butler MSS.; Taft to George Creel, Sept. 5, 1952, Box 4, Creel MSS.

13. Nixon had carefully avoided too close an association with McCarthy, however. *New York Times*, July 11, 12, 20, 1952; Washington *Post*, July 12, 1952.

14. *New York Times*, July 12, 27, Aug. 10, 1952; Washington *Post*, July 13, 1952. An alternative "three C" formula added "change"; Senator Mundt proposed "seven C's." Milwaukee *Journal*, Sept. 14, 1952; *New York Times*, Sept. 9, 1951.

15. Washington *Post*, Sept. 2, Nov. 21, 1951; *New York Times*, Sept. 30, Nov. 21, 27, Dec. 23, 1951; Milwaukee *Journal*, Aug. 24, 1951.

16. *New York Times*, March 30, April 30, June 7, 23, July 6, 13, 1952.

17. *Ibid.*, March 20, 21, 1952. See also *ibid.*, April 7, 18, June 24, 1952; Washington *Post*, June 7, 1952.

18. *New York Times*, July 24, Aug. 3, 1952. Stevenson also vetoed a bill requiring Illinois state employees to take a loyalty oath. *Ibid.*, June 27, 1951.

19. White said there "could be no conceivable doubt" of his story's "authenticity," but he conceded that it should have read: "no endorsement for either the views or the methods" of McCarthy. Leo Katcher and William V. Shannon wrote that Nixon "fed" the story to White, then "denied it when the pressure was put on." *Ibid.*, Aug. 22–24, 26, 1952; New York *Post*, Oct. 2, 1952.

20. Washington *Post*, Sept. 27, Oct. 1, 14, Nov. 17, 1951.

21. Milwaukee *Journal*, Aug. 22, 1951; *New York Times*, Oct. 13, 25, Dec. 16, 1951; Washington *Post*, Oct. 30, 1951, Jan. 31, 1952; valuable on this aspect of the campaign is O'Brien, "The Anti-McCarthy Campaign in Wisconsin," pp. 97–100.

Retrospectively, Kohler believed the Democrats were more interested in dividing the GOP; he may also have been less serious about a contest with McCarthy than the press thought. Walter J. Kohler to author, July 19, 1971; memorandum, Kohler to Sherman Adams, April 27, 1959, courtesy of Gov. Kohler.

22. *New York Times,* June 26, Aug. 14, 24, 31, Sept. 1, 1952; Milwaukee *Journal,* Sept. 3, 4, 1952; O'Brien, "The Anti-McCarthy Campaign in Wisconsin," pp. 101–3.

23. Milwaukee *Journal,* Sept. 7, 19, 1952; Washington *Post,* Nov. 9, 1951, July 9, 18, 1952; Frances Rose to Julius Edelstein, July 6, 1951, Series 5, Box 37, ADA MSS; Miles McMillin to Thomas N. Duncan, April 10, 1952, File A, Box 8, C.O.P.E. Papers, AFL-CIO MSS, State Historical Society of Wisconsin.

24. Milwaukee *Journal,* Sept. 14, 1952; Washington *Post,* Sept. 17, Oct. 9, 1952.

25. Milwaukee *Journal,* Sept. 10, 1952; *New York Times,* Sept. 10, 1952; Oshinsky, "Wisconsin Labor and the Campaign of 1952," pp. 111–12.

26. *Christian Science Monitor,* Sept. 10, 1952; *New York Times,* Aug. 29, 1952; Indianapolis *Star,* Sept. 11, 1952; Mundt to Arthur Summerfield and Wayne Hood, Aug. 28, 1952, Mundt MSS, "GOP Speakers Bureau, 1952 Campaign."

27. *New York Times,* Aug. 23, 1952.

28. Washington *Post,* Sept. 10, 11, 1952; Indianapolis *Star,* Sept. 10, 1952; Hughes, *The Ordeal of Power,* p. 41; Cutler, *No Time for Rest,* p. 287.

29. Milwaukee *Journal,* Sept. 12, 1952; Washington *Post,* Sept. 11, 13, 1952.

30. Milwaukee *Journal,* Sept. 10, 1952; memorandum, Hugh Scott to Sherman Adams, Sept. 15, 1952, Alpha File, Eisenhower Papers, Dwight D. Eisenhower Library.

31. Washington *Post,* Sept. 11, 1952; Hughes, *Ordeal of Power,* pp. 41–42; Eisenhower, *Mandate for Change,* p. 317; cf. Elmer Davis radio script, Aug. 1, 1952, Box 23, Davis MSS.

32. St. Louis *Post-Dispatch,* Oct. 3, 1952; Milwaukee *Journal,* Sept. 12, 17, Oct. 1, 3, 1952; Walter J. Kohler to author, July 19, 1971.

33. New York *Post,* Oct. 3, 1952; Milwaukee *Journal,* Oct. 3, 1952; Kohler memorandum to Adams, April 27, 1959; Eisenhower, *Mandate for Change,* pp. 318–19; cf. Sherman Adams, *Firsthand Report,* pp. 30–31; Parmet, *Eisenhower and the American Crusades,* p. 131. Griffith, "The General and the Senator," pp. 23–29, is a valuable account of the episode.

34. Milwaukee *Journal,* Oct. 3, 1952; St. Louis *Post-Dispatch,* Oct. 3, 1952; Kohler memorandum to Adams, April 27, 1959.

35. Kohler memorandum; sixth draft of speech to be delivered in Milwaukee, "Communism and Freedom," n.d., OF 101-GG, Eisenhower Papers; Milwaukee *Journal,* Oct. 4, 1952; cf. Griffith, "The General and the Senator," p. 27.

36. New York *Post,* Oct. 6, 1952; Griffith, "The General and the Senator," p. 28; St. Louis *Post-Dispatch,* Oct. 4, 1952; Milwaukee *Journal,* Oct. 4, 1952.

37. Washington *Post,* Oct. 10, 14, 1952; cf. St. Louis *Post-Dispatch,* Oct. 15, 1952.

38. St. Louis *Post-Dispatch,* Oct. 14, 1952; Washington *Post,* Oct. 11, 18, 1952.

39. St. Louis *Post-Dispatch,* Oct. 27, 1952; Washington *Post,* Nov. 1, 2, 1952.

40. *New York Times,* Aug. 3, 15, 1952.

41. *Ibid.,* Aug. 10, 1952; Indianapolis *Star,* Sept. 7, 1952; St. Louis *Post-Dispatch,* Oct. 1, 1952.

42. *New York Times,* Aug. 13, 14, 1952; Washington *Post,* Sept. 7, 1952; Nixon to George Creel, Aug. 30, 1952, Box. 4, Creel MSS.

43. Washington *Post,* Sept. 20, 1952; Milwaukee *Journal,* Sept. 20–22, 1952.

44. *New York Times,* Sept. 24, 1952.

45. New York *Post,* Oct. 2, 1952; Washington *Post,* Oct. 10, 1952; St. Louis *Post-Dispatch,* Oct. 17, 1952; Milwaukee *Journal,* Oct. 24, 1952.

46. *New York Times,* Sept. 4, 21, 1952; Milwaukee *Journal,* Sept. 18, 30, Oct. 16, 1952.

47. *New York Times,* Oct. 8, 27–29, 1952; St. Louis *Post-Dispatch,* Oct. 25, 1952; New York *Post,* Oct. 28, 1952. McCarthy used the "Alger/Adlai" slip or a variation of it on several other occasions—e.g., St. Louis *Post-Dispatch,* Oct. 18, Nov. 1, 1952; *Arizona Republic,* Oct. 19, 1952; Indianapolis *Star,* Oct. 21, 1952.

48. Milwaukee *Journal,* Oct. 28, 29, 1952; *Newsday,* quoted in New York *Post,* Oct. 30, 1952.

49. *New York Times,* Oct. 7, 29, 1952; Seattle *Times,* Oct. 24, 1952; *Christian Science Monitor,* Oct. 7, 1952.

50. *New York Times,* Oct. 5, 7, 10, 12, 1952; Washington *Post,* Oct. 5, 1952; St. Louis *Post-Dispatch,* Oct. 19, 1952.

51. *New York Times,* Aug. 28, 29, Sept. 11, 19, Oct. 5, 1952; Milwaukee *Journal,* Oct. 8, 9, 16, 1952; cf. Washington *Post,* Oct. 12, 16, 1952.

52. *New York Times,* Sept. 13, 20, 30, Oct. 1, 1952; Washington *Post,* Sept. 30, 1952 (cf. Oct. 8, 1952).

53. *New York Times,* Oct. 8, 10, 11, 15, 23, 1952.

54. Washington *Post,* Oct. 20, 1952; *New York Times,* Oct. 24, 1952.

55. Washington *Post,* Sept. 5, 1952; *New York Times,* Oct. 11, 1952. Beset by angry rebuttals from Columbia, Sparkman explained that he had not meant to malign that institution, but to reveal the absurdity of the "McCarthyism which Eisenhower has embraced." Seattle *Times,* Oct. 13, 1952.

56. *New York Times,* Sept. 10, 12, Oct. 14, 1952.

57. *Public Papers of the Presidents of the United States: Harry S. Truman, 1952–1953* (Washington, D.C., 1966), pp. 831–32, 858.

58. *Ibid.,* pp. 634–35, 709–11.

59. *Ibid.,* pp. 856–57.

60. *Ibid.,* pp. 579–80, 598, 895; cf. *ibid.,* pp. 855, 891, 1011.

61. *Ibid.,* pp. 1011, 1047.

62. *Ibid.,* pp. 940–41, 1042; St. Louis *Post-Dispatch,* Oct. 2, 6, 1952; Milwaukee *Journal,* Oct. 24, 1952; *New York Times,* Oct. 28, 1952.

63. Milwaukee *Journal,* Sept. 21, Oct. 22, 24, 1952. Both O'Brien, "The Anti-McCarthy Campaign in Wisconsin, 1951–1952," pp. 104, 106–7, and Oshinsky, "Wisconsin Labor and the Campaign of 1952," p. 113, stress that McCarthy's foes were aware of the futility of contesting the effectiveness or ethics of McCarthy's anticommunism and emphasized instead his poor voting record on issues of concern to Democratic interest groups.

64. Fairchild charged McCarthy with "tearing around the country" to avoid owning up to a "miserable" voting record. Milwaukee *Journal,* Sept. 24, 25, 27, Oct. 21, 1952; Matusow, *False Witness,* pp. 138–48; Washington *Post,* Oct. 8, 1952.

65. Milwaukee *Journal,* Sept. 17, 21, 25, 1952; *New York Times,* Sept. 18, 1952; St. Louis *Post-Dispatch,* Oct. 1, 1952.

66. Bean, *Influences in the 1954 Mid-Term Elections,* p. 20; Milwaukee *Journal,* Sept. 18, 1952; *Arizona Republic,* Oct. 19, 1952.

67. Milwaukee *Journal,* Oct. 14, 15, 1952; Washington *Post,* Sept. 6, 1952; *New York Times,* Oct. 25, 1952; (Butte) *Montana Standard,* Oct. 13, 15, 1952; Seattle *Times,* Oct. 23, 1952. McCarthy also spoke in Utah, New Mexico, and, under nonpartisan auspices, in Texas.

68. Hartford *Courant,* Oct. 14, 1952; *New York Times,* Oct. 25, 1952; Seattle *Times,* Oct. 23, 24, 1952.

69. St. Louis *Post-Dispatch,* Nov. 1, 1952; Detroit *Free Press,* Oct. 10, 1952; Indianapolis *Star,* Oct. 21, 1952; Wheeling *Intelligencer,* Oct. 22, 1952.

70. This juxtaposition of friend and foe was bizarre even for McCarthy. Transcript, "Spots on Radio," n.d. [1952], Box 216-1, Langer MSS.

71. Hartford *Courant,* Oct. 1, 29, 1952; *New York Times,* Oct. 1, 1952; Milwaukee *Journal,* Sept. 3, 1952; St. Louis *Post-Dispatch,* Oct. 1, 1952.

72. St. Louis *Post-Dispatch,* Oct. 1, 3, 11, 17, 1952.

73. The *Post-Dispatch* thought Symington "went too far" in making the Marcantonio comparison. *Ibid.,* Oct. 2, 14, 15, 21, 1952.

74. Seattle *Times,* Oct. 2, 25, 28, 1952; *New York Times,* Oct. 5, 1952. More frequently, Cain hit Jackson as a "spender" and captive of the unions, while Jackson alleged that Cain had done little for the state.

75. Mansfield also chided Ecton for doing nothing for his constituents. *Montana Standard,* Oct. 22, 23, 29, 1952.

76. *Arizona Republic,* Oct. 10, 15, 19, 21, 29, Nov. 2, 1952.

77. *New York Times,* Oct. 7, 11, 1952; Indianapolis *Star,* Sept. 6, 9, 11, 12, 26–28, Oct. 24, 28, Nov. 1, 1952.

78. Cleveland *Plain Dealer,* Oct. 4, 1952; Milwaukee *Journal,* Sept. 4, 1952; press release, Oct. 22–23, 1952, Box 301, DiSalle MSS, Ohio Historical Society. McCormick had endorsed these Senators while refusing to support Eisenhower.

79. Detroit *Free Press,* Oct. 2, 4, 8, 20, 26, 27, Nov. 1, 2, 6, 1952.

80. Washington *Post,* Sept. 7, 18, Oct. 24, 1952.

81. *New York Times,* Oct. 19, 1952; Wheeling *Intelligencer,* Oct. 18, 28, 29, Nov. 1, 3, 1952.

82. Whalen, *Founding Father,* pp. 424–25, 430–31; Washington *Post,* Sept. 18, Nov. 6, 1950; St. Louis *Post-Dispatch,* Oct. 29, 30, 1952; *Arizona Republic,* Oct. 27, 1952; New York *Post,* Oct. 24, 1952.

83. *Arizona Republic,* Oct. 17, 1952; Washington *Times-Herald,* Jan 28, 1952 (William Fulton), clipping in File 4, Drawer 3, NCEC MSS. In one very guarded statement distributed only to a limited group of Jewish constituents, JFK rapped Lodge for using "McCarthy tactics" in a handbill which had suggested that Joseph P. Kennedy was anti-Semitic. Whalen, *Founding Father,* p. 426.

84. Hyman, *Lives of William Benton,* p. 480; Brock, *Americans for Democratic Action,* pp. 184–85; Whalen, *Founding Father,* pp. 427–29; ACLU "Questionnaire for Presidential, Vice-Presidential and Senatorial Candidates for 1952 Elections," n.d., answered and enclosed in Kennedy letter of Oct. 23, 1952, vol. 34 (1952), ACLU MSS.

85. Milwaukee *Journal,* Oct. 30, 1952; Hartford *Courant,* Oct. 12, 18, 19, 30, 1952.

86. Hartford *Courant,* Oct. 5, 8, 12, 14, 19, 21, 22, Nov. 2, 1952.

87. *Ibid.,* Oct. 20, Nov. 2, 1952; Indianapolis *Star,* Nov. 5, 1952; Washington *Post,* Oct. 30, 1952.

88. *New York Times,* Nov. 5, 6, 1952; Milwaukee *Journal,* Nov. 6, 1952; Bean, *Influences,* pp. 8–18; Rogin, *The Intellectuals and McCarthy,* pp. 86, 91–94. McCarthy's mediocre showing may have stemmed partly from his casual campaign and from the fact that he, unlike other GOP candidates, faced a well-known opponent (Milwaukee *Journal,* Nov. 8, 1952).

89. Indianapolis *Star,* Sept. 21, 1952; Lester Hunt to Wandell Elliot, March 12, 1954, Hunt MSS; *Arizona Republic,* Nov. 8, 1952.

90. Hartford *Courant,* Nov. 5, 1952; Benton to Maurice Rosenblatt, n.d. [ca. April 1953], Box 4, Benton MSS; John Howe to William T. Evjue, Jan. 19, 1954, *ibid.;* Bean, *Influences,* pp. 23–24.

91. Bean, *Influences*, pp. 23–24; Polsby, "Toward an Explanation of Mc-Carthyism," pp. 266–68; Benton to Herbert H. Lehman, Nov. 29, 1952, copy in Nevins Research File, Drawer 2, Lehman MSS; St. Louis *Post-Dispatch*, Nov. 9, 1952; *New York Times*, Nov. 5, 1952.

92. For the difficulties in analyzing this phenomenon, see Miller, "Presidential Coattails," pp. 353–68.

93. Indianapolis *Star*, Oct. 19, 1952; Washington *Post*, Nov. 7, 1952 (Alsops).

94. Kelso, "The 1952 Elections in Arizona," p. 101; Washington *Post*, Nov. 6, 1952; *Arizona Republic*, Nov. 2, 6, 1952.

95. C. C. Smith, "The 1952 Elections in Nevada," pp. 118–19; Washington *Post*, Nov. 7, 1952.

96. Merrill, "The 1952 Elections in Utah," pp. 127, 130; Washington *Post*, Nov. 5, 1952.

97. Hinckley, "The 1952 Elections in Wyoming," pp. 135–36. O'Mahoney believed that the "Eisenhower avalanche" buried him, but his administrative assistant thought that McCarthy was a weightier factor. O'Mahoney to Carl Hayden, Nov. 14, 1952, Box 135, Hayden MSS; memorandum, Stephen J. Spingarn to Murphy, Lloyd, Bell, et al., Nov. 24, 1952, Internal Security, Spingarn Papers.

98. Bone, "Western Politics and the 1952 Elections," p. 95. Two who failed to benefit from the Ike landslide, Cain and Ecton, were not particularly effective candidates who faced experienced, powerful Congressmen noted for an ability to produce for their constituents. Pat Hurley of New Mexico was hurt by opposition from the regular organization. Karlen, "The 1952 Elections in Montana," p. 116; Daniel M. Ogden, Jr., "The 1952 Elections in Washington," p. 134; Judah, "The 1952 Elections in New Mexico," pp. 120–21. See also De Grazia, *The Western Public*, pp. 11, 14–15.

99. Bean, *Influences*, pp. 18–23.

100. Harris, *Is There a Republican Majority?* pp. 203–4, 223.

101. *Ibid.*, p. 32; Campbell, Converse, Miller, and Stokes, *The American Voter*, pp. 50–51; De Grazia, *The Western Public*, pp. 43–45; cf. Washington *Post*, Jan. 21, 1953 (Gallup); Stouffer, *Communism, Conformity, and Civil Liberties*, pp. 59, 68.

102. Harris, *Is There A Republican Majority?* pp. 88–93, 100–1; Lubell, *Revolt of the Moderates*, pp. 71–74, 269; Daniel Bell, ed., *The Radical Right*, especially Seymour Martin Lipset, "Three Decades of the Radical Right," pp. 391–421; Rogin, *McCarthy and the Intellectuals*, pp. 238–39, 246, and *passim*.

103. Indianapolis *Star*, Sept. 2, 1952 (Pegler), Sept. 11, Oct. 16, 1952 (Pegler); *Newsweek*, 41 (April 27, 1953): 32; *New York Times*, Jan 18, 1953 (White); *Look*, 17 (June 16, 1953): 32. In the first article, White listed Benton, McFarland, Schricker, and O'Mahoney as 1952 casualties; in the second, he had Moody and

Lodge in mind as additional McCarthy victims. Unsigned memorandum, n.d. [1953], "The 'Power' of McCarthy," File 9, Drawer 1, NCEC MSS.

104. St. Louis *Post-Dispatch*, Oct. 31, 1952 (Lubell); Lubell, *Revolt of the Moderates*, pp. 38–39; Campbell, Converse, et al., *The American Voter*, pp. 45–46, 50; Harris, *Is There A Republican Majority?* pp. 38–40.

105. Humphrey to Eugene Matters, July 20, 1953, Box 97, Humphrey MSS.

106. Benton to Maurice Rosenblatt, n.d. [ca. April 1953], Box 4, Benton MSS; Rosenblatt to Gifford Phillips, Aug. 31, 1953, File 4, Drawer 1, NCEC MSS.

107. Bean, *Influences;* memorandum, Howe to Benton, April 23, May 7, 8, 1954; Howe to Harry Scherman, June 7, 1954; Joseph C. Harsch to Howe, June 22, 1954; Louis Bean to Howe, July 9, 1954, all Box 4, Benton MSS.

CHAPTER 9 ". . . A REPUBLICAN PROBLEM"

1. St. Louis *Post-Dispatch*, Oct. 10 (Lippmann), 18, 1952; Washington *Post*, Nov. 3, 1952 (Alsops); Hartford *Courant*, Jan. 15, 1953; Cleveland *Plain Dealer*, Nov. 8, 1952.

2. Eisenhower to Harry Bullis, May 18, 1953, OF 99-R, Eisenhower Papers, Eisenhower Library.

3. Donovan, *Eisenhower*, p. 248; Hughes, *Ordeal of Power*, pp. 66, 92; Adams, *Firsthand Report*, pp. 135–36, 140; Parmet, *Eisenhower and the American Crusades*, p. 248; Washington *Post*, July 5, 1953; Hall to Eisenhower, Dec. 21, 1953, GF 171, Eisenhower Papers.

4. *New York Times*, June 28, July 9, 26, 1953; Hughes, *Ordeal of Power*, p. 94; Adams, *Firsthand Report*, pp. 139–40; Mazo and Hess, *Nixon*, pp. 132–36.

5. Gerald D. Morgan to Rep. Jacob K. Javits, Nov. 28, 1953, OF 99-P, Eisenhower Papers; President's News Conference of June 17, 1953, *Public Papers of the Presidents of the United States. Dwight D. Eisenhower, 1953* (Washington, D.C., 1960), p. 426 (cited hereafter as *Eisenhower Papers*).

6. Eisenhower to Harry Bullis, May 28, 1953, OF 99-R, Eisenhower Papers; Donovan, *Eisenhower*, p. 249; cf. Hughes, *Ordeal of Power*, p. 92.

7. *New York Times*, July 12, 1953; cf. Pusey, *Eisenhower the President*, p. 274; Watkins, *Enough Rope*.

8. *New York Times*, Jan. 23, Feb. 22, 26, 28, 1953; Beal, *John Foster Dulles*, pp. 138ff. Dulles, of course, sought to avoid the raveled relations with Congress which had ensnarled Acheson. Washington *Post*, April 17, 1953 (Lippmann).

9. Memorandum, Charles S. Willis, Jr., to Bernard Shanley, April 22, 1953, OF 103-P, Eisenhower Papers. For Doerfer's later difficulties, see Frier, *Conflict of Interest in the Eisenhower Administration*, ch. 13. McCarthy's support of the efforts of the Hearst interests to obtain a channel in Milwaukee also took on a sinister cast.

Griffith, *Politics of Fear,* p. 236; Frank Zeidler to Norman Thomas, March 19, June 1, 1953, Box 73, Thomas MSS.

10. *Arizona Republic,* Nov. 8, 1952; Indianapolis *Star,* Nov. 9, 1952; Washington *Post,* Jan. 2, 3, 9, 12, 26, 1953; *New York Times,* Jan. 6, 23, 1953.

11. John J. Gunther memorandum, "Congressional Investigations," n.d. [Feb. 1953], Series 5, Box 30, ADA MSS; Washington *Post,* Jan. 10, 14, 31, 1953; Elmer Davis, radio script of Jan. 23, 1953, Box 24, Davis MSS; *Cong. Record,* 83d Cong., 1st Sess., 99 (Jan. 29, 1953): 603–4, (Jan. 30, 1953): 698–706; Taft quoted in Rovere, *Senator Joe McCarthy,* pp. 187–88; cf. Griffith, *Politics of Fear,* pp. 207–10.

12. *New York Times,* Jan. 26, Feb. 5–8, 1953; Washington *Post,* Jan. 27, Feb. 4, 1953; U.S. Senate, Committee on Government Operations, Permanent Subcommittee on Investigations, *State Department—Files Survey,* 83d Cong., 1st Sess., 1953. Other hearings of the same subcommittee will be designated hereafter as "PSI."

13. C. D. Jackson to John Foster Dulles, Feb. 19, 1953, OF 8-D, Eisenhower Papers; PSI, *State Department Information Program—Voice of America,* pp. 1–11, 151–211, 224. Senator Taft thought "the whole outfit ought to be abolished and a brand new start made outside the State Department." Taft to Norman Thomas, March 20, 1953, Box 73, Thomas MSS.

14. PSI, *State Department Information Centers;* Washington *Post,* Feb. 14, 20, March 25, 27, April 25, June 14, 1953; *New York Times,* March 3, June 16, 22, 1953.

15. Washington *Post,* April 10, 22, 26, 1953; G. David Schine to Charles F. Willis, Jr., May 15, 1953, OF 150-C-1, Eisenhower Papers.

16. Among the objections voiced against Conant were his critical views of parochial education, initial support for harsh treatment of postwar Germany, and his call for an American breed of radicalism. Washington *Post,* Feb. 3, 4, 7, 1953; McCarthy to Eisenhower, Feb. 3, 1953; McCarthy to Sherman Adams, Feb. 4, 1953, both in GF 9-D-1, Eisenhower Papers.

17. Washington *Post,* March 18, 19, 21, 24–26, 28, 1953; *Cong. Record,* 99 (March 20, 1953): 2155–57, (March 25, 1953): 2277–2300, (March 27, 1953): 2374–92; William S. White, *The Taft Story,* pp. 230–39. See also Bohlen, *Witness to History,* ch. 18.

18. Washington *Post,* March 29, 31, April 2–4, 1953; President's New Conference of April 3, 1953, *Eisenhower Papers, 1953,* pp. 153–55.

19. *Eisenhower Papers, 1953,* p. 415; *New York Times,* June 15, 17, 18, 1953; President's News Conference of June 17, 1953, *Eisenhower Papers, 1953,* pp. 426–38; cf. *ibid.,* pp. 465–67, 477.

20. Carl Hayden also helped shape the Democratic strategy. Frank J. Kendrick, "The Senate and Senator Joseph R. McCarthy," *Proceedings of the Minnesota Academy of Science,* vol. 32, no. 1 (1964): 63; *New York Times,* Jan. 7, 1954; first

Mitchell quote in memorandum, John Howe to William Benton, Jan. 13, 1954, Box 4, Benton MSS; Mitchell to Adlai E. Stevenson, July 23, 1953, Case 88, Drawer 1, Stevenson MSS, Illinois State Historical Library; Mitchell to Hayden, Dec. 17, 1954, Box 135, Hayden MSS.

21. Richard Russell to Clyde Hoey, Nov. 14, 1952, Box 6, Hoey MSS; White, *The Professional,* pp. 49–50; memorandum, Howe to Benton, Jan. 13, 1954, Box 4, Benton MSS; cf. *New York Times,* Jan. 3, 7, 1954.

22. Lehman and McCarthy also tangled several times over the latter's charges that the New Yorker had abused his franking privilege. *Cong. Record,* 99 (March 25, 1953): 2299–2300, (June 11, 1953): 6386–91, (June 15, 1953): 6459–61, (July 7, 1953): 8056–57, (July 20, 1953): 9179, (July 21, 1953): 9352–54; Washington *Post,* April 30, 1953.

23. *Cong. Record,* 99 (June 16, 1953): 6610–11, (July 2, 1953): 7863–65, (July 10, 1953): 8424–30; Kerr speech, Jackson Day Banquet, April 4, 1953, Kerr MSS.

24. Hoey to Mrs. P. H. Winston, May 3, 1954, Box 35, Hoey MSS; Hoey to John B. Graham, March 20, 1954, *ibid.;* Fulbright to John Huenefeld, March 2, 1953, Fulbright MSS; Fulbright to William Benton, March 4, 1953, Box 4, Benton MSS.

25. Hunt to Zan Lewis, Feb. 24, 1953, Hunt MSS; Fulbright to Mrs. Jesse Murphy, March 4, 1953, Fulbright MSS, Fulbright to Benton, March 4, 1953, Box 4, Benton MSS; Humphrey to Paul F. Schmidt, Dec. 15, 1953, Box 97, Humphrey MSS.

26. Hunt to Charles E. Hanner, July 15, 1953, Hunt MSS; Humphrey to Paul F. Schmidt, Dec. 15, 1953, Box 97, Humphrey MSS; Humphrey to Mr. and Mrs. Warren Seulowitz, June 1, 1953, *ibid.; New York Times,* Feb. 22, 1953.

27. Anderson to Mrs. James Calvin Hobart, Jan. 12, 1953, Box 283, Anderson MSS; Hoey to J. R. Still, Oct. 1, 1953, Box 2, Hoey MSS; cf. Hubert Humphrey to Kathleen Arnes, Sept. 23, 1953, Box 97, Humphrey MSS.

28. Anderson to Mrs. J. M. Stoney, March 11, 1953, Box 283, Anderson MSS; Hoey to Mrs. Alex S. Davis, May 4, 1954, Box 35, Hoey MSS; Hoey to Miss Gertrude Neill, May 7, 1954, *ibid.*

29. Hoey to Hoyt McAfee, March 6, 1953, Box 34, *ibid.* Hoey had also wanted to quit the parent Government Operations Committee, but he was persuaded to stay in order to "bolster" it. Washington *Post,* Jan. 13, 1953.

30. *New York Times,* Jan. 14, 1953; Washington *Post,* Jan. 14, 1953.

31. For a helpful analysis of the "McCarthy balance" at this stage, see Griffith, *Politics of Fear,* pp. 196–207, 224. Cf. unsigned, undated draft of memorandum, [ca. Feb.–March 1954], File 10, Drawer 1, NCEC MSS; *New York Times,* Feb. 22, 1953.

32. John Howe to Benton, June 2, 1953, Box 4, Benton MSS; Benton to Howe, June 9, 1953, *ibid.*

33. Minutes, ADA Executive Meeting, Aug. 26, 1953, Series 2, Box 35, ADA MSS; Edward D. Hollander to Frederick E. Bauer, Jr., Dec. 4, 1953, Series 2, Box 25, *ibid.;* cf. memorandum, Hollander to Robert R. Nathan, Sept. 24, 1953, Series 2, Box 35, *ibid.;* ADA press release, June 9, 1953, "Editorial and Reply Printed in Washington *Evening Star,"* Series 5, Box 39, *ibid.*

34. Richard Rovere to Arthur Schlesinger, March 30, 1952; copy, Schlesinger to Sidney Hook, April 1, 1952; Hook to Rovere, April 2, 1952; Draft of Minutes for Planning Conference, American Committee for Cultural Freedom, March 1, 1952; Dwight Macdonald, "Notes on Meeting of Committee for Cultural Freedom at the Columbia Club," April 23, 1952, all Box 3, Rovere MSS. Also see Lasch, *The Agony of the American Left,* ch. 3.

35. Humphrey to Dr. Frederick J. Kottke, March 8, 1954, Box 109, Humphrey MSS.

36. Maurice Rosenblatt to Gifford Phillips, Aug. 31, 1953, File 4, Drawer 1, NCEC MSS; George Agree to Rosenblatt, Nov. 16, 1953, *ibid.*

37. Other Clearing House participants included, on occasion, Michael Straight of the *New Republic,* John Howe, and Henry Kaiser. Agree to Oscar Hammerstein II, Dec. 11, 1959, File 7, Drawer 4, NCEC MSS; undated list, "Clearing House Group," File 10, Drawer 1, *ibid.;* "Confidential Memorandum #1, n.d. [ca. Aug. 1954], File 10, Drawer 1, *ibid.*

38. Rosenblatt to Phillips, Aug. 31, 1953.

39. Robert R. Nathan, memorandum, March 4, 1953, File 10, Drawer 1, NCEC MSS.

40. *New York Times,* June 19, July 9, 1953; *American Mercury,* 77 (July 1953): 3. On Matthews, see Kempton, *Part of Our Time,* ch. 5.

41. *New York Times,* July 3, 4, 8, 9, 1953; George Agree to Benton, July 23, 1953, Box 5, Benton MSS; [NCEC], *Congressional Report,* vol. 2, no. 4 (July 23, 1953); memorandum, John Howe to Benton, July 10, 1953, Box 4, Benton MSS; personal interview with Gerhard P. Van Arkel (Aug. 26, 1968); *Cong. Record,* 99 (July 9, 1953): 8278–79.

42. *New York Times,* July 10, 1953; Hughes, *Ordeal of Power,* pp. 94–96; telegram, Msgr. John A. O'Brien, Rabbi Maurice N. Eisendrath, and Dr. John Sutherland Bonnell to Eisenhower, July 9, 1953, OF 133-E-1, Eisenhower Papers; telegram, Eisenhower to same, July 9, 1953, *ibid.*

43. *Congressional Report,* vol. 2, no. 4 (July 22, 1953); cf. Griffith, *Politics of Fear,* pp. 229–34.

44. Some Democrats disapproved of the boycott, fearing it would inject partisanship into the situation. *New York Times,* July 11, 12, 1953; but cf. Washington *Post,* July 12, 1953.

45. Robert B. Downs to Eisenhower, June 15, 1953; Eisenhower to Downs, June 24, 1953; Len Arnold to Emmet John Hughes, July 9, 1953, all in PPF 47, Ei-

senhower Papers; Hughes, *Ordeal of Power*, p. 94; *New York Times*, June 27, July 11, 12, 1953.

46. Matthews's attacks on the clergy (this was not the first) had struck a tender chord in the Protestant South. *New York Times*, July 12, 31, 1953; Doris Fleeson and Thomas L. Stokes in Washington *Evening Star*, July 15, 17, 1953, clippings in File 4, Drawer 3, NCEC MSS; Washington *Post*, July 12, 1953; *Cong. Record*, 99 (July 10, 1953): 8472.

47. Washington *Post*, June 16, 1953.

48. *Ibid.*, July 25, 1953; *New York Times*, July 25, 1953.

49. *Congressional Report*, vol. 2, no. 4 (July 22, 1953); *Cong. Record*, 99 (July 13, 1953): 8619–21, (July 16, 1953): 8939–41, (July 20, 1953): 9185; memorandum, Thomas Wheeler to Benton and Howe, July 31, 1953, Box 4, Benton MSS. Bundy, like others winged during the McCarthy era, emerged a full-fledged hawk in the Vietnam age.

50. *New York Times*, July 11, 17, 20, 1953.

51. *Ibid.*, July 12, 16, 17, 20, 26, 1953.

52. Hunt to Charles E. Hanner, July 15, 1953, Hunt MSS; Humphrey to Dr. Charles M. Turck, July 17, 1953, Box 97, Humphrey MSS; Washington *Post*, Aug. 23, 1953.

53. PSI, *Security—Government Printing Office*.

54. PSI, *Communist Infiltration Among Army Civilian Workers*.

55. PSI, *Security—United Nations*, p. 1 and passim.

56. Secretary of the Army Robert T. Stevens, who witnessed the session, defended his officers limply on the grounds that, while their answers had not been "fully satisfactory to the committee," they had tried to cooperate. PSI, *Communist Infiltration in the Army*, pp. 86, 101, 105, and passim. For an earlier flare-up with an Army witness, see PSI, *Communist Infiltration Among Army Civilian Workers*, p. 16.

57. The witness "broke down," it developed, as a result chiefly of grief over the recent death of a parent. *New York Times*, Oct. 13–18, 1953. Also see the articles by Peter Kihss in *ibid.*, Jan. 11–14, Nov. 21, 1954.

58. *Ibid.*, Nov. 5, 1953. For the conflicting efforts to tone down the Monmouth probe and to secure special handling for Schine, see U.S. Senate, Committee on Government Operations, Special Subcommittee on Investigations, *Special Senate Investigation on Charges and Countercharges Involving: Secretary of the Army Robert T. Stevens, John G. Adams, H. Struve Hensel and Senator Joe McCarthy, Roy M. Cohn and Francis P. Carr*, 83d Cong., 2d Sess., 1954. Cited hereafter as *Army-McCarthy Hearings*.

59. *New York Times*, Nov. 7, 8, 1953. Democrats noted that the speech came after GOP defeats in New Jersey and Wisconsin elections, yet in time for a congressional contest in California.

60. *Ibid.*, Nov. 7–12, 17, 18, 25, 1953; President's News Conference of Nov. 18, 1953, *Eisenhower Papers, 1953*, p. 782.

61. *New York Times*, Nov. 26, 1953; memorandum, C. D. Jackson to General Persons, Oct. 1, 1953, OF 133-E, Eisenhower Papers; C. D. Jackson, "December 1, 1953—Draft—Press Conference Statement," Box 25, Bryce Harlow Papers, Eisenhower Library.

62. Memorandum, Stanley M. Rumbough, Jr., and Charles Masterson to Murray Snyder, Dec. 1, 1953, "Responding to Senator McCarthy," OF 99-R, Eisenhower Papers; Donovan, *Eisenhower*, p. 249; President's News Conference of Dec. 2, 1953, *Eisenhower Papers, 1953*, pp. 801-3; *New York Times*, Dec. 4, 1953.

63. Jackson to Sherman Adams, Nov. 25, 1953, quoted in Adams, *Firsthand Report*, p. 136; Parmet, *Eisenhower and the American Crusades*, pp. 337, 340.

64. *New York Times*, Dec. 20, 1953, Jan. 5–7, 1954; Leonard W. Hall to Eisenhower, Dec. 21, 1953, GF 171, Eisenhower Papers; Cohn, *McCarthy*, pp. 111–12; Mazo, *Richard Nixon*, pp. 132–33. Cohn reports a further mediation effort by the President's brother Milton, but the younger Eisenhower denied so doing. Parmet, *Eisenhower and the American Crusades*, p. 338.

65. *New York Times*, Nov. 30, 1953, Jan. 7, 1954; Washington *Post*, Jan. 2, 3, 1954.

66. *New York Times*, Jan. 1, 2, 5, 7, 1954; Washington *Post*, Jan. 3, 1954; cf. Paul Douglas and Hubert Humphrey press release, March 8, 1954, Douglas MSS.

67. Ellender's opposition to McCarthy was of some duration. In the midst of the Fort Monmouth hearings, he had assailed the "airing of old charges." *New York Times*, Nov. 8, 1953, Jan. 5, 8, 1954; Washington *Post*, Jan. 5, 1954.

68. *New York Times*, Dec. 9, 1953, Jan. 1, 1954; Hendrickson to Paul Douglas, Jan. 12, 1954, Douglas MSS; Homer Ferguson to John W. Bricker, March 10, 1954, Box 105, Bricker MSS; Flanders radio speech, week of March 7, 1954, Box 154, Flanders MSS.

69. *New York Times*, Jan. 5, 9, 23, 24, 26, 31, 1954.

70. *Ibid.*, Jan. 28, 31, 1954; Washington *Post*, Jan. 8, 12, 1954; "Statement by Senator Hayden," n.d. [Feb. 1954], Box 120, Hayden MSS; Hayden to James Harris, March 1, 1954, Box 128, *ibid.; Cong. Record*, 100 (Feb. 2, 1954): 1103; Hoey to Mrs. Doris Betts, Feb. 16, 1954, Box 35, Hoey MSS.

71. *New York Times*, Oct. 19, 1953, Jan. 19, 1954; "Preliminary Report on Robert E. Lee," Dec. 17, 1953, File 9, Drawer 1, NCEC MSS; Lucille Lang to Senator Monroney, Oct. 14, 1953, File 4, Drawer 2, *ibid.; Congressional Report*, vol. 3, no. 1 (Feb. 17, 1954); *Cong. Record*, 100 (Jan. 25, 1954): 683–98; cf. Griffith, *Politics of Fear*, pp. 235–37. On Lee and H. L. Hunt, see Lee to George Creel, June 25, 1953, Box 4, Creel MSS.

72. *New York Times*, Oct. 24, Nov. 7, Dec. 17, 1953; Fact Sheet, Research Division, Democratic National Committee, March 2, 1954, "The Republican 'Security

Risk' Hoax Background," Box 134, Hayden MSS; *Eisenhower Papers, 1954,* p. 12.

73. Washington *Post,* Jan. 1, Feb. 1 (Drummond, Alsops), Feb. 3 (Childs), 6, 16, 18, 19, 1954; series by Anthony Lewis, Washington *News,* Dec. 21–24, 28–29, 1953, Jan. 4, 6, 1954, reprinted in *Cong. Record,* 100 (Jan. 25, 1954): 710–16.

74. *New York Times,* Nov. 25, 26, 30, 1953, Jan. 10, 22, 24, Feb. 4, 1954.

75. *Cong. Record,* 100 (Jan. 25, 1954): 707–8, (Feb. 8, 1954): 1482–84, 1514; untitled, mimeographed background material, Democratic Senatorial Campaign Committee, Feb. 9, 1954, Box 134, Hayden MSS; Hayden to Wesley Bolin, Feb. 15, 1954, Box 14, *ibid.;* Washington *Post,* Feb. 10, 11, 15, 1954.

76. *New York Times,* Jan. 23, 27, 1954.

77. The army finally caught up to Peress after his promotion and ordered his separation by March 31; his discharge thus came about two months early. PSI, *Communist Infiltration in the Army* 83d Cong., 2d Sess., 1954, pp. 107–8, 123–57.

78. *New York Times,* Feb. 22, 25, 1954; Michael Straight, *Trial by Television,* pp. 60–61; Karl Mundt to Fred Christopherson, March 1, 1954, 66A191, Box 6, Mundt MSS; Mundt to Judge Alex Rentto, March 1, 1954, *ibid.*

79. Hunt to Robert T. Stevens, Feb. 25, 1954, Hunt MSS; Straight, *Trial by Television,* p. 61; Washington *Post,* Feb. 25, 1954; Statement by the Secretary of the Army, Feb. 25, 1954, OF 3-A, Eisenhower Papers; *New York Times,* Feb. 26, 1954; Mundt to Fred Christopherson, March 1, 1954, 66A191, Box 6, Mundt MSS.

80. Adams, *Firsthand Report,* pp. 143–45; *Army-McCarthy Hearings,* pp. 355, 1378–86, 1476–1512; *New York Times,* March 5, 12, 13, 1954. The "Chronology" is printed in *Army-McCarthy Hearings,* pp. 135–42.

81. Mundt to John O'Donnell, May 1, 1954, 66A191, Box 6, Mundt MSS; *Army-McCarthy Hearings,* pp. 1–26, 28.

82. *New York Times,* June 23, Aug. 7, 15, 21, Sept. 1, 1954; Mundt to Ray Jenkins, June 30, Aug. 5, 1954; telegram, Jenkins to Mundt, July 21, 1954; Mundt to J. Mark Trice, Aug. 23, 1954, all in 66A191, Box 6, Mundt MSS; U.S. Senate, Committee on Government Operations, Special Subcommittee on Investigations, *Charges and Countercharges Involving Secretary of the Army Robert T. Stevens, John G. Adams, H. Struve Hensel and Senator Joe McCarthy, Roy M. Cohn and Francis P. Carr,* 83d Cong., 2d Sess., 1954.

83. *New York Times,* June 19, 1954; *Army-McCarthy Hearings,* pp. 2426–30. In alluding to Fisher, McCarthy violated his pledge to Cohn, who had struck a bargain with Welch not to raise the subject. Welch's decision not to have Fisher assist him had previously been reported in the papers. Cohn, *McCarthy,* pp. 200–3; *New York Times,* April 16, 1954.

84. G. D. Wiebe, "The Army McCarthy Hearings and the Public Conscience," *Public Opinion Quarterly,* 21 (Winter 1958–59): 490–502; Sevareid, news analysis, May 11, 1954, Box 15, Sevareid MSS.

85. *New York Times,* March 7, 11, 14, 16, 1954; *Eisenhower Papers, 1954,* p. 300. For an overgenerous assessment of the impact of Stevenson's speech, see Brown, *Conscience in Politics,* ch. 2.

86. *New York Times,* March 11, 14, 1954; Mundt to Fred C. Hubbard, March 11, 1954, 66A191, Box 6, Mundt MSS.

87. *New York Times,* March 6, 11, 14, 1954. Fred W. Friendly, *Due to Circumstances Beyond Our Control . . . ,* ch. 2; Benton to Millard Tydings, April 5, 1954, Box 4, Benton MSS; memorandum, John Howe to Benton, June 10, 1954, *ibid.*

88. *New York Times,* Feb. 26, March 14, 1954; *Army-McCarthy Hearings,* pp. 2119–26, 2143–47 (Symington quoted on p. 2120); draft of letter (unused), Clifford to Mundt, n.d. [ca. June 1954], Army-McCarthy, 1954, Clifford Papers, Truman Library.

89. *New York Times,* March 13–15, 21–26, 31, 1954.

90. *Ibid.,* Feb. 24, March 11–14, 1954.

91. *Army-McCarthy Hearings,* pp. 2119–27, 2156, 2227–34, 2240, 2281, 2603.

92. *Ibid.,* pp. 58–60, 659–62, 682, 934–36, 977, 993, 1004, 1280, 2813, 2980.

93. *Ibid.,* pp. 727–28, 783–84, 2613–17; *New York Times,* June 12, 1954; cf. Cohn, *McCarthy,* pp. 70–72.

94. *Army-McCarthy Hearings,* pp. 258, 1722, 2062.

95. *Ibid.,* pp. 2241, 2281–84.

96. Gallup poll, Aug. 22, 1954, File 7, Drawer 3, NCEC MSS; Julie Kirlin to Leonard Hall, March 11, 1954, GF 171, Eisenhower Papers; copy, Frank Sulloway to Hall, March 10, 1954, *ibid.; New York Times,* March 3, 27, 1954.

97. Bender to Eisenhower, May 7, 1954, OF 138, Eisenhower Papers; telegram, F. Peavey Heffelfinger to Karl Mundt, May 6, 1954, 66A191, Box 6, Mundt MSS; Mundt to Alf M. Landon, May 1, 1954, *ibid.;* John Vorys to Robert Royce, May 3, 1954, Box 39, Vorys MSS, Ohio Historical Society.

98. Memorandum, John Howe to William Benton, May 8, 1954, Box 4, Benton MSS; Hugh Butler to Harry Simon, May 14, 1954, Box 358, Butler MSS; Butler to Ray McConnell, May 15, 1954, *ibid.;* Thomas E. Martin to Dr. Virgil M. Hancher, May 29, 1954, University of Iowa Presidential Papers, 1953–54; *New York Times,* April 27, May 21, June 20, 1954; Thelen and Thelen, "Joe Must Go," pp. 185–209.

99. Bennett's chief concern was to forbid commercial sponsorship of telecasts of Senate business. The Republican Policy Committee also proposed a code of committee conduct. Press release, Prescott Bush speech, Cheshire, Conn., May 15, 1954, Bush MSS, Connecticut State Library; H. Alexander Smith, "Memorandum re Possible speech on the McCarthy Issues," March 30, 1954, Box 139, Smith MSS;

Smith to Bennett, May 25, 1954, Box 157, *ibid.; New York Times,* May 19, June 29–July 2, July 7, 8, 12, 14, 15, 1954.

100. *New York Times,* June 19–20, July 1, 13, 16, 20, 1954.

101. La Venia had belonged briefly to the American Law Students Association; Mc-Carthy had found this organizational tie suspicious in others. *Ibid.,* June 19, July 16, 17, 21, 22, 24, 30, Aug. 11, 1954; Mundt to Brewster, Aug. 21, 1954, 66A191, Box 6, Mundt MSS; copies, Mundt, Margaret Chase Smith, and Dirksen to Mc-Carthy, all Aug. 4, 1954, 67A1541, Box 27, Mundt MSS. On these battles over staff and procedure, see Griffith, *Politics of Fear,* pp. 266–68.

102. *New York Times,* Aug. 15, 1954.

CHAPTER 10 ". . . CONTRARY TO SENATORIAL TRADITIONS"

1. Flanders, *Senator from Vermont; New York Times,* July 31, 1954; Parmet, *Eisenhower and the American Crusades,* pp. 42–44, 301–3, 314; AP biographical sketch, Box 101; Flanders to Paul Hoffman, Oct. 21, 1951, Box 105; Flanders to Eisenhower, Feb. 4, 1954, Box 115; Flanders to Sen. Edward Martin, Dec. 22, 1954, Box 109; Flanders to Dorothy Thompson, April 13, 1953, Box 111, all in Flanders MSS, Syracuse University (as are all Flanders MSS citations unless otherwise noted).

2. Flanders to Benton, Nov. 3, 1958, Box 102; Flanders to Paul Hoffman, Oct. 15, 21, 1951, Box 105; radio broadcasts, weeks of May 7, July 23, 1950, Box 151, all in Flanders MSS.

3. *Cong. Record,* 100 (March 9, 1954): 2886, (June 1, 1954): 7389–90, (June 11, 1954): 8032–33; *Army-McCarthy Hearings,* pp. 2559–60. Valuable on Flanders's crusade against McCarthy is Griffith, *Politics of Fear,* ch. 9.

4. *New York Times,* June 13–16, 22, 27, July 14–15, 1954; Ralph E. Flanders Oral History Memoir, Columbia Oral History Collection, pp. 10, 13, 34–35; *Cong. Record,* 100 (July 14, 1954): 10478; William Frye, memorandum, n.d. [July 23, 1954], File 10, Drawer 1, NCEC MSS.

5. *New York Times,* June 18, 1954; Maurice Rosenblatt to Joseph Shane, June 30, 1954, File 10, Drawer 1, NCEC MSS; Rosenblatt to Dean Clara Mayer, June 22, 1954, *ibid.;* Humphrey to Mr. and Mrs. Roy Delin, July 9, 1954, Box 109, Humphrey MSS.

6. *New York Times,* June 16, July 11, 18, Aug. 3, 1954; Rosenblatt to Dean Clara Mayer, June 22, 1954; *Congressional Report,* vol. 3, no. 2 (July 2, 1954).

7. *New York Times,* June 15–16, July 14, 1954; Rosenblatt to Mayer, June 22, 1954.

8. Rosenblatt to Frank Edwards, July 7, 1954; Rosenblatt to Mark Ethridge, July 9, 1954; Rosenblatt to Mayer, June 22, 1954; memorandum, George Agree to Rosenblatt and Larry Henderson, n.d. [early July 1954], all File 10, Drawer 1, NCEC MSS.

9. "Memorandum on Flanders Resolution," July 22, 1954, *ibid.; New York Times,* July 17–18, 1954; *Cong. Record,* 100 (July 20, 1954): 10993.

10. "Memorandum on Flanders Resolution," July 22, 1954; Rosenblatt to Marshall Field, July 22, 1954; Rosenblatt to Mayer, June 22, 1954, all File 10, Drawer 1, NCEC MSS; *New York Times,* July 18–20, 1954.

11. *New York Times,* Aug. 1, 3, 1954; list attached to unsigned memorandum to Don Montgomery and John Edelman, July 26, 1954, File 10, Drawer 1, NCEC MSS; William Frye, press release, July 27, 1954, *ibid.*

12. Rosenblatt to Marshall Field, July 22, 1954, and (attached) "Memorandum on Flanders Resolution"; "Proposed Budget" (June 25–Aug. 10, 1954), n.d.; "Confidential Memorandum #1," n.d. [ca. Sept. 1954]; Rosenblatt to Mayer, June 22, 1954, and attached "Chronology," all in File 10, Drawer 1, NCEC MSS.

13. "Memorandum on Flanders Resolution," July 22, 1954, *ibid.;* Donald Jenks to G. Jared Ingersoll, July 22, 1954, *ibid.; New York Times,* July 22, 1954; Humphrey to Dr. Charles J. Turck, July 21, 1954, Box 109, Humphrey MSS.

14. *New York Times,* July 30, 1954; memorandum to Don Montgomery and John Edelman, July 26, 1954, and attached list, File 10, Drawer 1, NCEC MSS.

15. *Cong. Record,* 100 (July 30, 1954): 12729–31, 12736–42, (July 31, 1954): 12893–97; *New York Times,* July 30, 1954; H. Alexander Smith, "Memorandum Re McCarthy Situation," July 11, 1954, Box 139, Smith MSS; Smith to McCarthy, July 17, 1954, *ibid.*

16. Wayne Morse's insistence upon "procedural safeguards" also swayed his colleagues. *Cong. Record,* 100 (July 30, 1954): 12732–36, (July 31, 1954): 12919–21, (Aug. 2, 1954): 12968–72; *New York Times,* July 31, Aug. 1, 1954; Clinton P. Anderson to Ivan L. Carbine, Aug. 4, 1954, Box 283, Anderson MSS; Robert E. Kerr to C. D. Maupin, Aug. 6, 1954, Kerr MSS.

17. *Cong. Record,* 100 (July 31, 1954): 12917, (Aug. 2, 1954): 12943–44, 12966, 12971–81, 12984–89; *New York Times,* Aug. 1–3, 8, 11, 1954; Washington *Post,* Aug. 6, 1954; Rosenblatt to Flanders, n.d. [July 1954], File 10, Drawer 1, NCEC MSS; William Frye, memorandum, n.d. [July 23, 1954], *ibid.;* Lehman to Harry Stanfield, Aug. 3, 1954, Washington Files, Miscellaneous #2, McCarthy and McCarthyism, Lehman MSS.

18. Senators Millikin and George, the early favorites, begged off on grounds of poor health. *New York Times,* Aug. 4–6, 1954; White, *Citadel,* pp. 129–31; personal interview with Edwin C. Johnson (Aug. 7, 1967).

19. *New York Times,* Aug. 7–8, 1954; Humphrey (form letter) to Joseph G. Stiepan, Aug. 18, 1954, Box 109, Humphrey MSS; Flanders radio speech, week of Aug. 15, 1954, Box 154, Flanders MSS.

20. "We are not unmindful," Watkins told Flanders, "of *his* genius for disruption." *New York Times,* Aug. 7–8, 10, 16, 1954; Maurice Rosenblatt to Paul Hoffman, Aug. 26, 1954, File 4, Drawer 1, NCEC MSS; [Francis Case,] minutes, meet-

ing of the Committee on Censure Resolution #301, Aug. 6, 1954, Drawer 60, Case MSS, Dakota Wesleyan University.

21. *New York Times*, Aug. 25, 1954; minutes, meetings of the Committee on Censure Resolution #301, Aug. 9, 14, 17, Sept. 6, 1954, Drawer 60, Case MSS.

22. Senator Ervin, it developed, had also confessed having "formed an unfavorable opinion" of McCarthy. U.S. Senate, *Hearings before a Select Committee to Study Censure Charges*, 83d Cong., 2d Sess., 1954, pp. 18–19, 35–38; *New York Times*, Aug. 31, Sept. 1, 8, 1954.

23. *New York Times*, Sept. 1–2, 20, 1954.

24. U.S. Senate, *Report of the Select Committee to Study Censure Charges*, 83d Cong., 2d Sess., 1954; *New York Times*, Aug. 6, 1954; White, *Citadel*, pp. 126, 133.

25. Flanders to Watkins, Sept. 11, 1954, File 4, Drawer 1, NCEC MSS; Watkins to David O. Ensign, Dec. 3, 1954, Box 23, Watkins MSS, Brigham Young University; memorandum, Rosenblatt to Paul Hoffman, Oct. 8, 1954, File 10, Drawer 1, NCEC MSS; copy, Julius C. C. Edelstein to Arthur Schlesinger, Jr., Nov. 11, 1954, Box 5, Benton MSS; Griffith, *Politics of Fear*, pp. 301–3. The ADA also took care to "keep in the background." Edward Hollander to Schlesinger, Aug. 11, 1954, Series 5, Box 30, ADA MSS.

26. *Cong. Record*, 100 (Aug. 11, 1954): 14099, 14103, 14129–34, 14145, 14148–50, 14159, (Aug. 12, 1954): 14200. A useful analysis of the passage of the Communist Control Act is Griffith, "The Political Context of McCarthyism," pp. 32–34.

27. *Cong. Record*, 100 (Aug. 12, 1954): 14208–11, 14219–22, 14229–34.

28. *Ibid.*, 100 (Aug. 16, 1954): 14639–58; *New York Times*, Aug. 17, 1954.

29. *Cong. Record*, 100 (Aug. 17, 1954): 14711–15, 14718, 14722–23, 14726, 14729, 14849–51, (Aug. 19, 1954): 15102, 15105, 15121, 15236–37.

30. *Ibid.*, 100 (Aug. 16, 1954): 14646–48, 14651, (Aug. 17, 1954): 14724; *New York Times*, Aug. 18, 1954; Humphrey to Mrs. L. H. Lackore, Sept. 18, 1954; to David B. Leonard, Sept. 20, 1954; to Thomas McEnroe, Sept. 11, 1954; to Marvin Rosenberg, Aug. 27, 1954; to Joseph Goldberger, Sept. 25, 1954, all in Box 104, Humphrey MSS.

31. *Wall Street Journal*, Aug. 19, 1954; Max M. Kampelman to Carl A. Auerbach, Dec. 29, 1954, Box 117, Humphrey MSS; *New York Times*, Aug. 14, 1954.

32. Democratic National Committee, Fact Sheet, "The Democratic Record Against Communism in America," Dec. 9, 1953, Charles Murphy Papers, Smear Tactics—Political Libel; copy, Mitchell to Lyndon B. Johnson, Jan. 7, 1954, Box 104, Anderson MSS; *New York Times*, June 28, Aug. 22, 1954.

33. *New York Times*, June 20, Sept. 17, 19, 24, 29, Oct. 31, 1954; telegram, McCarthy to Joseph T. Meek, Nov. 1, 1954 (with text of telegram to Douglas), 1954

Senatorial Campaign Data, Box 1, Meek MSS, Chicago Historical Society. Meek later regretted that McCarthy had not campaigned in Chicago. Meek to Robert Humphreys, Dec. 3, 1954, *ibid*.

34. *New York Times*, Sept. 24, Oct. 10, 12, 17, 23, 1954; Democratic National Committee, "Special Memorandum—The Facts About the Nixon Campaign Role," Nov. 12, 1954, Murphy Papers, Smear Tactics—Political Libel.

35. *New York Times*, Oct. 14, 24–25, 1954.

36. *Ibid.*, Sept. 19, Oct. 11, 17, 19, 24, 27, 30, 1954; speech, state convention, June 12, 1954, 1954 Senatorial Campaign Data, Box 1, Meek MSS; speech, Illinois Federation of Women's Republican Clubs, Sept. 8, 1954, *ibid*.

37. CIO Legislative Department, "1954 Opinion Survey," n.d., Paul Douglass MSS; Campbell and Cooper, *Group Differences in Attitudes and Votes*, pp. 66–67, 78, 83, 121; *New York Times*, Oct. 10, 1954 (White); see also Stouffer, *Communism, Conformity, and Civil Liberties*, pp. 59, 68, 71. Campbell and Cooper do not specify *how* their respondents believed the Republicans "mishandled McCarthy."

38. *New York Times*, Sept. 24–26, 1954; Fulbright to William Benton, Sept. 18, 1954, Fulbright MSS; *Congressional Report*, vol. 3, no. 3 (Nov. 19, 1954).

39. *Cong. Record*, 100 (Nov. 8, 1954): 15851, (Nov. 9, 1954): 15911, (Nov. 10, 1954): 15952–54, (Nov. 12, 1954): 15988–89, (Nov. 15, 1954): 16020–21, (Nov. 16, 1954): 16059, 16071; Watkins to President David O. McKay, Dec. 31, 1954, Box 23, Watkins MSS.

40. *Cong. Record*, 100 (Nov. 8, 1954): 15850; *New York Times*, Nov. 9, 1954; Hubert Humphrey to Henry Mayers, Dec. 6, 1954, Box 109, Humphrey MSS; Julius Edelstein to John Howe, Nov. 17, 1954, Washington Files, Misc. #2, McCarthy and McCarthyism, Lehman MSS; copy, Edelstein to Arthur Schlesinger, Jr., Nov. 11, 1954, Box 5, Benton MSS; cf. *New York Times*, Nov. 11, 1954.

41. References for speeches from *Cong. Record* 100: Lehman (Nov. 10, 1954): 15957–58, (Nov. 30, 1954): 16220–22; Fulbright (Nov. 30, 1954): 16195–201; Ervin (Nov. 15, 1954): 16018–22; Ed Johnson (Nov. 29, 1954): 16156–58; Lennon (Nov. 18, 1954): 16137–38; Daniel (Dec. 1, 1954): 16328–39; Long (Dec. 1, 1954): 16290–91; Lyndon Johnson (Dec. 1, 1954): 16292–93.

42. Memorandum, John Howe to William Benton, Nov. 24, 1954, Box 5, Benton MSS; Maurice Rosenblatt to Marshall Field, Nov. 19, 1954, File 10, Drawer 1, NCEC MSS; *New York Times*, Nov. 14, 18, 1954; H. Alexander Smith Diary, Nov. 16, 18, 1954, Smith MSS; note, "RN" [Nixon] to Smith, Nov. 18, 1954, and attached "Proposed Speech" (for McCarthy) by O. K. Armstrong, Box 139, Smith MSS; Edward Bennett Williams, *One Man's Freedom*, pp. 67–68; Jack Bell, *Mr. Conservative*, pp. 99–101; Mundt to Ernest Vessey, Dec. 4, 1954, 66A191, Box 6, Mundt MSS; *Cong. Record*, 100 (Dec. 1, 1954): 16330, 16335–36.

43. A motion to table the Zwicker count lost, 55 to 33. "Statement by Senator Francis Case," Nov. 23, 1954, Drawer 60, Case MSS; Case, "Memorandum on

Dates and Data on Zwicker-Peress matter IN TWO LIGHTS," Nov. 16, 1954, *ibid.;* Mundt to A. W. Odell, Nov. 16, 1954, 66A191, Box 33, Mundt MSS; Humphrey to Stewart M. Hockin, Dec. 6, 1954, Box 109, Humphrey MSS; Max M. Kampelman to Roger E. Joseph, Dec. 22, 1954, Box 108, *ibid.; New York Times,* Nov. 12, 14, 1954; *Cong. Record,* 100 (Dec. 2, 1954): 16370.

44. *Cong. Record,* 100 (Dec. 2, 1954): 16392. The Independent Morse accounted for the 67th vote. The recently deceased Pat McCarran would have opposed censure.

45. Watkins to M. E. Dalton, Dec. 9, 1954, Box 23, Watkins MSS; *New York Times,* Dec. 3, 5, 1954; *Cong. Record,* 100 (Dec. 2, 1954): 16392–95. Watkins noted that "condemned" was "the historical word used in censure resolutions."

46. Norman Thomas column for Dec. 9, 1954, Box 78, Thomas MSS; Lehman to Dr. Lewis Perry, Dec. 10, 1954, Washington Files, Misc., McCarthy and McCarthyism, Lehman MSS; Daniel to Humphrey, Jan. 4, 1955, Box 121, Humphrey MSS; *Cong. Record,* 101 (Jan. 10, 1955): 167–68, (Jan. 14, 1955): 361.

47. U.S. Senate, Committee on Government Operations, Subcommittee on Reorganization, *Commission on Government Security,* 84th Cong., 1st Sess., 1955; *Cong. Record,* 101 (June 27, 1955): 9240; *New York Times,* Nov. 11, 1955.

48. U.S. Senate, Committee on Post Office and Civil Service, Subcommittee to Investigate the Government Employee Security Program, *Administration of the Federal Employees' Security Program,* 84th Cong., 1st Sess., 1956; U.S. Senate, Judiciary Committee, Subcommittee on Constitutional Rights, *Security and Constitutional Rights,* 84th Cong., 1st Sess., 1956; Ralph S. Brown, Jr., *Loyalty and Security,* pp. 58–59; Kemper, *Decade of Fear,* chs. 5–6.

49. *New York Times,* Nov. 6, 25, 28, Dec. 19, 21–29, 1954, Jan. 1, 8, 10, 15–16, March 18, June 3, Sept. 20, 1955; U.S. Senate, Judiciary Committee, Internal Security Subcommittee, *Strategy and Tactics of World Communism: The Significance of the Matusow Case,* 84th Cong., 1st Sess., 1955; Matusow, *False Witness* (New York, 1955).

50. *Cong. Record,* 100 (Nov. 15, 1954): 16030–31, (Nov. 18, 1954): 16130–31; *ibid.,* 101 (June 22, 1955): 8960; Washington *Post,* June 26, 1955.

51. McCarthy speech, Sertoma International, Chicago, Dec. 5, 1955, File 7, Drawer 4, NCEC MSS; McCarthy speech, Tulsa, Dec. 7, 1955, *ibid.;* McCarthy to Estes Kefauver, Dec. 2, 1955, National Security II, Kefauver MSS; McCarthy press release, Nov. 25, 1955, Box 160, Hennings MSS.

52. *New York Times,* Dec. 3, 5, 8–9, 1954; McCarthy to Eisenhower, March 10, May 18, 1955; Wilton B. Persons to McCarthy, March 24, 1955; memo by "G," May 21, 1955, all OF 154-H, Eisenhower Papers; McCarthy to Eisenhower, Sept. 21, 1955, OF 104-J, *ibid.;* Rovere, *Senator Joe McCarthy,* pp. 238–40.

53. Humphrey to Mrs. Herman Brandt, Aug. 14, 1954, Box 109, Humphrey MSS; *New York Times,* March 6–7, 1955; Ralph S. Brown, Jr., "Regression in the Wright Report," pp. 253–56; Murphy, *The Constitution in Crisis Times,* pp. 320–37.

54. Edward Hollander to Robert L. Harper, Sept. 1, 1954, Series 2, Box 52, ADA MSS; Hennings to Marvin Bank, April 25, 1955, Box 73, Hennings MSS; Scott to Mrs. Jane Winston, Aug. 8, 1955, Box 113, Scott MSS, North Carolina State Department of Archives and History, Raleigh.

EPILOGUE

1. Mundt to James A. McFarland, Dec. 14, 1954, 66A191, Box 33, Mundt MSS. For criticism of the Eisenhower Administration, see Dorsen and Simon, "McCarthy and the Army," pp. 21–28; Schlesinger, *The Imperial Presidency*, pp. 156–58; Interview with Clark Mollenhoff, Karl E. Mundt Oral History Project, Dakota State College.

2. Rovere, *Senator Joe McCarthy*, pp. 232–54; Cohn, *McCarthy*, ch. 19; Washington *Daily News*, Aug. 29, 1956, clipping in Philleo Nash Papers, Truman Library; Ralph E. Flanders Memoir, Columbia Oral History Project, pp. 15–16; personal interview with Arthur V. Watkins (June 23, 1967); Drew Pearson press release, Washington Merry-Go-Round, May 7, 1957, Box 4, Benton MSS.

Bibliography

I   MANUSCRIPTS

AFL-CIO MSS, State Historical Society of Wisconsin.
American Civil Liberties Union MSS, Princeton University.
Americans for Democratic Action MSS, State Historical Society of Wisconsin.
Clinton P. Anderson MSS, Library of Congress.
Alben Barkley MSS, University of Kentucky.
William E. Benton MSS, State Historical Society of Wisconsin.
John W. Bricker MSS, Ohio Historical Society.
Prescott Bush MSS, Connecticut State Library.
Hugh Butler MSS, Nebraska Historical Society.
Paul M. Butler MSS, University of Notre Dame.
Francis Case MSS, Dakota Wesleyan University.
Clark Clifford Papers, Harry S. Trumen Library.
Tom Connally MSS, Library of Congress.
George Creel MSS, Library of Congress.
Jonathan Daniels MSS, University of North Carolina.
Elmer Davis MSS, Library of Congress.
Democratic National Committee Clipping File, Truman Library.
Michael V. DiSalle MSS, Ohio Historical Society.
Helen Gahagan Douglas MSS, University of Oklahoma.
Paul Douglas MSS, Chicago Historical Society.
John Foster Dulles MSS, Princeton University.
Papers of Dwight D. Eisenhower, Eisenhower Library.
    David W. Kendall Files.

George Elsey Papers, Truman Library.
Ralph E. Flanders MSS, State Historical Society of Wisconsin.
Ralph E. Flanders MSS, Syracuse University.
J. William Fulbright MSS, Washington, D.C. (now at University of Arkansas).
Fund for the Republic MSS, Princeton University.
Frank P. Graham MSS, University of North Carolina.
Theodore Francis Green MSS, Library of Congress.
Bryce Harlow Papers, Eisenhower Library.
Carl Hayden MSS, Arizona State University.
Robert C. Hendrickson MSS, Syracuse University.
Thomas C. Hennings MSS, University of Missouri.
Bourke B. Hickenlooper MSS, Washington, D.C. (now at Herbert C. Hoover Library).
Clyde Hoey MSS, Duke University.
Hubert H. Humphrey MSS, Minnesota Historical Society.
Lester C. Hunt MSS, University of Wyoming.
Patrick J. Hurley MSS, University of Oklahoma.
Irving M. Ives MSS, Cornell University.
Jefferson D. Johnson, Jr., MSS, Duke University.
Estes Kefauver MSS, University of Tennessee.
James E. Kem MSS, University of Missouri.
Robert S. Kerr MSS, University of Oklahoma.
Harley M. Kilgore MSS, Franklin D. Roosevelt Library.
Harley M. Kilgore MSS, University of West Virginia.
William L. Langer MSS, University of North Dakota.
Herbert H. Lehman MSS, Columbia University.
Scott W. Lucas MSS, Illinois State Historical Library.
Douglas MacArthur MSS, MacArthur Memorial Library, Norfolk, Va.
Pat McCarran MSS, Division of Archives, Office of the Secretary of State of Nevada.
John F. X. McGohey Papers, Truman Library.
J. Howard McGrath Papers, Truman Library.
Joseph T. Meek MSS, Chicago Historical Society.
Eugene Millikin MSS, University of Colorado Law School.
Stephen A. Mitchell Papers, Truman Library.
Blair Moody MSS, Michigan Historical Collections, Ann Arbor.
Karl E. Mundt MSS, Dakota State College.
Charles S. Murphy Papers, Truman Library.
National Committee for an Effective Congress (NCEC) MSS, Washington, D.C.

Joseph C. O'Mahoney MSS, University of Wyoming.
Claude Pepper MSS, Federal Records Storage Center, Alexandria, Va.
Political Campaign Literature, North Carolina State Department of Archives and History.
Records of the President's Commission on Internal Security and Individual Rights (Nimitz Commission), Truman Library.
Presidential Papers, University of Iowa.
Richard H. Rovere MSS, State Historical Society of Wisconsin.
W. Kerr Scott MSS, North Carolina State Department of Archives and History.
Eric Sevareid MSS, Library of Congress.
H. Alexander Smith MSS, Princeton University.
Stephen J. Spingarn Papers, Truman Library.
Elbert D. Thomas MSS, University of Oklahoma.
Elmer Thomas MSS, University of Oklahoma.
Norman Thomas MSS, New York Public Library.
Edward Thye MSS, Minnesota Historical Society.
Papers of Harry S. Truman, Truman Library.
    Martin L. Friedman Files.
    David D. Lloyd Files.
    Charles S. Murphy Files.
    Philleo Nash Files.
Millard E. Tydings MSS, University of Maryland.
Arthur H. Vandenberg MSS, William Clements Library, University of Michigan.
A. Devitt Vanech Papers, Truman Library.
John Vorys MSS, Ohio Historical Society.
Arthur V. Watkins MSS, Brigham Young University.
William W. Waymack MSS, State Historical Society of Iowa.
Kenneth Wherry MSS, University of Nebraska.
Alexander Wiley MSS, State Historical Society of Wisconsin.

II   GOVERNMENT DOCUMENTS

U.S. Congress. *Congressional Record*, vols. 92–102, 1946–1956.
U.S. House of Representatives: Committee on the Judiciary. *Report of Sub-committee IV of the Committee on Judiciary pursuant to H. Res. 430*, 79th Cong., 2d Sess., 1946.
—— *Report No. 1595*, 80th Cong., 2d Sess., 1948.
—— *Report No. 1753, Directing the Secretary of Commerce to Transmit to the House of Representatives a Certain Letter with Respect to Dr. Edward U. Condon*, 80th Cong., 2d Sess., 1948.

—— *State, Justice, Commerce, and the Judiciary Appropriation Bill, Fiscal Year 1949. Report* [To accompany H.R. 5607], 80th Cong., 2d Sess., 1948.

U.S. Senate. Committee on Armed Services. *Malmedy Massacre Investigation. Report . . . ,* 81st Cong., 1st Sess., 1949.

—— Committee on Armed Services. *Nomination of Anna M. Rosenberg To Be Assistant Secretary of Defense. Hearings . . . ,* 81st Cong., 2d Sess., 1950.

—— Committee on Banking and Currency. *Study of Reconstruction Finance Corporation. Lustron Corp.—Transportation Contract. Hearings . . . ,* 81st Cong., 2d Sess., 1950.

—— Subcommittee of the Committee on Foreign Relations. *Nomination of Philip C. Jessup to be United States Representative to the Sixth General Assembly of the United Nations. Hearings . . . ,* 82d Cong., 1st Sess., 1951.

—— Subcommittee of the Committee on Foreign Relations. *State Department Employee Loyalty Investigation. Hearings . . .* pursuant to S. Res. 231, 81st Cong., 2d Sess., 1950.

—— Committee on Foreign Relations. *State Department Employee Loyalty Investigation. Report . . .* pursuant to S. Res. 231, 81st Cong., 2d Sess., 1950.

—— Committee on Government Operations. Permanent Subcommittee on Investigations. *Communist Infiltration Among Army Civilian Workers. Hearings . . . ,* 83d Cong., 1st Sess, 1953.

—— Committee on Government Operations. Permanent Subcommittee on Investigations. *Communist Infiltration in the Army. Hearings . . . ,* 83d Cong., 1st and 2d Sess., 1953–1954.

—— Committee on Government Operations. Permanent Subcommittee on Investigations. *Control of Trade with the Soviet Bloc. Hearings . . . ,* 83d Cong., 1st Sess., 1953.

—— Committee on Government Operations. Permanent Subcommittee on Investigations. *Security—Government Printing Office. Hearings . . . ,* 83d Cong., 1st Sess., 1953.

—— Committee on Government Operations. Permanent Subcommittee on Investigations. *Security—United Nations. Hearings . . . ,* 83d Cong., 1st Sess., 1953.

—— Committee on Government Operations. Permanent Subcommittee on Investigations. *State Department Files Survey. Hearings . . . ,* 83d Cong., 1st Sess., 1953.

—— Committee on Government Operations. Permanent Subcommittee on Investigations. *State Department Information Centers. Hearings . . . ,* 83d Cong., 1st Sess., 1953.

—— Committee on Government Operations. Permanent Subcommittee on Investigations. *State Department Information Program*—Voice of America. Hearings . . . , 83d Cong., 1st Sess., 1953.

—— Committee on Government Operations. Permanent Subcommittee on Investigations. *Subversion and Espionage in Defense Establishments and Industry. Hearings* . . . , 83d Cong., 1st and 2d Sess., 1954.

—— Committee on Government Operations. Special Subcommittee on Investigations. *Charges and Countercharges Involving Secretary of the Army Robert T. Stevens, John G. Adams, H. Struve Hensel and Senator Joe McCarthy, Roy M. Cohn and Francis P. Carr. Hearings* . . . , 83d Cong., 2d Sess., 1954.

—— Committee on Government Operations. Special Subcommittee on Investigations. *Special Senate Investigation on Charges and Countercharges Involving: Secretary of the Army Robert T. Stevens, John G. Adams, H. Struve Hensel, and Senator Joe McCarthy, Roy M. Cohn, and Francis P. Carr. Senate Report 2507*, 83d Cong., 2d Sess., 1954.

—— Committee on Government Operations. Subcommittee on Reorganization. *Commission on Government Security*. 84th Cong., 1st Sess., 1956.

—— Committee on the Judiciary. Subcommittee on Constitutional Rights. *Security and Constitutional Rights. Hearings* . . . , 84th Cong., 1st Sess., 1956.

—— Committee on the Judiciary. Subcommittee on Internal Security. *The Amerasia Papers: A Clue to the Catastrophe of China*, 2 vol., 91st Cong., 1st Sess., 1970.

—— Committee on the Judiciary. Subcommittee on Internal Security. *Strategy and Tactics of World Communism: The Significance of the Matusow Case*. 84th Cong., 1st Sess., 1955.

—— Committee on Post Office and Civil Service. Subcommittee to Investigate the Government Employee Security Program. *Administration of the Federal Employees' Security Program*. 84th Cong., 1st Sess., 1956.

—— Committee on Rules and Administration. Subcommittee on Privileges and Elections. *Investigation of Joseph R. McCarthy. Hearings* . . . on S. Res. 187, A Resolution to Investigate Senator Joseph R. McCarthy to Determine Whether Expulsion Proceedings should be Instituted, 82d Cong., 2d Sess., 1952.

—— Committee on Rules and Administration. Subcommittee on Privileges and Elections. *Investigation of Senators Joseph R. McCarthy and William Benton. Report*, 82d Cong., 2d Sess., 1952.

—— Committee on Rules and Administration. Subcommittee on Privileges and Elections. *Maryland Senatorial Election of 1950. Hearings* . . . pursuant to S. Res. 250, 82d Cong., 1st Sess., 1951.

—— Committee on Rules and Administration. *Maryland Senatorial Elec-*

tion of 1950. Report . . . pursuant to S. Res. 250, 82d Cong., 1st Sess., 1951.

—— *Report of the Select Committee to Study Censure Charges,* 83d Cong., 2d Sess., 1954.

—— Select Committee to Study Censure Charges. *Hearings on S. Res. 301,* 83d Cong., 2d Sess., 1954.

U.S. Department of State. *Department of State Bulletin,* vol. XXII, 1950.

—— *United States Relations with China With Special Reference to the Period 1944–1949.* Washington, D.C.: Government Printing Office, 1949.

III   BOOKS, ARTICLES AND DISSERTATIONS

Abell, Tyler, ed. *Drew Pearson Diaries, 1949–1959.* New York: Holt, Rinehart and Winston, 1974.

Abels, Jules. *Out of the Jaws of Victory.* New York: Holt, 1959.

Acheson, Dean. *Present at the Creation: My Years in the State Department.* New York: Norton, 1969.

Adams, Sherman. *Firsthand Report: The Story of the Eisenhower Administration.* New York: Harper, 1961.

Adler, Selig. *The Isolationist Impulse: Its Twentieth-Century Reaction.* New York: Abelard-Schuman, 1957.

Anderson, Jack and Ronald W. May. *McCarthy: The Man, the Senator, the "Ism."* Boston: Beacon Press, 1952.

Auerbach, Jerold S. *Labor and Liberty: The La Follette Committee and the New Deal.* Indianapolis: Bobbs-Merrill, 1966.

Barth, Alan. *The Loyalty of Free Men.* New York: Viking, 1951.

Beal, John Robinson. *John Foster Dulles: 1888–1959.* New York: Harper, 1959.

Bean, Louis H. *Influences in the 1954 Mid-Term Elections.* Washington, D.C.: Public Affairs Institute, 1954.

Bell, Coral. *Negotiation from Strength: A Study in the Politics of Power.* New York: Knopf, 1963.

Bell, Daniel, ed. *The Radical Right.* Garden City, N.Y.: Doubleday, 1963.

Bell, Jack. *Mr. Conservative: Barry Goldwater.* Garden City, N.Y.: Doubleday, 1962.

Bendiner, Robert. "Anything Goes in Pennsylvania," *Nation,* 171 (Oct. 28, 1950), 385–88.

Berelson, Bernard R., Paul F. Lazarsfeld, and William N. McPhee. *Voting: A Study of Opinion Formation in a Presidential Campaign.* Chicago: University of Chicago, 1954.

Berman, William C. "Civil Rights and Civil Liberties," in Richard S.

Kirkendall, ed., *The Truman Period as a Research Field*. Columbia, University of Missouri Press, 1967.

Bernstein, Barton J. "America in War and Peace: The Test of Liberalism," in Bernstein, ed., *Towards a New Past: Dissenting Essays in American History*. New York: Random House, 1968.

Bohlen, Charles E. *Witness to History, 1929–1969*. New York: Norton, 1973.

Bone, Hugh D. "The 1950 Elections in Washington," *Western Political Quarterly*, 4 (March, 1951), 94.

Bontecou, Eleanor. *The Federal Loyalty-Security Program*. Ithaca, N.Y.: Cornell University Press, 1953.

Boorstin, Daniel J. *The Image; or, What Happened to the American Dream*. New York: Atheneum, 1962.

Bowles, Chester. *Promises to Keep: My Years in Public Life, 1941–1969*. New York: Harper & Row, 1971.

"Bowman, Alfred" [Miles McMillin]. "The Man Behind McCarthy— Coleman of Wisconsin," *Nation*, 178 (March 24, 1954), 236–37.

Branyan, Robert L. and R. Alton Lee. "Lyndon B. Johnson and the Art of the Possible," *Southwestern Social Science Quarterly*, 45 (December 1964), 213–25.

Brazil, Burton R. "The 1950 Elections in California," *Western Political Quarterly*, 4 (March 1951), 67.

Brock, Clifton. *Americans for Democratic Action: Its Role in National Politics*. Washington, D.C.: Public Affairs Press, 1962.

Brown, Ralph S., Jr. *Loyalty and Security: Employment Tests in the United States*. New Haven: Yale University, 1958.

—— "Regression in the Wright Report," *Bulletin of the Atomic Scientists*, 13 (September 1957), 253–56.

Brown, Stuart Gerry. *Conscience in Politics: Adlai E. Stevenson in the 1950's*. Syracuse: Syracuse University Press, 1961.

Buckley, William F., Jr. and L. Brent Bozell. *McCarthy and His Enemies: The Record and Its Meaning*. Chicago: Regnery, 1954.

Burns, James MacGregor. *The Deadlock of Democracy: Four-Party Politics in America*. Englewood Cliffs, N.J.: Prentice-Hall, 1963.

Calkins, Fay. *The CIO and the Democratic Party*. Chicago: University of Chicago Press, 1952.

Campbell, Angus, Philip E. Converse, Warren E. Miller, and Donald E. Stokes. *The American Voter*. New York: Wiley, 1960.

Campbell, Angus and Homer Cooper. *Group Differences in Attitudes and Votes*. Ann Arbor: Institute for Social Research, University of Michigan, 1956.

Campbell, Angus, Gerald Gurin, and Warren E. Miller. *The Voter Decides*. Evanston, Ill.: Row Peterson, 1954.

Cantril, Hadley, ed. *Public Opinion, 1935–1946*. Princeton, Princeton University Press, 1951.

Caridi, Ronald J. *The Korean War and American Politics: The Republican Party as a case study*. Philadelphia: University of Pennsylvania Press, 1968.

Carr, Robert K. *The House Committee on Un-American Activities, 1945–1950*. Ithaca, N.Y.: Cornell University Press, 1952.

Cater, Douglass. "The Captive Press," *Reporter*, 2 (June 6, 1950), 17–20.

—— *The Fourth Branch of Government*. Boston: Houghton Mifflin, 1959.

—— "Is McCarthy Slipping?" *Reporter*, 5 (Sept. 18, 1951), 25–26.

—— "A Senate Afternoon: The Red Hunt," *Reporter*, 3 (Oct. 10, 1950), 27–30.

—— "Senator Cain: Washington Hamlet," *Reporter*, 6 (Sept. 7, 1952), 15.

Chase, Harold W. "Controlling Subversive Activities: An Analysis of the Efforts of the National Government to Control the Indigenous Communists, 1933–1954," Ph.D. dissertation, Princeton University, 1954.

Clubb, O. Edmund. *The Witness and I*. New York: Columbia University Press, 1974.

Cohn, Roy. *McCarthy*. New York: New American Library, 1968.

Cook, Fred J. *The Nightmare Decade: The Life and Times of Senator Joe McCarthy*. New York: Random House, 1971.

Cooke, Alistair. *A Generation on Trial*. New York: Knopf, 1951.

Costello, William. *The Facts About Nixon: An Authorized Biography*. New York: Viking, 1960.

Cotter, Cornelius P. and Malcolm Smith. "An American Paradox: The Emergency Detention Act of 1950," *Journal of Politics*, 19 (February 1957), 20–33.

Crabb, Cecil V., Jr. *Bipartisan Foreign Policy: Myth or Reality?* Evanston, Ill.: Row Peterson, 1957.

Cutler, Robert M. *No Time for Rest*. Boston: Little, Brown, 1966.

David, Paul T., Malcolm Moos, and Ralph M. Goldman, eds. *Presidential Nominating Politics in 1952*. Vol. IV: *The Middle West*. Baltimore, Johns Hopkins University Press, 1954.

Davies, Richard O. *Housing Reform During the Truman Administration*. Columbia: University of Missouri Press, 1966.

—— "Social Welfare Policies," in Richard S. Kirkendall, ed., *The Truman Period as a Research Field*. Columbia, University of Missouri Press, 1967.

Davis, Elmer. *But We Were Born Free*. Indianapolis: Bobbs-Merrill, 1954.

De Grazia, Alfred. *The Western Public: 1952 and Beyond*. Stanford: Stanford University Press, 1954.

"Democrats Fume at McCarthy, But He has Them Terrorized," *Newsweek*, 38 (Aug. 20, 1951), 19.

Dies, Martin. *The Trojan Horse in America*. New York: Dodd, Mead, 1941.

Doherty, Herbert L. "Liberal and Conservative Voting Patterns in Florida," *Journal of Politics*, 14 (August 1952), 403–17.

Donovan, Robert J. *Eisenhower: The Inside Story*. New York: Harper, 1956.

Dorsen, Norman and John G. Simon. "McCarthy and the Army: A Fight on the Wrong Front," *Columbia University Forum*, 7 (Fall 1964), 21–28.

Eisenhower, Dwight D. *The White House Years: Mandate for Change, 1953–1956*. Garden City, N.Y.: Doubleday, 1963.

Ekirch, Arthur A., Jr. *The Decline of American Liberalism*. New York: Atheneum, 1966.

"The Elections," *Nation*, 171 (Nov. 18, 1950), 451–52.

Epstein, Benjamin R. and Arnold Forster. *The Trouble-Makers*. Garden City, N.Y.: Doubleday, 1952.

Epstein, Leon D. *Politics in Wisconsin*. Madison: University of Wisconsin Press, 1958.

Evans, Rowland and Robert D. Novak. *Lyndon B. Johnson: The Exercise of Power*. New York: New American Library, 1968.

Evjue, William T. *A Fighting Editor*. Madison: Wells Printing Company, 1968.

—— "Young Bob," *Nation*, 176 (March 7, 1953), 200.

Felknor, Bruce. *Dirty Politics*. New York: Norton, 1966.

Fenton, John. *Politics in the Border States*. New Orleans: Hauser Press, 1957.

Fenton, John M. *In Your Opinion. . . .* Boston: Little, Brown, 1960.

Fiedler, Leslie. *An End to Innocence*. Boston: Beacon Press, 1955.

Flanders, Ralph E. *Senator from Vermont*. Boston: Little, Brown, 1961.

Flynn, John T. *The Road Ahead*. New York: Devin-Adair, 1949.

Freeland, Richard M. *The Truman Doctrine and the Origins of McCarthyism: Foreign Policy, Domestic Politics, and Internal Security, 1946–1948*. New York: Knopf, 1972.

Fried, Richard M. "Young Bob La Follette and Wisconsin Progressivism, 1925–1946." Masters essay, Columbia University, 1965.

Friendly, Alfred. "The Noble Crusade of Senator McCarthy," *Harpers*, 201 (August 1950), 34–42.

Friendly, Fred W. *Due to Circumstances Beyond Our Control. . . .* New York: Random House, 1967.

Frier, David A. *Conflict of Interest in the Eisenhower Administration.* Ames: Iowa State University Press, 1969.

Gaddis, John Lewis. *The United States and the Origins of the Cold War, 1941–1947.* New York: Columbia University Press, 1972.

Gilpin, Robert. *American Scientists and Nuclear Weapons Policy.* Princeton: Princeton University Press, 1962.

Goldman, Eric F. *The Crucial Decade—and After; America, 1945–1960.* New York: Knopf, 1960.

Goodman, Walter. *The Committee: The Extraordinary Career of the House Committee on Un-American Activities.* New York: Farrar, Straus and Giroux, 1968.

Gore, Leroy. *Joe Must Go.* New York: Julian Messner, 1954.

Graebner, Norman. *The New Isolationism.* New York: Ronald Press, 1956.

Griffith, Robert. "The General and the Senator: Republican Politics and the 1952 Campaign in Wisconsin," *Wisconsin Magazine of History,* 54 (Autumn 1970), 23–29.

—— "The Political Context of McCarthyism," *Review of Politics,* 33 (January 1971), 24–35.

—— *The Politics of Fear: Joseph R. McCarthy and the Senate.* Lexington: University of Kentucky Press, 1970.

Hamby, Alonzo L. *Beyond the New Deal: Harry S. Truman and American Liberalism.* New York: Columbia University Press, 1973.

Harper, Alan D. *The Politics of Loyalty: The White House and the Communist Issue, 1946–1952.* Westport, Conn.: Greenwood, 1969.

Harris, Louis. *Is There a Republican Majority?* New York: Harper and Row, 1956.

Heald, Robert L. and Lyon L. Tyler. "The Principle Behind the Amerasia Case," *Georgetown Law Journal,* 39 (1951), 181–215.

Hinckley, John T. "The 1952 Elections in Wyoming," *Western Political Quarterly,* 6 (March 1953), 135–38.

Hoving, John. "My Friend McCarthy," *Reporter,* 2 (April 25, 1950), 28–31.

Hughes, Emmet John. *The Ordeal of Power: A Political Memoir of the Eisenhower Years.* New York: Atheneum, 1963.

Hyman, Sidney. *The Lives of William Benton.* Chicago: University of Chicago Press, 1969.

Johnson, Haynes and Bernard M. Gwertzman. *Fulbright the Dissenter.* Garden City, N.Y.: Doubleday, 1968.

Johnson, Roger T. *Robert M. La Follette, Jr., and the Decline of the Progressive Party in Wisconsin.* Madison: State Historical Society of Wisconsin, 1964.

Jonas, Frank H. "The Art of Political Dynamiting," *Western Political Quarterly,* 10 (June 1957), 374–91.

—— "The 1950 Elections in Utah," *Western Political Quarterly,* 4 (March 1951), 81–91.

—— "Setting the Stage for the Political Dynamiter," in Jonas, ed., *Political Dynamiting.* Salt Lake City: University of Utah Press, 1970.

Judah, Charles. "The 1952 Elections in New Mexico," *Western Political Quarterly,* 6 (March 1953), 120–23.

Karlen, Jules A. "The 1952 Elections in Montana," *Western Political Quarterly,* 6 (March 1953), 113–17.

Keeley, Joseph. *The China Lobby Man: The Story of Alfred Kohlberg.* New Rochelle, N.Y.: Arlington House, 1969.

Kelley, Stanley, Jr. *Professional Public Relations and Political Power.* Baltimore: Johns Hopkins University Press, 1956.

Kelso, Paul A. "The 1952 Elections in Arizona," *Western Political Quarterly,* 6 (March 1953), 100–02.

Kemper, Donald J. *Decade of Fear: Senator Hennings and Civil Liberties.* Columbia: University of Missouri Press, 1965.

Kempton, Murray. *Part of Our Time: Some Monuments and Ruins of the Thirties.* New York: Simon and Schuster, 1955.

Kendrick, Frank J. "McCarthy and the Senate." Ph.D. dissertation, University of Chicago, 1962.

—— "The Senate and Senator Joseph R. McCarthy," *Journal of the Minnesota Academy of Science,* vol. 32, no. 1 (1964), 60–67.

Key, V. O., Jr. *Southern Politics in State and Nation.* New York: Knopf, 1949.

Kirkendall, Richard S., ed. *The Truman Period as a Research Field: A Reappraisal, 1972.* Columbia: University of Missouri Press, 1974.

Kirschten, Ernest. "Donnell Luck and Missouri Scandal," *Nation,* 171 (Oct. 14, 1950), 332–34.

Kirwin, Harry W. *The Inevitable Success: Herbert R. O'Conor.* Westminster, Md.: Newman Press, 1962.

Kogan, Herman. "Illinois: A Sorry Choice," *Nation,* 171 (Oct. 21, 1950), 262–64.

La Feber, Walter. *America, Russia, and the Cold War, 1945–1971.* New York: Wiley, 1972.

La Palombara, Joseph G. "Pressure, Propaganda and Political Action in the Election of 1950," *Journal of Politics,* 14 (May 1952), 305–25.

Lasch, Christopher. *The Agony of the American Left.* New York: Random House, 1969.

Latham, Earl. *The Communist Controversy in Washington from the New Deal to McCarthy.* Cambridge: Harvard University Press, 1966.

Lilienthal, David E. *The Journals of David E. Lilienthal*. Vol. II: *The Atomic Energy Years, 1945–1950*. New York: Harper and Row, 1964.

Lubell, Samuel. *The Future of American Politics*. 3d ed., rev. New York: Harper and Row, 1965.

—— *Revolt of the Moderates*. New York: Harper, 1956.

Luthin, Reinhard H. *American Demagogues—Twentieth Century*. Boston: Beacon Press, 1954.

"The McCarthy Issue . . . Pro and Con," *US News & World Report*, 31 (Sept. 7, 1951), 24–41.

McCoy, Donald R. *Landon of Kansas*. Lincoln: University of Nebraska Press, 1966.

McGill, Ralph. "Can He Purge Senator Pepper?" *Saturday Evening Post*, 222 (April 22, 1950), 33.

McLellan, David S. and John W. Reuss. "Foreign and Military Policies," in Richard S. Kirkendall, ed., *The Truman Period as a Research Field*. Columbia: University of Missouri Press, 1967.

McMillan, Taylor. "Who Beat Frank Graham?" Unpublished manuscript, University of North Carolina Political Studies Program, Research Report #1, May 20, 1959.

McPhee, William N. and William A. Glaser, eds. *Public Opinion and Congressional Elections*. New York: Free Press, 1962.

Maddox, Robert James. "Keeping Cool with Coolidge," *Journal of American History*, LII (March 1967), 772–80.

Malafronte, Anthony F. "Claude Pepper, Florida Maverick: The 1950 Florida Senatorial Primary." Masters essay, University of Miami, 1964.

Martin, Boyd A. "The 1950 Elections in Idaho," *Western Political Quarterly*, 4 (March 1951), 76–79.

Martin, Curtis. "The 1950 Elections in Colorado," *Western Political Quarterly*, 4 (March 1951), 73–75.

Matthews, Donald R. *U.S. Senators and Their World*. Chapel Hill: University of North Carolina Press, 1960.

Matusow, Harvey. *False Witness*. New York: Cameron and Kahn, 1955.

Mazo, Earl and Stephen Hess. *Nixon: A Political Portrait*. New York: Popular Library, 1968.

Merrill, M. R. "The 1952 Elections in Utah." *Western Political Quarterly*, 6 (March 1953), 127–30.

Meyer, Karl E. "The Politics of Loyalty: From La Follette to McCarthy in Wisconsin, 1918–1952." Ph.D. dissertation, Princeton University, 1956.

Miller, Warren E. "Presidential Coattails: A Study in Political Myth and Methodology," *Public Opinion Quarterly*, 19 (Winter 1955–56), 353–68.

Moos, Malcolm, ed. *H. L. Mencken on Politics: A Carnival of Buncombe*. New York: Random House, 1960.

Murphy, Paul L. *The Constitution in Crisis Times, 1918–1969*. New York: Harper and Row, 1972.

National Council of Churches of Christ in the U.S.A. *Churches and Church Membership in the United States; an enumeration and analysis by counties, states and regions*. New York: National Council of Churches, 1956.

Neuberger, Richard L. "Stand-off in the Northwest," *Nation,* 171 (Oct. 30, 1950), 334–36.

O'Brien, Michael. "The Anti-McCarthy Campaign in Wisconsin, 1951–1952," *Wisconsin Magazine of History,* 56 (Winter 1972–1973), 91–108.

—— "McCarthy and McCarthyism: The Cedric Parker Case, November 1949," in Robert Griffith and Athan Theoharis, eds., *The Specter: Original Essays on the Cold War and the Origins of McCarthyism*. New York: New Viewpoints, 1974.

—— "Senator Joseph R. McCarthy and Wisconsin: 1946–1957." Ph.D. dissertation, University of Wisconsin, 1971.

Ogden, August Raymond. *The Dies Committee: A Study of the Special House Committee for Investigation of Un-American Activities, 1938–1944*. Washington, D.C.: Catholic University Press, 1945.

Ogden, Daniel M., Jr., "The 1952 Elections in Washington," *Western Political Quarterly,* 6 (March 1953), 131–35.

Oshinsky, David M. "Wisconsin Labor and the Campaign of 1952," *Wisconsin Magazine of History,* 56 (Winter, 1972–1973), 109–18.

Otto, Robert L. "The Maryland Senatorial Election of 1950: Butler vs. Tydings." Masters essay, University of Maryland, 1962.

Packer, Herbert L. *Ex-Communist Witnesses*. Stanford: Stanford University Press, 1962.

Parenti, Michael. *The Anti-Communist Impulse*. New York: Random House, 1969.

Parmet, Herbert S. *Eisenhower and the American Crusades*. New York: MacMillan, 1972.

Paterson, Thomas G. "The Dissent of Senator Claude Pepper," in Paterson, ed., *Cold War Critics: Alternatives to American Foreign Policy in the Truman Years*. Chicago: Quadrangle, 1971.

Patterson, James T. *Mr. Republican: A Biography of Robert A. Taft*. Boston: Houghton Mifflin, 1972.

Peterson, F. Ross. *Prophet Without Honor: Glen Taylor and the Fight for American Liberalism*. Lexington: University of Kentucky Press, 1974.

Phillips, Cabell. *The Truman Presidency: The History of a Triumphant Succession*. New York, Macmillan, 1966.

Pollard, James E. "The White House News Conference as a Channel of

Communication," *Public Opinion Quarterly*, 15 (Winter, 1951–1952), 661–78.

Polsby, Nelson W. "Towards an Explanation of McCarthyism," *Political Studies*, 8 (October 1960), 250–71.

Potter, Charles E. *Days of Shame*. New York: Coward-McCann, 1965.

Pratt, William C. "Senator Glen H. Taylor: Questioning American Unilateralism," in Thomas G. Paterson, ed., *Cold War Critics: Alternatives to American Foreign Policy in the Truman Years*. Chicago: Quadrangle, 1971.

Price, H. D. "The Negro and Florida Politics, 1944–1954," *Journal of Politics*, 17 (May 1955), 198–220.

―――― *The Negro in Southern Politics: A Chapter of Florida History*. New York: New York University Press, 1957.

Pusey, Merlo J. *Eisenhower the President*. New York: Macmillan, 1956.

Reeves, Thomas C. *Freedom and the Foundation: The Fund for the Republic in the Era of McCarthyism*. New York: Knopf, 1969.

Ripley, Randall B. *Power in the Senate*. New York: St. Martin's, 1969.

Rogin, Michael P. *McCarthy and the Intellectuals: The Radical Specter*. Cambridge: MIT Press, 1967.

Rorty, James and Moshe Decter. *McCarthy and the Communists*. Boston: Beacon Press, 1954.

Ross, Irwin. *The Loneliest Campaign: The Truman Victory of 1948*. New York: New American Library, 1968.

Rovere, Richard H. *Senator Joe McCarthy*. Cleveland: World, 1959.

Schattschneider, E. E. *Party Government*. New York: Holt, Rinehart and Winston, 1942.

Schlesinger, Arthur M., Jr. *The Age of Roosevelt: The Coming of the New Deal*. Boston: Houghton Mifflin, 1958.

―――― *The Age of Roosevelt: The Politics of Upheaval*. Boston: Houghton Mifflin, 1960.

―――― *The Imperial Presidency*. Boston: Houghton Mifflin, 1973.

Schmidt, Karl M. *Henry Wallace: Quixotic Crusader 1948*. Syracuse: Syracuse University Press, 1960.

Schonberger, Howard B. "The General and the Presidency: Douglas MacArthur and the Election of 1948," *Wisconsin Magazine of History*, 57 (Spring 1974), 201–19.

Schriftgeisser, Karl. *The Lobbyists: The Art and Business of Influencing Lawmakers*. Boston: Little, Brown, 1951.

Schuyler, George S. *Black and Conservative*. New Rochelle, N.Y.: Arlington House, 1966.

Scoble, Harry M. *Ideology and Electoral Action: A Comparative Study of the National Committee for an Effective Congress.* San Francisco: Chandler, 1967.

Seib, Charles B. and Alan L. Otten. "Fulbright: The Arkansas Paradox," *Harpers,* 212 (June 1956), 60–66.

Service, John S. *The Amerasia Papers: Some Problems in the History of US-China Relations.* Berkeley: University of California Press, 1971.

"Shellacking for Tydings," *Newsweek,* 36 (Nov. 13, 1950), 25.

Shelton, Willard. "Nine G.O.P. Senate Freshmen," *Reporter,* 6 (April 1, 1952), 10–12.

Sherrill, Robert and Harry W. Ernst. *The Drugstore Liberal: Hubert H. Humphrey in Politics.* New York: Grossman, 1968.

Smith, C. G. "The 1952 Elections in Nevada," *Western Political Quarterly,* 6 (March 1953), 117–20.

Smith, Carl O. and Stephen B. Sarasohn. "Hate Propaganda in Detroit," *Public Opinion Quarterly,* 10 (Spring 1946), 24–52.

Smith, Margaret Chase. *Declaration of Conscience.* Edited by William C. Lewis, Jr. Garden City, N.Y.: Doubleday, 1972.

Steinke, John M. "The Rise of McCarthyism." Masters essay, University of Wisconsin, 1960.

Steinke, John and James Weinstein. "McCarthy and the Liberals," *Studies on the Left,* vol. 2, no. 3 (1962), pp. 43–50.

Stoesen, Alexander Rudolph. "The Senatorial Career of Claude D. Pepper." Ph.D. dissertation, University of North Carolina, 1964.

Stouffer, Samuel A. *Communism, Conformity, and Civil Liberties.* New York: Doubleday, 1955.

Straight, Michael. *Trial by Television.* Boston: Beacon Press, 1954.

"Taft and McCarthy," *Life,* 31 (Oct. 1, 1951), 32.

Tanner, William Rudolph. "The Passage of the Internal Security Act of 1950." Ph.D. dissertation, University of Kansas, 1971.

Tanner, William R. and Robert Griffith. "Legislative Politics and 'McCarthyism': The Internal Security Act of 1950," in Griffith and Athan Theoharis, eds., *The Specter: Original Essays on the Cold War and the Origins of McCarthyism.* New York: New Viewpoints, 1974.

Thelen, David P. and Esther S. Thelen. "Joe Must Go: The Movement to Recall Senator Joseph R. McCarthy," *Wisconsin Magazine of History,* 49 (Spring 1966), 185–209.

Theoharis, Athan. "Document: Attorney General Clark, Internal Security, and the Truman Administration," *New University Thought,* 5–6 (Spring 1968), 16–23.

—— "The Escalation of the Loyalty Program," in Barton J. Bernstein, ed.,

Politics and Policies of the Truman Administration. Chicago: Quadrangle, 1970.

—— "The Rhetoric of Politics: Foreign Policy, Internal Security, and Domestic Politics in the Truman Era, 1945–1950," in Barton J. Bernstein, ed., *Politics and Policies of the Truman Administration*. Chicago: Quadrangle, 1970.

—— *Seeds of Repression: Harry S. Truman and the Origins of McCarthyism*. Chicago: Quadrangle, 1971.

—— "The Threat to Civil Liberties," in Thomas G. Paterson, ed., *Cold War Critics: Alternatives to American Foreign Policy in the Truman Years*. Chicago: Quadrangle, 1971.

—— *The Yalta Myths: An Issue in U.S. Politics, 1945–1955*. Columbia: University of Missouri Press, 1970.

Truman, David B. *The Congressional Party*. New York: Wiley, 1959.

Truman, Harry S. *Memoirs*. Vol. II: *Years of Trial and Hope*. Garden City, N.Y.: Doubleday, 1956.

Tsou, Tang. *America's Failure in China, 1941–1950*. Chicago: University of Chicago Press, 1963.

Tyler, Gus. "The Mid-Term Paradox," *New Republic*, 123 (Nov. 27, 1950), 14–15.

Vandenberg, Arthur H., Jr., ed. *The Private Papers of Senator Vandenberg*. Boston: Houghton Mifflin, 1952.

"War on McCarthy," *Newsweek*, 35 (May 15, 1950), 24–26.

Watkins, Arthur V. *Enough Rope: The Inside Story of the Censure of Senator Joe McCarthy*. Englewood Cliffs, N.J.: Prentice-Hall, 1969.

Wechsler, James A. *The Age of Suspicion*. New York: Random House, 1953.

Wentworth, Evelyn L. "County Alignments in Maryland Elections, 1934–1958." Masters essay, University of Maryland, 1962.

—— *Election Statistics in Maryland, 1934–1958*. College Park: University of Maryland, 1962.

Westerfield, H. Bradford. *Foreign Policy and Party Politics: Pearl Harbor to Korea*. New Haven: Yale University Press, 1955.

Whalen, Richard. *The Founding Father: The Story of Joseph P. Kennedy*. New York: New American Library, 1964.

White, William S. *Citadel: The Story of the U.S. Senate*. New York: Harper, 1956.

—— *The Professional: Lyndon B. Johnson*. Boston: Houghton Mifflin, 1964.

—— *The Taft Story*. New York: Harper and Row, 1954.

Whiteford, Daniel F. "The American Legion and McCarthyism," *Continuum*, 6 (Autumn 1968), 326–35.

"Why Not Spank Him" *Collier's*, 128 (Aug. 18, 1951), 74.

Wiebe, G. D. "The Army-McCarthy Hearings and the Public Conscience," *Public Opinion Quarterly*, 21 (Winter 1958–1959), 490–502.

Williams, Edward Bennett. *One Man's Freedom*. New York; Atheneum, 1962.

Williams, N. Bancroft. "An Examination of the Factors Leading to the Defeat of Millard E. Tydings in the Maryland Senatorial Election of 1950." Masters essay, Loyola College (Baltimore), 1966.

Williams, T. Harry. *Huey Long*. New York: Knopf, 1969.

Wolfskill, George. *The Revolt of the Conservatives: A History of the American Liberty League, 1934–1940*. Boston: Houghton Mifflin, 1962.

Yarnell, Allen. *Democrats and Progressives: The 1948 Presidential Election as a Test of Postwar Liberalism*. Berkeley: University of California Press, 1974.

Young, Roland. *Congressional Politics in the Second World War*. New York: Columbia University Press, 1956.

IV   ORAL HISTORY MEMOIRS AND PERSONAL INTERVIEWS.

Kenneth M. Birkhead Oral History Interview. Truman Library.

Prescott Bush Oral History Memoir. Columbia Oral History Collection.

Roscoe Drummond Oral History Memoir. Columbia Oral History Collection.

Adrian S. Fisher. Personal interview, Aug. 27, 1968.

Ralph E. Flanders Oral History Memoir. Columbia Oral History Collection.

Edward Folliard Oral History Memoir. Columbia Oral History Collection.

G. W. Foster, Jr., Oral History Interview. Cornell Oral History Project.

Donald Hansen Oral History Interview. Truman Library.

Carlisle Humelsine Oral History Interview. Cornell Oral History Project.

Edwin Johnson. Personal interview, Aug. 7, 1967.

Walter H. Judd. Telephone interview, Aug. 22, 1973.

Max Lowenthal Oral History Interview. Truman Library.

Jack K. McFall Oral History Interview. Cornell Oral History Project.

Jack K. McFall Oral History Interview. Truman Library.

Miles McMillin Oral History Interview. Cornell Oral History Project.

Clark Mollenhoff Oral History Interview. Karl E. Mundt Library, Dakota State College.

Charles S. Murphy Oral History Interview. Truman Library.

Congressman Claude D. Pepper. Personal interview, June 27, 1967.

Maurice Rosenblatt. Personal interview, June 27, 1967.

Morris H. Rubin Oral History Interview. Cornell Oral History Project.

Leverett Saltonstall Oral History Memoir. Columbia Oral History Collection.

H. Alexander Smith Oral History Memoir. Columbia Oral History Collection.

Stephen J. Spingarn Oral History Interview. Truman Library.

Edward Thye Oral History Memoir. Columbia Oral History Collection.

Norman Thomas. Personal interview, Nov. 29, 1966.

Gerhard P. Van Arkel. Personal interview, Aug. 26, 1968.

Arthur V. Watkins. Personal interview, June 23, 1967.

INDEX

Abt, John, 232

Acheson, Dean G.: and China White Paper, 4; defines U.S. defense perimeter, 13-14; remarks on Alger Hiss, 14; attacked by Republicans, 14, 66-67, 107; attacked on Gubitchev case, 15; appointment of, 21; McCarthy attacks, 43, 46, 130, 131, 175, 223; and loyalty files issue, 58; notes McCarthy's sources, 58-59; defended by Democrats, 70, 157-58; "sells" foreign policies, 70; blamed for Korean War, 102; National Press Club speech, 107; attacked by Capehart, 117; criticized, 134; and Tom Connally, 141; under attack (late 1950–early 1951), 156-59; twits Senator Taft, 157; position improves, 159; clears O.E. Clubb, 170; scores attacks on State Department, 174; Stassen mentions, 189; Benton defends, 197; attacked in 1952 campaign, 232; and William Bundy, 270; on proper committee to hear McCarthy charges, 326n

Adams, John G.: and Army-McCarthy fight, 280, 284; resignation urged, 281

Adams, Sherman: in 1952 campaign, 230; and Army response to McCarthy, 280-81

Agnew, Spiro T., 315

Agree, George, 265

Aiken, Sen. George: on Tydings probe, 92; in 1950 campaign, 120; signs Declaration of Conscience, 333n

Alexander, Rev. "Bill," 112

Alsop, Stewart, 54

Amerasia: case of stolen documents, 6-7; and loyalty program, 22; investigated by Tydings committee, 77-78, 85; 1950 grand jury findings on, 85, 93

American Bar Association, 98

American Civil Liberties Union: on Truman and civil Liberties, 106; supports PCISIR, 164; sends out questionnaire, 246

American Committee for Cultural Freedom, 265

American Jewish Committee, 164

American Labor Party, 20

American Legion: puts on Mosinee pageant, 1; hears Truman speech, 173, 176; and McCarthy, 178n

American Liberty League, 7

American Library Association, 268-69

American Mercury, 267

Americans for Democratic Action (ADA): and Wallace in 1948 campaign, 18; as 1950 campaign issue, 113-14; local chapter aids Tydings, 131; criticism of loyalty program, 162, 169; as 1952

tested, 267; resignation accepted, 268; Budenz consults, 331*n*

Matusow, Harvey: campaigns for McCarthy, 239; admits perjury, 311

May, Ronald W., 266

Maybank, Sen. Burnet R.: antipathy toward McCarthy, 40; defends Conant, 269

Mechling, Thomas, 240, 249

Meek, Joseph T., 305, 380*n*

Mencken, H. L., 7

Meyer, Rep. John A., 125-26, 129, 130

Michigan: 1950 campaign in, 113-14; 1952 campaign in, 241, 244-45, 248

Miller, Mrs. Ruth McCormick, 127, 133

Millikin, Sen. Eugene D., in 1950 campaign, 111-12, 120

Mills, Herman L., 126

Milne, Edward, 208

Milwaukee *Journal*: on McCarthy in 1946, 37; on 1950 campaign, 116

Missouri: 1950 campaign in, 117-18; 1952 campaign in, 241, 242, 248

Mitchell, Rep. Hugh, 243

Mitchell, Kate, 6

Mitchell, Stephen A.: on McCarthy as GOP responsibility, 260; on Army-McCarthy dispute, 283; warns of GOP redbaiting, 303

Monaghan, Hugh M., II, 126, 129, 130

Monroney, Sen. A. S. "Mike": in 1950 campaign, 112; and Maryland election probe, 141; and Maryland Report, 149; on Margaret Smith resignation, 206; presses discharge motion, 206-7; resigns from Privileges and Elections Subcommittee, 211; attacks McCarthy, 252; protests McCarthy CIA probe, 270; ready to confront McCarthy (1953), 272; opposes R. E. Lee appointment, 277; offers aid to Flanders, 293; on censure resolution, 297; opposes referral of censure motion, 297*n*

Montana: 1952 campaign in, 240, 243, 248; 1954 campaign in, 305

Moody, Sen. A. E. Blair, 241, 244-45

Moore, Ewell, 145-46

Moore, John: commends Benton restraint, 203; and McCarthy's finances, 208, 359*n*; shifted from Gillette subcommittee, 210

Morgan, Edward P.: hired by Tydings Committee, 63; attacked by Jenner, 75; plans attack on McCarthy, 79; drafts report, 86

Morgan, Gerald, 280

Morris, Robert, 331*n*

Morse, Sen. Wayne: on probe of McCarthy charges, 54, 327*n*; on attack on Marshall, 192; offers censure specifications, 297, 299; and Communist Control Act, 301, 302; signs Declaration of Conscience, 333*n*; in debate on S. Res. 301, 378*n*; on censure, 381*n*

Mosinee, Wisc., 1-2

Moss, Annie Lee, 285

Muir, Jean, 103

Mundy, Cornelius P., 147

Mundt, Sen. Karl E.: attacks Hiss, 12; on L. Duggan death, 13; on Hiss case, 43; hits Democrats, 48; on Korea as political issue, 102; on veto of McCarran Act, 121; seeks backing for McCarthy, 227; and "chicken luncheon," 279-80; in Army-McCarthy hearings, 281, 282; regrets McCarthy's excesses, 283; on effect of Army hearings, 287; seeks to avert censure, 309; on Francis Case, 309; on censure, 314; in 1952 campaign, 363*n*

Mundt-Ferguson-Johnston bill, 104-5

Mundt-Nixon bill, 104

Murchison, Clint, 133

Murphy, Charles S., 81-82

Murphy, Gov. Frank, 10

Murray, Sen. James A.: defends Acheson, 158; McCarthy mentions, 241; in 1954 campaign, 303, 305, 306

Murrow, Edward R., 283